Reluctant Remilitarisation

Reluctant Remilitarisation

Transforming the Armed Forces in Germany, Italy and Japan after the Cold War

FABRIZIO COTICCHIA,
MATTEO DIAN AND
FRANCESCO NICCOLÒ MORO

EDINBURGH
University Press

Edinburgh University Press is one of the leading university presses in the UK. We publish academic books and journals in our selected subject areas across the humanities and social sciences, combining cutting-edge scholarship with high editorial and production values to produce academic works of lasting importance. For more information visit our website: edinburghuniversitypress.com

Edinburgh University Press Ltd
The Tun – Holyrood Road
12(2f) Jackson's Entry
Edinburgh EH8 8PJ

Typeset in 11/13 Adobe Garamond by
Cheshire Typesetting Ltd, Cuddington, Cheshire, and
printed and bound in Great Britain

A CIP record for this book is available from the British Library

ISBN 978-1-4744-6727-8 (hardback)
ISBN 978-1-4744-6729-2 (webready PDF)
ISBN 978-1-4744-6730-8 (epub)

Contents

Graphs and Tables

Graphs

Tables

Acknowledgements

We would like to thank Pietro Batacchi, Vincenzo Bove, Andrea Catanzaro, Giampiero Cama, Edoardo Corradi, Jason Davidson, Marco Di Giulio, Mauro Gilli, Ina Kraft, Hugo Meijer, Gianpaolo Misseritti, Nicoletta Pirozzi, Chiara Ruffa, Andrea Ruggeri, Olivier Schmitt, Francesco Vignarca and Valerio Vignoli for comments and suggestions. We would also like to thank Michela Ceccorulli, Tom Dyson, Giampiero Giacomello, Sonia Lucarelli, Patrick Mello, Giulio Pugliese and Corey Wallace who participated in the workshop 'Reluctant Military Powers: Defence Transformation in Germany, Italy, and Japan', held in Bologna, 14 and 15 November 2019. Matteo Mazziotti di Celso provided great research assistance for the book. At EUP, Sarah Foyle, Ersev Ersoy and Jenny Daly provided important support at different stages of the production of the manuscript. The authors also wish to thank an anonymous reviewer for the very helpful suggestions and remarks.

Fabrizio Coticchia would like to thank Hans Peter Kriemann and the Zentrum für Militärgeschichte und Sozialwissenschaften der Bundeswehr for the amazing support provided as a visiting scholar in Potsdam. Fabrizio Coticchia thanks the University of Genoa that provided the grant for 'Curiosity Driven' ('Divergent Paths: Understanding post-Cold War Italian and German Defence Policy'), which has been crucial for this research. Fabrizio thanks his parents for the constant help over all these years.

Francesco N. Moro and Matteo Dian would like to thank Marco Valigi for his precious support in managing the AlmaIdea 2017 'Protagonisti riluttanti. La trasformazione della difesa in Italia, Giappone e Germania' grant generously offered by the University of Bologna and that importantly contributed to this research.

Fabrizio dedicates this book to Gisella and Francesco, 'always'.

Francesco dedicates this book to Rebecca and Cecilia, for their unwavering support.

Matteo dedicates this book to his parents and Karina.

Chapter 1

Introduction: Military Transformation in Germany, Italy and Japan

1.1 Military transformation in three unlikely candidates

In the last three decades, the defence policies of all the countries that prevailed in the Cold War have undergone dramatic changes. In few states, however, was this change more radical than in Germany, Italy and Japan. After their defeat in the Second World War, the three countries adopted constitutions that severely constrained the use of military force and developed national narratives that made the very idea of waging war a taboo. Their armed forces were designed primarily to intervene against a conventional, large-scale Soviet threat. They also had in common relatively low defence spending and budgets that were heavily biased towards personnel costs. In addition, in Germany and Italy the ranks were filled through conscription, which, in both countries, served to demonstrate the view that the civic duty of democratic countries with a troubled past was to produce harmonious relations between post-war societies and the armed forces.[1] Japan did not adopt conscription, and with the economic growth of the country most Japanese did not find the professional armed forces attractive. With a few exceptions, during the Cold War the armed forces of the three countries remained in their own respective bases, waiting for a call to fight a large-scale war that never came, and in which they would have likely played a secondary role.

In the 1990s, however, everything seemed to change. The end of the Cold War and the ensuing regional crises, 9/11 and the rise of China (to name just the most immediately dramatic changes in the global and regional security environments) affected these countries in different ways, but for all three they represented a time of reckoning. Regional crises ranging from the post-Arab uprisings of 2011 to North Korean nuclear ambitions profoundly influenced the perceptions of security in the three countries. Broadly speaking, Germany, Italy and Japan went from being 'security consumers' to more active 'regional security providers' or, at least (and here some ambiguities arise), they were called to assume the role both by certain domestic actors and by their major ally (the United States).

Since the early 1990s, territorial defence has ceased to be a core mission of the Italian armed forces. Italy participated in the first military operation of the post-bipolar world (the intervention against Iraq in 1991) and took an active role in the UNITAF and UNISOM missions in Somalia from 1992 to 1995. The engagement in Iraq (Operations Desert Shield and Desert Storm) represented a turning point in Italian defence policy, as Italian aircraft were involved in combat operations for the first time since the Second World War. Since the mid-1990s, what Italy defined as 'peace missions' (that is, military operations abroad), generally as a part of UN- or NATO-led coalitions, become the main task of the Italian armed forces. Italy became the leading country in manifold NATO missions, from Kosovo to Iraq. Italy also suspended conscription at the beginning of the new century. The Mediterranean increasingly became the pivotal focus for Italian defence policies due to emerging factors. The Arab Spring, the NATO intervention in Libya and the Syrian civil war heightened regional instability, intensifying the influx of migrants and refugees. This led to the need to develop capabilities and missions aimed at patrolling the waters between Italy and North Africa.

For Japan, with the emergence of the Chinese threat to the southwestern islands of the Japanese archipelago, the Japan Self-Defence Forces (JSDF) began a process of re-orientation aimed at rebalancing its military doctrine and force structures away from the north and towards the southwestern quadrant. This change of geographical orientation is associated with a shift of resources away from ground forces to an increased emphasis on the role of the Japan Maritime Self-Defence Force (MSDF) and the Air Self-Defence Force (ASDF).

Change was less clear-cut for Germany. Territorial defence remained the core mission up to 2003, and force structure and doctrines continued to regard defence from external threats to the eastern border as the main mission. In the period between 2003 and 2014, due to Germany's participation in the NATO-led International Security Assistance Force (ISAF) mission in Afghanistan, counterinsurgency and crisis management took on importance as core missions. The Ukraine crisis in 2014 and the Russian seizure of Crimea motivated Germany to focus once more on territorial defence and the threat posed by Russia. Germany was more reluctant in the 1990s and engaged in military action (for the first time since the Second World) in the Balkans (especially in Kosovo, 1999).

Both Italy and Germany took part in NATO's largest operation ever, in Afghanistan, and Italy intervened in Iraq (2003) and led the United Nations Interim Force (UNIFIL) in Lebanon (2006) and Libya (2011). Conscription, a cornerstone of German defence, was finally suspended in 2011 (as it had been in Italy several years earlier). After the approval of the law on peacekeeping operations (PKOs) in 1992, the JSDF took part in several UN-led PKOs, including in Cambodia, Mozambique and the Golan Heights in the 1990s, and in East Timor, Nepal, Sudan and Haiti in the 2000s and early 2010s. Moreover, a small contingent of the Japan Ground Self-Defence Force (GSDF) was dispatched to Iraq between 2004 and 2006, and the MSDF contributed to the war effort in Afghanistan with a refuelling mission between 2001 and 2004. Lastly, the *Jietai* were involved in multiple humanitarian assistance/disaster relief missions (HA/DR), such as those in Thailand and Indonesia (2004–2005), Haiti (2010) and the Philippines (2013). It is important to note that, unlike Italy and Germany, Japan never deployed its troops in scenarios characterised by high levels of conflict or in situations in which ongoing insurgencies determined an increased risk of reporting casualties (see Table 1.1 for a summary of interventions).

In this process, the three countries reformed both the structure of their forces and their military doctrines. Rather than a complete abandonment of previous structures, practices and guiding principles (such as pacifist standards and ideals), this was a re-elaboration (carried out in different ways and at different times), prompted by the need to assume a more active role in the security of their regions in the face of emerging, albeit very dissimilar, challenges.

The purpose of this book is to address how military transformation took place in Germany, Italy and Japan after the end of the Cold War. Empirically, the book reconstructs how two major domains within defence policy – military doctrine and force structure – have evolved in over three decades. In other words, we look at how the armed forces, and the political decision makers in charge of them, have renewed their vision of their mission, the nature of the military engagements they will face and the approach they must adopt (doctrine). The traditional notion of 'which wars to fight, and how' does not apply here since, as we shall see, actual combat is just one of the missions envisaged in this new context. Moreover, we show how military means have evolved, how the budget has been allocated and what type of military assets have been acquired and developed to face the challenges identified (force structure). Given the radical transformation that Germany, Italy and Japan have had to undertake, by tracing

Table 1.1 Participation in military missions

Mission	Italy	Germany	Japan
Iraq 1990/1991	✓ (Air strikes)	✗ (Financial support)	✗ (Financial support)
Somalia 1992/1994	✓ (Boots on the ground)	✓ (Humanitarian aid, logistical support, Navy)	✓
Bosnia 1995	✓ (PKO)	✓ (PKO)	✗
Albania 1997	✓ (Lead country)	✗	✗
Kosovo 1999	✓ (Air strikes)	✓ (Air strikes)	✗
Afghanistan	✓ (Combat)	✓ (PKO)	✗ (JSDF refuelling missions)
Iraq 2003/2006	✓ (Combat)	✗	✓ (Medical treatment, logistical support)
Lebanon 2006	✓ (PKO, lead country)	✓ (Logistical support, Navy)	✓ (Logistical support)
Libya 2011	✓ (Air strikes)	✗	✗
Iraq 2014	✓ (no air strikes)	✓ (no air strikes)	✗

Source: Authors' elaboration

their stories side by side we can identify the factors that have shaped each trajectory. Somewhat surprisingly, nevertheless, given their past similarities, these stories have never been told together until now.

The book does not provide a unified theory of change, but it contains original theoretical insights. In a nutshell, we show how in existing literature certain key elements can be identified that underpin defence policy change, such as the role of external factors (from threats to alliances), domestic constraints (from different 'parliamentary war powers' to cultural factors) and military organisations (due to learning processes, for example). We argue that although it is essential to take these factors into account, a long-term analysis of the process of change reveals that such occurs when several factors transpire in a given moment of time, and that at such times, in order to support change and establish trajectories, a series of self-enforcing mechanisms emerge, which then become difficult to alter. The terminology and insights of historical institutionalism will be used to analyse defence policy change, adopting a nuanced view of how change occurs and avoiding simplifications that might result from dichotomising what change is or losing a key evolutionary perspective.

This book also provides insights into three different 'middle powers',[2] how they define their role in the regional and global security environments, how they plan to use the armed forces in this contest, and how they have reformed their armed forces to achieve these new aims. The volume shows how, by looking at the different trajectories undertaken in the past three decades by Germany, Italy and Japan, we can begin to understand not only their respective paths but also their current positions and the potential of the same to help the countries adapt in the face of a changing environment. The analysis presented in this book may help to pave the way for new avenues of research. First, a similar analysis could be extended to other countries in Europe, such as Spain or Poland, or in East Asia, such as South Korea. Secondly, further research may be needed to analyse how military innovations generated in the last years of the wars in the Middle East and Central Asia, and lessons learned during these conflicts, have been institutionalised. Lastly, this research could be integrated with an effort to reach a more coherent theoretical synthesis between organisational studies and studies on military innovation.

This chapter introduces the comparative analysis on the process of military transformation in the cases of Italy, Germany and Japan. It first highlights the scholarly debate that can help to identify and address questions on military transformations. It then delves into what exactly we intend by 'military transformation', focusing on force doctrine and structure. The third section describes the research design, looking at some of the main choices made to respond to the key questions raised and describing the sources. Lastly, an outline of the book is provided.

1.2 Defining and explaining 'military transformation'

Military transformation is a complex concept. Often used indiscriminately to refer to both changes occurring at the tactical level and major overhauls in defence policy, the notion has been as successful as it is vague. Recent research has focused on causal mechanisms to provide explanations of military 'innovation and adaptation',[3] mainly examining empirically the operations of the 'war on terror' as crucial case studies.[4] The assessment of the impact of these missions on the armed forces (especially the institutionalisation of the adaptations), the role of organisational learning, along with further comparative perspectives, are considered the most promising avenues for further research.[5]

Before it can be analysed, 'military transformation' must be first operationalised. In short, we define military transformation as the part of a defence policy that relates to doctrine and force structure. Specifically, the first dimension we look at is the evolution of military doctrines, as institutional operationalisation of the cognitive frameworks, and preferences of the political and organisational leadership for its executing arms on the battlefield. Military doctrines (a fundamental element of innovation and learning) emerge from official documents and statements. In terms of results, we aim to explore the evolution of the main conceptual references through which doctrines have been redefined in the three countries since the post-Cold War period.[6] The second dimension we observe is force structure. Here we explore the transformation of force levels and the changes in the distribution of human and material resources.

Based on existing research, the book will consider different drivers of change. Today there are numerous studies on the elements that drive military transformation, but three broad sets of factors seem to play a key role. These are the evolution of the external environment; domestic institutional and ideational drivers; and organizational factors. Changes at the international level also shape the evolution of the role and the mission requirements of armed forces. The demise of the Soviet threat combined with the rise of civil conflicts led to a broad reconfiguration of the role of the armed forces. In the 1990s, the armed forces began to re-organise with the aim of promoting peacekeeping and stabilisation missions abroad. This was particularly the case with the German and (especially) Italian forces, deployed in the Balkans and in Africa, and, to a lesser extent, the Japanese armed forces, which began to be involved in peacekeeping operations in Southeast Asia and in the Middle East.[7] The terrorist attack on 11 September 2001 and the subsequent conflicts in Afghanistan and Iraq substantially accelerated the need for military transformation, placing counterinsurgency at the centre of the process of transformation. During these last years, the emphasis on counterinsurgency has drastically diminished in favour of a return to policies focused on deterrence and security competition among great (or super) powers.[8] The rise of China in Asia and the new Russian aggressiveness, culminating with the invasion of Ukraine, have determined the need for a broad recalibration of the task of the armed forces, which are again beginning to consider the need to deter adversaries and to protect the national territory as their mission's main obligation. Thus, territorial defence (especially in the case of Germany) re-affirms its relevance.

As for external factors, alliances are unquestionably important also, given that the three countries analysed all belong to a security alliance, with Italy and Germany members of NATO and Japan part of a bilateral security alliance with the United States. Alliance dynamics are a key part of the explanation for a number of reasons. The very existence of a security alliance alters the strategic calculus of a country.[9] First, the perceived severity of external threats is mitigated by the reliance of allies. Secondly, at operational level, one of the major consequences of alliance politics is that weapons procurement is heavily influenced by the need to achieve a certain level of interoperability with allies' forces. And, lastly, alliance politics can also shape national doctrines. The conceptual references first developed at multinational level can later be adopted by allies in their national strategic elaboration.[10]

The second set of drivers often considered in studies on force transformation (and, more broadly, defence policy change) features institutional and ideational drivers, particularly legal, political and institutional constraints and strategic cultures. Italy, Germany and Japan shared similar experiences of defeat during the Second World War and of rebirth as pacifist countries in the post-war period.[11] Consequently, the development of post-war military strategies, as well as the transformation of their militaries, has been deeply influenced by pacifist and anti-militarist orientations. The regulatory influence of the wartime past has shaped the strategic cultures of the three countries in rather different ways. Strategic culture has generally been identified as a driver of the propensity to intervene (or not) in Italy, Germany and Japan.[12] Deep-rooted convictions can be *strategically* reinterpreted by the elite to legitimise policy changes. For example, the narrative of Italy as a 'pacifist country', as well as the 'peace and humanitarian missions', are stratagems built intentionally on the basis of a specific set of values (such as peace, multilateralism and so on). Likewise, in Germany the storyline of 'civilian power' was built on the main aspects of the national strategic culture. Similarly, the expansion of Japan's security role in Asia has been legitimised under the rubric of 'proactive contribution to peace'. On the whole, strategic culture in each country has gradually evolved due to different factors, such as (1) shifting domestic political equilibria, with the decline and even disappearance of the radical leftist political narratives; and (2) generational changes that led to the emergence of both public opinion and elites that were increasingly removed from a direct experience of the wartime past. The literature has explored the ways in which defence policy may be a reflection of military and strategic culture.[13] On the other hand, other 'domestic constraints', which could represent fundamental drivers of change, have often been underestimated in IR and FP analyses.[14] The literature has given growing attention to the influence exerted by domestic factors (such as the role of parliamentary oversight) in shaping foreign and defence policy.[15] Institutional constraints on executive autonomy may clearly affect governments' room to manoeuvre in foreign policy. The three cases under investigation in this research reveal very different levels of 'parliamentary war powers' that are worth examining in detail.

Lastly, several studies have highlighted how organisational drivers must be included in the analysis of military transformation.[16] Armed forces are formed by several bureaucracies that can promote innovation or resist it. Especially in a context characterised by shrinking budgets, each service fights to preserve its own resources. This can lead to resisting innovations that would be likely to reduce both military utility and the status of certain branches or services. Competing for resources and status, however, can also have the opposite effect of encouraging innovation. The literature on military innovation shows how informal and formal mechanisms shape adaptation and organisational learning.[17] Within organisational factors, the process of learning from past experiences is central. Military institutions are essentially learning organisations. Consequently, they seek to adapt through a process of emulation and trial and error. Complex organisations such as armed forces can 'forget' the lessons learned from previous experiences if they are not able to institutionalise them and thereby make them available to new members when old members are assigned to other posts or functions or retire. The purpose here is to assess whether, and how, prolonged experience linked to deployment (as in the case of Italy, for example) has impacted transformation. In other words, by looking at how operational experience and bottom-up feedback promotes innovation at institutional level, and in structuring organisational learning we can examine the different degrees of adaptation that occurred in the three cases.[18]

1.3 Argument(s), contribution and research design

While this book does not necessarily aim to put forward a new comprehensive theory of military transformation, it does intend to offer several original contributions. From the empirical point of view, it fills a gap in the literature by proposing a comparison between Italy, Germany and Japan.[19] It also offers a different perspective compared with recent comparative analyses on Japan and Germany. For instance, the recent *Reluctant Warriors*, by Sakaki, Maull, Lukner, Krauss and Berger, focuses mainly on the domestic legitimacy of the armed forces, arms export policies and decisions on interventions, without any specific focus on military doctrine and force structures.[20] Previous studies, meanwhile, have largely investigated the impact of regulatory aspects and domestic identities regarding foreign policy choices.[21] We intend here to contribute also to the theoretical debate on military transformation and, more generally, on security policies. While considering the three major sets of drivers mentioned above, the book also builds on a historical institutionalist approach; it aims to highlight the role of regulatory, institutional and organisational legacies, and looks at how these legacies contribute to shaping contemporary policy choices by restricting or enabling a given course of action, particularly when it comes to the use of force.

Contemplating legacies does not mean merely emphasising the weight of the past, or continuity. Rather, the book highlights the centrality of critical junctures, path dependence and positive feedback dynamics, which help to explain both continuity and change and, often, the layering of different strategies as the outcome of a process that follows multiple incentives and constraints.[22] Especially in the realm of military transformation, when and how certain policy decisions take place is crucial, since they have a significant influence on the ensuing events. Critical junctures, such as the decision to take part in Desert Storm in 1991, are crucial for Italy and Germany in determining (different) trajectories that are inherently difficult to reverse. This implies that the historical context cannot simply be dismissed as just a background to the analysis. On the contrary, locating the international and domestic context of key policy choices enables us to describe the main trajectories of change, while at the same time focusing on the causal mechanism at play. Moreover, the timing and sequencing regarding policy choices and critical junctures also make it possible to compare different processes of the institutionalisation of practices and processes of innovation. Lastly, these elements lead to underlining the role of agents as protagonists of key policy decisions, whether it regards decisions related to the use of force or longer and more incremental processes of organisational innovation.

Path dependent processes can be described as characterised by three different phases: an initial event, representing a critical juncture, which triggers the creation of a new path; a period of reproduction, in which the initial trajectory is reinforced; and a new event that leads to the end of the path. From this point of view, this book aims to highlight how different choices made at critical times for the three countries' foreign policies have generated several distinct mechanisms and several trajectories of positive feedback and path dependent effects. Consequently, it attempts to identify how early developments become deeply embedded in national contexts, modifying the incentive structures for policymakers, and altering the pattern of following events and the perception of the legitimacy of courses of action.

By carefully tracing the mechanisms at play to shape the trajectories followed by the three countries we also provide a contribution to FPA scholarly debate on the impact of domestic factors on foreign and defence policy.[23] Indeed, the book focuses on the interplay between international pressures (allies and perceived threats) and domestic and organisational drivers and constraints (cultural and institutional factors, along different military experiences and their feedbacks) to properly assess relevant policy decisions adopted in military affairs by Germany, Italy and Japan in the post-Cold War era.

Sources for this book are diverse. First, we have relied on literature by IR and military historians which analyses the three countries separately (or, in rare cases, in pairs). These sources constitute the core of Chapter 2, dealing with the Cold War period. The rest of the empirical chapters, especially Chapters 4, 5 and 6, rely more extensively on primary sources. The bulk of the material here comes from official documents and statements, which provide useful guidance in tracing the evolution of the three countries' military doctrines and force structures. The three countries have endeavoured to maximise their transparency and the effectiveness of their strategic communication to explain to experts and to the wider public their policy choices and to legitimise their initiatives in the field of security and defence. Japan is the country that has made the most significant effort in this direction. The Japanese Ministry of Defence publishes yearly a 'Defence of Japan' White Paper, which accompanies the 'Blue Paper' of the Ministry of Foreign Affairs. Likewise, key documents such as the National Defence Plan Guidance and the Mid-Term Defence Programme, or the National Security Strategy, are also released to the public after their adoption. Germany and Italy have produced less official defence documents, but focus on articulating the most significant policy changes through the publication of detailed White Papers. For Germany, the most significant examples are the White Papers of 2006 and 2016 and the policy guidelines of 2003 and 2011. Similarly, the Italian Ministry of Defence has produced a 'Libro Bianco' (White Paper) only twice, in 2002 and 2015, as well as a few other significant documents such as the Chief of Defence Concepts. The book also draws on more than thirty semi-structured interviews[24] with ministers, MPs, experts, practitioners and military officers in Germany, Italy and Japan (see List of Interviewees, below).

1.4 Plan of the book

The rest of the book is organised as follows. Chapter 2 describes how the security policies of the three countries were restricted by regulatory and institutional factors during the post-war period. Their common experience of defeat, occupation and political reform led Italy, Germany and Japan to develop both cultures of anti-militarism and a pacifist public opinion and to adopt significant constitutional limits that substantially constrained their security policies. In this sense, Article 9 of the Japanese constitution and Article 11 of the Italian constitution are very similar in that both declare that the country will not use force as a means of resolving international disputes. In Germany, Article 26 of the *Grundgesetz* (Basic Law) also explicitly states that 'Acts tending to and undertaken with intent to disturb the peaceful relations between nations, especially to prepare for a war of aggression, shall be unconstitutional.' This chapter highlights the similarities and differences between these elements, underlining how such factors decisively contributed to shaping security policies in the three countries in question.

Chapter 3 introduces the theoretical framework of the book, which is briefly sketched in the previous pages. First, it outlines the *explanandum* of the research, the process of military transformation. The book considers mainly military doctrine and budget and force structures as primary elements of military transformation. Secondly, the chapter introduces the main drivers of change, dividing them into external (security environment, threats, influence of allies), regulatory, technological and organisational factors.

Chapter 4 traces the evolution of the military doctrines and force structure in Germany. Berlin was relatively slow to adapt to post-Cold War realities. The *Bunderswehr* continued to maintain the central role of territorial defence throughout the 1990s. Germany's participation in the NATO mission to Kosovo and, especially, involvement in the ISAF mission in Afghanistan constituted key critical junctures. In the 2010s, Germany developed a doctrine oriented to crisis management and 'stabilisation operations' (later finally suspending conscription). This trend was partially reversed after the Ukraine crisis, which, along with other factors, contributed to a return to (the never-vanished) territorial defence as its main objective. Scarce resources, limited operational experience and constant domestic (both institutional and cultural) constraints played a vital role in maintaining the 'traditional' trajectory adopted by a militarily reluctant Germany after the fall of the Berlin Wall.

Chapter 5 traces the evolution of Italian defence in the post-Cold War. Italy was the country that adapted most quickly to the post-bipolar environment, offering a significant contribution to the US-led coalition during the Gulf War. Since then, Italy's armed forces have embraced a military doctrine largely characterised by stabilisation and peacekeeping missions. In the aftermath of 9/11, the Italian armed forces sought to further adapt their defence model to cater to new threats by developing an effective and efficient military instrument based on a 'holistic approach' geared to performing a wide spectrum of multi-dimensional operations. 'Power projection', which was confirmed in Italy's *Libro Bianco* 2015 and remained at the centre of Italian doctrine through the 2010s, focused primarily on the Mediterranean as a key strategic region for Italy. The chapter traces the parallel evolution of doctrine and force structure, highlighting how the latter – while profoundly changed – did not always keep pace with the former, leaving unresolved certain questions regarding the ability of the Italian armed forces to effectively face multiple crisis scenarios. Resource constraints heavily affect this outcome, but the reconstruction of the trajectory of Italian force transformation also shows how past decisions play a key role in determining how the process of transformation has unfolded.

Chapter 6 focuses on Japan. Japan's military doctrine has undergone an even more radical redefinition, transcending several of the post-war regulatory and institutional constraints and embracing a role of 'active contributor to peace' in the Indo-Pacific region. In terms of timing, Japan more closely resembles Germany than Italy. With the emergence of the threats presented by China and North Korea in the 2000s and 2010s, Japan introduced its most important policy changes, such as the acquisition of ballistic defence systems, the legalisation of 'collective self-defence' and the shift to 'dynamic deterrence' as the core mission of the JSDF. Overall, the re-emergence of great power rivalry has significantly affected Japan and Germany, reducing the centrality of peacekeeping operations in favour of deterrence and the defence of the integrity of the national territory. The chapter highlights how Japan adapted its force structure to cope with the threat posed by China and another significant military power, North Korea. It invested in sectors such as missile defence, intelligence, surveillance and reconnaissance (ISR), cyber, space, amphibious capabilities, air superiority jet fighters and attack submarines.

The Conclusion wraps up the narratives of the previous chapters, highlighting similarities and differences in the trajectories undertaken by the three countries. The section reveals the main findings of the empirical analysis, which has illustrated how Germany, Japan and Italy addressed dissimilar critical junctures which were then followed by different patterns of institutionalisation, with diverse self-reinforcing feedbacks. Along with the 'legacies in action', the interaction between international and domestic factors profoundly shaped – in distinctive ways – the evolution of doctrines and force structure in each country.

The chapter then stresses how future research could develop this and related topics. Lastly, the Conclusion sums up with a brief synthesis of how three decades of transformation affect the prospects for action and further reform in the current, and fast-evolving, global security environment.

Notes

1. S. Pfaffenzeller (2010). 'Conscription and Democracy: The Mythology of Civil–Military Relations', *Armed Forces & Society* 36(3): 481–504.
2. The literature has often adopted the term 'middle power' to describe the three countries. For instance, in the case of Italy, see F. Andreatta (2001), 'Italy at the Crossroad: The Foreign Policy of a Medium Power after the Cold War', *Daedalus* 130: 45–66; L. Ratti (2011). 'Italy as a Multilateral Actor: The Inescapable Destiny

of a Middle Power', in M. Carbone (ed.). *Italy in the Post Cold War Order*. Lanham, MD: Lexington Books, 123–40; M. Siddi (2019). 'Italy's "Middle Power" Approach to Russia', *The International Spectator* 54(2): 123–8; G. Giacomello and B. Verbeek (eds) (2020), *Middle Powers in Asia and Europe in the 21st Century*. Lanham, MD: Lexington Books. Yet other scholars have emphasised the need to better engage with the middle power theory (MPT), providing a nuanced understanding of the international hierarchy, moving beyond the strict traditional tripartition of great, middle and small powers. See, for instance, G. Abbondanza (2020), 'Middle Powers and Great Powers through History: The Concept from Ancient Times to the Present Day', *History of Political Thought* 41(3): 397–418; G. Abbondanza (2021), 'The Odd Axis: Germany, Italy, and Japan as Awkward Great Powers', in G. Abbondanza and T. S. Wilkins (eds), *Awkward Powers: Escaping Traditional Great and Middle Power Theory*. London: Palgrave Macmillan, 3–39.

3. For a detailed debate on the concepts of transformation, adaptation and innovation, see W. Murray (2001), *Military Adaptation in War*. Cambridge: Cambridge University Press; T. Farrell, S. Rynning and T. Terriff (2013), *Transforming Military Power since the Cold War: Britain, France, and the United States, 1991–2012*. Cambridge: Cambridge University Press. For a seminal paper reviewing the different perspectives in the literature, see A. Grissom (2006), 'The Future of Military Innovation Studies', *Journal of Strategic Studies* 29(5): 905–34.

4. Recent analyses include D. Barno and N. Bensahel (2020), *Adaptation Under Fire: How Military Change in Wartime*. New York: Oxford University Press; T. G. Mahnken (ed.) (2020), *Learning the Lessons of Modern War*. Stanford, CA: Stanford University Press.

5. See M. van der Vorm (2021). 'The Crucible of War: What Do We Know About Military Adaptation?' *Journal of Advanced Military Studies* 12(1): 197–209.

6. E. Kier (1995), 'Culture and Military Doctrine: France between the Wars', *International Security* 19(4): 65–93; J. Russell (2020). *Innovation, Transformation, and War: Counterinsurgency Operations in Anbar and Ninewa Provinces, Iraq, 2005–2007*. Stanford, CA: Stanford University Press.

7. F. Coticchia and F. N. Moro (2015), *The Transformation of Italian Armed Forces in Comparative Perspective: Adapt, Improvise, Overcome?* Abingdon: Routledge; A. Sakaki, H. W. Maull, K. Lukner, E. S. Krauss and T. U. Berger (2019), *Reluctant Warriors: Germany, Japan, and their US Alliance Dilemma*. Washington DC: Brookings Institution Press; H. N. Fujishige, Y. Uesugi and T. Honda (2022), *Japan's Peacekeeping at a Crossroads: Taking a Robust Stance or Remaining Hesitant?* Basingstoke: Palgrave Macmillan.

8. E. A. Colby and A. V. Mitchell (2020), 'The Age of Great-Power Competition', *Foreign Affairs* 99(1):118–30. For a detailed analysis of the concept of 'great powers' or 'super power', see Abbondanza, 'Middle Powers and Great Powers through History, 397–418.

9. G. H. Snyder (1984), 'The Security Dilemma in Alliance Politics', *World Politics* 36(4):, 461–95; G. H. Snyder (1997). *Alliance Politics*. Ithaca, NY: Cornell University Press; O. Schmitt (2018), *Allies that Count: Junior Partners in Coalition Warfare*. Washington, DC: Georgetown University Press; M. Dian and H. Meijer (2020), 'Networking Hegemony: Alliance Dynamics in East Asia', *International Politics* 57(2): 131–49; M. Rapp-Hooper (2020), *Shields of the Republic: The Triumph and Peril of America's Alliances*. Cambridge, MA: Harvard University Press; J. Davidson (2020). *America's Entangling Alliances: 1778 to the Present*. Washington, DC: Georgetown University Press.

10. L. Simón, A. Lanoszka and H. Meijer (2021), 'Nodal Defence: The Changing Structure of US Alliance Systems in Europe and East Asia', *Journal of Strategic Studies* 44(3): 360–88; A. Lanoszka (2022), *Military Alliances in the Twenty-First Century*. New York: John Wiley.

11. For comparisons between the Italian and the Japanese case, see S. Beretta, A. Berkofsky and F. Rugge (eds) (2014), *Italy and Japan: How Similar Are They? A Comparative Analysis of Politics, Economics, and International Relations*. Berlin: Spinger; R. J. Samuels (2003), *Machiavelli's Children: Leaders and Their Legacies in Italy and Japan*. Ithaca, NY: Cornell University Press.

12. P. Ignazi, G. Giacomello and F Coticchia (2012), *Italian Military Missions Abroad: Just Don't Call It War*. Houndmills: Palgrave Macmillan; P. J. Katzenstein (1996), *The Culture of National Security: Norms and Identity in World Politics*. New York: Columbia University Press.

13. A. King (2006), 'Towards a European Military Culture?' *Defence Studies* 6(3): 257–77.

14. H. Biehl, B. Giegerich and A. Jonas (eds) (2013), *Strategic Cultures in Europe: Security and Defence Policies across the Continent*. Wiesbaden: Springer; J. Kaarbo (2015), 'A Foreign Policy Analysis Perspective on the Domestic Politics Turn in IR Theory', *International Studies Review* 17(2): 189–216. On Italy, see M. Carbone (2007), 'The Domestic Foundations of Italy's Foreign and Development Policies', *West European Politics* 30(4): 903–23.

15. For a comprehensive review, see P. A. Mello and D. Peters (2018), 'Parliaments in Security Policy: Involvement, Politicisation, and Influence', *British Journal of Politics and International Relations* 20(1): 1–16. See also the seminal R. D. Putnam (1988), 'Diplomacy and Domestic Politics: The Logic of Two-Level Games', *International Organization* 42(3): 427–60.

16. S. Griffin (2017), 'Military Innovation Studies: Multidisciplinary or Lacking Discipline', *Journal of Strategic Studies* 40(1): 198–203.

17. S. Catignani (2012), '"Getting COIN" at the Tactical Level in Afghanistan: Reassessing Counterinsurgency Adaptation in the British Army', *Journal of Strategic Studies* 35(4): 513–39.

18. Grissom, 'The Future of Military Innovation Studies'.

19. A recent exception is Abbondanza, 'The Odd Axis', 3–39.

20. For previous analyses covering two of the three cases, see Sakaki et al., *Reluctant Warriors*.

21. T. U. Berger (1998), *Cultures of Antimilitarism: National Security in Germany and Japan*. Baltimore, MD: Johns Hopkins University Press; Katzenstein, *The Culture of National Security*.

22. J. Gerring (2010), 'Causal Mechanisms: Yes, But . . .', *Comparative Political Studies* 43(11): 1499–526; P. Pierson (2000), 'Not Just What, But When: Timing and Sequence in Political Processes,' *Studies in American Political Development* 14(1): 72–92; P. Pierson (2004), *Politics in Time: History, Institutions and Social Analysis*. Princeton, NJ: Princeton University Press; S. D. Hyde and E. N. Saunders (2020). 'Recapturing Regime Type in International Relations: Leaders, Institutions, and Agency Space', *International Organization* 74(2): 363–95.

23. Kaarbo, 'A Foreign Policy Analysis Perspective on the Domestic Politics Turn in IR Theory'.

24. On qualitative interviews, see, among others, N. K. Denzin and Y. S. Lincoln (2011). *The SAGE Handbook of Qualitative Research*. Los Angeles, CA: Sage.

Chapter 2

Historical Background: The Cold War and Beyond

Germany, Italy and Japan emerged shattered from the Second World War. The cost of defeat was obviously immense in human, social and economic terms, yet the institutional and, more broadly, political fabric was also in shreds. As defeated powers, their militaries were not faring any better. The forty and more years that followed were characterised by a process of reconstruction that proceeded at least in part asymmetrically across the different domains and countries. The Cold War and its logic had a disproportionate impact on how these processes occurred. The United States was first of all an occupying power that gave a vital impulse to redesigning the institutions and rebuilding the economies. It was also the major ally in a new confrontation that required the armed forces of the three defeated powers to play some role in facing the new enemy. The evolutionary trajectory of the defence policy and armed forces in the Cold War was also deeply affected by domestic factors. The legacy of defeat in the Second World War and, in time, the development of domestic political preferences over the functions and structure of the new armed forces, which is also connected with the reinterpretation of this legacy, decisively contributed to shape that course. In this chapter we shall provide an overview of these trajectories, focusing, for each case, on how the external and domestic environments (co)evolved and describing the key features of the armed forces, their structure, budget and doctrine for the Cold War.

2.1 Germany

2.1.1 External environment and alliances

The foreign and defence policy of the Federal Republic of Germany was 'unnaturally constrained'[1] during the Cold War, with a sort of 'semi-sovereignty in strategic affairs'.[2] The Wehrmacht surrendered in May 1945, while the victorious powers occupied the country. The aim of the Allies, as reported in the final communiqué at the Potsdam Conference, was to extirpate German militarism and Nazism, disarming and demilitarising the country while 'continuing control over Germany's ability to conduct war'.[3] Germany's leaders emerged from Nazism with the intent to embrace democracy and pacifism as 'core political values in Germany's foreign-policy role concept' and become a trustworthy partner in the international community, even if this meant accepting restrictions on West Germany's autonomy in defence and foreign policy matters.[4] Domestic and international factors deeply affected the German armed forces in this phase. The process of 'de-Nazification' (*Entnazifizierung*) began at a domestic level, while the mounting international tension that culminated with the 'Berlin Blockade' (June 1948–May 1949) made clear the new reality of the Cold War.[5] In 1949, the Federal Republic of Germany (FRG) and the German Democratic Republic (GDR) were established. The Western Allies approved the German Constitution (the Basic Law), which then came into force. While the Western rhetoric still supported a potential reunification of Germany, clearly the focus was on the communist threat. However, in the late 1940s, potential Soviet aggression was not considered a great danger as long as the memory of war (both inside and outside Germany) was still vivid and, consequently, West German rearmament was blocked. Moreover, Chancellor Adenauer was not keen on German rearmament, believing rather that Germany should have provided a contingent for an integrated European army, in return for complete sovereignty.[6] Adenauer had three main aims: to obtain greater commitment from the United States; to prevent Germany from becoming the battlefield between the United States and the USSR; and to regain German sovereignty.[7] The outbreak of the Korean War fostered the controversial process of German rearmament,[8] highlighting the risks of conflict in the heart of Europe. This was only a few years, in fact, after the end of the Nazi regime and the commitment (made at Potsdam) to demilitarisation.[9] Initially, West Germany had no national armed forces, with the Federal Border Guard being created in 1951. Conscious of the need for Germany's contribution in defending Europe from the Soviets, NATO military planners, in an effort to increase troop strength, advocated the 'renunciation of the policy of German demilitarization and acceptance of the participation of the FRG in the defence of Western Europe'.[10] However, this led to differences between Paris and Washington over the timing of German rearmament. The kind of German military integration that was 'needed to keep Germany from having a capability for independent action' (that is, a German national army or something deeply integrated at multinational level) was a vital issue that was also debated by the Pentagon and the Department of State.[11] France was concerned that such a move would provoke a tough reaction from Moscow. Yet although the Allies and the German leaders agreed on the need for restrictions on German forces, due to the increasing Cold War tensions, the establishment of the German armed forces (the Bundeswehr) was eventually accepted by all.[12]

To address the issue of rearmament, in 1950 Adenauer established a government office to design the new German armed forces. Such a move was not public, although it was known to the Allies. The so-called 'Himmerod memorandum', based on advice by former Wehrmacht senior officers, represented a crucial base for the future of the West German armed forces.[13] At international level, Germany approved the 'Eden Plan' that supported German national forces under NATO command and, together with France, Great Britain, Italy and the Benelux countries, was part of the West European Union (WEU).[14] While the proposed treaty of the European Defence Community (EDC), which included Germany, was rejected by the French parliament, further international agreements substantially confirmed the process that led to the end of 'occupation forces'. The Allies maintained forces in Germany, however, continuing to occupy West Berlin, and the Bundeswehr was subject to a number of restrictions, especially in terms of force levels, deployment and military capabilities (including NBC weapons[15]). Only parts of the Territorial Defence forces remained under national command, while the combat units of the Bundeswehr were assigned to NATO command. As stated by the former Chief of Staff of the British Sector of Berlin, Geoffrey Van Orden, the Bundeswehr (created in 1955) 'was a product of the conflicting Allied desires to oppose the Soviet threat while containing Germany. The nature of the German armed forces was largely determined by Alliance requirements and constrained by safeguards designed to prevent a resurgence of German militarism.'[16]

At domestic level, while parties such as the SPD and a large percentage of public opinion were sceptical towards rearmament, the popularity of Chancellor Adenauer and rising Cold War tensions (and the war in Korea in 1950) allowed the government to secure a majority in parliament to sustain this new course.[17] There were, however, restrictions. First, on how force should be used: the first Defence Supplement to the Basic Law (the German Constitution) authorised the creation of armed forces 'for defence' in accordance with Articles 26 and 87a of the Basic Law, allowing the use of the military only for defensive purposes.[18] Secondly, although the FRG recovered its sovereignty in the 1950s, its armed forces were placed under the direct command of NATO.[19] The Bundestag approved German participation in NATO in 1954, and in 1955 Germany became a member. The army was central in this process and, as recently remarked, the Bundeswehr served 'as a political means of integrating with the West'.[20] Moreover, the aims of the German armed forces overlapped with those of NATO. The main role of the Bundeswehr, in fact – to ward off a potential Soviet attack with a large conventional army – was basically the central aim of the Alliance itself.[21] While the Bundeswehr has been equipped with nuclear-capable missiles since the end of the 1950s, the nuclear warheads remained under American control.[22] Bonn recognised 'that nuclear weapons were vital to German security'.[23] Yet, despite such support for the US and NATO nuclear umbrella, German leaders disagreed with Washington on the fact that a 'nuclear war could be controlled'.[24]

The restrictions that characterise the re-birth of the German military proved to be long-lasting. While German industry had already recovered in the 1950s, the defence sector – which had already started to produce high-level military assets such as battle tanks and a missile-armed tank destroyer – was continued to be affected by the post-war regulation for a while.[25] Moreover, although international demands on Germany for a greater military contribution increased, especially since the 1960s, German military activities outside the country and the NATO area were not permitted, even when the FRG became a UN member (1973). A decision by the Federal Security Council of 1982 confirmed this restrictive view, denying Germany participation in any intervention except in self-defence.[26] Thus, despite some pressures,[27] and contrary to allies such as Italy (see below), FRG cabinets 'formally decided to interpret the Constitution as prohibiting any German participation in out-of-area missions',[28] a position that was maintained until the decision adopted by the Constitutional Court in July 1994. Indeed, rising Cold War tensions in the 1980s, while fostering some changes at domestic level on the issue of pacifism, did not alter Bonn's reluctance. With the end of the Cold War and the reunification of the country, German defence faced new challenges: transforming (and downsizing) the Bundeswehr and creating the 'army of unity'.[29] The East German Armed Forces, or NVA, ceased to exist on 3 October 1990. Up until then, the strength of the Bundeswehr amounted to under 500,000 soldiers, half of whom were conscripts. Yet in view of the demographic decline this level of force was not considered as sustainable.[30]

2.1.2 Strategic culture and institutional constraints

The West German Armed Forces were placed under supranational (NATO) command, while, more than anywhere else, civilians were subjected to constant monitoring, especially through parliament. The German 'civilian power narrative', which was largely shared across the political spectrum and considered vital to German identity, was based on the following principles: multilateralism; NATO control over the Bundeswehr; a strictly defensive mission; and the primacy of civilian means.[31] A global role outside NATO by West German political leaders was not considered conceivable. The explicit formulation of national security interests was avoided by endorsing multilateral institutions.[32] Germany's national interests were 'routinely defined in terms of norms and values, such as its close integration with the West', while 'the pacifist impulse implied a strong preference for political solutions'.[33]

Whereas, on account of the restricted duties of the German forces, the literature on the military transformation of the Bundeswehr during the Cold War is limited, the scholarly debate on the 'new German strategic culture' is extensive. This subject has attracted interest for mainly two reasons. First, the difference between the pre- and post-Second World War situation is remarkable, from the fanatic militarism of Nazi Germany to the widespread pacifism and anti-militarism of the FRG. Secondly, despite increasing international threats, and despite also pressure from the Allies to increase its military contribution, Germany has been reluctant to use armed forces as an instrument of foreign policy for decades, testifying to the socialisation and institutionalisation of this new strategic culture established after the Second World War.[34]

The starting-point for understanding German strategic culture is obviously the Second World War and the *Stunde Null* ('zero hour', 8 May 1945), which represents 'the total physical, moral and psychological devastation and trauma that prevailed in Germany at the close of the Second World War'.[35] The *Primat der Politik* (primacy of politics) and the repudiation of militarism are the clear consequences of the *Stunde Null* that shaped the creation of the new armed forces.[36] For decades, military affairs in Germany were conducted under a '*Denkverbot*' (ban on thinking). In short, the legacy of the Second World War and the Nazi regime radically affected the birth and development of West German defence policy.[37] The new strategic culture is based on four major principles. First, 'Venusian values'[38] and 'anti-militarism'[39] emerged as key norms behind the restraints of West Germany in the field of security. The ban on wars of aggression, the cornerstone of this view, is enshrined in Article 26 of the Federal Constitution. Secondly, multilateralism has been a key element of German political culture.[40] The Federal Republic's security identity became a 'substitute identity', since it was 'intimately bound up with the greater Western cause'. The subordination of national troops to the NATO command well illustrates this condition.[41] This is the core of *Genscherism*, an approach named after the former Minister of Foreign Affairs, who maintained that diplomacy and cooperation – rather than the military – were the only legitimate tools of foreign policy.[42] Thirdly, clear civilian control of the armed forces, enshrined in the role assigned to the Bundestag by the constitution.[43] Fourthly, a leitmotif for the 'intellectual, political and moral reform of the military was *Innere Führung* and *Bürger in Uniform* (Citizen in Uniform)'.[44] *Innere Führung* has been variously translated as 'inner guidance', 'moral leadership', 'leadership and civic education', and 'leadership and character training'.[45] Democratisation of the armed forces was to be achieved through mandatory military service (Article 12 of the Basic Law) with male conscription (*Wehrpflicht*) to 'prevent the Bundeswehr from becoming a state within a state'.[46] In so doing, the Bundeswehr broke with a past marked by the involvement of the Wehrmacht in the crimes of the Nazi regime, but also by the ideal of the apolitical soldier of the *Reichswehr* in the Weimar Republic.[47] As the official presentation of the Bundeswehr states, 'obedience and the performance of duty are important military virtues, but they have their limits. These virtues no longer apply if they would result in violation of key values of the Basic Law. In particular, these values include respecting human dignity, observing the rule of law and international law, rejecting any despotism or tyranny, and commitment to freedom and peace.'[48]

This new image of the Bundeswehr helped to 'narrow' the gap with public opinion. In August 1975, 74 per cent of the population considered the armed forces of the FRG as 'important'.[49] During the Cold War, 'there was a relatively settled period throughout which the foundational elements and the external environment were largely mutually reinforcing'.[50] On the whole, the armed forces established in 1956 'with defence as their core mission' met quite large-scale approval within society.[51] However, German public opinion devoted very limited attention to defence policy, with a few exceptions, such as the debate on the German defence budget.[52] During the Cold War, popular support for Bonn's alliance framework increased. Partly due to the perception of the threat, a public consensus was emerging in Germany to support the status of being a US ally. Whereas in 1961 a slight majority was in favour of remaining neutral rather than allying with the United States, by 1981 this had substantially changed, with 55 per cent preferring the existing alliance against 31 per cent in favour of neutrality.[53] As in other European countries, the crisis of the 'Euro-missiles' fuelled public interest in security issues, paving the way for the development of the peace movement and the protests against intermediate-range nuclear missiles.[54] In 1977, in fact, after the Soviets deployed 400 intermediate-range SS-20 missiles, NATO decided to deploy Tomahawk Cruise missiles and Pershing II 'Euro-missiles' in Europe (and West Germany).[55] Although the resulting protests were unsuccessful, they influenced the domestic scenario, demonstrating how forty years after the end of the Second World War pacifism was still a core value in German domestic politics.

Institutions embraced and acted upon pacifist values.[56] Special attention had to be given to what Buras and Longhurst called an 'observable policy of the German strategic culture': stringent parliamentary control over the Bundeswehr.[57] Apart from the aforementioned Basic Law, other provisions and institutional tools deserve consideration. First of all, supervision of the armed forces 'rests primarily with two parliamentary committees, Budgetary[58] and Defence, and with the Parliamentary Commissioner for Military Affairs, commonly known as the *Ombudsman*'.[59] The Ombudsman, who is elected by the Bundestag, is 'responsible for protecting the basic rights of soldiers and for the practical application of the principles of *Innere Führung*', reporting annually to parliament and thus increasing parliamentary control over the armed forces.[60] The Parliamentary Commissioner for the Armed Forces[61] plays 'an important role in upholding the principles of leadership development and civic education in the Bundeswehr'.[62] In addition, according to the Basic Law, it is parliament, rather than the executive branch, that determines the existence of a state of defence. Moreover, the rights and duties of soldiers are defined in the 'Soldier's Law' (March 1956).[63] Lastly, although the 'civilian' strategic culture was broadly supported by parties and leaders during the Cold War, 'not all German political actors are necessarily constrained and restrained in a similar fashion'.[64] For instance, the CDU/CSU and SPD diverged over defence policy, both during and after the period of rearmament. As of the late 1950s, following the party congress at Bad Godesberg, the SPD accepted in principle the government's concept of rearmament and NATO membership.[65] On the whole, that is, since there were two camps: on the left the pacifists, who were very keen to avoid any attempt to use force as a foreign policy tool; and, on the other side, the conservatives, who were mainly concerned with Germany's commitment within the Western community and alliances.[66]

2.1.3 Key features of the armed forces and doctrines in West Germany

The UNSCOM operation (Iraq 1991), established for the purpose of monitoring chemical, biological, radiological and nuclear (CBRN) weapons in Iraq, was the Bundeswehr's first military mission abroad. During the Cold War, FRG troops were never deployed for military operations beyond domestic borders. The army was trained for high-intensity conventional conflict scenarios, but it was never actually used on the ground during military crises.[67] This did not mean that the armed forces of the FRG had no role or did not undergo transformations. Without the Bundeswehr and German participation in NATO, 'the West could have neither contained nor, if war had occurred, stopped the Soviet Army from overrunning most if not all of Western Europe'.[68] Thus, the Bundeswehr was 'organized, structured and equipped for one purpose: territorial defence'.[69] On accession to the WEU and NATO, the Bundeswehr was limited to a maximum of twelve divisions, while its peacetime strength could not exceed 500,000.[70] The command of the Bundeswehr was assigned to the Minister of Defence during peacetime and to the Chancellor in case of war, and both answered to the Bundestag. All the units were to operate under NATO structure and command in times of war.[71] The Bundeswehr, in fact, did not have a General Staff. Difficulties were overwhelming in the early years.[72] It was almost impossible for the West German armed forces to reach their full capacity of 500,000 troops without conscription, which came into effect in 1957, one year after the Bundeswehr was established.[73]

By early 1964, the originally planned structure composed of twelve divisions comprising around 415,000 officers and enlisted personnel was finally complete.[74] In addition, German leaders agreed to expand the West German army's territorial militia and reserves, mirroring to an extent the US Army National Guard. Perception of Soviet aggressiveness profoundly influenced the evolution of the German military.[75] The Bundeswehr, which since the 1970s has developed into the largest Western European armed forces, provided a significant contribution to NATO's land forces and integrated air defence in Central Europe. In the 1980s, its army was composed of '12 divisions with 36 brigades and over 7,000 tanks and other armoured vehicles, its *Luftwaffe* had 15 flying combat units, and its navy had around 1,000 combat aircraft, 18 surface-to-air missile battalions, and naval units with some 40 missile boats and 24 submarines, as well as several destroyers and frigates'.[76] This was in part due to an annual increase in defence spending of around 3 per cent in the two decades before the end of the Cold War, making Germany the third largest spender in NATO,[77] while reducing its expenditure to GDP.

In this context, the trajectories of the individual services differed from those at the very beginning of the post-Second World War era. The 'Himmerod Conference' proved to be crucial in plotting these paths.[78] 'As the main combat objective of the armed forces in the event of attack was "to restore the integrity of the territory", the army was the largest of the three services, with an authorized peacetime strength of 340,000 men.'[79] Due to its previous experience in the Second World War with ground mechanised manoeuvre warfare, and considering the thousands of tanks that the Warsaw Pact maintained in East German, the focus was clearly on armoured and mechanised units and anti-tank equipment. The *Bundesmarine* (navy) was designed to have a small force operating in the Baltic and North Sea.[80] The rearmament of the navy was facilitated by the post-Second World War maintenance of minesweeping flotillas manned by former German naval officers.[81] The German Minesweeping Service Authority (GM/SA) had been renamed the Minesweeping Group Cuxhaven in 1947, under the supervision of the Allied Control Commission, and assisted the US Navy.[82] With the FRG's accession to NATO, American military assistance increased, delivering equipment such as inshore minesweepers, patrol boats and other types of vessel.[83] In the 1950s, the coastguard was integrated into the new Bundesmarine, with the Baltic and North Sea being its exclusive areas of operation.[84] In the 1970s, the Bundesmarine represented one-third of NATO's naval forces in the North, North Atlantic and Baltic seas, while in the 1980s, German naval forces began operating alongside NATO allies in blue waters.[85] Nevertheless, the limits posed by budget restrictions made it difficult to modernise equipment. With the *Bundesluftwaffe* (*Luftwaffe*; airforce), the idea of German military leaders was to equip it with American aircraft, dispense with the old organisation, and adopt the logistical and organisational structure of the United States Air Force (USAF), with air defence delegated to the Allies.[86]

While the Bundeswehr rejected the 'US model' (partly on the grounds that German-made equipment was deemed to be superior), the Luftwaffe opted to imitate the USAF in terms of tactics and equipment. According to a major study on the topic, the reasons behind the different attitudes of the two services towards their US counterparts were both psychological (the former army officers who had built the new West German army, in fact, 'did not feel any inferiority' and firmly believed that the 'German army of World War II had been, man for man and unit for unit, the better army'[87]) and economic. Indeed, while German companies were able to produce high-quality modern arms for the army (the Leopard I battle tank, for example) this was not the case with the aeronautical industry. Luftwaffe officers realised that the only way they could catch up technologically and learn how to fight a modern air war would be to copy the Americans. Consequently, German–American collaboration between the air forces was constantly advocated. From the US standpoint, the major difficulties were regarded as budgetary limits and bureaucratic issues in rearmament, in a context where civilians had total administrative control.[88] On the whole, the overall integration and interoperability between the Bundeswehr and the NATO forces represented a crucial element in understanding the complex transformation of West German military units. Since the beginning of the bipolar era, German strategies and doctrines have been crafted within US and NATO frameworks, from the 'forward strategy' and 'flexible response' of the 1960s.[89] For example, since the end of the 1950s the strategy of 'massive retaliation' (with a rapid and, indeed, massive nuclear response in case of a military attack) was conceived as a vital insurance for West Germany. Beyond deterrence, 'flexible response' required the use of a conventional response, involving a rethinking of tasks.[90]

Yet in some fields Germany contributed decisively to developing doctrine, rather than merely 'downloading' it. In the 1980s, for example, the United States developed the Air–Land Battle doctrine 'that departed from the notion that the battle would be won in a main battle area. Instead, future battles would not be restricted to traditional notions of front lines and rear areas'.[91] The debate on a new 'offensive' doctrine lost its salience in West Germany when the Berlin Wall collapsed. The Bundeswehr agenda ceased to be concerned exclusively with the Cold War context and began to focus on the problems posed by reunification with East Germany.[92] Despite integration with the Allies, there were also continual clashes and divergences regarding planning. In the 1950s, German political and military leaders, clearly concerned about the risk of fighting a nuclear war on German soil, were disconcerted to see NATO's lines of defence being moved further into West Germany, leaving large sections of territory potentially outside the defence perimeter.[93] Indeed, they criticised the doctrine of mobile defence, calling for strong fortified positions and the holding of terrain, and then successfully established that all West German territory had to be included in the collective defence. Although the bulk of armaments were provided with American aid and German soldiers were trained under the direction of the US Army until 1957, German operational concepts and previous military experiences (such as on the Eastern Front during the Second World War) played a vital role in the planning of Bundeswehr operations.[94] The White Paper of 1970 affirmed the relevance of the German armed forces as a national institution, aiming to achieve a growing normalisation in military affairs.[95] In 1972, under an SPD government, the Bundeswehr underwent a reform.[96]

A major problem that was emerging regarded conscription. In the early 1970s, due to rising personnel costs the proportion of the budget spent on military hardware fell to below 30 per cent of the overall defence budget.[97] Reducing personnel costs thus became an important, and constant, goal for Bonn.

2.2 Italy

2.2.1 External environment and alliances

Italian defence policy in the Cold War was profoundly influenced by the experience of the Second World War. The 'political and psychological heritage of the war and fascism', together with severe economic restrictions and domestic tensions, fostered a 'general reshaping of the role of the armed forces in public life'.[98] Italy delegated its external security to the United States and NATO, choosing the 'Western front' shortly after the Second World War. Rome, however, still maintained a low international profile to limit tensions within the domestic political arena (marked by the presence of the major communist force in Western Europe), thus constraining the role of the military. Consequently, Italian foreign and defence policy in the Cold War period was affected by the constant contrast between the goals it pursued in international affairs (mainly through alliances) and on the domestic front.[99] Since the mid-1960s, and especially in the 1980s, Italy had promoted greater activism, particularly in the Mediterranean, and this activism bolstered attempts to reform and modernise its armed forces in the last years of the bipolar era. However, there is a stark contrast between the Cold War and the last three decades; until 2020, in fact, Italy has participated in 151 military missions abroad, 132 of which (87.4 per cent) began in the post-Cold War period.[100]

After the end of the Second World War, Italy struggled to recover its international status. With the 1947 Paris Peace Treaty, Italy managed to maintain its territorial integrity, opposing the demands made by France and Yugoslavia, but suffered considerable de-militarisation.[101] The intent of the Allies was to dismantle the fascist army, but also to leave a force large enough to guarantee public order and to defend the borders, thus supporting Washington and London in future war scenarios. Italy's optimism (or perhaps illusion) regarding the treaty evaporated after its ratification, sparking protests against an 'unjust peace',[102] with the Trieste issue still unsolved (see below). Not until it was admitted to the UN in 1955 did Italy completely regain its freedom of executive action, albeit still under the rigid international restrictions of the Cold War.

Two major factors affected Italian defence policy in the early post-Second World War years. The first was Italy's position in the Western bloc, which was formalised when it joined the Atlantic Treaty and NATO. Italy's inclusion in the treaty right from the start was the result of complex negotiations conducted in 1947–1948, which have been the subject of extensive historiographical debate.[103] Italy entered the North Atlantic Treaty in 1949 and NATO in the following year as one of its founding members. The main task of the Italian armed forces in the Cold War was to protect NATO's southeastern border from a possible Warsaw Pact invasion.[104] The 'fear of subversion' triggered by the large communist presence in Italy, and the victory of the Christian Democrats (DC) in the 1948 parliamentary elections, were decisive factors in achieving this. On the one hand, in fact, Italy was perceived as being in need of support, while, on the other hand, the governing coalition provided the Allies, primarily the United States, with enough assurances in terms of effective cooperation and willingness to comply with their requests.[105] What matters here is that once the decision to incorporate Italy was made (both by the other Western powers and by the Italian government), it had a wide-ranging impact on Italian defence policy, as NATO soon became of pivotal importance both in the devising of doctrine and as a reference point in the adopting of standards for the Italian armed forces.[106] The second factor that profoundly impacted Italian defence policy was the perception of threats. Italy was aware of its own vulnerability, which was determined partly by its geography. Historical research on the period has tended to downplay the idea that the Soviet Union represented an immediate danger in the eyes of Italian policymakers, especially just after the Second World War. Besides the preservation of territorial integrity, the most important fronts in Italian foreign policy focused on Austria due to the problems of the Südtirol/Alto Adige German-speaking minority, and Yugoslavia, with the leading issue being the status of the city of Trieste. The problem of Austria was addressed through bilateral negotiations and international agreements (the new Austrian Republic was to become a neutral state in 1955), which left Südtirol as a question of internal security, though with important foreign policy ramifications. In terms of defence policy, the most relevant aspect here is the use of army units in the region, especially after the onset of attacks, beginning in 1957, by a newly established secessionist movement, the *Befreiungsausschuss Südtirol* (South Tyrolean Liberation Committee).

Yugoslavia represented a more pressing problem, and arguably the most real military threat to Italian territory in the first decades of the Cold War. Trieste was jointly liberated from German forces by Anglo-American forces and Yugoslav (communist) partisans led by Marshal Tito, resulting in a de facto partition of the city, which was then declared Free Trieste Territory (FTT), a buffer zone between Italy and Yugoslavia.[107] Although in 1954 a Memorandum of Understanding de facto solved the issue by dividing the FTT into two areas, the Trieste question made it clear to Italian policymakers that they would have to be prepared to deal with some of the most strategic areas for Italy somewhat autonomously from NATO. Through the decades, and with the gradual improvement of Italian–Yugoslavian relations, the issue of the 'Eastern flank' would repeatedly be supplanted by that of the 'Southern front', with an ambiguous search for some level of strategic autonomy in the region.[108]

The evolution of the Cold War had a great impact on Italian defence. In particular, the US military presence in the country,[109] either direct or under the NATO umbrella, had a significant effect not only in guaranteeing Italian territorial defence (which, as mentioned earlier, was never a major concern of Italian and allied policymakers), but also in fostering connections between the US military and their Italian counterparts. The growing Italian armed forces benefited from the US presence in terms of training programmes aimed at teaching Italian soldiers to operate the mainly US-built military hardware (from artillery to aircraft) that was shipped to Italy in those years.[110] These relationships were often operational and geared to training on the ground and technical issues, and solidified over time as US military deployment in Italy increased from the mid-1950s, consistent with changes in US and NATO doctrine. The creation of a Southern European Task Force (SETAF), with a military base established in northeast Italy[111] which took place after Austria was neutralised and Allied troops were removed, was the most visible sign of a nationwide American presence on Italian soil including important naval bases in Sicily and Sardinia, in the following years. From the viewpoint of the Allies, primarily the United States and the United Kingdom, Italy's geopolitical position in the Mediterranean was a key military asset in naval operations and the maintaining of forward air bases.

Political and economic developments in the Middle East had the effect of increasing this centrality, but also created contrasts between US and Italian foreign policy preferences. On the one hand, in fact, the United States regarded Italy as a 'privileged' partner in the region, seeing the country's position and the web of relationships it had with the Arab world as a valuable asset.[112] At the same time, however, it was keen to prevent Italy's agendas in energy politics (specifically oil) and the Arab–Israeli conflict from becoming too autonomous. On the subject of energy, US–Italian relations were strained by the fact that the policies adopted by the Italian state-owned corporation ENI with oil-producing countries on the allocation of royalties were in contrast – being more generous – to those of the leading

US companies.[113] Concerning the Arab–Israeli conflict and the Palestinian question, meanwhile, Italian policy tended to be more fairly balanced than that of the United States (which sided more and more with Israel), due to both international and domestic pressure. The need to maintain good relations with Arab countries, together with the *Partito Comunista Italiano*'s (PCI) pro-Palestinian views, often prompted Italian governments to seek a more accommodative stance towards Arab and Palestinian positions than their major ally.[114] Most of these alignments (and re-alignments), however, had limited impact on defence policy itself, with NATO representing a constant benchmark for the Italian armed forces in their procurement decisions, doctrinal evolution and training cooperation (see below). From a military standpoint, the centrality of the Middle East in Italian foreign policy can also be seen in the military engagements in the region in the 1980s. Two events signalled the commitment of the Italian armed forces in the region and its pursuit of an autonomous (though by no means independent) role. First, Italy joined the Multinational Force and Observers (MFO), which operated in Sinai in 1982 to guarantee compliance with the 1978 Camp David Accords signed by Egypt and Israel, providing mostly naval assets. Secondly, and most importantly, the deployment of Italian forces in Lebanon in 1982 on two missions (August–September 1982 and September 1982–March 1984). These were the 'first international military interventions in which Italy deployed a large number of troops after WWII'.[115]Although these missions (see below) profoundly affected the Italian idea of strategy, operations continued to be influenced by the logic of the Cold War.[116]

Lastly, nuclear issues were of great importance in shaping the relationship between Italy and the United States in the Cold War.[117] Italy had hosted US weapons on its soil since the 1950s, and some leading policymakers viewed favourably the idea of building a European mechanism overseeing nuclear weapons.[118] No such solution ever succeeded, however, as all plans for the 'collective' supervision and management of nuclear weapons were immediately rejected by the United States. The so-called Euro-missiles,[119] ground-launched cruise missiles carrying nuclear warheads which were installed in Europe in the late 1970s, again suggested that the Italian cabinets and defence establishment might have been willing to make concessions to the domestic political consensus (the PCI and an anti-nuclear mass movement that coalesced on that very issue as of 1979) on some foreign policy issues and rhetoric, but not on what was deemed central to maintaining Italy's place in the Atlantic Alliance and what was perceived as a preferential relationship with the United States.[120] The different cabinets that dealt with the question, in fact, consistently demonstrated that despite frustration over specific issues of varying importance, Italy would not consider any alternative to the bilateral relationship with the United States, which continued to be regarded as the cornerstone of Italian 'nuclear policy' in the context of its broader defence policy.

2.2.2 Strategic culture and institutional constraints

Historical memories played a vital role in affecting the Italian strategic culture. According to the Ministry of Defence, in the Second World War Italy lost 320,000 soldiers (including partisans) and 160,000 civilians. While repudiating war as a 'normal' tool of international politics, Italian elites moved from the fascist culture to the 'culture of peace'.[121] There is a general consensus in literature that multilateralism, peace and humanitarianism were the main values of the Italian strategic culture in the Cold War.[122] A 'non-military', 'accommodationist' strategy culture emerged in Italy after the Second World War.[123] The legacy of fascism and the traumatic experience of the war and its catastrophic end[124] helped to 'bury nationalism',[125] with the crisis of Trieste (1952–1954) representing the last public attempt to openly assert national needs.[126] The rejection of nationalism also made it almost impossible to talk about national interests. Even the very concept of nation lacked legitimacy,[127] with scholars discussing the emergence of a 'multilateralist ideology'.[128] In short, several authors have pointed out how nationalism was 'camouflaged under internationalist clothes', which were (and in part still are) Atlanticism, Europeanism and 'Third-Worldism' (that is, a 'positive attitude' towards the so-called 'Third World'). The role of Catholic and communist political cultures was also essential in shaping Italian defence and foreign policy during the Cold War.[129] Indeed, pacifism and internationalism were fundamental values shared by the parties,[130] while 'proletarian internationalism' merged with 'Christian Ecumenism'.[131] In a context that had been characterised for decades by fierce opposition on the part of the PCI (which at its height represented a third of the electorate) to Italy's membership in the Western bloc, there was still common ground between 'internationalism and Christian values'.[132] This led to the adoption of a consensual approach by parties regarding defence issues, limiting the debate and the potential consequences of open divergences in the bipolar context.[133] The 'peace framework' has always represented the basis for a common approach in international politics.[134] This framework has clearly been present since the very beginning, and was visibly represented by the constitution. The main political parties shared the ethical repudiation of war as a means of advancing national interests.

At the same time, however, the defence of the homeland was a 'sacred duty of citizens' (Article 52). Moreover, parliamentary authorisation was required for ratifying treaties, thus limiting freedom of executive action (Article 80). The vote by parliament was clearly necessary in declaring a state of war (Article 78). The post-war 'consensus' was formalised in Article 11 of the Italian constitution drafted in 1946/7, which states: 'Italy rejects war as an instrument of aggression against the freedom of other peoples and as a means for the settlement of international disputes.' The second paragraph of the Article, however, allows for active participation in international organisations for the purpose of 'ensuring peace and justice among the Nations'. Like the rest of the constitution, Article 11 is the result of a compromise between political parties. The DC, in fact, supported (and were in turn supported by) the US-led emerging Western bloc, while the PCI and the *Partito Socialista Italiano* (PSI, Socialist Party) upheld democracy but had strong ties with the Soviet Union. This was a sort of 'dual loyalty' towards both the nation and the international actor (Washington or Moscow) that supported the Italian parties.[135] The PCI did not favour disarmament, rather supporting conscription; 'popular armed forces' and the 'democratisation of the army' were the objective, as opposed to a professional army separate from society.[136]

On the whole, regardless of the abovementioned Articles, defence policy had a marginal role in the constitutional debate and 'scepticism and indifference' towards military affairs were dominant in the Cold War.[137] Furthermore, the image of the armed forces during the Cold War was far from positive, as for decades they remained almost invisible in the face of an indifferent public opinion that considered them at best useless, and at times even dangerous,[138] with certain of their members being associated with attempts to destabilise the new democracy.[139] Despite such 'scandals', this general lack of interest towards the armed forces was instrumental in delegating a large part of the organisation of the military system to the generals. In short, defence was removed from the debate, even when pressing issues were at stake. For instance, the dramatic problem regarding veterans and prisoners-of-war (the Germans had captured approximately 650,000 soldiers, while others returned to Italy from Australia only in 1947) was paradoxically disregarded by public attention.[140] In the late 1970s and early 1980s this situation began to change. The large mobilisation of protests against the installation at Comiso (Sicily) of US missiles with nuclear warheads is essential in understanding the evolution of Italian strategic culture and the constant relevance of the peace framework. Indeed, from the initial parliamentary decision in 1979 until the dismantling of the intermediate-range nuclear missiles in 1987, Italy was constantly characterised by protests and rallies attended by thousands of people.[141] Hundreds of 'peace committees' were set up, with communists, radicals and also Catholics proclaiming their opposition.[142] The issue of peace became 'dominant in the public debate', with a number of protests denouncing not only the decision to instal the cruise missiles but also the overall logic and risks of the Cold War.[143] Pacifist movements also began to protest strongly against procurement policies (for example, the acquisition of F-16 fighter planes), demonstrating in front of US/NATO bases.[144] But while dramatic and controversial circumstances occasionally caused a temporary rise in the public interest in defence policy during the bipolar era, the overall attention of the Italian parliament on military affairs remained extremely low.

A crucial element that interacts with 'strategic culture' is the institutional context, and especially the role played by political parties and parliaments. While Italy's low profile in defence policy was related to international restrictions and cultural characteristics, poor parliamentary supervision also limited public engagement in this domain.[145] A lack of professionalism on the part of the MPs in the field, lack of control over the government in terms of institutional infrastructure, capabilities, resources and willingness, and a consensual approach adopted by the parties in order to avoid open conflict were the main characteristics of the parliamentary role with regard to Italian defence.[146] In the early years of the Cold War, despite the goal of the new democracy to 'establish control over the military', there was little actual supervision, and assembly debates tended to develop into just 'skirmishes' between pro- and anti-NATO MPs.[147] Later, with the introduction of substantial domestic political changes,[148] parliamentary attention of defence policy increased, and the *Leggi promozionali* (promotional laws, or bills of rearmament) for the army, navy and air force, as well as the *Libro Bianco* (Italy's White Paper on Defence) introduced in 1977, marked the beginning of discussions on the structure of the armed forces. It was not until the 1980s, however, that comprehensive debates and reforms took place. Overall, parliament and political elites allowed the armed forces considerable autonomy in organising themselves – a permanent trait in Italy since the liberal era.[149] In the early decades of the republic, for instance, policymakers did not actually discuss in detail the model for the large armed forces after the end of the Second World War – a model which, as shown below, was clearly unsustainable.

2.2.3 The evolution of the armed forces: structure and doctrine

Italian strategic documents, as well as the overall debate on defence, were extremely limited after the Second World War.[150] Today, however, the fairly extensive academic studies written on the subject have shed light on various aspects relating to the structure and doctrine of the forces in the Cold War period. In what military historian Nicola Labanca calls the 'reconstruction phase' (1945–1948),[151] despite the lack of resources, the general staff was more inclined to focus on building larger armed forces rather than small but well-equipped units. In this phase, the armed forces were also a way of providing employment for a substantial number of people.[152] This approach was also supported by the political leaders who, focusing their efforts on restoring international status, failed to see the value of more effective but smaller forces. As Italy did not have possibility of rebuilding its forces without external support, 'supervision by the Allies' was crucial.[153] After the war and the Treaty of Paris, the Italian armed forces were considerably reduced. The main limitations regarded the navy (which, for example, was not allowed to have submarines), partly because the army and the air force had suffered greater damage in the war.[154] Subsequently, NATO membership 'promoted the transformation of the forces', setting new goals and providing new equipment and support.[155]

Besides the military contribution, in the early 1950s, Minister of Defence Randolfo Pacciardi also played a crucial role in supporting the need for large forces, notwithstanding the limited responsibilities. World tensions (rearmament prompted by the Korean War, the Soviet nuclear bomb and Communist China) clearly favoured this approach. De Gasperi supported Pacciardi's request despite a degree of opposition within the government, tripling military expenses[156] but avoiding open parliamentary discussion on the matter.[157] This approach did not prove to be sustainable, and in the second half of the 1950s, while modernising the forces with American support, the Italian army was forced to 'scale down its former expectations', amending programmes and cutting down on the number and size of the divisions.[158]

In the 1950s, one element emerged that continues to affect the entire history of Italian defence: personnel expenses were higher than those allocated to investments and equipment.[159] In this period, however, the attention including that of the Allies, was on the army more than the navy, since the main threat came from northeastern Europe rather than from the Mediterranean Sea. It was during these years that Italy agreed to host US nuclear missiles on its soil.[160] The pursuit of greater cost-effectiveness continued in the mid-1960s, with Italy's efforts to reorganise its forces accelerating at the end of the decade. The 'restructuring' of the armed forces was also necessary to adequately implement NATO's requests (such as the doctrine of Flexible Response) in alignment with the military growth of the Soviets. At the same time, political and military elites pushed for the modernisation of equipment. For instance, the rising Soviet military presence in the Mediterranean and the obsolescence of some of the assets demanded greater investment in the navy. The army, paying the price for its decision to focus on large forces, was having to deal with problems clearly caused by inefficiency and ineffectiveness.

As mentioned earlier, the very first in-depth parliamentary debates (along with the *Leggi Promozionali* and the *Libro Bianco*) and strategic documents on defence and military issues made their appearance in the mid-1970s. The army, which was based on conscription (a military service of eighteen months, subsequently reduced to twelve), counted 260,000 units. The modernisation of the forces continued in the 1970s with new submarines, Leopard tanks and F-104 aircraft, while the military budget was increased.[161] In 1974, the navy's White Paper paved the way for the building of Italy's first aircraft carrier, the *Giuseppe Garibaldi* (which was deployed in 1983).[162]

Doctrinal changes accompanied these transformations and were incorporated in the White Paper issued in 1977. Prudence dominated, with the preservation of the tenets of post-war policy regarding the use of military force 'only to defend national institutions, as distinguished between "war" functions (such as halting external aggression, guaranteeing territorial integrity and so on) and "peace" functions (such as controlling the borders and protecting vital infrastructures)'.[163] While the 'defensive posture' was still paramount, the document stressed the need for a 'radical renovation'[164] of Italian defence due to the 'obsolescence'[165] of the military system and a severely imbalanced budget in which a huge percentage was allocated to personnel. Lastly, the *Libro Bianco* aimed to overturn the image of the armed forces as a body separate from society. In short, the White Paper launched the 'reorganisation' of the forces, in keeping with the requests put forward by the services, which were to contribute to defining the last phase of the Cold War.[166]

From 1976 to 1989 the Italian military underwent a considerable transformation, essentially as a result of three main aspects: changes in the international scenario (both regarding the bipolar confrontation and the instability on the southern front); an initial military thrust with the operation(s) in Lebanon (1982–1984) and other minor missions (Red Sea, Persian Gulf); and the White Paper published in 1985. As we have seen, Italy agreed to instal Euro-missiles on its territory. The main commands of the armed forces were all still based in northern Italy, but increasing attention and concern were being directed to the Mediterranean. Despite the Sigonella episode mentioned earlier, and the national political and diplomatic activism in the Middle East, the Italian foreign and defence policy of the 1980s remained firmly bound, and subordinated, to the United States. In other words, the Cold War logic still dominated the decisions adopted by Rome regarding the international context.[167] Moreover, despite attempts at reforms, modernisation and a first military action, there were still several long-standing problems such as inter-service rivalries and the general inefficiency of the military assets. Defence budgets also reflected four decades of evolution in defence. Nascia and Pianta identify several phases of military budget:

> the Atlantic rearmament under De Gasperi (1948–1950, 4% of the GDP, 18% of the public budget); the period of consolidation and 'stability' (1951–1958, expenses at 20% of the public budget); the 'strengthening' phase (1959–1973, with a new increase in military expenses but also in GDP and public budget, which moved the figure to 3% and 12%, respectively); the reduction of 1974–1975 (with a 11% drop in defence budget) after a new increase (1976–1980, around 3.5% of the GDP per year). Lastly, in 1981–1988 the highest military expenses were incurred, due partly to the return of the Cold War rearmament, with a yearly increase of 4.8%. This was followed by a reduction in the late 1980s and, after the collapse of the Berlin Wall, a considerable drop (around 12%) until the mid 1990s, before expenses were stabilised (1.5% of the GDP). Once again, only by considering the interaction between the international context (structure, alliances, threats, and so on) and the logic of the domestic scenario can we comprehend the results of Italian defence policy.[168]

The same is true for overseas military operations. While for decades a low profile and a static approach characterised Italian defence, which remained constantly at an 'embryonic level' during the bipolar era,[169] the 1980s began to see an increase in military dynamism.[170] Italian troops were deployed in Malta, Sinai, the Red Sea and, especially, Lebanon as part of the UNIFIL mission). In the two missions in Lebanon (the first in August–September 1982 and the second from September 1982 to March 1984), around 8,000 Italian military personnel were involved in the operations, with one soldier killed during a patrol. The first operation, undertaken within the so-called Multinational Force and with domestic bipartisan consensus, addressed the issue of the fighters of the Palestinian Liberation Organisation (PLO). The goal of the second operation was to support the new Lebanese government in gaining stabilisation. After the attacks on American and French troops and the Soviet Union's growing support of Syria, the context changed considerably, including from the Italian perspective. Cold War logic still played a massive role, while the level of risk for the troops increased considerably. As a result, Italy pulled out. Generally speaking, the first important mission abroad increased the debate on Italian defence, urging the re-examination of the country's role and military capabilities and the reforms that were needed to address rising threats abroad. Thus, the *Libro Bianco* (1985), which laid out in a clear form such views, represented the perfect bridge between Italian Cold War policy and the new national approach that was to develop with the end of the bipolar confrontation. The document, which was drafted by Minister of Defence Spadolini after the missions in Lebanon, discussed for the very first time a new role for the Italian armed forces, introducing the concept of joint operations. Interoperability among services became crucial in Italian defence.[171] The *Libro Bianco*, while recognising certain existing weaknesses (such as anti-aircraft or anti-tank missiles, for example) insisted on deployability as a new key feature for operations, which would no longer be based on a clear distinction between 'peacetime' and 'wartime'. A joint approach was deemed central to operations, with function, rather than services, becoming the cornerstone of planning.[172]

In this new framework, nevertheless, differentiation between services remained important. While the army enjoyed a degree of autonomy from the Allies (for example, in forward defence and territorial defence), this was not the case with the navy, nor the air force,[173] which was still dependent on NATO, especially with regard to activities that required high-end technologies, such as reconnaissance.[174] One newly introduced service was *Forza di Intervento Rapido* (FIR, or rapid deployment force), created for peacekeeping and for guaranteeing the security of Italian citizens abroad. However, the Additional Note to the 1987 defence budget still considered the FIR as functionally and financially part of 'territorial defence'.[175] Unlike the French *Force d'Action Rapide*, therefore, the Italian FIR was conceived as a force for mobile national territorial defence rather than for missions abroad.[176] This is an example of a broader ambiguity. Although the *Libro Bianco* called for the modernisation of military assets, the gap between the actual force size and financial resources remained considerable. Consequently, Italian defence continued to be affected by a problematic interaction between a large army with resources unbalanced in favour of personnel and the pressing need for transformation.

2.3 Japan

2.3.1 The external environment and alliances

Post-war Japan is generally described as a *heiwa kokka*, a peace-loving nation. In keeping with this identity, during the Cold War period Japan developed a low defence posture prompted by the need to guarantee the country's security while minimising both economic costs and strategic risks. Operating within these limits, Japan developed – especially during the last two decades of the Cold War – a significant and technologically sophisticated military force, despite severe restrictions in terms of procurement and operational functions. This approach was the result of the political choices of the Japanese leadership, which were heavily influenced by both external and domestic restrictions. The relationship with the United States and the evolving Cold War security environment were the two most important features of Japan's strategic landscape.

The country was occupied by the United States from September 1945 to April 1952.[177] This occupation was effectively divided into two distinct phases. During the first, the process of demilitarisation and the democratisation of Japan's political system, as well as its society and economic system, were at the centre of US priorities. This period culminated with the approval of the new Japanese constitution, which introduced universal suffrage, promoted the establishment of new and free political parties and trade unions, limited the role of the emperor and set strict restrictions on the role of the military. This phase came to an end in late 1947. The mounting Cold War rivalry and the emergence of the strategy of containment led the United States to deeply reconsider the priorities of the occupation. Like Germany, in this new context Japan was no longer considered as merely a dormant enemy, but rather as a part of the main bulwark against the expansion of communism and Soviet influence in Asia.[178] The second phase was characterised by the 'Reverse Course' policy that shifted the focus of the occupation away from the process of democratisation and demilitarisation to pursue the new strategic priorities generated by the looming Cold War geopolitical rivalry. Consequently, economic recovery and industrial reconstruction, as well as integration in the 'anticommunist camp', became the main objectives of the occupation.[179] To speed up the recovery process, all attempts to radically decentralise the Japanese economic and industrial system by dismantling the *zaibatsu*, the giant industrial conglomerate that was regarded as one of the main causes of the war, were shelved. At the same time, the US authorities sought to groom new allies within the country, on the one hand, by promoting the 'Red Purge' that led to the exclusion of all communists from public office,[180] and, on the other, by supporting the emergence of a centre-right coalition that in 1955 led to the founding of the Liberal Democratic Party (LDP, *Jimintō*), which was to become the dominant party of the Japanese post-war democracy.[181]

These tendencies were further fuelled by the outbreak of the Korean War. The conflict had several consequences for Japan. First, it contributed to Japanese economic recovery, since a large part of Japanese exports in this period was related to US military procurement.[182] More importantly, the war accelerated the consolidation of the Cold War military alignments as it convinced US leaders of the urgent need to establish a system of alliances that could guarantee both the protection and control of US anti-communist partners in the period following the end of the occupation.[183] This led to the signing, in September 1951, of the Treaty of San Francisco, which re-established peaceful diplomatic relations between Japan and the other signatories.[184] Contextually, Japan signed the Security Treaty that established its alliance with the United States.[185] The 1951 Security Treaty, however, did not include a formal and explicit security clause and granted the United States police powers within Japan as well as unrestricted use of military bases, including the stationing of nuclear weapons. At the end of the occupation, the United States kept over 200,000 troops stationed in the country to protect it and to safeguard Washington's presence and influence Japan's foreign and security policies.[186] The original treaty was renegotiated in the late 1950s, resulting in the signing of the Mutual Security Treaty (*Anpo* in Japanese) in 1960. This treaty, which is still in effect today, included an asymmetric security clause that bound the United States to protect Japan while denying the right of the latter to collective self-defence, which was prohibited under Article 9 of the constitution. With the *Anpo*, Japan granted the United States the use of the bases and gradually assumed responsibility for its defence against external aggression.[187] The content of the treaty, as well as the history of the negotiations leading up to it, provide an important insight into Japan's strategic priorities during the Cold War.

Once Tokyo secured the protection of the United States, its main priority was, on the one hand, to avoid being caught up in the conflicts stemming from Cold War rivalry, and, on the other, to minimise the impact of defence expenditure on Japan's recovery and fast-paced development. Japan therefore opposed both collective security clauses and a degree of interoperability and military integration present in other US alliances.[188] This approach was influenced by the fact that the Japanese perception of threat differed considerably from that of the United States, especially during the 1950s and 1960s. After the Korean War, adopting the 'domino theory' approach, the United States began to consider every possible advancement of communist influence as a significant threat, blurring all distinction between the defence of fundamental and marginal interests and areas. Moreover, US policymakers largely underestimated internal fractures and tensions within the communist bloc. Tokyo, while considering the external environment dangerous, had a much narrower perception of the main threats to its security. Both the Soviet Union and China were considered threatening. Nevertheless, it was estimated that neither of them were willing to directly attack Japanese territory. Moreover, the Japanese leadership never shared the political and strategic views of the domino theory. On the contrary, since the early 1950s Japan's policies and statements largely predicted that China would not have accepted a position of subordination to the USSR in the longer term, anticipating the Sino–Soviet split of the 1960s.[189] This divergence in threat perception and policy priorities become clear during the 1960s and, particularly, the Vietnam War. The strategy of flexible response and the domino theory prompted the United States, as Kennedy argued, to 'pay any price and bear every burden' to demonstrate their credibility and resolve in the fight against communism. This resulted in Washington becoming caught up in the war in Vietnam to prevent the other dominoes, primarily Japan, from falling.[190] This approach did not reassure Japan. Both the political elite and the public feared more the risk of becoming entrapped in an unwanted conflict and the escalation of tension between the blocs than the advance of communism in relatively secondary theatres. Thus, Japan tried to minimise its role in the conflict, which was limited to the use of bases.[191]

The strategic environment was the area in which Japanese foreign and defence policies evolved most significantly in the late 1960s and early 1970s. The Vietnam War demonstrated the logical and strategic failure of the flexible response and the domino theory. Consequently, the United States needed to rethink its approach to containment and go back to distinguishing between fundamental and secondary interests and theatres, while making its grand strategy politically and economically sustainable. The initial effect of this process was the Guam Doctrine, namely, the declaration that while the United States pledged to maintain the credibility of the alliances, the Asian allies would need to provide the manpower and the resources for their own defence. For Japan this represented an important turning point. For the first time, Japanese policymakers feared being abandoned by the United States. Moreover, the Guam Doctrine gave the United States more leverage with Tokyo, leading to the first requests for more equitable burden-sharing within the alliance.[192]

Nixon's visit to China in 1972 marked a second important turning point. In the longer term, Japan benefited enormously from the resumption of bilateral relations with the People's Republic of China (PRC), a policy that it had advocated since the 1950s.[193] In the short term, as Edwin O. Reischauer stated at the time, due to the failure on the part of the Nixon administration to either consult or inform the Japanese government, 'the Japanese confidence in the reliability of the American defence commitment was seriously damaged'.[194] Moreover, America's opening up to China led Tokyo to believe that Japan's centrality in the US strategy in Asia could be undermined.

The 1970s, however, did not bring only bad news for Japan. Lingering doubts about US commitment were compensated by the relaxation of tensions generated by the superpower détente of the 1970s, which led to the regulating of competition between the United States and the Soviet

Union. Moreover, Japan was quick to follow in America's footsteps with China, recognising the PRC in 1972 and ultimately signing a Treaty of Peace and Cooperation in 1978.[195] In the late 1970s, while bilateral relations with Beijing improved, several factors, such as the decline and eventual demise of the global détente, the Soviet military rebalancing towards Asia prompted by its rivalry with China, and an extensive naval build up, led to a deterioration of the security environment in East Asia.[196]

In this context, the United States and Japan agreed to a substantial updating of their alliance, approving the Guidelines in 1978.[197] The document institutionalised the Japanese commitment to achieve the capacity to autonomously defend itself against direct invasion and established the possibility of joint military planning and exercises, which were previously excluded. In addition, the Maritime Self-Defence Force (MJSDF, the Japanese navy) began to patrol and defend the sea lines of communication around Japan and the main straits of the Japanese Archipelago.[198] These breakthroughs enabled Japan to cooperate more closely with the United States in the last decade of the Cold War when the Soviet threat appeared to be on the rise, especially after the shooting down of a South Korean civilian airliner in 1983 and the deployment of SS-20 IRBM missiles in the Soviet Far East.

2.3.2 Strategic culture and institutional constraints

Strategic incentives and systemic restrictions are filtered through the lenses of domestic debate, norms and ideas. This was particularly significant for post-war Japan, where defence policies were deeply influenced by war memories and anti-militarist sentiments, and also by institutional restrictions which limited the role of the JSDF.[199] Article 9 of the post-war constitution is institutionally and symbolically at the centre of Japanese anti-militarism. The Article states that 'the Japanese people forever renounce war as a sovereign right of the nation and the threat or use of force as means of settling international disputes'. Moreover, 'land, sea and air forces, as well as other war potential, will never be maintained. The right of belligerency of the state will not be recognized.'[200]

The official reinterpretation of the Article has varied significantly.[201] In the early post-war years, the establishment of armed forces was considered illegal. The first interpretations in 1952 and 1954 determined that Japan could own independent armed forces, but could not develop 'war potential' (senryoku). This introduced the possibility of establishing the JSDF with the minimum level of capabilities needed to defend the national territory. Interpretations offered in 1954 and confirmed in

1968 determined that Japan could not perform any collective defence, nor deploy armed troops abroad. Consequently, its defence policies had to be exclusively defence-oriented (*senshu bōei*), that is, geared only to protecting the national territory from external attack, without retaining offensive and power projection capabilities.[202]

Besides Article 9, other articles of the constitution also limited the country's defence policies. The most significant of these is probably Article 66, which establishes strict civilian control over the military, banning all uniformed personnel from serving in government positions. The purpose of this was to avoid the risk of repeating the military take-over of the government that had led to Japan's imperialism in the 1930s. Based on this principle of direct control over the military, up until 2007 Japan was prevented from formally having an autonomous Ministry of Defence. The Defence Agency that coordinated defence policies was placed directly under the control of the prime minister. Within the JDA, the effective policy planning was assigned to the Internal Bureau, which was made up exclusively of civilians. Moreover, officials from other ministries, primarily those of foreign affairs, finance, and industry and trade were seconded to key positions in the Defence Agency to ensure supervision and control.[203]

Aside from the legal interpretation of Article 9 and other institutional arrangements, the debate on the Japanese post-war identity was particularly intense. Progressive forces, comprising the socialist and communist parties, trade unions and anti-bases and anti-nuclear movements, advocated that Japan needed to break completely away from the legacy of wartime militarism and aggression to build a peace-loving, neutral and unarmed country. They opposed the alliance, the presence of US bases and the very existence of the JSDF, which they saw as a possible cause of involvement in a new conflict.[204]

Conservative forces promoted a very different post-war identity, rooted in a distinctive interpretation of the Japanese pre-war and wartime experience. The conservative coalition of forces that consolidated around the LDP was also supported by the *Keidanren* (Japanese Business Federation) and by grassroots associations such as the *Jinja honchō* (Association of Shinto Shrines) and the *Nippon Izokukai* (War-Bereaved Families Association). This coalition shared the belief that Japan did not conduct a war of aggression but was driven to war by the brutality of international politics and the aggression of Western imperialism. Moreover, the sacrifice of the wartime generation needed to be remembered and honoured, since it constituted the foundation of post-war prosperity.[205]

From this point of view, the alliance was deemed a necessary, albeit temporary, tool for promoting the reconstruction of the country and its economic development while protecting it from Soviet and Chinese threats. In the longer term, Japan would eventually return to more autonomous foreign and defence policies, more fitting for its status and prestige.

Most of the post-war governments, generally led by the LDP, sought to both react to the evolving external environment and to find a compromise between these opposing interpretations of Japanese identity. Key post-war prime ministers such as Yoshida Shigeru and his supporters Ikeda Hayato and Sato Eisaku held the middle ground, very pragmatically promoting and institutionalising a strategy that would later be called the Yoshida Doctrine.[206] They fundamentally disagreed with progressive ideas such as unarmed neutrality and promoted the creation and the consolidation of the alliance, which guaranteed Japan security while allowing it to concentrate on economic development. At the same time, they upheld Article 9 and the other legal limits as useful instruments both for diffusing US pressure to contribute more to regional security and for appeasing the opposition from the Left. Ultimately, they managed successfully to navigate through the multiple risks they were facing during the Cold War: they provided security for the country without over-burdening it economically; maintained stable relations with Washington without being caught up in existing conflicts; and found a compromise between progressive anti-militarism and the conservative will to return to a more autonomous and active role in international affairs.

During the Vietnam War, when both fears of entrapment and domestic political pressures from progressive forces were at their peak, Japanese policymakers opted to establish new limits to the country's defence policies, contributing to a new wave in the institutionalisation of Japanese anti-militarism. In 1967, the Sato government approved the Three Non-Nuclear Principles, on the basis of which Japan would not produce, possess or store nuclear weapons on its soil. In the same year it adopted the Three Principles on Arms Exports, banning the export of arms or other defence materials to communist bloc countries that could be involved in a conflict or subject to UN sanctions. Subsequently, in 1976, this principle was extended to include not only the communist bloc but all countries. Furthermore, in 1969, Japan declared its commitment not to use space for military purposes.[207] In the 1980s, until the end of the Cold War, most of these restrictions remained in place, despite the intention of the leadership to assume a more visible security role in the alliance and in the region.

2.3.3 Key features of the armed forces in Japan

Even though the role of the JSDF was limited by the institutional and political restrictions described above, throughout the Cold War Japan gradually developed a reliable, well-equipped and technologically advanced armed force. As Graph 2.1 shows, despite several institutional and regulatory restrictions the Japanese defence budget increased steadily to exceed $40 billion during the 1980s. The 1 per cent GDP ceiling on defence expenditure was offset by the high-paced economic growth the country was experiencing at the time. Japan had the fifth largest economy by 1960 and the second by 1970.

During the first decades of the post-war period, however, the process of reconstruction of the Japanese armed forces was prudent and incremental. The Japanese Self-Defence Forces were constituted only in 1954, almost a decade after the end of the war.[208] Moreover, during the years of the occupation, the US authorities had dismantled a large part of the Japanese industrial and technological potential associated with the defence sector, further delaying the process of reconstruction.[209]

In 1956, the government led by Kishi Nobusuke[210] approved the first of several Build-Up Plans. These documents defined the size, role and resources of the armed forces for a period varying from three to five years. The main purpose of the first plan was to rebuild several core capabilities for repelling a limited-scale attack on Japanese territory.[211] It called for an increase in military personnel to compensate for the reduction in US troops in Japan, which dropped from 200,000 at the end of the occupation to 90,000 in 1959. The First Build-Up Plan also established the Basic Conditions for Self-Defence, namely, the conditions under which Japan could use force to defend itself: a direct external attack; the lack of any other means than war for repelling it; and the minimum level of violence needed to stop it. In 1957, Kishi Nobosuke's government approved the Basic Policy for National Self-Defence, whose goal was to prevent aggression through 'the establishment of efficient defensive capabilities in accordance with the nation's strength and situation'.[212]

The Second Build-Up Plan (1960–1964), issued after the signing of the Mutual Security Treaty, defined the JSDF's role as 'coping with aggression using limited conventional means on a scale no larger than localized warfare' and 'delaying aggression in support of US forces'. In these first two build-up plans the navy and the air force were assigned a very limited role in supporting the defence of the national territory in case of direct attack.

The total number of military personnel rose from 190,000 in 1957 to 248,000 in 1964, remaining more or less stable between 240,000 and 250,000 troops for the rest of the Cold War period. These numbers are significantly lower compared with Germany and Italy.

The Third Build-Up Plan (1964–1969) introduced deterrence as a further objective for the JSDF and stressed the aim of increasing self-reliance for the defence of the national territory against a limited conventional attack. This plan led to the procurement of Nike-Hercules missiles, which could potentially be fitted with nuclear weapons, and F-105 and F-4 fighter planes that could be used as bombers, thus generating a heated debate on the JSDF's increased 'war potential'. The JMSDF saw an expansion of its role with the purpose of 'increasing the ability to defend coastal areas, straits and surrounding waters', as well as protecting maritime commercial transportation. For this purpose it was equipped with new capabilities, such as surface-to-air missiles and anti-submarine warfare, as well as eleven attack submarines.[213]

Lastly, this plan also emphasised the need to achieve long-term autonomy in the technological and industrial fields.[214] This objective, however, would largely be undermined by the approval of the Three Principles of Arms Export in 1967.[215]

The Fourth Plan (1972–1976) proved to be even more controversial than the previous plan. JDA director (and later prime minister) Nakasone Yasuhiro, in an attempt to react to Nixon's policies, advanced the concept of autonomous defence (*jishu bōei*). Unlike previously, autonomy was conceived not just from a technological and industrial viewpoint, but also in terms of actual military capabilities and associated with the objective of minimising the country's reliance on the alliance.[216]

Nakasone's early drafts included the idea of pursuing naval and air superiority in the areas surrounding Japan, and also of substantially extending the operational range of the JMSDF to protect the sea lanes of communication (SLOCs) 'up the Malacca Strait'. These drafts involved doubling the budget over a period of four years and acquiring platforms such as nuclear-powered submarines, helicopter carriers and new fighter aircraft.[217]

Plans for autonomous defence were opposed by a wide coalition of forces. As expected, progressive forces regarded the idea as a betrayal of the country's anti-militarist identity and a violation of the constitutions. The plan also met with considerable resistance within the government, particularly by the Ministry of Finance, which opposed the inflation of the budget, and even within the JDA and the JSDF. Several authoritative voices within the Japanese defence community, such as Kaihara Osamu and Kubo Takuya, criticised the concept of autonomous defence on the grounds that it risked over-extending the mission of the JSDF, generating a security dilemma with Japan's neighbours and dangerously moving away from the centrality of territorial self-defence. Ultimately, the Fourth Build-Up Plan largely reflected the concerns of the forces that argued against autonomous defence. Some of the concepts associated with autonomous defence would resurface in the following decades, such as sea control and patrol of the SLOCs, while others, such as minimising reliance on the United States, would prove to be impractical, with Japan moving towards greater integration and interoperability in the following decade. The final procurement decisions in that period reflected the compromise between these different positions. For example, the navy procured seven Uzushio-class and the first of ten Yūshio-class submarines, but none of the platforms that were considered offensive, such as the helicopter carriers, were procured.

The disputes caused by the Fourth Build-Up Plan led to a general rethinking of Japanese defence planning and the approval of the National Defence Programme Outline (NDPO, also called *Taikō*), which brought an end to the succession of defence build-up programmes and defined the optimum size and composition of Japan's military forces.[218]

The document contained two parts. The first, described the main purposes of the Japanese security policies. It confirmed the centrality of the concept of 'exclusively defence-oriented defence' (*senshu bōei*).[219] As Richard Samuels argues, this confirmed Japan's 'hedgehog posture', which focused on developing capabilities for territorial defence while refraining from procuring weapons systems or developing any plans relating to offence, power projection, deterrence by punishment or other 'offensive' purposes.[220] The second part of the NDPO introduced the concept of 'standard defence force' (*Kibanteki Boeiryoku Koso*), which would become central in the next three decades. This idea reflected that in peacetime the country should maintain the minimal level of capabilities required to exercise 'defence-oriented' defence, without adapting to the level of external threat posed by neighbouring powers. In so doing, Japan would be able to expand its capabilities in the event of increasing tensions or the possibility of conflict.[221]

This meant that the JSDF would stop focusing on quantitative expansion and concentrate on creating a 'small but high-quality force'. The NDPO also represented a rejection of the concept of autonomy as proposed by Nakasone in the early 1970s, since it reasserted the alliance's need for deterrence and for the repelling of large-scale threats, and argued against the pursuit of complete autonomy in the context of the defence industry.[222] As regard the JMSDF (navy) and the JASDF (air force), the NDPO requested the consolidation of their capacities to perform sea control in the Sea of Japan and especially around the major straits, in order to deter possible Soviet harassment of Japanese shipping.[223] This mission would be expanded in 1978 with the introduction of joint patrol of the SLOCs together with the US Navy. For this purpose, the NDPO stressed the need to improve the capabilities of the navy, with particular emphasis on the acquisition of attack submarines and surface vessels suitable for anti-submarine and anti-air system (such as SAMs) warfare.

During the 1980s, with the onset of the Second Cold War, the increasing military presence of Soviet forces in the Far East and the division of labour institutionalised by the 1978 guidelines, as well as the emergence of 'anti-mainstream'[224] leaders in the LDP (such as Nakasone Yasuhiro), led to a steady, albeit not radical, departure from the previous approaches. In 1981, Prime Minister Suzuki pledged to defend the SLOCS within 1,000 nautical miles of Japan. Nakasone, during his visit to Washington in 1983, confirmed Suzuki's pledge and declared that Japan would act as an 'unsinkable aircraft carrier' and would assume total control of its straits and of the Sea of Japan. In the following months, he reacted to the SS-20 crisis with the statement that 'the security of the West is indivisible'. The identification of Japan with the ideological Cold War struggle was unprecedented and signalled the desire to move away from a post-war anti-militarist posture and turn Japan into an active security provider in the region that would characterise the country's leadership in the twenty-first century.[225]

Nakasone's plans to overcome post-war pacifism and the Yoshida Doctrine did not succeed in the short term, since the combined presence of regulations, institutions and political resistance did not lead to any meaningful rupture with the past.[226] However, during the 1980s the JSDF proceeded to quietly improve its capabilities and expand its role, redefining the limits imposed by the concepts of exclusively defence-oriented defence and standard defence force.[227] By the end of the Cold War, Japan had sixty destroyers (three times more than the US 7th Fleet), fifteen attack submarines and 100 P-3 patrol aircraft (five times more than the 7th Fleet), as well as 200 F-15 and 100 F-4 jet fighters, more than the United States deployed in the entire Far East. These capabilities went beyond mere defence-oriented defence and enabled Japan to patrol, autonomously or in cooperation with the 7th Fleet, vast areas of the northwest Pacific, as well as the East China Sea, and to provide an air defence screen against Soviet incursion over Hokkaido.[228]

2.4 Conclusions

The sections above summarise how the international environment and domestic contexts co-evolved and outline the evolution of defence policy, and, more specifically, the role and structure of the armed forces in the three countries. Even at first glance, there are numerous elements of similarity, as defence budgets showed somewhat similar – and limited relatively to GDP – sizes and trends, and so did the structure of forces.

Although with different degrees of intrusiveness, the United States played a key role in the rearmament of the three countries, creating and then consolidating a bond between the US armed forces and those of the three countries that well outlasted the Cold War. Going beyond the macro-level evidence set out above, in the last few decades several high-level officers in Germany, Italy and Japan completed parts (in some cases key parts) of their education and/or training in the United States or – in the case of German and Italian officers – were deeply involved in NATO structures. Similarly, the three countries developed pacifist political cultures that were widely shared across the political spectrum. Over time, relatively low defence expenditures (vis-à-vis other public budget entries and those relating to the Allies) also contributed to limiting the debate on defence to small circles, with the public often given a very broad sketch of how the armed forces were developing. In some phases of the Cold War this was a delicate matter, especially for Germany and Italy, when the United States requested an increase in defence commitments in the early 1960s, as it created the need to balance American demands with a set of interests and preferences that were entrenched in the major political parties and public opinion. In Japan, public opinion and opposition parties not only squarely rejected the possibility of any direct military involvement, but they also criticised the use of bases during the Vietnam War and contested the legitimacy of the alliance with the United States, as testified by the mass demonstrations against the ratification of the alliance treaty in Tokyo in 1960.[229]

However, the above analysis also identifies some key differences that go beyond geographical positioning and the threat environment. Although they all upheld the constitutional principles on the 'non-use' of armed forces as foreign policy tools, domestic institutions differed in practice. Since the 1960s, Italy has felt less restricted than Germany and Japan with regarding to taking part with its military in missions within the UN framework. In addition, and in relation to this, being less occupied with territorial defence than Germany and Japan, Italy began developing skills in peacekeeping missions by specialising a small part of its large conscription-based forces.

Looking at their military budgets and force numbers also gives us an insight into their differences. As Graph 2.1 shows, as of the late 1960s, the Japanese defence budget, while remaining inferior to West Germany's, was superior to the Italian budget. Since early 1960s, Japan has embraced the 1 per cent ceiling established at that time, thereby limiting its military budget to 1 per cent of GDP. This limit, however, was largely offset by the exceptional economic growth the country experienced in the following three decades. Consequently, by the end of the Cold War the JSDF had become a highly sophisticated force in terms of capabilities and technology, despite the many practical limitations caused by a lack of

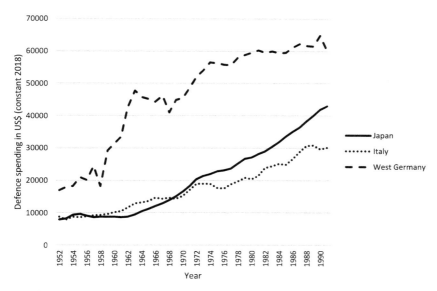

Graph 2.1 Defence expenditures in Germany, Italy and Japan during the Cold War
Source: Author's elaboration on Correlates of War Project data.

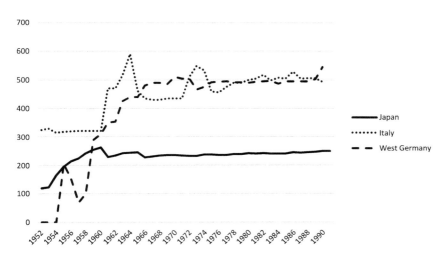

Graph 2.2 Total military personnel in Germany, Italy and Japan during the Cold War
Source: Author's elaboration on Correlates of War Project data.

operational experience and the pacifist institutional restrictions. Germany and Italy had two conscription-based forces that progressively diverged as Italy slowly but significantly moved towards operations in the field of crisis management (on overall force levels, see Graph 2.2). Italy thus had the only forces that were tested in the field, and its main problem was how to reconcile a large, underfunded military with new tasks that were to be performed by highly skilled and effective units. German forces, meanwhile, remained focused on territorial defence until 1989, a mission that enjoyed a high level of political consensus and for which they were seemingly well-prepared. On the other hand, and for these very reasons, they were relatively unprepared for a wholly new security environment and its drastically changed requirements.

Notes

1. G. Van Orden (1991), 'The Bundeswehr in Transition', *Survival* 33(4): 352.
2. T. Noetzel and B. Schreer (2008), 'All the Way? The Evolution of German Military Power', *International Affairs* 84(2): 212.
3. 2 August 1945, reported in M. A. Lytle and T. L. and Cockman (1989), 'An Institutional Evolution: The Bundeswehr – A New German Army', *Defence Analysis* 5(3): 207–20.
4. H. Maull (2000), 'Germany and the Use of Force: Still a "Civilian Power"?' *Survival* 42(2): 66.
5. The NSDAP (the Nazi Party) was banned 'while government officials and high-ranking military officers were brought to justice by special war crimes tribunals'. See the official reconstruction provided by the German Armed Forces: 'The Establishment of the Bundeswehr', available at: https://www.bundeswehr.de/en/about-bundeswehr /history/establishment-of-the-bundeswehr. See also M. Rink (2015), *Die Bundeswehr 1950/55–1989*. Munich: De Gruyter Oldenbourg.
6. On the 'package deal', see Lytle and Cockman, 'An Institutional Evolution', 209.
7. L. J. Daugherty (2011). '"The Tip of the Spear": The Formation and Expansion of the Bundeswehr, 1949–1963', *Journal of Slavic Military Studies* 24(1): 149.
8. On German rearmament debate, see, among others, Lytle and Cockman, 'An Institutional Evolution'; D. C. Large (1996), *Germans to the Front: West German Rearmament in the Adenauer Era*. Chapel Hill: University of North Carolina Press; M. Trachtenberg (1999), *A Constructed Peace: The Making of the European Settlement, 1945–1963*. Princeton, NJ: Princeton University Press; I. W. Trauschweizer (2008), 'Learning with an Ally: The U.S. Army and the Bundeswehr in the Cold War', *Journal of Military History* 72(2): 477–508; Rink, *Die Bundeswehr 1950/55–1989*; M. Sanding and R. Schlaffer (2015), *Die Bundeswehr 1955–2015: Sicherheitspolitik und Streitkräfte in der Demokratie*. Freiburg im Breisgau: Rombach.
9. Van Orden, 'The Bundeswehr in Transition'.
10. Lytle and Cockman, 'An Institutional Evolution', 209.
11. M. Trachtenberg and C. Gehrz (2003), 'America, Europe and German Rearmament, August–September 1950', in M. Trachtenberg (ed.), *Between Empire and Alliance: America and Europe during the Cold War*. New York: Rowman & Littlefield, 1–23.
12. G. Kümmel (2003), 'The Winds of Change: The Transition from Armed Forces for Peace to New Missions for the Bundeswehr and Its Impact on Civil–Military Relations', *Journal of Strategic Studies* 26(2): 9.
13. J. Corum (2004), 'Building a New Luftwaffe: The United States Air Force and Bundeswehr Planning for Rearmament, 1950–60', *Journal of Strategic Studies* 27(1), 89–113. Adenauer appointed the Christian Democrat MP Theodor Blank as the 'Chancellor's Commissioner for Questions with Regard to the Strengthening of Allied Troops'. In 1955, this government office was renamed the 'Federal Ministry

of Defence'. In this phase, despite the fact that the *Sozialdemokratische Partei Deutschlands* (SPD) opposed rearmament, it participated in committees for discussing the issue. See R. J. Evans (1977), 'The Creation of the Bundeswehr: Ensuring Civilian Control', *RUSI Journal* 122(3): 33–7.

14. On this process, see Lytle and Cockman, 'An Institutional Evolution', 209.
15. The Bundeswehr has been equipped with missiles capable of carrying nuclear warheads since 1958, but the warheads were under US control. Van Orden, 'The Bundeswehr in Transition', 361.
16. Van Orden, 'The Bundeswehr in Transition'.
17. 'Realizing that they had little chance of halting the creation of armed forces in Germany, SPD leaders began to play more constructive roles in the mid-1950s in setting up the legal framework of rearmament.' Sakaki et al., *Reluctant Warriors*, 26.
18. On this point see F. Berenskoetter and B. Giegerich (2010), 'From NATO to ESDP: A Social Constructivist Analysis of German Strategic Adjustment after the End of the Cold War', *Security Studies* 19(3): 407–52.
19. Maull, 'Germany and the Use of Force', 56–80.
20. Daugherty, 'The Tip of the Spear', 175.
21. On this point, see Berenskoetter and Giegerich, 'From NATO to ESDP'.
22. Van Orden, 'The Bundeswehr in Transition'.
23. Van Orden, 'The Bundeswehr in Transition', 358.
24. Daugherty, 'The Tip of the Spear', 169.
25. Corum, 'Building a New Luftwaffe', 96.
26. A. Hoffmann and K. Longhurst (1999), 'German Strategic Culture and the Changing Role of the Bundeswehr', *WeltTrends* 22: 149.
27. Despite being asked by the United States, Germany refused to support missions for clearing the Persian Gulf of mines laid during the Iran–Iraq War in 1987, and also ignored requests from the UN Secretary General to provide a military contribution to UN peacekeeping operations. Bonn deployed exclusively non-military personnel (in Namibia and Central America). For additional details, see again Maull, 'Germany and the Use of Force'.
28. Maull, 'Germany and the Use of Force'.
29. See again the official reconstruction provided by the German Armed Forces: 'The establishment of the Bundeswehr', available at: https://www.bundeswehr.de/en/abo ut-bundeswehr/history/establishment-of-the-bundeswehr.
30. Van Orden, 'The Bundeswehr in Transition'.
31. Berenskoetter and Giegerich, 'From NATO to ESDP'.
32. The Adelphi Papers (1993). *Domestic Sources of German Security Policy*. For Biehl et al., both Germany and Italy conceive security policy as international bargaining. Both are interested 'in being perceived as reliable partners, without focus on their specific national interests'. See Biehl, Giegerich and Jonas, *Strategic Cultures in Europe*.
33. Maull, 'Germany and the Use of Force'.
34. R. Baumann and G. Hellmann (2001), 'Germany and the Use of Military Force: "Total War", the "Culture of Restraint" and the Quest for Normality', *German Politics* 10(1): 62.
35. K. Longhurst (2004), *Germany and the Use of Force*. Manchester: Manchester University Press, p. 24.
36. Ibid.
37. As Kümmel and Lehonard interestingly point out: 'In contrast to the monuments of World War I, which are marked by patriotism and also by righteous defiance, the World War II memorials are focused on mourning and are characterized by a strange speechlessness. Instead of celebrating the soldiers' sacrifices, they mourn the victims of the war.' See G. Kümmel and N. Leonhard (2005), 'Casualties and Civil–Military

Relations: The German Polity between Learning and Indifference', *Armed Forces & Society* 31(4): 513–35.

38. A. Malici (2006), 'Germans as Venutians: The Culture of German Foreign Policy Behavior', *Foreign Policy Analysis* 2(1): 37–62.

39. Berger, *Cultures of Antimilitarism*.

40. J. S. Duffield (1999), 'Political Culture and State Behavior: Why Germany Confounds Neorealism', *International Organization* 53(4): 781; Miskimmon, *Germany and the Common Foreign and Security Policy of the European Union*, 187.

41. Hoffmann and Longhurst, 'German Strategic Culture and the Changing Role of the Bundeswehr', 147.

42. The Adelphi Papers (1993), *Domestic Sources of German Security Policy*, 6.

43. 'These norms are a product of the breakdown in moral obligation, caused by World War II.' See S. Dalvi (1998), 'The Post-Cold War Role of the Bundeswehr: A Product of Normative Influences', *European Security* 7(1): 102.

44. Hoffmann and Longhurst, 'German Strategic Culture and the Changing Role of the Bundeswehr', 147.

45. For a review, see Evans, 'The Creation of the Bundeswehr', 33–7.

46. Dalvi, 'The Post-Cold War Role of the Bundeswehr', p. 102. See also Hoffmann and Longhurst, 'German Strategic Culture and the Changing Role of the Bundeswehr', 147; Kümmel, 'The Winds of Change'.

47. See again at: https://www.bundeswehr.de/en/about-bundeswehr/history/establishment-of-the-bundeswehr.

48. The official website of the Bundeshwer presents the members of the military resistance (such as Colonel Count von Stauffenberg) as models of 'exemplary soldierly and ethical attitude in German (military) history'. See at: https://www.bundeswehr.de/en/about-bundeswehr/history/establishment-of-the-bundeswehr.

49. Evans, 'The Creation of the Bundeswehr', 37.

50. Longhurst, *Germany and the use of force*, 40.

51. Kümmel, 'The Winds of Change'.

52. Ibid., 13.

53. Sakaki et al., *Reluctant Warriors*, 31.

54. H. Haftendorn (1984). 'Germany and the Euromissile Debate', *International Journal* 40(1): 68–85; D. Cortright (2008), *Peace: A History of Movements and Ideas*. Cambridge: Cambridge University Press; N. D. Cary (2019), 'On the Political Decision-making Process see Helmut Schmidt, Euromissiles, and the Peace Movement', *Central European History* 52(1): 148–71.

55. H. Jeffrey (1991), *War by Other Means: Soviet Power, West German Resistance, and the Battle of the Euromissiles*. New York: Free Press.

56. Biehl, Giegerich and Jonas, *Strategic Cultures in Europe*.

57. P. Buras and K. Longhurst (2004), 'The Berlin Republic, Iraq, and the Use of Force', *European Security* 13(3): 216–17.

58. On the financial control of the Bundestag over the defence budget during the Cold War, see M. Wörner (1974), 'Parliamentary Control of Defence: The German Example', *Survival* 16(1): 13–16.

59. Evans, 'The Creation of the Bundeswehr', 34.

60. Ibid., 35.

61. According to Lytle and Cockman, 'the Commissioner and his staff were initially perceived by the military leadership as a hostile agency', but this changed after the concepts of 'Innere Fuhrung' were assimilated. Lytle and Cockman, 'An Institutional Evolution', 217.

62. See at: https://www.bundeswehr.de/en/about-bundeswehr/history/establishment-of-the-bundeswehr.

63. In terms of civilian control, the Advisory Council on Leadership Development and Civic Education is another advisory body that advises the Federal Minister of

Defence on matters of 'leadership development and civic education' through expert opinions and recommendations. Ibid.

64. See S. C. Hofmann (2019), 'Beyond Culture and Power: The Role of Party Ideologies in German Foreign and Security Policy', *German Politics* 30(1): 51–71.
65. See Sakaki et al., *Reluctant Warriors*, 31–2.
66. A. Dalgaard-Nielsen (2005), 'The Test of Strategic Culture: Germany, Pacifism and Pre-emptive Strikes', *Security Dialogue* 36(3): 339–59.
67. T. Dyson (2011, 'Managing Convergence: German Military Doctrine and Capabilities in the 21st Century', *Defence Studies* 11(2): 244–70.
68. Daugherty, 'The Tip of the Spear', 148.
69. B. S. Seibert (2012), 'A Quiet Revolution', *RUSI Journal* 157(1): 60.
70. Ibid.
71. Lytle and Cockman, 'An Institutional Evolution'.
72. Corum, 'Building a New Luftwaffe', 90.
73. Rink, '*Die Bundeswehr 1950/55–1989*. The threshold of 500,000 was reached only after many years. See Graph 2.1.
74. The forces would have been put under the control of the West German government in case of war. Daugherty, 'The Tip of the Spear', 175.
75. Ibid., 176–7.
76. See Bundeswehr, 'The Bundeswehr in the Cold War', available at: https://www.bundeswehr.de/en/about-bundeswehr/history/cold-war.
77. Van Orden, 'The Bundeswehr in Transition', 363.
78. Corum, 'Building a New Luftwaffe'.
79. R. Cox (1975), 'A New Self-confidence in the Bundeswehr', *RUSI Journal* 120(4): 61.
80. At the Himmerod Conference, holding the northern flank (the Baltic coast) was conceived as crucial, and the possibility of engaging in a war of manoeuvre against the Soviets in the Baltic influenced the development of the West German navy. For a review on the West German naval rearmament, see D. B. Snyder (2002), 'Arming the Bundesmarine: The United States and the Build-up of the German Federal Navy, 1950–1960', *Journal of Military History* 66(2): 477–500.
81. Corum, 'Building a New Luftwaffe', 101.
82. Snyder, 'Arming the Bundesmarine'.
83. Ibid.
84. Cox, 'A New Self-Confidence in the Bundeswehr'.
85. Ibid.
86. Corum, 'Building a New Luftwaffe'.
87. Ibid., 95.
88. Ibid.
89. See Sanding and Schlaffer, *Die Bundeswehr 1955–2015*.
90. Ibid.
91. Ibid.
92. Seibert, 'A Quiet Revolution', 60–9.
93. Trauschweizer, 'Learning with an Ally', 477–508.
94. Ibid., 479.
95. Lytle and Cockman, 'An Institutional Evolution'.
96. Van Orden, 'The Bundeswehr in Transition', 363.
97. Cox, 'A New Self-Confidence in the Bundeswehr', 58.
98. L. Nuti (2006). 'Linee generali della politica di difesa italiana (1945–1989)', in L. Goglia, R, Moro and L. Nuti (eds) (2006), *Guerra e Pace nell'Italia del Novecento*. Bologna: Il Mulino, 463–504.
99. L. Goglia, R. Moro and L. Nuti (eds) (2006), *Guerra e Pace nell'Italia del Novecento*. Bologna: Il Mulino.
100. See V. Vignoli and F. Coticchia (2022), 'Italy's Military Operations Abroad (1945–2020): Data, Patterns, and Trends', *International Peacekeeping* 29(3): 436–62.

101. P. Rainero and R. Albertini (2005), *Le forze armate e la nazione italiana*. Roma: Commissione Italiana di Storia Militare. The last years of war, after the armistice of 1943, were marked by the ambiguity of co-belligerence. Despite the tactical need to win the war and political aims for future cooperation with Rome in the post-war period, the Allies avoided seeking any significant Italian military support after 1943, partly because they (especially the United Kingdom) wanted Rome to pay a price for the war while reducing Italian influence in the Mediterranean.

102. The leader of the Italian Socialist Party, Pietro Nenni, said: 'Fascist Italy lost the war, anti-fascists cannot lose the peace.' Quoted in M. Cuzzi (2005), 'L'opinione pubblica e le clausole del trattato di Parigi', in P. Rainero and R. Albertini (eds), *Le forze armate e la nazione italiana*. Roma: Commissione Italiana di Storia Militare, 75–110.

103. P. Pastorelli (2011), 'De Gasperi, the Christian Democrats and the Atlantic Treaty', in E. Di Nolfo (ed.), *The Atlantic Pact Forty Years Later*. New York: De Gruyter, 209–19; E. T. Smith (1983), 'The Fear of Subversion: The United States and the Inclusion of Italy in the North Atlantic Treaty', *Diplomatic History* 7(2): 139–56; A. Varsori (2011), 'The First Stage of Negotiations: December 1947 to June 1948', in E. Di Nolfo (ed.), *The Atlantic Pact Forty Years Later*. New York: De Gruyter, 19–40; A. Varsori (1992), 'Italy and Western Defence 1948–55: The Elusive Ally', in B. Heuser and R. O'Neill (eds), *Securing Peace in Europe, 1945–62*. London: Palgrave Macmillan, 196–221.

104. The army (with the support of the US Air Force) was given the task of defending the Italian northeastern border, while the navy was to control the Adriatic Sea and the Strait of Otranto, focusing on the Mediterranean. The role of the air force was exclusively supportive. On the whole, the Italian armed forces had a tactical, non-strategic role within NATO. See G. Oliva (2016), '70 anni. 1946–2016: Le forze armate dell'Italia Repubblicana', *Informazioni della Difesa* 2/2016: 8–23; L. Nuti (1989), *L'esercito italiano nel secondo dopoguerra: 1946–1950: La sua ricostruzione e l'assistenza militare alleata*. Rome: Stato maggiore dell'esercito, Ufficio storico; N. Labanca (2011), 'Defence Policy in the Italian Republic: Frames and Issues', UNISCI Discussion Papers', No. 25 (January), Madrid.

105. Smith, 'The Fear of Subversion'; Nuti, *L'esercito italiano nel secondo dopoguerra*, ch. 5.

106. See V. Ilari (1987), 'The New Model of Italian Defence, Doctrinal Options, Issues and Trends', *International Spectator* 22(2): 81.

107. K. Ruzicic-Kessler (2014), 'Italy and Yugoslavia: From Distrust to Friendship in Cold War Europe', *Journal of Modern Italian Studies* 19(5): 641–64.

108. See A. Carati, M. Merlati and D. Vignati (2021), 'Freer When Constrained? Italy and Transatlantic Relations during the Cold War', *Journal of Modern Italian Studies* 26(3): 314–32.

109. The Korean War made it clear that concrete support of the Alliance, rather than mere membership, was vital. This explains the military agreement with Washington on US and NATO bases on Italian soil. See Nuti, *Le linee generali della politica di difesa italiana (1945–1989)*.

110. D. A. Carter (2015), 'Forging the Shield: The US Army in Europe, 1951–1962', *US Army in the Cold War Series* 45(3): 232.

111. L. Nuti (1998), 'Commitment to NATO and Domestic Politics: The Italian Case and Some Comparative Remarks', *Contemporary European History* 7(3): 361–77.

112. D. Caviglia and M. Cricco (2006), *La diplomazia italiana e gli equilibri mediterranei: la politica mediorientale dell'Italia dalla guerra dei Sei Giorni al conflitto dello Yom Kippur (1967–1973)*. Roma: Rubbettino Editore, 82.

113. Enrico Mattei, CEO of ENI, has often been seen as trying to carve out an autonomous role for Italy in the region beyond the energy arena, similar to what French President De Gaulle did in a politico-military context. See, for example, G. Salame (1994), 'Torn between the Atlantic and the Mediterranean: Europe and the Middle East in the post-Cold War Era', *Middle East Journal* 48(2): 226–49.

114. Caviglia and Cricco, *La diplomazia italiana e gli equilibri mediterranei.*
115. E. Calossi, F. Calugi and F. Coticchia (2013), 'Peace and War in Political Discourse of Italian Marxist and post-Marxist Parties', *Contemporary Italian Politics* 5(3): 309–24, 365.
116. Initially, all the Italian political parties supported the operation, including the PCI. Later, however, when the international context changed, the domestic debate also altered accordingly.
117. On this subject see, in particular, L. Nuti (2007), *La Sfida Nucleare: La Politica Estera Italiana e Le Armi Atomiche, 1945–1991.* Bologna: Il Mulino; E. Bini, I. Londero and G. Iannuzzi (2017), *Nuclear Italy: An International History of Italian Nuclear Policies during the Cold War.* Trieste: EUT Edizioni.
118. L. Nuti (2016), 'Extended Deterrence and National Ambitions: Italy's Nuclear Policy, 1955–1962', *Journal of Strategic Studies* 39(4): 559–79.
119. The literature on the Euro-missiles is vast; for a summary that also addresses the role of Italy, see, for example, M. Gala (2017), 'Italy's Role in the Implementation of the Dual-Track Decision', in E. Bini, I. Londero and G. Iannuzzi (eds), *Nuclear Italy: An International History of Italian Nuclear Policies during the Cold War.* Trieste: EUT Edizioni, 151–62; M. Gala (2015), 'The Euromissile Crisis and the Centrality of the "Zero Option"', in L. Nuti, F. Bozo, M. P. Rey and B. Rother (eds), *The Euromissile Crisis and the End of the Cold War.* New York: Woodrow Wilson Center Press, ch. 9. For a broader perspective, see also A. Varsori (2022), *Dalla rinascita al declino.* Bologna: Il Mulino.
120. The most famous crisis with the United States was that involving the then Prime Minister Bettino Craxi over the management of Palestinian terrorists that had surrendered to Italian authorities after hijacking an Italian cruise ship and killing a US citizen on board in October 1985. The crisis almost led to a clash between US and Italian soldiers at the military base of Sigonella over the custody of the Palestinian commandos. A. Silj (1998), *L'alleato scomodo: I rapporti fra Roma e Washington nel Mediterraneo: Sigonella e Gheddafi.* Milan: Corbaccio. On US–Italy diplomatic crises over the Mediterranean and Middle East, see also P. Soave (2017), 'Power vs. Diplomacy, Globalism vs. Regionalism: United States and Italy Facing International Terrorism. The Sidra Crisis, 1986', *Nuova Rivista Storica* 101(1): 161–79.
121. Silj, *L'alleato scomodo*, 23.
122. For a review, see Ignazi et al. *Italian Military Operations Abroad*; P. Rosa (2014), 'The Accommodationist State: Strategic Culture and Italy's Military Behaviour', *International Relations* 28(1): 88–115.
123. Rosa, 'The Accommodationist State'; P. Rosa (2012), *Tra pacifismo e Realpolitik.* Roma: Rubettino, 113.
124. According to Battistelli, the armistice in 1943 was a betrayal of the pact between military institutions and the society, which was to be defended but instead was abandoned when the armed forces disappeared and the Nazis took control of large parts of Italy. See F. Battistelli (2003), *Gli italiani e la guerra.* Roma: Carocci.
125. M. De Leonardis (2014), *Guerra Fredda e interessi nazionali.* Roma: Rubettino, 20. On the debate on the consequences of fascism and the war, as well as the alleged 'death of the homeland' after the armistice see, among others, A. Panebianco (1997). *Guerrieri Democratici.* Bologna: Il Mulino; E. Di Nolfo (2006), 'Guerra, Stato e Nazione nel secondo dopoguerra', in L. Goglia, R. Moro and L. Nuti (eds), *Guerra e Pace nell'Italia del Novecento.* Bologna: Il Mulino, 227–50.
126. De Leonardis, *Guerra Fredda e interessi nazionali.*
127. Rosa, *Tra pacifismo e Realpolitik.*
128. F. Battistelli (2003), 'L'opinione pubblica italiana e la difesa', *Quaderni di sociologia* 32/2003: 8–36.
129. Panebianco, *errieri Democratici.*

130. G. Mammarella and P. Cacace (2008), *La politica estera dell'Italia: Dallo stato unitario ai giorni nostri.* Bari: Laterza.
131. Calossi et al., 'Peace and War in Political Discourse'.
132. Panebianco, *Guerrieri Democratici.*
133. C. D'Amore (2001), *Governare la difesa: Parlamento e politica militare nell'Italia repubblicana.* Milano: Franco Angeli.
134. Calossi et al., 'Peace and War in Political Discourse'.
135. Di Nolfo, 'Guerra, Stato e Nazione nel secondo dopoguerra', 249.
136. On this point see, among others, Rosa, *Tra pacifismo e realpolitik*, 113; Nuti, *L'esercito italiano nel secondo dopoguerra 1946–1950.*
137. Goglia, Moro and Nuti, *Guerra e pace nell'Italia del Novecento*, 17.
138. Battistelli, 'L'opinione pubblica italiana e la difesa'.
139. See, among others, N. Labanca (ed.) (2009), *Le armi della Repubblica: dalla Liberazione ad oggi.* Turin: UTET.
140. See A. M. Isastia (2005), 'Forze armate e società: Il ritorno dei reduci tra indifferenza e rimozione', in P. Rainero and R. Albertini (eds), *Le forze armate e la nazione italiana.* Roma: Commissione Italiana di Storia Militare, 29–48.
141. On public opinion and the case of the Euromissiles, see F. Battistelli and P. Isernia (1990). *I movimenti pacifisti ed antinucleari in Italia 1980–1988.* Roma: Cemiss; P. Isernia (1996). *Dove gli angeli non mettono piede: Opinione pubblica e politiche di sicurezza in Italia.* Milano: FrancoAngeli; P. Bellucci (1998), *Difesa, politica e società: la politica militare italiana tra obiezione di coscienza e professionalizzazione delle Forze armate.* Milano: FrancoAngeli.
142. On the Italian peace movement at that time, see D. Della Porta and D. Rucht (1992), 'Movimenti sociali e sistema politico: Un confronto tra Italia e Germania', *Rivista Italiana di Scienze Politiche* 22(3): 501–37; Cortright, *Peace: A History of Movements and Ideas.*
143. A. Catanzaro and F. Coticchia (2018). *Al di là dell'Arcobaleno: I movimenti pacifisti italiani tra ideologie e contro-narrazioni strategiche.* Milano: Vita e Pensiero.
144. Ibid.
145. For the most comprehensive analysis of the role of parliament concerning defence policy, see E. Ertola (2020), *Democrazia e difesa: Il controllo parlamentare sulla politica militare (1948–2018).* Milano: Unicopli.
146. Ertola, *Democrazia e difesa;* D'Amore, *Governare la Difesa.*
147. The general view was that crucial decisions had been already taken 'abroad'. Ertola, *Democrazia e difesa*, 101.
148. It is worth noting that in the 1970s the PCI changed its attitude (becoming less hostile) towards Italian membership of NATO.
149. N. Labanca (2005), 'Nota sui bilanci militari della Repubblica', in P. Rainero and R. Albertini (eds), *Le forze armate e la nazione italiana.* Roma: Commissione Italiana di Storia Militare, 224–55.
150. For an overview on Italian defence doctrines during the Cold War, see, among others, F. Coticchia (2013), *Qualcosa è cambiato: L'evoluzione della politica di difesa italiana dall'Iraq alla Libia (1991–2011).* Pisa: Pisa University Press; L. Caligaris and C. M. Santoro (1986), *Obiettivo difesa: Strategia, direzione politica, comando operativo.* Bologna: Il Mulino; E. Cerquetti (1975), *Le forze armate italiane dal 1945 al 1975: Strutture e dottrine.* Milano: Feltrinelli; Ilari, 'The New Model of Italian Defence'.
151. Labanca, 'Defence Policy in the Italian Republic', 1.
152. Ibid.
153. Nuti, *L'esercito italiano nel secondo dopoguerra 1946–1950.*
154. Ibid. On the air force, see P. Rainero and R. Albertini (eds), *Le forze armate e la nazione italiana.* Roma: Commissione Italiana di Storia Militare, 191–223. On the navy, see R. B. La Racine (2005), 'Il rapporto tra la Marina e la Nazione', in P. Rainero and

R. Albertini (eds), *Le forze armate e la nazione italiana*. Roma: Commissione Italiana di Storia Militare, 157–89.

155. Labanca, 'Defence Policy in the Italian Republic', 7.
156. Oliva, '70 anni. 1946–2016: Le forze armate dell'Italia Repubblicana'.
157. Nuti, L. (1989). *L'esercito italiano nel secondo dopoguerra 1946–1950*, 233.
158. Labanca, 'Defence Policy in the Italian Republic', 9. Labanca emphasises how two defence ministers left their mark on this period: Paolo Emilio Taviani (1953–1958), who advocated the downsizing of the army; and Giulio Andreotti (1959–1966 and 1974).
159. Labanca, 'Defence Policy in the Italian Republic', 10.
160. See Nuti, *La sfida nucleare*.
161. Oliva, '70 anni. 1946–2016: Le forze armate dell'Italia Repubblicana'.
162. The new Italian aircraft carrier, the *Cavour*, was deployed in 2010–2011. The *Garibaldi* was an ASW carrier that could carry STO/VL aircraft.
163. Coticchia and Moro, *The Transformation of Italian Armed Forces in Comparative Perspective*.
164. White Paper (1977), 94.
165. White Paper (1977), 232.
166. In 1975, land forces were reduced by around one-third and almost 60 per cent were mechanised, while the light infantry brigades were assigned secondary tasks. Ilari, 'The New Model of Italian Defence', 82.
167. Labanca talks about 'parochial illusions of national autonomy'. Labanca, 'Defence Policy in the Italian Republic', 18.
168. On this subject see, among others, L. Nascia and M. Pianta (2009), 'La spesa militare in Italia, 1949–2008', in N. Labanca (ed.), *Le armi della Repubblica: dalla Liberazione a oggi*. Turin: UTET.
169. L. Calligaris (1990, 'La politica militare', in B. Dente (ed.), *Politiche pubbliche in Italia*. Bologna: Il Mulino, 93.
170. During the Cold War Italian forces were deployed in the following operations: Somalia (UN, 1950–1960); Egypt (UNEF, 1956–1957; MFO, 1982–; Red Sea, 1988); Lebanon (UNTSO, 1958–2015; UNOGIL, 1958; UNIFIL, 1979–; Lebanon I, 1982; Lebanon II, 1982–1984); India (UNMOGIP, 1959–); Laos (UN, 1959); DRC (UNOC, 1960–1964); Yemen (UNYOM, 1963–1964); Malta (MICTM, 1973–1988; DIATM, 1981–1988; MIATM, 1988); Iraq (UNIIMOG, 1988–1991); Namibia (UNTAG, 1989–1990); Afghanistan (UNOCA, 1989–1990). For additional details, see Vignoli and Coticchia, 'Italy's Military Operations Abroad'. The Italian navy has also been deployed in national missions, such as: 1940s in the Adriatic Sea; a humanitarian operation in 1979 in Vietnam (saving almost 1,000 of the so-called 'boat people'). See, above all, La Racine, 'Il rapporto tra la Marina e la Nazione'.
171. To encourage joint operations, a bill was previously approved in the 1980s to assign responsibility for general and financial inter-services planning to the Chief of Defence Staff.
172. Ilari, 'The New Model of Italian Defence', 80.
173. At that time the main assets were Tornados, F-104s and AM-Xs.
174. Ilari, 'The New Model of Italian Defence', 85.
175. Ibid.
176. Ibid.
177. M. Schaller (1985), *The American Occupation of Japan: The Origins of the Cold War in Asia*. Oxford: Oxford University Press; J. W. Dower (2000), *Embracing Defeat: Japan in the Wake of World War II*. New York: W. W. Norton.
178. M. P. Leffler (1992), *A Preponderance of Power: National Security, the Truman Administration, and the Cold War*. Stanford, CA: Stanford University Press; M. J. Hogan (1998), *A Cross of Iron: Harry S. Truman and the Origins of the National Security State, 1945–1954*. New York: Cambridge University Press.

179. M. Schaller (1997), *Altered States: The United States and Japan since the Occupation.* Oxford: Oxford University Press; D. L. Barnes (2017), *Architects of Occupation: American Experts and Planning for Postwar Japan.* Ithaca, NY: Cornell University Press.

180. J. W. Dower and H. Tetsuo (2007), 'Japan's Red Purge: Lessons from a Saga of Suppression of Free Speech and Thought', *Asia-Pacific Journal: Japan Focus*, 5(7): 1–7.

181. E. S. Krauss and R. J. Pekkanen (2011), *The Rise and Fall of Japan's LDP: Political Party Organizations as Historical Institutions.* Ithaca, NY: Cornell University Press.

182. K. B. Pyle (2007), *Japan Rising: The Resurgence of Japanese Power and Purpose.* New York: Public Affairs.

183. M. J. Green (2017), *By More than Providence: Grand Strategy and American Power in the Asia Pacific since 1783.* New York: Columbia University Press; V. D. Cha (2016). *Powerplay: The Origins of the American Alliance System in Asia.* Princeton, NJ: Princeton University Press.

184. Communist countries as well as countries involved in conflicts, such as South Korea, did not sign the treaty.

185. The US–Japan alliance established in 1951 represented the first element in the 'San Francisco System' of alliance, also known as the 'Hub and Spokes architecture', which included also bilateral treaties signed with the Philippines (1951), the Republic of China (1951, abrogated with the Recognition of the PRC in 1979), the ANZUS (New Zealand abrogated the treaty in 1984, while Australia remains part of the pact signed in 1951).

186. J. Swenson-Wright (2005), *Unequal Allies? United States Security and Alliance Policy toward Japan, 1945–1960.* Stanford, CA: Stanford University Press.

187. R. Buckley (1995), *US–Japan Alliance Diplomacy 1945–1990.* Cambridge: Cambridge University Press; M. Dian (2014), *The Evolution of the US–Japan Alliance: The Eagle and the Chrysanthemum.* Oxford: Chandos.

188. Swenson-Wright, *Unequal Allies?*; W. LaFeber (1998), *The Clash: US-Japanese Relations throughout History.* New York: W. W. Norton.

189. J. W. Dower (1988), *Empire and Aftermath: Yoshida Shigeru and the Japanese experience, 1878–1954.* Cambridge, MA: Harvard University Press.

190. J. L. Gaddis (2005), *Strategies of Containment: A Critical Appraisal of American National Security Policy during the Cold War.* New York: Oxford University Press.

191. Schaller, *Altered States.*

192. A. Iriye (1992), *China and Japan in the Global Setting.* Cambridge, MA: Harvard University Press.

193. The Japanese government had already resolved to recognise the PRC during the negotiations leading to the San Francisco Peace Treaty and was induced by the United States to recognise Taiwan. Y. Soeya (1998), *Japan's Economic Diplomacy with China, 1945–1978.* Oxford: Oxford University Press; N. B. Tucker (1984), 'American Policy toward Sino-Japanese Trade in the Post-War Years: Politics and Prosperity', *Diplomatic History* 8(3): 183–208.

194. H. A. Kissinger (1979), *The White House Years.* Boston, MA: Little Brown, 219.

195. A. Iriye (1990), 'Chinese–Japanese Relations, 1945–90', *China Quarterly* 124(4): 624–38; Soeya, *Japan's Economic Diplomacy with China, 1945–1978.*

196. R. L. Garthoff (1985), *Detente and Confrontation: American–Soviet Relations from Nixon to Reagan.* Washington, DC: Brookings Institution Press.

197. The guidelines for the Alliance would again be updated in 1997 and 2015, marking major turning points in the redefinition of the scope of the Alliance and the different areas of bilateral cooperation.

198. M. J. Green and K. Murata (1998), *The 1978 Guidelines for the US–Japan Defence Cooperation Process and the Historical Impact*, GWU Working Paper No. 17. Washington, DC: George Washington University; A. Patalano (2008), 'Shielding

the "Hot Gates": Submarine Warfare and Japanese Naval Strategy in the Cold War and Beyond (1976–2006)', *Journal of Strategic Studies* 31(6): 859–95.

199. During the post-war period the Japanese armed forces were referred to as Japanese Self-Defence Forces, or *Jieitai*.

200. 200. Office of the Prime Minister of Japan, the Japanese constitution, available at: https://japan.kantei.go.jp/constitution_and_government_of_japan/constitution _e.html.

201. Unlike in Italy and Germany, in Japan the official interpretation of the constitution is not provided by the Constitutional Court but by the Cabinet Legislation Bureau, an agency of the executive branch.

202. J. P. Boyd and R. J. Samuels (2005), *Nine Lives? The Politics of Constitutional Reform in Japan*. Honolulu, HI: East West Center.

203. S. A. Smith (2019), *Japan Rearmed: The Politics of Military Power*. Cambridge, MA: Harvard University Press.

204. M. Dian (2017), *Contested Memories in Chinese and Japanese Foreign Policy*. Oxford: Elsevier; J. A. Stockwin (1968), *The Japanese Socialist Party and Neutralism: A Study of Political Party and Its Foreign Policy*. Melbourne: Melbourne University Press; K. Szczepanska (2014), *The Politics of War Memory in Japan: Progressive Civil Society Groups and Contestation of Memory of the Asia-Pacific War*. London: Routledge. On the anti-base movement in Japan, see S. Kawana and M. Takahashi (eds) (2020), *Exploring Base Politics: How Host Countries Shape the Network of US Overseas Bases*. London: Routledge; G. McCormack and S. O. Norimatsu (2018), *Resistant Islands: Okinawa Confronts Japan and the United States*. New York: Rowman & Littlefield.

205. F. Seraphim (2006), *In War Memory and Social Politics in Japan, 1945–2005*. Cambridge, MA: Harvard University Press.

206. R. J. Samuels (2007b), *Securing Japan: Tokyo's Grand Strategy and the Future of East Asia*. Ithaca, NY: Cornell University Press.

207. A. L. Oros (2008), *Normalizing Japan: Politics, Identity, and the Evolution of Security Practice*. Stanford, CA: Stanford University Press.

208. R. D. Eldridge and P. Midford (eds) (2017), *The Japanese Ground Self-defense Force: Search for Legitimacy*. New York: Palgrave Macmillan.

209. Dower, *Embracing Defeat*.

210. During the wartime period, Kishi Nobusuke was Deputy Minister of Development for the Manchukuo region and Minister of Transportation. In 1945, he was identified as a Class A war criminal and imprisoned. He was released in 1948. He served as prime minister from 1957 to 1960. He was the maternal grandfather of Prime Minister Abe Shinzo.

211. Dian, *The Evolution of the US–Japan Alliance*; R. J. Samuels (1994), '*Rich Nation, Strong Army': National Security and the Technological Transformation of Japan*. Ithaca, NY: Cornell University Press.

212. A. L. Oros (2017), *Japan's Security Renaissance: New Policies and Politics for the Twenty-first Century*. New York: Columbia University Press, 40.

213. A. Patalano (2019), '"The Silent Fight": Submarine Rearmament and the Origins of Japan's Military Engagement with the Cold War, 1955–76', *Cold War History* 21(1): 1–21. The MSDF, particularly with the development of submarines, is the branch of the JSDF that managed to elude the anti-militarist restrictions and move beyond exclusively defence-oriented defence.

214. Samuels, '*Rich Nation, Strong Army*'.

215. These three principles prevented Japan from exporting any type of defence equipment, thus limiting Japanese firms to producing for the JSDF. This led to an increase in the costs of development and production, and consequently lowered Japan's chances of achieving a high degree of technological autonomy in the field of defence.

216. Samuels, '*Rich Nation, Strong Army*'.

217. E. Graham (2005), *Japan's Sea Lane Security: A Matter of Life and Death?* London: Routledge.
218. The NDPO (which, in 2004, became the NDPG, National Defence Plan Guidance) has been re-formulated five times: in 1995 under Murayama; in 2004 under Koizumi Junichiro; in 2010 (now referred to as NDPG) under Kan; and in 2013 and 2019 under Abe. Since 2022, the NDPG has been renamed National Defence Strategy, following the American title.
219. T. Kawasaki (2001), 'Japan and Two Theories of Military Doctrine Formation: Civilian Policymakers, Policy Preference, and the 1976 National Defence Program Outline', *International Relations of the Asia-Pacific* 1(1): 67–93.
220. Samuels, *'Rich Nation Strong Army'.*
221. This meant abandoning the idea of the Basic Defence Force Concept (*Shoyo Boeiryoku Koso*) incorporated in the Build-Up Plans, by which Japanese strength was to be adapted to the capabilities of potential enemies. Y. Chijiwa (2016), 'Unfinished "Beyond-the-Threat Theory": Japan's "Basic Defence Force Concept" Revisited', *NIDS Journal of Defense and Security* (17): 83–101.
222. On the contrary, as Samuels describes, Japan would continue the process of indigenisation and diffusion of technology acquired by the United States through co-production and licensed production.
223. The NDPO envisaged the need for sixty major surface vessels, to be organised into four escort flotillas to conduct ASW operations, and six attack submarines which would remain active at all times to patrol Japan's main straits.
224. Nakasone, former director of the JDA in the early 1970s, was prime minister of Japan from 1982 to 1987. The mainstream leaders in the LDP identified with Yoshida's approach to foreign and security policies geared to limiting Japan's role, minimising risks and focusing on economic development. The anti-mainstream leaders, such as Nakasone and Kishi, were associated with the pursuit of a more autonomous and active role in security policies and attempts to overcome pacifist and anti-militarist regulations. On this point, see R. J. Samuels (2007), 'Securing Japan: The Current Discourse', *Journal of Japanese Studies* 33(1): 125–52.
225. Graham, *Japan's Sea Lane Security*
226. On this point, see K. B. Pyle (1987), 'In Pursuit of a Grand Design: Nakasone between the Past and the Future', *Journal of Japanese Studies* 13(2): 243–70.
227. During his five years in office, Nakasone managed to obtain a 36 per cent increase in the defence budget, symbolically exceeding 1 per cent in 1983.
228. A. Patalano (2015). *Post-War Japan as a Sea Power: Imperial Legacy, Wartime Experience and the Making of a Navy.* London: Bloomsbury.
229. D. Williams and R. Kersten (eds) (2004), *The Left in the Shaping of Japanese Democracy: Essays in Honour of JAA Stockwin.* London: Routledge.

Chapter 3

Military Transformation: Drivers and Sequences

3.1 Introduction

The book draws on historical institutionalism in addressing military transformation in Germany, Italy and Japan. Put simply, we emphasise the importance of the past in explaining the different countries' trajectories in terms of defence policy. The weight of historical legacies sets such trajectories, which can change at specific moments – critical junctures – due to events and decisions that alter or transform the path to adapt it over time. Once a new path is taken, it undergoes a series of evaluations to strengthen and develop it, resulting in trajectories which remain relatively stable over time. As Pierson said, 'it is not just a question of what happens but when it happens'.[1] As we shall see later, for example, if we look at the macro-picture we can see how the prominent elements of continuity in defence policies across the three countries, as discussed in the previous chapter, altered decisively with the Italian participation in the Gulf War (1991). Italy's decision to intervene set in motion a series of changes in the Italian armed forces (experiencing combat operations for the first time since the Second World War) that put Italy on a different course from that of (its) past. In this phase, previous operational experiences such as the Italian participation in UNIFIL (1982), which was at the time a relatively minor engagement, helped to organise and prepare the Italian armed forces for future missions.[2] This was *not* the case – or at least not at this time – with Germany and Japan.[3] While the end of the Cold War undoubtedly led to a general rethinking of defence policies, transformation in these two countries was largely shaped by the legacy of the past, both in terms of its pace (slow) and its reach (limited).

In this broad picture, two things should be pointed out. First, this change in the armed forces did not necessarily take place at the same time as the transformation of the international system brought about by the end of the Cold War. The end of the bipolar confrontation certainly provided a stimulus – and several Western countries attempted to exact what was then called the 'peace dividend' by cutting their defence budgets[4] – but major transformations in doctrine and force structure occurred at different times in different countries. Secondly, while external factors are powerful drivers of change, if we look at how they combine with internal dynamics we have a more accurate picture of the timing and direction of such change.

As we shall see, literature on defence policy and force transformation has now widely addressed what the different domestic drivers of change might be. It has failed, however, to thoroughly analyse the impact of legacies and show the different mechanisms through which change can occur and then be locked in to establish a new stable trajectory. We maintain that using an historical institutionalist framework to understand force transformation helps in at least two ways. First, it enables the timing and contents of the reforms undertaken to be untangled. Secondly, looking at legacies is essential to observe how (once measures to implement change are taken) they perpetuate: self-enforcing mechanisms play a key role both in explaining when and how change occurs. Along with Schieder, we believe that historical institutionalism can be a 'useful theoretical framework for analysing foreign policy', offering 'pertinent tools for studying processes and institutional dynamics' on foreign and defence policy.[5]

In short, the purpose of this section is to build the analytical blocks to show how specific configurations of factors, and their timing, can lead to military transformation. While we do not provide a unified theory of change, we focus on specific factors that account for foreign and defence policy systems, such as decision-making structures, belief systems and implementation, taking into consideration conditions and contingencies.[6] In particular, we highlight how timing and sequences matter in order to explain how in different contexts external and internal factors interact in bringing about change, and which mechanisms can set a country's armed forces sustainably on a new trajectory. To do so, we first reconstruct the major explanations that currently address force transformation. Namely, we look at the impact of external factors, such as the international system and alliance structure, at the weight of cultural and institutional factors, and at the influence of operational experience on organisational change. The aim is not to provide a complete analysis of these factors, which has been done extensively elsewhere, but rather to show how all three sets of factors can be used to explain the major transformations addressed here and highlight the major changes with the past where relevant, focusing on those in the external environment. Following this, we introduce the major tenets and findings of literature on historical institutionalism. We show how such an approach holds promising, yet relatively unexplored, insights into the study of defence policy (and, more specifically, force transformation), contributing to the development of existing analyses. Finally, we discuss how this framework can effectively apply to military transformation in Germany, Italy and Japan.

3.2 What drives change? The factors underlying military transformation

3.2.1 The external environment: international system, new threats, and military change and alliance structure after the Cold War

The debate on the 'sources of military doctrine' has long maintained that external factors play a central role in shaping key aspects of military strategies. If we break down the concept of 'external environment' into two main sub-dimensions – threats and alliance structures – we can see that within both it is possible to observe how geographical factors as well as technological changes can affect military transformation.

With reference to the threat environment, a classic study by Posen argues that the position of a country in the international system is a primary driver of doctrinal development and provides the starting point for most neorealist-based analyses of military change.[7] Posen claims that, when faced with external constraints, military innovation will take place as political leaders directly interfere with the military's allocation of resources and doctrinal production, thus removing bureaucratic constraints (see below). Later studies have shown how other aspects of defence policy are also affected by this type of innovation dynamics, which has been a popular subject with scholars studying strategic innovation.[8] The basic principle of this approach is that the intensity of competition in international politics – and in the military domain – creates a powerful motivation to 'adapt or die'.

In the period in question, three key changes took place which clearly impacted force transformation from this perspective. First, the demise of the Soviet Union led to the unprecedented US dominance in international politics. Although the definition of unipolarity in reference to the post-Cold War period has been the subject of intense debate,[9] it is commonly held that the new phase introduced unparalleled opportunities for military action by the United States and its allies. Beginning with the Gulf War, the United States and its (European) allies have conspicuously intervened in various forms in the Balkans and sub-Saharan Africa. It is widely agreed, both in policy circles and in the academic literature studying the phenomenon, that the most immediate consequence of this systemic change was a profound transformation in the nature of military operations and, with it, the type of armed forces required to carry them out.[10] The new approach demanded a distancing from at least some of the tenets of Cold War defence posture in order to maximise deployment capabilities, thus strengthening the ability to operate out-of-area in multifaceted missions where the strictly military, 'kinetic' dimension of applying force was one of the several activities armed forces could have been required to perform. It involved, in other words, both a territorial and a functional reconfiguration of the military's core operations, which would be extended far beyond the defence of national territory and would include a range of non-combat missions.

Secondly, while the 1990s were largely characterised by the apogee of so-called liberal interventionism, in 2001 the 9/11 attacks and the response of the US administration drastically changed the general intervention rationale, with the 'Global War on Terror' (GWOT) substituting the humanitarian paradigm.[11] The conventional and (except for the Gulf War) limited interventions of the 1990s gave way to the GWOT, with a more intense (in terms of troops deployment) and more combat-oriented use of military force in a range of complex operations, both conventional (for example, the first phases of the wars in Afghanistan, in autumn 2001 and especially Iraq, in spring 2003) and unconventional. This major change, however, had the effect of strengthening the aforementioned trends. The 'boots on the ground' policy that characterised the most intense phase of counterinsurgency in Iraq and later in Afghanistan required, *mutatis mutandis*, the ability to deploy large contingents to perform various activities ranging from counterterrorism at the tactical level to security assistance for reconstruction.[12]

Thirdly, the rise of China – arguably the most visible phenomenon of the last decade – is inevitably reshaping the global security environment.[13] Further, a 'return of geopolitics',[14] often discussed with reference to resurgent Russian ambition, has been cited in reference to the end of the unipolar era and a shift towards a more multipolar world in which regional powers with revisionist goals might attempt to alter the (US-dominated) status quo.[15] The Indo-Pacific region is clearly central here, and has been widely perceived as the epicentre of this contest. While the challenges to the 'liberal' order are greater than those of a military system, this latter dimension is nonetheless central.[16] The impact on the armed forces is somewhat different from the previous changes, with increasing attention given to more traditional missions and missile and anti-missile technologies.

Also significant in this context is alliance structure. While a substantial body of scholarship has focused on the relationship between alliance politics and the conduct of military operations,[17] less attention has been given to how alliance dynamics can shape military transformation. The most immediate way is by de facto limiting the need for innovation on the part of countries that are part of asymmetrical military alliances. In fact, since most of the defence needs of minor allies are supplied by their major ally, they are relatively uninterested in taking on the hefty responsibilities (both financial and organisational) involved in transformation. As we saw in Chapter 2, this description clearly fits Germany and Italy during the Cold War. Similarly, Japan, up to the late 1980s, sought to minimise both the risks associated with Cold War rivalry and the financial burden relating to a main security role in the region. To do this, it maintained a strategy oriented exclusively towards self-defence and promoted several self-binding institutional constraints, limiting both the military budget and the role of the JSDF. In the post-Cold War period Japan has gradually overcome those limits, assuming a role of 'proactive contributor' to stability in the region. Moreover, the alliance in the late 1990s and the mid-2010s experienced two key instances of redefinition that expanded both the Japanese role and its level of military and political cooperation. Most recently, processes occurring at alliance level have been found to affect innovation and adaptation.[18] For instance, the approval of the 2015 guidelines led Japan to reconsider its military doctrine and focus more on the need to exercise deterrence against China's grey zone tactics. Previously, participation in the BMD, the US-led ballistic missile defence system, had deeply affected decisions regarding budget allocation and procurement. Similarly, the decision to procure F-35 fighters was consistent with the need to improve the level of interoperability with US forces. In addition, as highlighted in most studies,[19] the conspicuous involvement of US allies in complex operations on the ground during the GWOT – from Iraq to Afghanistan – has fostered a process of military innovation.

3.2.2 Strategic cultures and institutional arrangements

Different domestic factors have been widely thought to shape the many facets of military policy. The recent scholarly debate has highlighted an increasing focus in FPA literature on the role of domestic variables in explaining foreign and defence policy, with the aim of bridging the gap between comparative politics and IR by looking, for example, at the influence exerted by political parties or parliaments.[20] Here we explore two aspects of this impact on military transformation: strategic cultures and institutional arrangements.

Strategic cultures help decision-makers legitimise defence policies and military interventions by providing a comprehensive framework that outlines the values, interests and state goals of defence policy, as well as the instruments needed to employ it.[21] Besides the assumption that states are rational actors, ever since the seminal work by Snyder on Soviet doctrine,[22] security studies have focused on cultural factors, revealing how strategic cultures can condition countries in the shaping of their defence policies.[23] According to the 'strategic culture literature', defence policy decisions depend not only on pressure from the international system, but are also affected by the values and standards of the national strategic culture, which constitute the cognitive 'set of constraints and opportunities within which policy can be framed and implemented'.[24] The literature has also examined the individual beliefs and values of soldiers, assessing their sources and their influence over behaviour during both ground action and training.[25]

Constructivist studies have given great importance to demonstrating how ideas and beliefs play a significant role in concretely influencing defence policymaking,[26] illustrating how culture acts as a distinct national lens for shaping the perception of events.[27] For example, after unification, German foreign and defence policy[28] appeared incomprehensible to neorealist theory. Contrary to the expectations of a return to power politics, 'German state behaviour has been marked by a high degree of moderation and continuity with its record in the post-war era, exercising considerable restraint and circumspection in its external relations since 1990.'[29] In other words, German foreign policy, rather than embarking on power politics after the fall of the Berlin Wall, was still 'shaped by Venusian values: a high degree of moderation, restraint and circumspection, multilateralism'.[30] A number of scholars have pointed out how the post-1989 normalisation of memory did not dramatically alter the main elements of German strategic culture.[31] Similarly, Berger focused on the cultures of anti-militarism in Germany and Japan to explain post-Cold War continuity and restraint.[32] A strategic culture is a product of a broader political culture or 'situational context and is thus subject to change and modification'.[33] To Duffield, however, culture essentially promotes continuity in behaviour: 'Even as external circumstances change, decision makers may persist in defining problems in traditional ways, or they may continue to favour familiar approaches in trying to address new concerns.'[34]

Literature has used culture to explain variations in defence policy preferences and behaviour,[35] debating (1) a common definition of 'strategic culture', and (2) the possibility of empirically distinguishing between culture and behaviour. Regarding the first aspect, most definitions of strategic culture are based on the beliefs, values and standards of the use of force that are shared by the entire national community and rooted in history and political culture.[36] According to Gray, strategic culture is a set of 'attitudes, beliefs and procedures that a community learns, teaches and practices'.[37] Other scholars associate it more narrowly with the set of beliefs shared by members of the political and military elite,[38] while Doeser maintains that 'the concept of strategic culture focuses on a state's core beliefs and assumptions in military strategic matters'.[39] The second element, the controversial relationship between culture and behaviour, an ever-present topic in academic debate, has been emphasised by several 'generations'[40] of authors who have focused on the strategic cultures of states,[41] hegemony,[42] the 'measurement' of culture,[43] and competing sub-cultures.[44] The possibility (or impossibility) of separating – and thus empirically assess – cultural form from material and non-cultural factors is at the centre of the discussion. According to Johnston, 'culture either presents decision makers with a limited range of options or it acts as a lens that alters the appearance and efficacy of different choices'.[45] Thus, culture affects behaviours at the level of strategic preferences. However, for authors such as Gray, behaviour and culture are inseparable and, therefore, the former could be examined only by studying the context in which actors are 'en-cultured'.[46] Others emphasise how culture can 'directly influence collective behaviour' in several ways: from social identity that generates its interests to the perceptions of the external environment, affecting the evaluation of the available options.[47]

In short, we can distinguish between the scholars who 'view culture as the central independent variable explaining policy outcomes', and those who 'perceive culture as an intervening variable between the pressures of the international system and domestic policy response'.[48] Beyond definitions and possible empirical measurement, the literature has examined the potential sources of strategic culture, stressing the role of material and ideational conditions and devoting specific attention to historical experiences.[49]

Authors have empirically investigated the overall relationship between the historical experiences of a state and its cultural dispositions, highlighting the influence this relationship has over strategic behaviour.[50] For instance, Hyde-Price emphasises how attitudes towards armed forces by European states are 'rooted in 20th-Century history, particularly the experience of World War II'.[51] To 'Germany, the war led to the emergence of a strategic culture embracing civilian power, while France concluded that they needed military resources to defend their national interests'.[52] Moreover, 'Italy's defeat in 1945 favoured the establishment of an elite that opposed war and the use of force as a means of solving international disputes'.[53] However, after the fall of the Berlin Wall, Italy began to deploy troops in several military operations abroad, acting as 'international peace-keeper' but still remaining within the bounds of 'an *idealpolitik* model of strategic culture (a cooperative image of international politics and a propensity for non-coercive policy instruments)'.[54]

On the whole, did the post-Second World War 'cultural context of the losers' (Germany, Italy and Japan) impose a 'humanitarian strategic and military culture'[55] at the expense of martial attitudes? The existence of national styles in the defence domain has been long dominant in the analysis of countries like Germany and Japan,[56] while the impact of strategic culture has often been referred to as a key factor explaining diverse military policies between European states. Existing studies on Germany, for instance, have often compared it with France and the United Kingdom, using variables linked to strategic culture to explain the country's aversion to intervention in the post-Cold War environment. Katzenstein defined German foreign and security policy as 'tamed',[57] while Maull considered Berlin a 'civilian power reluctant to use military means as a foreign policy tool'.[58] Since the Second World War, 'antimilitarism and even pacifism have acquired strong roots in Germany . . . A not insignificant number of Germans have been inclined to consider peace an absolute value, rejecting the use of force.'[59] Germany's 'aversion to unilateralism, promotion of stability, general restraint in military matters', and anti-militarism were seen by Longhurst as containing the foundational elements of the German strategic culture.[60] After the Second World War, for Germans the 'possibility of drawing on national history as a source of national identity was denied'.[61] According to a number of scholars, however, the rupture after 1989 did not lead to a fundamental break in strategic culture, while 'militarism remained an illegitimate ideology'.[62] After 9/11, Germany 'appeared able to balance elements of its strategic culture', providing military support to allies while still maintaining 'a measured approach to the use of force'.[63]

Moreover, in the recent scholarly debate on Italian defence policy, particular importance is given to the role played by strategic culture in shaping political decisions and attitudes.[64] Authors examine the lens through which post-Cold War Italian leaders have perceived defence policy issues, stressing the persistence of multilateralism, peace and humanitarianism as the main values of Italian strategic culture.[65] Despite the significant transformation of Italian defence after the end of the bipolar era, 'the employment of the military instrument would be a by-product of the sedimentation within national strategic culture of global norms and values related to "humanitarian interventions" that Italy has shared and elevated as a potential determinant of foreign interventions'.[66] In other words, despite constant post-1989 military activism, Italy has maintained a 'humanitarian strategic and military culture'.[67] Accordingly, Italy intervenes abroad because of its post-Cold War specific strategic and military culture: 'a "cosmopolitan" understanding of security informs operations together with a sense of international/national responsibility to provide humanitarian assistance'.[68] Some have highlighted the 'accommodationist Italian strategic culture',[69] while others have focused on how global norms have been received (and then socialised) at domestic level. Multilateralism has remained the core aspect of the strategic culture of Italy, which became an international peacekeeper in the post-1989 era.[70]

The case of Japan displays even more clearly the role of the 'culture of anti-militarism' in shaping defence policies.[71] Japanese post-war pacifism, however, was by no means monolithic, nor uncontested. Different political groups interpreted the legacies of the wartime era in profoundly different ways. Progressives such as members of the Japanese Socialist Party, the Japanese Teachers' Union and the anti-base movement advocated strict adherence to Article 9, which stated that 'land, sea and air forces as well as any other war potential will not be recognised' and squarely denied the legitimacy of the JSDF and the US–Japan alliance. They upheld unarmed neutrality and the idea that Japan needed to be a 'peace-loving country' (*heiwa kokka*).[72] While the majority of public opinion shared these beliefs, especially during the Cold War, the conservative elite that guided the Liberal Democratic Party adopted a much more pragmatic stance. During the Cold War, their pacifism was instrumental in focusing on economic growth but also in manoeuvring through the dangers of the Cold War, diffusing US pressures to share the burden and the risk of being drawn into unwanted conflicts.[73] In the post-Cold War era, the decline of the Socialist Party and the political left-wing released what Arthur Stockwin defined as the 'political handbrake' for Japanese security policy.[74] While Japan promoted its process of 'normalisation', removing most of the institutional obstacles in favour of a more active foreign policy, it maintained that its main purpose remained the promotion of peace. The concept of 'proactive contribution to peace' promoted by Abe since 2015 represents the most significant example of how Japan managed to 'square the circle' between a much more active security policy and a still very influential pacifist and militarist strategic culture.[75]

Strategic culture has been identified as a driver of the propensity to intervene (or not) in Germany, Italy and Japan, while the question of how such a factor has affected force transformation has been studied relatively little. Lastly, to understand the ways through which non-material factors can shape defence policy we must focus on one topic that is often vaguely connected with strategic culture in the scholarly debate – strategic narratives.

Strategic narratives are stories that aim to make sense of the world by connecting different elements and imposing coherence on them. They have been defined as 'compelling storylines which can explain events convincingly and from which inferences can be drawn',[76] or – more concisely – as a 'sequence of events tied together by a plot line'.[77] To Miskimmon et al. strategic narratives are a 'means for political actors to construct a shared meaning of the past, present and future of international politics to shape the behaviour of domestic and international actors'.[78] Despite the still limited efforts to clarify the conceptual confusion about the relationship between strategic narratives and other terms (for example, frames, master-frames, etc.),[79] scholars shared the view that the general public makes sense of security issues through the use of stories.[80] Strategic narratives are strictly embedded in a given culture; they are built over existing concepts, ideas and thoughts, in keeping with common symbols, to express 'a sense of identity and belonging and communicate a sense of cause, purpose and mission'.[81] Therefore, by looking at the main frames that build strategic narratives we can reconstruct those ideas and values that condition a specific cultural context.

For example, the literature[82] has highlighted the features of the storylines crafted by political leaders in post-Cold War Italy for the purpose of increasing public and parliamentary support for military operations abroad. The strategic narrative of the 'peace mission' is clearly connected 'to the national political culture and ideology (pacifism, liberalism, and so on), which was free from the bipolar international and domestic constraints, but still coherent with the widespread bipolar values of "peace"'.[83] Schemas such as 'humanitarian aid' or 'multilateral framework' have been widely used (in a bipartisan way) to justify the new Italian military activism in the post-bipolar era. In short, the plots around which narratives are built represent the common knowledge of the member of a specific culture. As such, they can reveal the fundamental traits of identities.

Among the domestic factors that interact decisively with 'strategic culture' is the institutional context, and especially the role played by political parties and parliaments. As Biehl et al. correctly point out, 'the issue of political control of armed forces is often neglected in works on strategic culture'.[84] Institutional aspects have also been prominent in analyses of defence policy. While the importance of institutional accords is also integrated in other approaches, there are two major themes that deserve attention. First, several studies have insisted on the impact on innovation of civil–military relations. A consistent finding is that civilian leadership must be directly involved in military decision-making if innovations are to occur.[85] Different mechanisms may be invoked. Broadly speaking, civilian intervention is considered to be key to innovation in that it makes it possible to overcome the organisational inertia that would otherwise result in the perpetuation of conservative practices. Civilian intervention can re-allocate resources in two key areas: (1) budget allocation, thus modifying incentives across different services and programmes; and (2) officers' careers, by altering standard patterns that risk favouring continuity over the adoption of innovative practices.

A second theme, which is increasingly the subject of more studies, looks at how different 'domestic material power relations'[86] within democracies can lead to different defence policy outcomes. A large part of this literature focuses on the analysis of the foreign policy behaviour of European states after the end of the Cold War.[87] A recent element of debate here regards whether, and how, parliaments are valuable in shaping military interventions. Authors drawing from the 'neoclassical realism' approach, for example, have emphasised the intervening role of domestic power relations.[88] Literature on foreign policy analysis, having observed the abovementioned 'domestic turn'[89] after years of disciplinary divide, has given increasing attention to the role played by legislative assemblies in affecting foreign and defence policy.

According to the democratic peace theory, democratic institutions play a vital role because they help to convert the preferences of a war-averse population into specific policies adopted by leaders and cabinets.[90] More specifically, research has examined how domestic institutions affect foreign and defence policymaking, revealing a marked change in parliamentary control of post-Cold War military activism, from complete exclusion to veto power.[91] Besides the analysis of formal and legal aspects, Born and Hänggi introduced the influential threefold distinction between 'authority', 'ability' and 'attitude',[92] stressing the importance of resources or MPs' willingness and informal procedures. In short, parliaments can affect the propensity to undertake military interventions abroad because of the existence of 'formal (and informal) procedures' that constrain executive action.[93]

More generally, two major themes under the broad label of forces deployment are related to political institutions. First, different parliament–cabinet relations count in shaping the opportunity structure of the decision of executives to intervene. Facing stricter parliamentary scrutiny, executives will have more hurdles to jump if they want to intervene. The requirements of alliances can help to overcome these obstacles,[94] as can powerful motives for intervention that drive public opinion,[95] such as in the case of the Afghanistan intervention after 9/11. Moreover, as an increasing body of literature emphasises, the preferences of political parties also have an important impact on the decision to intervene.[96]

Indeed, the literature has empirically disproved the common idea that 'politics stops at the water's edge'. While global affairs and international governance have been more salient for parties, research has shown[97] that parties carry weight in foreign and security policy, identifying, for example, the patterns of disagreement between political parties and party families on foreign policy issues, such as military deployment. Going beyond the traditional 'hawks and doves divide', scholars emphasise the importance of the left–right dimension,[98] and especially those core values (for example, multilateralism and human rights) that explain the differences between parties in their views of military missions abroad.[99] Also in the cases of Italy and Germany, the literature has given increasing importance to the influence that political parties have over defence and security policies.[100] Consistent with Hoffman, it is worth pointing out that although elites are usually defined as a unit, the 'more political ideologies vary within a country, the less likely it is that national culture, power or role are able to capture foreign and security policy preferences and policies'.[101]

Secondly, parliaments that closely monitor the use of armed forces once missions are in place are able to deeply affect how military operations are conducted, from troop levels to rules of engagement (RoE). This scholarly debate has been less prominent in explaining other areas of defence policy, such as changes in doctrine, budgetary allocation and force structure. However, there are indications that different institutional arrangements, a different balance of forces between the executive and the legislative power, can influence the propensity to adapt by affecting the internal functioning of military institutions, or create other powerful incentives for military institutions to adapt to the wishes of the civilian leadership.[102]

Based on the recent literature,[103] in the cases in question we can expect a very different behaviour from parliaments. Indeed, while the German Bundestag is generally portrayed as an example of strict parliamentary supervision in defence policy, restraining executive autonomy, the role of monitoring by the Italian assembly in military affairs has been extremely limited, enabling governments to avoid audience costs and attribution of responsibility.[104]

In Japan, in the aftermath of the war, the military takeover of the civilian government was widely identified as one of the key causes of wartime imperialism and expansionism. As a consequence, the activities of the JSDF were limited by strict civilian control (*bunmin tōsei*) and bureaucratic control (*bunkan tōsei*) of the armed forces. The first principle led to the classifying of JSDF personnel as 'special civil servants' and the placing of the Japanese Defence Agency under the direct control of the

Office of the Prime Minister. The second principle resulted in the JDA being 'colonised' by bureaucrats of the ministries of Foreign Affairs and Finance. Moreover, contacts between uniformed personnel and the political leadership were filtered by the presence of civilian 'defence councillors' (*bōei sanjikan*), who further consolidated bureaucratic control of the activities of the JSDF. This system was reformed only with the creation of an independent Ministry of Defence in 2007. These mechanisms of civilian control were further modified when Abe Shinzo instituted the National Security Secretariat in 2013, allowing a limited number of uniformed officers to participate in meetings and offer direct advice on policy, while preserving strict civilian control over the military.[105]

The Japanese parliament, the National Diet, has also been instrumental in limiting the activities of the JSDF and guaranteeing civilian control as well as the respect of constitutional norms.[106] As Takako Hikotani argues, the Japanese Diet has had 'significant power to authorise (or not) actions by the SDF, through legislative action and authoritative statements on constitutional interpretation'.[107] Historically, its role in defence policy-making and its capacity to supervise policies outside the annual bill on the defence budget has been limited, partly due to the long-standing refusal by the opposition parties to recognise the legitimacy of the JSDF.[108] More recently, the security reforms promoted by Abe in 2015 have partially limited the Diet's authoritative power. Nevertheless, these restrictions have in part been compensated in terms of supervision by the increasing political salience of security matters, together with the practical need to authorise several deployments, new security agreements and the procurement of new weapons systems.[109]

3.2.3 Organisational dynamics and operational experience

Armed forces are constituted by several bureaucracies that can either promote or resist innovation. One way this general statement has been addressed is by separating *inter*-organisational from *intra*-organisational aspects in military transformation theories. Furthermore, literature has often distinguished between peacetime and wartime innovation – a distinction that has been made increasingly complicated by the nature of the post-Cold War environment in which, for the United States and several of its major allies, barely a year has passed without some sort of military engagement abroad (in this case with the partial exception of Japan).

Looking at inter-organisational factors, competing for resources may produce positive results due to competition between different services: within the area of defence, in fact, this rivalry leads to another 'adapt or die (or at least languish)' situation.[110] Empirical research following this approach has shown how – at least in the context of the post-war United States – rivalry among the air force, army and navy regarding which service should have ownership of nuclear weapons and missile technology has created powerful incentives to adopt effective solutions. This was perceived as essential by the different branches to avoid lagging behind and risk decreasing relevance and its very material consequences, thus fostering a race to innovate,[111] notably in the missile domain (a new technology where 'ownership' was not pre-ordained).

Otherwise, competition among services can stifle, rather than stimulate, innovation. Inter-service rivalry can lead to resistance to innovations that are expected to reduce the status and role of certain branches or services. One frequently mentioned mechanism is that jealousy among services over the potentially asymmetric distribution of benefits following the adoption of a new doctrine or weapons system can hinder innovation because policymakers are induced to mitigate conflict by keeping resource endowments stable and all (or at least most) parties satisfied. The price to pay for this avoidance of conflict and adoption of compromising solutions is that potential innovators and economies of scale are not favoured and, consequently, operational effectiveness is reduced.[112]

Intra-organisational factors have also received widespread attention. Literature on military innovation has dealt extensively with how internal informal and formal mechanisms shape adaptation and organisational learning, with a strong focus on the role played by culture, learning and the configuration of military officers' coalitions.[113] While definitions vary, military culture is generally intended as the set of beliefs that allows a (shared) understanding of the external environment and, more specifically, the nature of warfare.[114] In this sense, military organisations are the unit of reference for military culture (a lower level, that is, than strategic cultures). Military cultures, for example, have held the forefront of scholarly literature in explaining variation over adoption of military doctrine and effectiveness, operational practices and force structure.[115] The impact of culture on military doctrine has been widely discussed (for example, in studies on what motivated the preference for offensive doctrines in the First World War[116] and the inter-war period) in the context of the impact of organisational preferences on doctrinal developments and effectiveness, with attempts to show how different sets of beliefs affect the nature of past and future wars, or the importance to be attributed to bottom-up feedback.[117] Military culture has also been called upon more recently to explain variations in doctrine and operational practices in diverse settings, such as counterinsurgency[118] and peacekeeping operations.[119] Finally, cultural factors have been invoked to illustrate different ways of adopting technological innovations, for example, the ability to embed information and communication technologies within the armed forces.[120]

Closely related to the debate on culture, studies have been focusing on innovation and its links with learning processes. The interpretation of past experiences is considered to be central, with military institutions seen as essentially learning organisations.[121] This entails, first, looking at how learning occurs. Military organisations try to adapt through processes of trial-and-error by getting 'in contact' with their enemies (who are also adapting).[122] It has been also been shown that innovation can occur through emulation, potentially underpinned by different mechanisms depending on the nature of the adopters such as major or middle powers.[123] The analysis of learning processes also involves studying how complex organisations such as armed forces incorporate and institutionalise these lessons to ensure they are not 'forgotten' and are available to new members when the old members are assigned to other positions or departments, or retire. This requires examining the role of operational experience and bottom-up feedback in promoting innovation at institutional level and structuring organisational learning.[124]

Recent literature has highlighted how the eventual extra budget devoted to missions abroad (as occurred in the case of Italy) allowed armed forces further resources, as well as training and assets availability.[125] According to this perspective, military deployment has been instrumental in guaranteeing the overall sustainability of the troops (even in periods of general budget shrinking), indirectly fostering national industry.[126]

Another line of studies regards how innovation actually happens as a result of the internal dynamics of military organisations. Classic studies on innovation in peacetime discuss how the formation of specific coalitions among military officers can bring about innovation in peacetime.[127] Rosen's *Winning the Next War*, for example, focuses on the formation of a coalition among senior officers who envision a new 'theory of victory' (that is, ideas on what future warfare will look like and how it will be won) and mid-level/junior officers who embrace the new approach. If the senior officers are able to raise these officers to higher-ranking positions they can then build a coalition that will promote changes (and to do this they must win an intellectual struggle with other coalitions within the military).[128] In the context of intra-organisational politics, several studies have applied similar logics to innovation in relation to the adoption of new weapons systems and doctrines.[129]

3.3 Premises and promises of historical institutionalism in the comparative study of force transformation

Literature on historical institutionalism[130] is fairly extensive and hetero-geneous, but a good starting point is Paul Pierson's *Politics in Time*,[131] which contains several key elements that characterise the approach and are central to our reconstruction here. Three of these are particularly rel-evant: path dependence and its mechanisms; exogenous and endogenous drivers of change; and the timing and sequencing of change. We shall describe these briefly and then outline how the domain of defence policy, and specifically force transformation, can be studied within this analytical framework.

First, the concept of path dependence is a central tenet of historical institutionalism. The idea is intuitive: once a path is selected, there will be strong incentives to maintain that path and significant obstacles to reversing and changing it. By 'path' we refer mainly to strategic choices and specific institutional arrangements, while 'dependence' means that the trajectories have been shaped, in an inertial manner, by certain prior events.[132] This also means that the analysis of the 'original' choice and of the mechanisms of reproduction should be differentiated.[133] The reproduc-tion mechanisms underpinning such path dependence are diverse: con-cepts such as positive feedbacks, network effects, institutional matrixes[134] and lock-in effects[135] are often invoked. With regard to positive feedbacks, and the relative concepts of self-reinforcing sequences and increasing returns, the logic is that once choices are made that entail start-up costs, they become increasingly difficult to reverse. Events have an important effect on the shaping of those to come, since the incentive to follow a path is greater once it has been taken (or, vice versa, the costs involved in leaving it are higher). Rules are created that enforce themselves and, often, their makers. Standards of behaviour are adopted that create behavioural routines[136] and mental maps that are difficult to change as they respond to basic cognitive requirements.[137] The classic example is that of technological platforms: once a decision is made to adopt a given technology, it becomes increasingly complicated to change to a different one. Potentially large costs are involved in setting up the technology (fixed costs, for example), people have learned how to use a specific language or asset, and an ecosys-tem has been built around a platform that makes switching to a different one (which, in hindsight, might even be superior) very costly. This may also be applied to social organisations that are incorporated in a broader system (the concepts of 'institutional matrix' and 'network effects'): one piece becomes part of a web that cannot be easily disentangled.

Secondly, since to assert the idea of path dependence does not mean to deny that change occurs, historical institutionalist approaches have had to identify the reasons for change.[138] The literature on path dependence stresses two main trajectories of change: resorting to exogenous shocks, and/or relying on endogenous elements. Generally, institutional transformations occurring as a result of large-scale, often exogenous, shocks are defined as 'critical junctures'.[139] A critical juncture is an instance of uncertainty in which processes that are defined as 'path dependent' can experience change. Rather than setting institutions or policies on a new pre-determined trajectory, however, they make it possible for agents to reshape these trajectories in multiple ways.[140] In this sense, they are 'permissive conditions' that constitute the prerequisite for the production of change, as they 'increase the causal power for agency'.[141] Exogenous shocks include political transitions, which at a domestic level can be represented by changes in regime or early phases of state formation (such as independence from colonial rule), and at international level, most visibly through systemic change or extraordinary events (such as the abovementioned 9/11 terrorist attacks). On their own, these instances create space for agency which can then produce change, but they do not *cause* change.

Two caveats should be applied to this general framework. First, the fact that agents are able to produce change does not mean that they will have full control over the actual outcome (the new trajectory). In other words, there is no univocal or necessary direction to be taken that perfectly corresponds to the preference of the actors who make key decisions at critical junctures. They help to set in motion a new trajectory but are both still affected by the very context in which they act (see below) and unable to control the process as it unfolds in the future – where, once the trajectory is followed, their room for action diminishes. The second, which leads to the identification of the endogenous aspects of change, is that there is a significant distinction between the types of change that occur. Change can, in fact, be incremental (which is perfectly compatible with the functioning of institutions or policies once a path has been taken) or it can be radical – in other words, based on the definition of key choices that determine which path is taken.

There is a clear link here with endogenous sources of change. Even critical junctures that are generated exogenously are preceded by factors and conditions which help to set the context in which agents act when shocks create that space.[142] While in the literature there is an ongoing debate as to the extent of the impacts of endogenous factors, it is agreed that the effect is that the actors are bound to specific courses of action, limiting their cognitive frames or establishing legal and regulatory constraints. Even junctures do not occur in a vacuum, and while the perimeter of action is clearly determined by the extent of the shock, it also depends on the relative weight of these antecedent conditions. This is also why, although exogenous shocks may appear symmetrically to be in different contexts, it is still possible to observe a relevant variation in outcomes.

A third building block of historical institutionalist theories relates to the concepts of 'timing' and 'sequence'. As Pierson notes, the idea that the past matters should not lead to a simple assessment of how t_{-1} is affecting trajectories in t_n (this is what is mirrored in quantitative analysis by so-called 'lagged dependent variables'). Rather, *when* things happen does matter: the same events occurring in different timeframes might not have similar effects on subsequent events. Decisions do not occur – nor do they affect outcomes – independently from the moment (and, more broadly, the context) in which they are made.

The objective of empirical research in the light of this approach should then be to identify the specific ways in which time affects key political processes. In the light of this short summary of historical institutionalism, it might be somewhat surprising that such an approach is not used more often in analysing defence policy change.[143] Ultimately, many aspects of the domain lend themselves to be considered as 'path dependent'. The typical features of the military domain coincide exactly with (some of) Pierson's features of the political domain (of which they constitute a subset).[144] Indeed, Pierson mentions national defence as a typical public good that would in turn be subject to path dependence. The nature of public goods and the need for coordinated action to create and sustain them demand that there be relative stability in the actors producing them: alternatives might be too risky as they have no previous expertise on a subject. This is, again, a factor that makes the defence domain path dependent: expertise is essential, and relatively concentrated; thus, change cannot come (as it would, in theory, in other domains such as free markets) simply through competition. The defence domain is also 'institutionally dense': once institutions and policies are established, they become difficult to challenge, as they create coalitions and incentives that support them. Institutional density is linked to power asymmetries that in many cases give incumbents an advantage: setting rules further reinforces their power. Nowhere this is more visible – within military organisations – than in setting the rules for career promotions. Besides, informational asymmetries can also contribute to strengthening incumbents; in the defence sector, the complexity of the matter and the high entry costs for acquiring relevant knowledge help to create this entrenchment. This is all the more the case due to the complexity of the defence domain, where actors pursue multiple and not always consistent goals. In such context, on the one hand, high complexity requires stable procedures, while, on the other hand, monitoring and assessment – crucial elements of innovation – become very complicated.[145]

3.4 Critical junctures and military transformation in Germany, Italy and Japan

As noted, despite the promises, defence is not one of the themes analysed in the major studies on historical institutionalism.[146] In keeping with what we perceive to be a strong approach to the study of change in armed forces, we look at how it can be used to effectively analyse military transformation in Germany, Italy and Japan, to pave the way for the subsequent chapters that may in turn provide empirical evidence on the evolution of military doctrine and force structure.

How might this approach be used to shed light on force transformation? Along with Schieder, we believe that historical institutionalism provides 'a set of conceptual mechanisms and tools for understanding and explaining' foreign and defence policy.[147] As Pierson points out, path-dependent arguments are not simply descriptive, but make it possible to identify the mechanisms behind a given trajectory, how they operate and with what consequences.[148]

In relation to this, in the empirical chapters we examine the circumstances in which a given path is chosen and the temporal sequences of processes by which social patterns reproduce themselves. In other words, we investigate the conditions of the critical junctures and the self-reinforcing dynamics responsible both for placing the defence policies of the three countries on distinct long-term trajectories, and for the patterns of institutionalisation they have adopted. We investigate military transformation defined as the part of a defence policy that relates to doctrine and force structure, as defined in Chapter 1.

We show how, after the critical juncture that came about with the end of the bipolar era, the three countries chose specific paths from the various possible trajectories.[149] Operation Desert Storm (1991) was the first 'critical' juncture (in the case of Italy) because it triggered 'a process of positive feedbacks'.[150] Indeed, self-reinforcing feedbacks (which for Rome came from the development of a dynamic military policy in the 1990s and afterwards) then gained 'more and more predominance' on the adopted path over the alternatives.[151] Sequences have been crucial in understanding the different evolutions of the defence policies selected in Rome, Berlin and Tokyo. Italy (which had its first, albeit limited, operational experiences in the 1980s) adopted in 1990–1991 a trajectory based on 'expeditionary forces', while Germany and Japan remained focused on 'territorial defence' for many years, despite the transformation of the international system and growing external pressures. In Chapters 4, 5 and 6 we will look at the evolution of force structure and doctrines in the cases of Germany, Italy and Japan, respectively, observing their distinct paths over thirty years. We maintain that the trajectory established after the collapse of the bipolar era was consolidated in the years following in a path dependent process. The mechanisms that make 'timing' and 'sequence' crucial can be properly understood by examining both domestic and international contexts. On the one hand, alliances and international events and pressures are fundamental drivers for the defence policies of the three countries. On the other hand, in line with Hyde and Saunders, it is crucial to 'look at which domestic audiences constrain leader action . . . and at the domestic political institutions that govern the interactions between leaders, elites and mass public'.[152] In other words, we investigate the 'structural and strategic domestic sources of audience constraint'.[153] Generally, we examine the contexts *when* the relationship between those variables occur. Specifically, as mentioned above, we focus on the interaction among alliances and international pressure, strategic culture, narratives and institutional constraints and operational experience.

We argue that the very prudent trajectory of German defence policy after the collapse of the Berlin Wall highlights elements of path dependence. Indeed, the legacies and the unexploited 'window of opportunity' left by Desert Storm influenced the choice of path adopted by the Bundeswehr. The subsequent incremental changes occurring in the 1990s affected the slow trajectory of Berlin's security policy. Here, the dynamic interaction between relevant domestic constraints (the anti-military culture but also the parliamentary supervision that greatly reduced executive autonomy), very limited operational experience and external drivers hindered the possibility for many years of moving away from territorial defence as the main reference for doctrine and force structure.

We claim that, in the case of Italy, the 'institutionalisation' of 'an expeditionary defence policy' occurred due to a constant military engagement after the critical juncture of Desert Storm, in the 1990s and also in the new century, with the GWOT. In many ways, the Italian experience is unique inasmuch as operational experience played a much larger role than in Germany and Japan in shaping military transformation. This, in any case, was also allowed by domestic conditions, through the development of a 'peace and humanitarian narrative' shared even in combat scenarios by political parties and by governments that were not restrained by the limited parliamentary supervision and international pressures (such as requests from allies and multilateral organisations). We empirically illustrate how timing and sequence mattered in providing self-reinforcing feedbacks for the path adopted since the end of the Cold War.

Similarly, the Japanese case testifies to the importance of timing and sequencing as well as to the development of paths in response to key critical junctures. The decision not to participate in the first Gulf War sparked widespread debate on the role and responsibilities of the country in the post-Cold War order, and it paved the way for the first steps towards a broad acceptance of a role as an active contributor to regional and global peace and stability. However, despite the approval of the 1992 Peace Cooperation Law, Japan did not undergo the transition towards an expeditionary force similar to that enacted by Italy. The emergence of external threats from North Korea and China during the late 1990s provided a much greater motivation for transforming Japan's military doctrine and force structure than the military role of peacekeeping operations. The Third Taiwan Strait Crisis (1995–1996) and the Taepodong Shock (1998) represented a critical juncture for the evolution of Japanese defence policies, leading to the decision to develop the alliance with Washington.

In Japan, 9/11 and the rise of the GWOT also had a significant impact. As in the case of Italy, it led the country to consolidate the path it had embarked on in the late 1990s. Although Tokyo participated in the GWOT with a refuelling mission in support of US operations in Afghanistan and the deployment from 2004 to 2006 of its forces in Iraq, the consequences went beyond mere participation in and preparation for overseas missions. The perception of insecurity associated with 9/11 and the US external pressures determined by the GWOT empowered the part of the conservative elite who wanted to accelerate the 'normalisation' of the country's security policies. This led to significant changes in how Japan dealt with regional problems, such as North Korea and China. Moreover, the Japanese case is characterised by another critical juncture that involves both domestic politics and external factors. The period between the Triple Disaster of 3/11 and the election of Abe in 2012 represents a case in point. On the one hand, 3/11 contributed to a much more favourable perception of the JSDF and of the US–Japan alliance. On the other hand, it helped to create the political climate that would enable Abe Shinzo to advance a vast array of security reforms, thanks to which the role of the JSDF in regional security would be considerably expanded and the US–Japan alliance would be able to adopt new measures for dealing with the mounting threat posed by China's use of grey zone coercive strategies since the early 2010s.

3.5 Conclusion

What drives military transformation? There are several different factors that explain why and how change occurs in armed forces. Drawing from the existing literature, this chapter has focused on both the external environment (mainly threats and alliance structure) and the domestic context (largely cultural and institutional elements) and operational experience. Only by taking into consideration the dynamic interaction between international drivers and internal dynamics can the timing and direction of military transformation by properly assessed. The scholarly debate has widely highlighted how – since the end of the Cold War – the boundaries between domestic and foreign policy became extremely blurred, while the 'politicisation of international politics' made domestic players increasingly relevant.[154] In line with Balfour et al.: 'The end of the Cold War, European integration and wider patterns of globalisation have substantially increased interdependencies and broken down traditional borders between national and foreign policy.'[155]

The purpose of this chapter has been to provide a framework within which different domestic and international factors may be placed together to illustrate when and how change occurs. We maintain that through the lens of historical institutionalism the impact of past decisions, self-enforcing mechanisms and sequences can be taken into account. The legacy of the past largely shaped post-Cold War military transformation in Germany, Italy and Japan. Based on our framework we claim that, in the wake of the critical juncture that occurred with the end of the bipolar era, the three countries followed different trajectories that were later consolidated in a path dependent process. The mechanisms that reinforce those paths depend not only on 'timing' and 'sequence', but also on how the abovementioned domestic and international factors interact and affect defence policy. Therefore, the dynamic processes between external pressures, culture, institutions and operational experience set the conditions that allow a trajectory to begin and self-reinforcing dynamics to shape the path. We envisage that different 'timing' and 'sequence' (since the mid-1980s), along with a considerable executive autonomy (thanks to limited parliamentary supervision and a 'peace narrative') and a growing operational experience, will shape the Italian defence policy along the path of 'expeditionary forces' that dates back to the early 1990s, while Germany and Japan, due to their separate conditions and temporal sequences, will remain focused on 'territorial defence' for many years.

The empirical chapters will assess the transformations taking place in the three countries by looking at the evolution of doctrines and force structure, illustrating in detail how the mechanisms work and their consequences. Chapter 4 will highlight the slow transformation of German defence after unification, from the Karlsruhe landmark decision to the first significant missions in Kosovo and Afghanistan, amid the disinclined doctrinal adoption of a crisis management approach, the reluctant development of the so-called 'Munich consensus' and a persistent hesitancy in the use of force. Chapter 5 will illustrate the remarkable evolution of Italian defence policy since Desert Storm and the development of a doctrine based on expeditionary forces in the context of a growing and demanding operational experience in the 1990s and especially in the new century, up to the more recent phase of greater military prudence after the war in Libya. At the other end of the scale, the chapter will also reveal the obstacles to the parallel development of the Italian force structure. Lastly, Chapter 6 will examine the trajectory of Japanese defence, with special attention given to the critical juncture of the GWOT and the Abe era.

Notes

1. Pierson, *Politics in Time.*
2. As illustrated in Chapter 2, the Italian White Paper (1985) was profoundly affected by the military experience in Lebanon. Despite its relevance, the mission was an isolated event for Italian defence policy, which was still heavily influenced by Cold War logic.
3. The German government interpreted the constitution as prohibiting *all* German participation in out-of-area missions, thereby avoiding any kind of military involvement in Lebanon. On this point, see Maull, 'Germany and the Use of Force', 66.
4. S. Chan (1995), 'Grasping the Peace Dividend: Some Propositions on the Conversion of Swords into Plowshares,' *Mershon International Studies Review* 39 (S1): 53–95.
5. S. Schieder (2019), 'New Institutionalism and Foreign Policy', in K. Brummer, S. Harnisch, K. Oppermann and D. Panke (eds), *Foreign Policy as Public Policy.* Manchester: Manchester University Press, 126.
6. On middle-range theories and FPA, see S. Smith (1986), 'Theories of Foreign Policy: An Historical Overview', *Review of International Studies* 12(1): 13–29.
7. B. Posen (1986), *The Sources of Military Doctrine: France, Britain, and Germany between the World Wars.* Ithaca, NY: Cornell University Press.
8. For a review, see E. O. Goldman and R. B. Andres (1999), 'Systemic Effects of Military Innovation and Diffusion', *Security Studies* 8(4): 79–125.
9. G. J. Ikenberry (2018), 'The End of Liberal International Order?' *International Affairs* 94(1): 7–23; J. J. Mearsheimer (2019), 'Bound to Fail: The Rise and Fall of the Liberal International Order', *International Security* 43(4): 7–50.
10. For a summary see Farrell, Rynning and Terriff, *Transforming Military Power since the Cold War.*
11. See A. Geis, H. Müller and N. Schörnig (eds) (2013), *The Militant Face of Democracy: Liberal Forces for Good.* Cambridge: Cambridge University Press.
12. See, for example, the analysis by D. Kilcullen (2010), *Counterinsurgency.* New York: Oxford University Press; on the United States, see P. Cornish (2009), 'The United States and Counterinsurgency: "Political First, Political Last, Political Always"', *International Affairs* 85(1): 61–79; on the United Kingdom,

see T. Farrell and S. Gordon (2009), 'COIN Machine: The British Military in Afghanistan', *Orbis* 53(4): 665–83.

13. For a review on China's rise in international relations, see, for example, A. I. Johnston (2013), 'How New and Assertive is China's New Assertiveness?' *International Security* 37(4): 7–28; T. J. Christensen (2015), *The China Challenge: Shaping the Choices of a Rising Power.* New York: W. W. Norton; N. Silove (2016), 'The Pivot before the Pivot: US Strategy to Preserve the Power Balance in Asia', *International Security* 40(3): 45–88; J. C. Weiss and J. L. Wallace (2021), 'Domestic Politics, China's Rise, and the Future of the Liberal International Order', *International Organization* 75(2): 635–64.

14. For a detailed debate on this point, see, for example, R. Belloni, V. Della Sala and P. Viotti (eds) (2019), *Fear and Uncertainty in Europe: The Return to Realism?* Houndmills: Palgrave.

15. See, for example, W. R. Mead (2014), 'The Return of Geopolitics: The Revenge of the Revisionist Powers', *Foreign Affairs* 93(3): 69; S. Guzzini (ed.) (2012), *The Return of Geopolitics in Europe? Social Mechanisms and Foreign Policy Identity Crises.* Cambridge: Cambridge University Press.

16. Ikenberry, 'The End of Liberal International Order?'; Mearsheimer, 'Bound to Fail'.

17. See, for example, P. A. Weitsman (2013), *Waging War: Alliances, Coalitions and Institutions of Interstate Violence.* Stanford, CA: Stanford University Press; O. Schmitt (2019), 'More Allies, Weaker Missions? How Junior Partners Contribute to Multinational Military Operations', *Contemporary Security Policy* 40(1): 70–84; J. Davidson (2011), *America's Allies and War: Kosovo, Afghanistan, and Iraq.* Houndmills: Palgrave; M. E. Henke (2019), *Constructing Allied Cooperation: Diplomacy, Payments, and Power in Multilateral Military Coalitions.* Ithaca, NY: Cornell University Press; Lanoszka, *Military Alliances in the Twenty-First Century.*

18. See, for example, S. Rynning (2013), 'ISAF and NATO: Campaign Innovation and Organisational Adaptation', in T. Farrell, F. Osinga and J. A. Russell (eds), *Military Adaptation in Afghanistan.* Stanford, CA: Stanford University Press, 83–107.

19. On Italy see, for example, F. Coticchia and F. N. Moro (2016), 'Learning from Others? Emulation and Change in the Italian Armed Forces since 2001', *Armed Forces & Society* 42(4): 696–718.

20. See especially the seminal article on domestic factors and foreign policy analysis by Kaarbo, 'Foreign Policy Analysis Perspective on the Domestic Politics Turn in IR Theory'.

21. For a definition (*infra*), see, for example, A. I. Johnston (1995), 'Thinking about Strategic Culture', *International Security* 19(4): 32-64. See also T. Farrell (2005), *The Norms of War: Cultural Beliefs and Modern Conflict.* Boulder, CO: Lynne Rienner, 602

22. J. Snyder (1977), *The Soviet Strategic Culture.* Santa Monica, CA: Rand Corporation.

23. For a review, see J. S. Lantis (2002), 'Strategic Culture and National Security Policy', *International Studies Review* 4(3): 87–113.

24. F. Coticchia and F. N. Moro (2014), 'Transforming the Italian Armed Forces, 2001–2012: New Challenges and Budget Constraints', *International Spectator* 49(1): 133–48.

25. 'Military culture influences military behaviour by directly affecting soldiers' perceptions of operations' context'. C. Ruffa (2017), 'Military Cultures and Force Employment in Peace Operations', *Security Studies* 26(3): 394.

26. See, for example, Katzenstein, *The Culture of National Security*; E. Kier (2017), *Imagining War: French and British Military Doctrine between the Wars.* Princeton, NJ: Princeton University Press.

27. Berger, *Cultures of Antimilitarism.*

28. For a recent overview on IR theory and German foreign policy, see J. Eberle and A. Miskimmon (eds) (2022), *International Theory and German Foreign Policy.* London: Routledge.

29. Duffield, 'Political Culture and State Behavior', 767.
30. Malici, 'Germans as Venutians', 37–62.
31. Buras and Longhurst, 'The Berlin Republic, Iraq, and the Use of Force', 215–45.
32. Berger, *Cultures of Antimilitarism*.
33. Buras and Longhurst, 'The Berlin Republic, Iraq, and the Use of Force'.
34. Duffield, 'Political Culture and State Behaviour'.
35. On similarities and differences of manifold 'Cultural Approaches', see Duffield, 'Political Culture and State Behaviour'.
36. F. Doeser (2018), 'Historical Experiences, Strategic Culture, and Strategic Behaviour: Poland in the anti-ISIS Coalition', *Defence Studies* 18(4): 455.
37. C. S. Gray (1981), 'National Style in Strategy: The American Example', *International Security* 6(2): 21–47. Gray talks about 'dominant national beliefs' regarding strategic choices. To Rosa, the strategic preferences of actors are defined as 'the result of the interaction between the collectively shared images of the world and the available resources'. P. Rosa (2018), 'Patterns of Strategic Culture and the Italian Case', *International Politics* 55: 316–33. Also 'military culture has its roots in the early formative moments of an army'. Ruffa, 'Military Cultures in Peace and Stability Operations', 393.
38. W. Tow (1999), 'Strategic Cultures in Comparative Perspective', in K. Booth and R. Trood (eds), *Strategic Cultures in the Asia Pacific Region*. Basingstoke: Palgrave Macmillan, 320–44.
39. Strategic culture is viewed as an 'ideational context surrounding the decision-makers in a state at any one time'. Doeser, 'Historical Experiences, Strategic Culture, and Strategic Behaviour', 456.
40. For an updated review, see F. Doeser and J. Eidenfalk (2019), 'Using Strategic Culture to Understand Participation in Expeditionary Operations: Australia, Poland, and the Coalition against the Islamic State', *Contemporary Security Policy* 40(1): 4–29.
41. Snyder, *The Soviet Strategic Culture*. On American strategic culture, see Gray, 'National Style in Strategy'.
42. B. Klein (1988), 'Hegemony and Strategic Culture: American Power Projection and Alliance Defence Politics', *Review of International Studies* 14(2): 133–48.
43. See A. I. Johnston (1995), 'Thinking about Strategic Culture', *International Security* 19(4): 32–64. For a critical perspective, see A. Ghiselli (2018), 'Revising China's Strategic Culture: Contemporary Cherry-Picking of Ancient Strategic Thought', *China Quarterly* 233: 166–85.
44. Lantis, 'Strategic Culture and National Security Policy'.
45. Johnston, 'Thinking about Strategic Culture', 42
46. Consistent with this view, actors who are 'encultured' conduct behaviour. C. S. Gray (1999), 'Strategic Culture as Context: The First Generation of Theory Strikes Back', *Review of International Studies* 25(1): 55.
47. Duffield, 'Political Culture and State Behaviour'.
48. T. Dyson (2011), 'Condemned Forever to Becoming and Never to Being? The Weise Commission and German Military Isomorphism', *German Politics* 20(4): 545–67.
49. See J. S. Lantis (2014), 'Strategic Cultures and Security Policies in the Asia-Pacific', *Contemporary Security Policy* 35(2): 166–86; Doeser, 'Historical Experiences, Strategic Culture, and Strategic Behaviour'.
50. Doeser, 'istorical Experiences, Strategic Culture, and Strategic Behaviour'.
51. A. Hyde-Price (2004), 'European Security, Strategic Culture, and the Use of Force', *European Security* 13(4): 325.
52. Doeser, 'Historical Experiences, Strategic Culture, and Strategic Behaviour', 457.
53. Rosa, 'Patterns of Strategic Culture and the Italian Case'.
54. Ibid., 325.

55. F. Coticchia and M. Ceccorulli (2017). 'Stick to the Plan? Culture, Interests, Multidimensional Threats and Italian Defence Policy', *Italian Political Science Review* 47(2): 183–203.
56. Berger, *Cultures of Antimilitarism*; Katzenstein, *The Culture of National Security*.
57. P. J. Katzenstein (ed.) (1997), *Tamed Power: Germany in Europe*. Ithaca, NY: Cornell University Press.
58. Maull, 'Germany and the Use of Force', 64.
59. Duffield, 'Political Culture and State Behaviour', 780.
60. Longhurst, *Germany and the Use of Force*.
61. Buras and Longhurst, 'The Berlin Republic, Iraq, and the Use of Force'.
62. Longhurst, *Germany and the Use of Force*, 140.
63. Buras and Longhurst, 'The Berlin Republic, Iraq, and the Use of Force'. The most recent debate concerns the possible impact of the Russian invasion of Ukraine on German strategic culture. See T. Bunde (2022), 'Lessons (to be) Learned? Germany's Zeitenwende and European Security after the Russian Invasion of Ukraine', *Contemporary Security Policy* 43(3): 516–30.
64. See especially, Ignazi et al., *Italian Military Operations Abroad*; P. Pirani (2010), 'The Way We Were: The Social Construction of the Italian Defence Policy', *Modern Italy* 15(2): 217–30; F. Coticchia (2014), *La guerra che non c'era: opinione pubblica e interventi militari italiani dall'Afghanistan alla Libia*. Milano, EGEA; P. Rosa (2016), *Strategic Culture and Italy's Military Behaviour: Between Pacifism and Realpolitik*. Lanham, MD: Rowman & Littlefield.
65. Ignazi et al., *Italian Military Operations Abroad*.
66. Ceccorulli and Coticchia, 'Stick to the Plan?'
67. F. Coticchia and F. N. Moro (2020), 'From Enthusiasm to Retreat: Italy and Military Missions Abroad after the Cold War', *IPS - Italian Political Science* 15(1): 114–31.
68. Ceccorulli and Coticchia, 'Stick to the Plan?'
69. Rosa, 'The Accommodationist State', 88–115.
70. Ignazi et al., *Italian Military Operations Abroad*.
71. Berger, *Cultures of Antimilitarism*; Oros, *Normalizing Japan*; Y. Izumikawa (2010), 'Explaining Japanese Antimilitarism: Normative and Realist Constraints on Japan's Security Policy', *International Security* 35(2): 123–60.
72. Dian, *Contested Memories in Chinese and Japanese Foreign Policy*.
73. Izumikawa, 'Explaining Japanese Antimilitarism'; Samuels, *Securing Japan*.
74. J. A. Stockwin (2000), 'The Social Democratic Party (Former Japan Socialist Party): A Turbulent History', in R. J. Hrebenar (ed.), *Japan's New Party System*. Boulder, CO: Westview, 209–51.
75. L. Hagström and U. Hanssen (2016), 'War is Peace: The Rearticulation of "Peace" in Japan's China Discourse', *Review of International Studies* 42(2): 266–86.
76. L. Freedman (2006), *The Transformation in Strategic Affairs*. London: Routledge, 22.
77. C. Archetti (2017), 'Narrative Wars: Understanding Terrorism in the Era of Global Interconnectedness', in A. Miskimmon, B. O'Loughlin and L. Roselle (eds), *Forging the World: Strategic Narratives and International Relations*. Ann Arbor: University of Michigan Press, 220.
78. A. Miskimmon, B. O'Loughlin and L. Roselle (2017). 'Conclusions', in A. Miskimmon, B. O'Loughlin and L. Roselle (eds), *Forging the World: Strategic Narratives and International Relations*. Ann Arbor: University of Michigan Press, 321.
79. Attempts such as, for example, A. Miskimmon, B. O'Loughlin and L. Roselle (eds) (2017), *Forging the World: Strategic Narratives and International Relations*. Ann Arbor: University of Michigan Press; T. Colley (2017), 'Is Britain a Force for Good? Investigating British Citizens' Narrative Understanding of War', *Defence Studies* 17(1): 1–22. For an updated review (and conceptual clarification), see C. Catanzaro

and F. Coticchia (2021), 'The Fog of Words: Assessing the Problematic Relationship between Strategic Narratives, (Master) Frames, and Ideology', *Media, War & Conflict* 15(4): 427–49.

80. Freedman, *The Transformation in Strategic Affairs*.

81. Ibid., 2.

82. See Ignazi et al., *Italian Military Operations Abroad*, I; Coticchia, *La guerra che non c'era*; Catanzaro and Coticchia, *Al di là dell'Arcobaleno*.

83. Catanzaro and Coticchia, 'The Fog of Words, 17.

84. Biehl, Giegerich and Jonas, *Strategic Cultures in Europe*.

85. See, for example, P. D. Feaver (2011), 'The Right to be Right: Civil–Military Relations and the Iraq Surge Decision', *International Security* 35(4): 87–125; K. M. Zisk (1993), *Engaging the Enemy: Organization Theory and Soviet Military Innovation, 1955–1991*. Princeton, NJ: Princeton University Press; on non-Western cases, see also E. E. Laksmana (2017), 'Threats and Civil–Military Relations: Explaining Singapore's "Trickle Down" Military Innovation', *Defence & Security Analysis* 33(4): 347–65. A review of most studies is in Grissom, 'The Future of Military Innovation Studies'; Griffin, 'Military Innovation Studies', 196–224.

86. T. Dyson (2008), 'Convergence and Divergence in Post-Cold War British, French and German Military Reforms: Between International Structure and Executive Autonomy', *Security Studies* 17(4): 725–74.

87. D. P. Auerswald and S. M. Saideman (2014), *NATO in Afghanistan: Fighting Together, Fighting Alone*. Princeton, NJ: Princeton University Press.

88. From a neoclassical realist perspective, see, for example, Dyson, 'Managing Convergence', 244: 'low "executive autonomy" deriving from a set of restrictive domestic material power relations has slowed Germany's convergence with the dictates of international structure'. See also T. Dyson (2010), *Neoclassical Realism and Defence Reform in Post-Cold War Europe*. Basingstoke: Palgrave.

89. Kaarbo, 'Foreign Policy Analysis Perspective on the Domestic Politics Turn in IR Theory'.

90. M. W. Doyle (1986), 'Liberalism and World Politics', *American Political Science Review* 80(4): 1151–69.

91. For a recent review, see Mello and Peters, 'Parliaments in Security Policy', 3–18.

92. H. Born and H. Hänggi (2005), *The Use of Force under International Auspices*. Geneva: DCAF Policy Paper.

93. F. Coticchia and F. N. Moro (2020), 'Peaceful Legislatures? Parliaments and Military Interventions after the Cold War: Insights from Germany and Italy', *International Relations* 34(4): 482–503.

94. W. Wagner (2018), 'Is There a Parliamentary Peace? Parliamentary Veto Power and Military Interventions from Kosovo to Daesh', *British Journal of Politics and International Relations* 20(1): 121–34.

95. Kümmel and Leonhard, 'Casualties and Civil–Military Relations', 513–35.

96. B. C. Rathbun (2004), *Partisan Interventions: European Party Politics and Peace Enforcement in the Balkans*. Ithaca, NY: Cornell University Press; P. A. Mello (2014), *Democratic Participation in Armed Conflict*. Houndmills: Palgrave, 182. On coalition politics and the role of junior parties, see J. Kaarbo and R. K. Beasley (2008). 'Taking It to the Extreme: The Effect of Coalition Cabinets on Foreign Policy', *Foreign Policy Analysis* 4(1): 67–81; F. Coticchia and J. Davidson (2018), 'The Limits of Radical Parties in Coalition Foreign Policy', *Foreign Policy Analysis* 14(2): 149–68. For a recent review, see S. Oktay (2022), *Governing Abroad: Coalition Politics and Foreign Policy in Europe*. Ann Arbor: Michigan University Press.

97. For a recent review, see T. Raunio and W. Wagner (2020), 'The Party Politics of Foreign and Security Policy', *Foreign Policy Analysis* 16(4): 515–31.

98. See G. Palmer, T. London and P. Regan (2004), 'What's Stopping You? The Sources of Political Constraints on International Conflict Behaviour in Parliamentary

Democracies', *International Interactions* 30(1): 1–24. For a different view, see W. Wagner, A. Herranz-Surrallés, J. Kaarbo and F. Ostermann (2017). The Party Politics of Legislative–Executive Relations in Security and Defence Policy', *West European Politics* 40(1): 20–40.

99. See Rathbun, *Partisan Interventions;* T. Haesebrouck and P. A. Mello (2020), 'Patterns of Political Ideology and Security Policy', *Foreign Policy Analysis* 16(4): 565–86. A growing body of research has focused also on populist parties and foreign policy. See J. A. Verbeek and A. Zaslove (2015), 'The Impact of Populist Radical Right Parties on Foreign Policy: The Northern League as a Junior Coalition Partner in the Berlusconi Governments', *European Political Science Review* 7(4): 525–46; S. Destradi and J. Plagemann (2019), 'Populism and International Relations: (Un)predictability, Personalisation, and the Reinforcement of Existing Trends in World Politics', *Review of International Studies* 45(5): 711–30; F. Coticchia and V. Vignoli (2020). 'Populist Parties and Foreign Policy: The Case of Italy's Five Star Movement', *British Journal of Politics and International Relations* 22(3): 523–41.

100. For recent reviews, see F. Coticchia and V. Vignoli (2020), 'Italian Political Parties and Military Operations: An Empirical Analysis on Voting Patterns', *Government and Opposition* 55(3): 456–73; Hofmann, 'Beyond Culture and Power', 51–71; V. Vignoli (2022), *Conflitti consensuali: I partiti italiani e gli interventi militari.* Bologna: Il Mulino.

101. Hofmann, 'Beyond Culture and Power', 55.

102. Here the argument becomes a specification of the civil–military relations' 'model' described above. See, for example, D. D. Avant (1994), *Political Institutions and Military Change: Lessons from Peripheral Wars.* Ithaca, NY: Cornell University Press; F. Coticchia and F. N. Moro (2020), 'Aspiring and Reluctant Middle Powers?', in G. Giacomello and B. Verbeek (eds), *Middle Powers in Asia and Europe in the 21st Century.* Lanham, MD: Lexington Books, 57–76.

103. Coticchia and Moro, 'Peaceful Legislatures?'

104. Empirical analysis on Germany and Italy shows how different types of parliamentary involvement led in different cases to the restriction of freedom of action for executives. Ibid.

105. S. Schwenke (2020), 'Changing Civil–Military Relations in Japan: 2009–2012', *Australian Journal of International Affairs* 74(6): 704–20.

106. The Japanese Diet employed a 'positive list approach' that includes the need to formally approve not only deployments but also military agreements and decision on procurement.

107. T. Hikotani (2018), 'The Japanese Diet and Defence Policy-making', *International Affairs* 94(4): 791–814.

108. The Japanese Diet established a Standing Committee on Security only in 1991.

109. A. Catalinac (2016), *Electoral Reform and National Security in Japan: From Pork to Foreign Policy.* Cambridge: Cambridge University Press.

110. For a general treatment of interservice rivalry, see S. P. Huntington (1961), 'Interservice Competition and the Political Roles of the Armed Services', *American Political Science Review* 55(1): 40–52.

111. On how interservice rivalry can promote innovation, see H. M. Sapolsky (1971), *The Polaris System Development.* Cambridge, MA: Harvard University Press; M. H. Armacost (1969), *The Politics of Weapons Innovation: The Thor–Jupiter Controversy.* New York: Columbia University Press.

112. On the effect of interservice rivalry on the conduct of military operations, see, for example, I. Horwood (2010), *Interservice Rivalry and Airpower in the Vietnam War.* Fort Leavenworth, KS: Combat Studies Institute, US Army Command and General Staff College; A. J. Cumming (2010), *The Battle for Britain: Interservice Rivalry between the Royal Air Force and Royal Navy; 1909–40.* Annapolis, MD: Naval Institute Press, 2015.

113. Catignani, 'Getting COIN'.
114. W. Murray (1999), 'Does Military Culture Matter?' *Orbis* 43(1): 27. See also J. L. Soeters, D. J. Winslow and A. Weibull (2006), 'Military Culture', in G. Caforio (ed.), *Handbook of the Sociology of the Military*. Boston, MA: Springer, 237–54.
115. See, for example, Murray, 'Does Military Culture Matter?'
116. J. Snyder (1984), 'Civil–Military Relations and the Cult of the Offensive, 1914 and 1984', *International Security* 9(1): 108–46.
117. See, for example, W. Murray (1998), 'Armoured Warfare: The British, French and German Experiences', in W. R. Murray and A. R. Millett (eds), *Military Innovation in the Interwar Period*. Cambridge: Cambridge University Press, 6–49.
118. A. Long (2016), *The Soul of Armies: Counterinsurgency Doctrine and Military Culture in the US and UK*. Ithaca, NY: Cornell University Press.
119. Ruffa, 'Military Cultures in Peace and Stability Operations'.
120. D. Adamsky (2010), *The Culture of Military Innovation: The Impact of Cultural Factors on the Revolution in Military Affairs in Russia, the US and Israel*. Stanford, CA: Stanford University Press.
121. T. Dyson (2019), 'The Military as a Learning Organisation: Establishing the Fundamentals of Best-Practice in Lessons-Learned', *Defence Studies* 19(2): 107–29.
122. R. T. Foley, S. Griffin and H. McCartney (2011). '"Transformation in Contact": Learning the Lessons of Modern War', *International Affairs* 87(2): 253–70.
123. Coticchia and Moro, 'Learning from Others?' 696–718.
124. Grissom, 'The Future of Military Innovation Studies'; Catignani, 'Getting COIN'.
125. Coticchia and Moro, 'Learning from Others?'
126. We thank an anonymous reviewer for the suggestion on this point.
127. S. P. Rosen (1994), *Winning the Next War: Innovation and the Modern Military*. Ithaca, NY: Cornell University Press.
128. Rosen, *Winning the Next War*, 19–22.
129. For a review, see Grissom, 'The Future of Military Innovation Studies'.
130. Historical institutionalism is 'historical because it recognises that political development must be understood as a process that unfolds over time. It is institutionalism because it stresses that many of the contemporary implications of these temporary processes are embedded in institutions, whether these be formal rules or policy structures.' P. Pierson (1996), 'The Path to European Integration: A Historical Institutionalist Analysis', *Comparative Political Studies* 29(2): 126.
131. Pierson, *Politics in Time*.
132. J. Mahoney (2000), 'Path Dependence in Historical Sociology', *Theory and Society* 29(4): 507–48.
133. A. L. Stinchcombe (1987), *Constructing Social Theories*. Chicago, IL: University of Chicago Press; Mahoney, 'Path Dependence in Historical Sociology'.
134. D. C. North (1993), 'Toward a Theory of Institutional Change', *Political Economy: Institutions, Competition, and Representation* 31(4): 61–9.
135. W. B. Arthur (1989), 'Competing Technologies, Increasing Returns, and Lock-in by Historical Events', *Economic Journal* 99(394): 116–31.
136. S. E. Page (2006), 'Path Dependence', *Quarterly Journal of Political Science* 1(1): 87–115.
137. W. B. Arthur (1994), *Increasing Returns and Path Dependence in the Economy*. Ann Arbor: University of Michigan Press.
138. K. Thelen (2004). *How Institutions Evolve: The Political Economy of Skills in Germany, Britain, the United States, and Japan*. New York: Cambridge University Press.
139. G. Capoccia and R. D. Kelemen (2007), 'The Study of Critical Junctures: Theory, Narrative and Counterfactuals in Historical Institutionalism', *World Politics* 59(3): 341–69.

140. G. Capoccia (2016), 'Critical Junctures', in O. Fioretos, T. G. Falleti and A. Sheingate (eds), *The Oxford Handbook of Historical Institutionalism*. Oxford: Oxford University Press, 89–106.

141. H. D. Soifer (2012), 'The Causal Logic of Critical Junctures', *Comparative Political Studies* 45(12): 1572–97, 1574.

142. Slater and Simmons define these factors as the 'critical antecedent'; see D. Slater and E. Simmons (2010), 'Informative Regress: Critical Antecedents in Comparative Politics', *Comparative Political Studies* 43(7): 886–917. For a comprehensive analysis, see Soifer, 'The Causal Logic of Critical Junctures'.

143. This is true even for foreign policy. A recent, and rare, exception is Schieder, 'New Institutionalism and Foreign Policy'.

144. P. Pierson (2000), 'Increasing Returns, Path Dependence, and the Study of Politics', *American Political Science Review* 94(2): 251–67.

145. This type of reasoning is consistent with Betts' analysis of the problems in the very definition of what strategy is; R. K. Betts (2000), 'Is Strategy an Illusion?' *International Security* 25(2): 5–50.

146. See, for example, the invaluable *Oxford Handbook of Historical Institutionalism*, where defence policy is barely mentioned. O. Fioretos, T. G. Falleti and A. Sheingate (eds) (2016), *The Oxford Handbook of Historical Institutionalism*. Oxford: Oxford University Press. On foreign policy and historical institutionalism, see again Schieder, 'New Institutionalism and Foreign Policy'.

147. Schieder, 'New Institutionalism and Foreign Policy', 133.

148. Pierson, *Politics in Time*.

149. The literature widely emphasises how major events can create critical junctures.

150. Pierson, 'Not Just What, but *When*', 75.

151. According to Sydow et al., this potentially results 'in an organisational lock-in, understood as a corridor of limited scope of action that is strategically inefficient'. J. Sydow, G. Schreyogg and J. Koch (2009), 'Organisational Path Dependence: Opening the Black Box', *Academy of Management Review* 34(4): 696.

152. Hyde and Saunders, 'Recapturing Regime Type in International Relations', 371.

153. Ibid.

154. See, among others: M. Zürn (2014), 'The Politicization of World Politics and its Effects: Eight Propositions', *European Political Science Review* 6(1): 47–71; T. Raunio and W. Wagner (2017), 'Towards Parliamentarisation of Foreign and Security Policy?' *West European Politics* 40(1): 1–19.

155. R. Balfour et al. (2016), 'Europe's Troublemakers: The Populist Challenge to Foreign Policy', European Policy Center, Brussels, 19.

Chapter 4

Germany: To Crisis Management and Back

4.1 Force transformation in the 1990s

4.1.1 From non-intervention to limited commitment: German deployments and doctrine in the 1990s

With the end of the bipolar era and of 'existential threats to the territorial integrity of Germany',[1] several scholars and pundits expected a return to normalcy in international affairs leading to the remilitarisation of Berlin. Other observers were more sceptical, looking at long-term effects of the strategic culture, standards and institutions developed in the previous decades.[2] We show here how the trajectory of the 'still reluctant'[3] German post-Cold War defence policy illustrates elements of path dependence.[4] The *sequence of changes* that took place in the defence policy of the Berlin Republic can be understood only by examining the effects of the (self-reinforcing) decisions adopted at the beginning of the post-bipolar era. In fact, the role of legacies (see Chapter 2) and the unexploited 'window of opportunity' represented by Desert Storm strongly affected the specific path followed by German defence in the 1990s.[5] Subsequent incremental changes were made following the Constitutional Court ruling that formally allowed out-of-area operations and paved the way for German missions in the Balkans, which in turn began to bring about changes. In the first phase, domestic constraints (anti-militarism culture, institutional and political factors that limited the executive's autonomy, and shortfalls in terms of resources and capabilities) prevailed over the international pressures and occasions for more military activism. In 1994, the Defence White Paper posited that national territorial and alliance defence remained the core tasks of the Bundeswehr, with crisis management having a subsidiary role.[6]

The decisions adopted during the first years of the post-Cold War era, from Desert Storm to the military intervention in Kosovo, are thus essential to understanding the trajectory of the German military transformation. The Gulf War represented a crucial moment. In November 1989, the Berlin Wall collapsed, furthering the future re-unification of Germany, which occurred in October 1990. A couple of months earlier, the international arena was shaken by the Iraqi invasion of Kuwait. After UNSC resolutions, the United States led a large multinational operation against the Saddam Hussein regime. When the military intervention began at the beginning of 1991, Germany, unlike the other allies, did not take part in the operation.

When the crisis in the Middle East erupted, Germany (which during this phase was mainly focused on the complex goal of integrating the East German National People's Army, NVA)[7] was faced with a difficult decision: to risk either demonstrating a 'lack of solidarity' (during the complex process of German reunification) or abandoning the domestic *Kultur der Zurückhaltung* (culture of restraint)[8] by taking part in a military intervention that the majority of public opinion also opposed.[9] In 1991 (as would later be seen again in the future, such as in Libya in 2011), domestic concerns were clearly prioritised, despite pressure from the Allies, especially Washington.[10] The decision was linked to legacies, namely, institutional and cultural constraints and organisational aspects of the Bundeswehr, which was instrumental in affecting the abovementioned 'domestic–international balance', favouring a prudent approach. On the whole, despite the imminent end of the Cold War, Germany was not free to develop a distinctly different defence policy.[11] In particular, at the onset of the Gulf War, some members of the government (including the ministers of Foreign Affairs and Defence) opened up to the possibility of answering the US call for support.[12] However, Chancellor Helmut Kohl stressed the need for a constitutional change in order to be militarily involved in Desert Storm. In this context, the German cabinet did not see any possibility of 'negotiating' with its domestic constituency[13] and decided to cover part of the cost of the war, providing financial support to Desert Storm and humanitarian and mine-clearing activities in the region, as well as allowing the use of military bases on its territory for the operations.[14]

In short, during the Iraqi crisis German defence remained anchored to *Friedenspolitik* ('peace policy'). Then, German defence policy began to gradually change, facing a wholly new environment. A shift occurred after the Iraq War also in terms of German military presence abroad, with the Bundeswehr involved in out-of-area crisis management missions in the 1990s. For example, Berlin sent ships and planes (AWACS) to the Adriatic Sea in 1992 to implement the arms embargo in Yugoslavia, medical units were deployed within the UN mission in Cambodia, and hundreds of German soldiers participated (with 'logistical tasks') in the UN mission in Somalia in 1993.[15] Thus, German security policy 'began to acquire a more "normal" quality, as out-of-area missions became acceptable right across the political spectrum'.[16]

This process occurred at a time of profound transformation for the Bundeswehr, which was 'adjusting' to a major downsizing (see below)[17] that involved considerable changes in doctrine. The first evolution in terms of strategic reflection came about with the 'Stoltenberg Paper' (1992), drafted by the then Minister of Defence, who called for the Bundeswehr to adopt a more proactive role.[18] Thus, timing appears crucial due to the role played by legacies in the domestic context. After this, German doctrine progressed with the *Verteidigungspolitische Richtlinien* (Defence Policy Guidelines, VPR) at the end of 1992. VPR illustrated how Germany 'was encircled by friends . . . no longer exposed to a direct military threat involving an offensive war in Europe'.[19] The vital security interests identified in the document included the prevention and resolution of low-intensity conflicts, along with the development of the crucial relationship with NATO and the EU. The VPR seemed to reveal that the 'intensive war in Europe was gone after the end of the Cold War'.[20]

Change was gradual, 'a muddling through with a direction, with an aim to increase the role in international security'.[21] Again, legacies help to shed light on this slow and 'incremental' process: the Cold War structure of the Bundeswehr had to be adapted significantly in order to protect the abovementioned 'new security interests' (prevention, containment and resolution of crises and low-intensity conflicts) while, after the collapse of the Berlin Wall and the reunification process, the 'money was pulled out from the military', shutting down units.[22] At the same time, cultural and institutional constraints influenced the pace of evolution towards a German military dynamic role; as one German general emphasised, political leaders were reluctant to start deploying troops abroad 'because of the public opinion, due to historical burdens'.[23] The '*out-of-area-Debate*' of the 1990s confirms the relevance of domestic constraints.

Indeed, the new timid steps undertaken sparked harsh opposition in parliament, prompting cabinets to continue to stress the humanitarian dimension of the interventions, as in the case of the national contribution in Somalia. However, because of their political opposition to German military out-of-area operations, the Liberals (FDP) called on the Federal Constitutional Court to address the issue. By providing non-combat personnel for UN peacekeeping missions, such as in Somalia in 1993, it gradually pushed the limits of the Bonn Republic and provoked a domestic constitutional debate which eventually led to the removal of 'the legal obstacles for "out-of-area" engagement'.[24]

In fact, on 12 July 1994, the Federal Constitutional Court clearly stated that the missions respected the *Grundgesetz*.[25] The Court also set the conditions for the Bundeswehr's future participation in military interventions abroad, and included multilateralism, Bundestag approval, acting with the objective of promoting international peace and stability.[26] The judges in Karlsruhe affirmed that military deployment abroad required the vote of the Bundestag, which had the right of prior approval. The decision of the Court re-affirmed the 'legacy of parliamentary control of the military'.[27] Thus, the Bundeswehr became a parliamentary army: the court determined that 'there is no executive authority if this has not been previously constituted through an act of parliament'.[28]

Afterwards, the government's deployment policy was 'domesticated by the Bundestag' through extensive 'national caveats' on almost all deployments.[29] Remarkably, although institutional constraints deriving from post-Second World War legacies were revised, they clearly did not disappear, but rather paved the way for self-reinforcing feedback dynamics in the following years. Following the Court decision, in fact, German troops were deployed in a variety of multinational military operations throughout the 1990s.

Thus, the path of post-Cold War German defence policy was established, while self-reinforcing feedbacks allowed it to be consolidated in the 1990s, once a balance had been achieved between the Allies' requests, changing threats, an increasing awareness by parts of the German elite that a different role would have to be played in international security, and the domestic constraints that were deeply rooted in German history.[30] This new trajectory was characterised by German participation in the missions in the Balkans, deploying 4,000 soldiers in the peacekeeping mission and supporting aircraft in the NATO attacks against Bosnian Serbs in 1995.[31] Germany was also active in the diplomatic arena during the crisis in Bosnia and took part in NATO operations after the civil war.[32]

There was not an 'automatic reaction' towards operations abroad after the 1994 court ruling. Despite the intervention of the Federal Court, the government took a prudent attitude towards military involvement in the Balkans.[33] Indeed, Kohl, who was 'eager to keep the decision away from the general German elections in October 1994', stated that 'Germany's adjustment to new international responsibilities would not mean militarisation'.[34] In other words, the beginning of military operations was 'timid and cautious'.[35]

Moreover, despite the favourable new legal environment regarding German participation in operations in the Balkans, dozens of pacifist MPs opposed the deployment of the Bundeswehr, and the Greens and SPD were internally divided on the issues.[36] A *Denkverbot* ('ban on thinking' with regard to warfare) remained solid, effectively contrasting a more active military involvement abroad.[37] A 'humanitarian' narrative was crafted to support the development of a new, more dynamic defence policy regarding military involvement abroad. After Srebrenica, a debate emerged on the need to prevent massacres with the use of armed force. This was a turning point, arguably stronger than the pressure from the Allies. A different narrative that was consistent with German legacies shaped the public debate: 'noting signs of genocide in Bosnia, opposition to a mission averting the atrocities would betray Germany's historical responsibility of preventing another Auschwitz'.[38]

Doctrinal change was neither speedy nor straightforward. The Defence White Paper published in 1994, and other key documents throughout the decade, maintained territorial defence as the core of the Bundeswehr's missions, while mentioning contribution to NATO and European 'crisis management activities'.[39] No general doctrinal change, however, was in place, with most of the transformations taking place as the Bundeswehr was 'learning by doing'. German military doctrine 'remained mainly focused on conventional warfare'.[40] In other words, in the aftermath of the Cold War, Germany's military doctrine was mainly anchored to self-defence, largely avoiding the development of capabilities for power projection. The *Konzeptionelle Leitlinien zur Weiterentwicklung der Bundeswehr 1994* (Conceptual Guidelines for the Further Development of the Bundeswehr) and the *Bundeswehrplan 1997* continued to focus on crisis management abroad but as a lateral activity among German forces' tasks, while fundamental decisions on procurement were delayed. In conclusion, the German defence policy in the 1990s, as well as its doctrine, were characterised by 'change without disruption', by a 'gradualist approach' that addressed the pressure from abroad.[41]

In short, despite the significant changes in terms of military posture, several crucial aspects of the Bonn Republic still affected Berlin's defence policy and its doctrine. Legacies played a role in giving political leaders room to manoeuvre, beginning with the decision to (not) be involved in Desert Storm. First, 'scepticism' regarding the use of military force persisted. 'Germany's increasing participation in multilateral military missions has caused Germany to undertake a partial shift in its foreign policy, but it still holds on to the main principles, promoting an aversion to involvement in war-fighting.'[42] Humanitarian concerns increased in the German public due to tragic episodes of violence occurring from Africa to the Balkans. Overall, the German public continued to prefer humanitarian or peace-keeping operations 'rather than peace enforcement or combat mission'.[43] Secondly, Germany was hampered by scarce executive autonomy in the field of defence. In other words, 'low "executive autonomy" deriving from a set of restrictive domestic material power relations has slowed Germany's convergence with the dictates of international structure'.[44] The development of the stabilisation doctrine proceeded at a slower pace than in other European countries which, as of the early to mid-1990s, abandoned territorial defence in favour of crisis management.

In short, the legacy of the past determined the balance between the external requests and incentives for a new German military international role and the persisting domestic constraints. Despite the changes that were taking place and the new military operations that were conducted after the Constitutional Court's landmark decision, territorial defence remained the key reference of German doctrine.

4.1.2 Force structure and organisational change in the 1990s

The end of the bipolar confrontation, German re-unification and the first missions undertaken in the 1990s after the decision by the Karlsruhe Court, 'demanded' the transformation of the German military organisation. Balancing international pressures and domestic constraints, the Bundeswehr (which was still 'a tank-based force, tailored for confrontation with Soviet forces'[45]) required the 'most radical reform in Europe'.[46] For decades the German armed forces had been preparing to confront a Soviet attack, and were therefore not ready to quickly adapt to new tasks and structures for deployment abroad.[47] Moreover, the re-organisation of forces was heavily impacted by the pressing needs of reunification and the creation of the new armed forces for Germany, since almost half a million of soldiers were absorbed from the NVA.[48] Thus, while the regional and international post-Cold War environment appeared more favourable to German security, the expected changes were challenging and complex. Nevertheless, in the 1990s German decision-makers adopted manifold reforms (or, at least, planned reforms), geared to downsizing personnel and restructuring the armed forces.[49]

As illustrated in Graphs 4.1 and 4.2, the reduction in forces and decrease in military spending were significant. From the mid-1980s to the end of the 1990s, the German budget (out of GDP) halved.[50] Significant cuts were implemented especially with regard to military R&D and procurement, with several programmes shut down.[51] In the course of the 1990s, the number of active-duty personnel dropped, and by the end of the decade the Bundeswehr had a strength of less than 340,000.

Aside from the post-1989 peace dividend, however, if we are to clearly understand this decline we must not underestimate the legacy of the

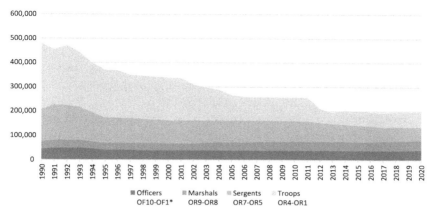

Graph 4.1 Personnel in the Bundeswehr by role, 1990–2020
Source: Authors' elaboration based on Bundesrat Reports.[52]

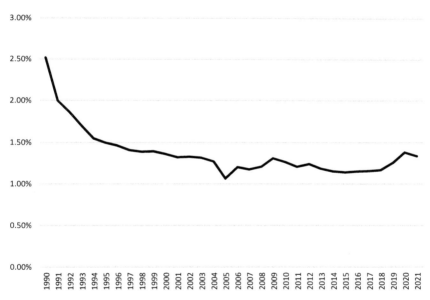

Graph 4.2 Germany's military expenditure as percentage of GDP
Source: Authors' elaboration based on SIPRI annual reports.

bipolar structure, along with bureaucratic politics (that is, the internal resistance to those reductions). First, personnel costs as a percentage of the budget rose sharply from 48.9 per cent in 1985–1989 to 61.5 per cent in 1995–1999).[53] Oddly enough, while troop numbers were cut,[54] the number of high-ranking generals remained the same.[55] It is worth noting that the disproportion of costs applied also to defence infrastructure. Secondly, 'Cold War procurement programmes' deeply affected the defence budget, limiting Berlin's room for manoeuvre. In other words, 'the pattern of resources' prevented the Bundeswehr from fully meeting the demands of the contemporary security environment.[56] Lastly, and similar to the case of Italy, Germany gradually developed two armies, 'comprising the larger and less well-equipped main defence forces with a substantial conscript element geared for territorial defence and the smaller, all-professional crisis reaction component, better equipped and prepared for out-of-area missions'.[57] Thus, the Bundeswehr became 'a two-class organisation',[58] with its bulk assigned to territorial defence.

Nevertheless, alongside the difficult evolution from a national defence force to an expeditionary army, some important new elements were introduced. In 1994, for example, the new German Army Operational Command was created, with the goal of unifying the command structure for all the services and sustaining operational capability also for operations outside NATO (such as UN missions). Likewise, the role of the chief of staff (*Generalinspekteur*) was reinforced, and in the same period the *Krisenreaktionskräfte* (Crisis Reaction Forces, KRK) was created, again with all the services, with the aim of promoting the capability of projecting force abroad with professional soldiers.

On the whole, if we examine the reforms of the Bundeswehr during the 1990s we can see that the process of adaptation of the forces was determined by four main issues: conscription, base closures, technological development and, as in the case of doctrine, the persistence of territorial defence. In all these aspects, legacy and self-reinforcing dynamics remained of key importance.

First, the draft was not abolished or suspended, despite pressures to adapt the organisation of the forces and reduce a clearly excessive conscription. There were growing doubts regarding the financial sustainability of conscription, which still caused a large part of the defence budget to be spent on manpower, thus reducing resources for new equipment and for R&D. Experts agreed that 'the maintenance of conscription threatens to jeopardise Germany's ability to effectively reform its armed forces for new tasks'.[59] In the 1990s, however, the majority of Germans were in favour of maintaining conscription.[60] The SPD and CDU/CSU pro-conscription consensus did not disappear with the end of the Bonn Republic.[61] The links between financial and social policy (which derives from the number of objectors providing cheap labour for the social system) 'created a powerful material constraint on the core executive's ability to create a fully professional armed force'.[62]

Secondly, and in relation to what has been said above, radical reforms in military base closures were avoided. While public opinion's general interest in military reforms (as opposed to the mobilisation for missions abroad) remained low, 'issues linked to daily life', such as the supposed closing down of bases, attracted attention and concern.[63] Local interests – especially in a federal state – were taken into consideration by the government. Moreover, with regard also to the defence policy reforms the Bundestag played a significant role. Indeed, German MPs were heavily focused on the needs of their constituency (such as preserving military bases and maintaining local military industries), thus hindering drastic reforms for electoral reasons.[64]

Thirdly, Germany did not embrace the post-Desert Storm military technological innovation, and the Revolution in Military Affairs (RMA)[65] debate did not affect Germany's defence industrial strategy after the end of the Cold War. Apart from a crucial limiting of defence funding,[66] the German establishment perceived the RMA almost as a 'myth', while German defence companies focused mainly on adapting their activity to the restructuring of the national procurement budget.[67] German defence ministers in the 1990s were not promoters 'of a Bundeswehr transformation process in the style of the American transformation'.[68] The lack of military involvement in the Iraqi War also limited the expansion of the debate on the RMA in the new Berlin Republic.

Lastly, and most importantly, territorial defence (as the doctrine observed) still profoundly influenced the organisation of the forces. Again, the Cold War legacies were instrumental in affecting the balance between domestic constraints and international pressures to force transformation. As we have seen, the evolution came about thanks to several reforms adopted to improve the possible deployability of the Bundeswehr. However, the changes were not 'structural'[69] and the reforms adopted in the 1990s 'did the minimum to respond to the new security environment'.[70] German domestic constraints still opposed pressures for adapting the armed forces, framing 'the realm of possibility'.[71] The Kultur der Zurückhaltung (culture of restraint) in foreign and security policy and conservative political leadership, along with financial limitations and bureaucratic opposition to jointness and to the restructuring of the budget for reducing infrastructure and personnel costs, were all constraints that hindered force transformation. By the end of the decade the Bundeswehr was 'oversized, ill-structured and ill-equipped'.[72] The absence of an imminent threat to security also affected the perceived sense of 'urgency' for reforming the armed forces. Path dependent mechanisms continued to influence the intensity of the shift, partly due to the very limited German military involvement in operations abroad. Thus, positive feedback on the adoption of a new path were scarce or totally lacking, while 'military leaders have had few opportunities to learn from crises and to adjust their routines and procedures'.[73] For example, the fact that the

Bundeswehr was not involved in Desert Storm limited German interest in the RMA.

At the same time, although the convergence between territorial defence and the NATO framework was still high after the end of the Cold War, top-down pressures regarding the adaptation of forces to crisis management were growing.[74] Moreover, German public opinion agreed on a more active role of the Bundeswehr, but within the UN framework and for non-combat interventions such as monitoring cease-fire agreements and assisting police forces.[75] These were the first steps along the path towards the 'normalisation' of German security policy.[76]

In conclusion, German defence was adapted in the post-bipolar era, 'both in terms of the reform of the Bundeswehr and in security policy thinking'.[77] However, despite gradual reforms and transformation, the post-Cold War window of opportunity to make further changes was not exploited.[78] Indeed, 'hamstrung by low executive autonomy', Germany's political elite lacks the will and ability' to overcome domestic cultural, bureaucratic and financial constraints.[79] Hence, the development of the process towards 'crisis management' in the 1990s was hindered.[80] In sum, the Cold War legacies were of value to armed forces that were 'organised, structured and equipped for one purpose: territorial defence'.[81]

4.2 The Bundeswehr in the new century

4.2.1 German doctrinal change across the new century, 1999–2003: the Kosovo watershed

Kosovo represented 'a critical juncture in the post-Cold War adaptation of German security policy',[82] and Bundeswehr participation in combat operations 'amounted to crossing the Rubicon'.[83] Did German defence policy deviate from its trajectory after Kosovo and Afghanistan, in the post 11/9 scenario? Did the military intervention in Kosovo, and later in Afghanistan profoundly alter German doctrine? To answer these questions we focus on the observable manifestations of defence transformation that took place in Germany at the beginning of the new century, emphasising the constant relevance of legacies 'in action', with reproduction mechanisms underpinning the path established at the beginning of the 1990s.

External events and pressure from allies still played a role. Indeed, the crises in the Balkans and NATO involvement in the operation against Serbia demanded actual military participation of Germany in a combat operation. This time, Germany played a direct role in contributing to regional stability.[84] The intervention in Kosovo illustrated how 'external pressures and the growing expectations from its allies' caused a moving away from the old 'cheque-book diplomacy' adopted, for example, in 1991.[85] New 'security threats', namely, the fear of massive flows of refugees from the region, had a role in the German decision.[86] To be fair, despite the importance of national involvement in combat operations, Germany played a mainly 'support role' in Kosovo,[87] providing fourteen Tornado planes, mainly for electronic reconnaissance and countermeasures against Serbian air defences.[88] Along with combat activities, the Bundeswehr was involved in providing humanitarian support to Albanian refugees. After the air strikes ('Operation Allied Force'), the UN authorised the (NATO-led) 'Kosovo Force' (KFOR).

The Kosovo intervention nevertheless represented a relevant change in German defence policy. The 1999 campaign demonstrated that public opinion was willing to support the use of military power, even without a UN resolution – something that would have been 'impossible' nine years earlier.[89] In addition, over 60 per cent of German public opinion was in favour of intervention (with support declining after air strikes).[90] On the other hand, the 'culture of restraint' did not disappear and the narrative of 'civilian power' persisted. Yet, despite an increasingly favourable public opinion towards Bundeswehr participation in peacekeeping and peace enforcement, the general opposition to 'real war-fighting involving ground troops remained firmly entrenched'.[91] The centre-left executive focused on the frame of humanitarian intervention to convince the 'pacifist strands' of the Greens and Social Democrats.[92] Chancellor Gerhard Schröder (SPD) saw a 'moral obligation' for Germany to stop the slaughter in Kosovo, and Minister of Foreign Affairs Joschka Fischer (Green Party) emotionally evoked the German past ('never again Auschwitz and ethnic cleansing').[93] The military operation was described as a tool to protect civilian populations and to avoid 'a second Srebrenica'.[94] Thus, the feedback on the humanitarian action developed in Bosnia in the 1990s after Srebrenica reinforced the narrative that allowed the German government to overcome domestic opposition to a more active military role, while still assuming the image of 'civilian power'.[95] The executive carefully avoided military terms relating to war, preferring expressions like 'robust deployment'.[96] Humanitarian reasons (such as 'protecting people on the ground'), as well as the 'never more Auschwitz' narrative, played a vital role.[97] For example, Fischer stressed 'the moral and political responsibility for Germany to safeguard peace in the world', aiming to overcome the 'Greens' pacifist position'.[98]

Observers are divided over the degree of change that occurred with the German intervention in Kosovo, with some arguing that Kosovo marked

a break with the tradition of military reticence[99] and others considering the shift that took place in Kosovo as more symbolic than real.[100]
Undoubtedly, Germany's new, increased disposition to consider using
the armed forces abroad was still ruled by criteria such as the multilateral framework.[101] In short, the main elements of German strategic culture were 'reinterpreted and reapplied'[102] through adjustments, while an
overall 'reticence' continued to govern German participation in military
operations.[103]

Institutional factors also played a role in this phase. The legacy of the
decision adopted by the Constitutional Court was more to do with 'how'
interventions should be carried out than 'whether' they should occur at
all. The 'constitutionally enshrined role of the Bundestag to decide on
military operations . . . complicates Germany's ability to plan and coordi-
nate with allies' the undertaking of missions if at any time the Bundestag
can oppose Bundeswehr actions.[104] Moreover, the role of parliament was
reinforced, with the executive being 'forced' to openly discuss the details
of the missions before a 'pacifist opposition'.[105] A multilateral framework
was still perceived as a necessity for the approval of the Bundestag.[106]
Moreover, parliament constantly monitored the deployment of troops
and their activities, severely limiting their flexibility and margin of
manoeuvre.

Albeit limited for the above reasons, after 1999 German doctrine did
undergo change. The 'Weiszäcker Commission' (2000), led by a former
Federal president, emphasised the need for the German armed forces
to distinguish between 'Main Defence Forces' and 'Crisis Reaction
Forces', reducing the total number of troops. In addition, in his review,
Generalinspekteur (Inspector General) Hans-Peter von Kirchbach
pointed out the current limitations of the Bundeswehr in effectively
implementing crisis reaction forces.[107] Lastly, several weeks later, SPD
Defence Minister Scharping delivered a paper with additional recommendations for the Bundeswehr, aiming to support the mobility of the
armed forces geared to addressing crises abroad, thereby contributing
effectively to EU and NATO efforts. Scharping concluded 'that the
Bundeswehr was still organised for Cold War scenarios', that 'it lacked
the necessary capabilities for crisis management tasks and that interoperability with Germany's allies was severely under threat'.[108] Despite
all these efforts to promote change, the core tenet continued to be
major emphasis upon territorial and collective defence.[109] In short, the
Bundeswehr 'has undergone a conservative adaptation' and its doctrine
was *not* substantially 'revised'.[110]

4.2.2 The new century: Afghanistan and beyond

The German military doctrine began to undergo more significant revision in the new century, when the new military commitment in Afghanistan accelerated the 'expeditionary' requirement for the armed forces, a trend that was also reflected in doctrines such as the Defence Policy Guidelines of 2003 and later the White Paper of 2006.[111] The intervention in Afghanistan was the most important and dramatic mission undertaken by the Bundeswehr since the end of the Cold War.[112] Although it was present with the allies in Afghanistan, Germany did not participate in the US-led military operation in Iraq. The US unilateral intervention in Iraq (2003), in fact, would have represented a major break with the German multilateral foreign policy tradition, which rejects preventive military interventions.

At the same time, Germany was intensely focused on developing the European Security and Defence Policy and EU crisis management capabilities, which were more in tune with the Berlin Republic and its civilian narrative than the NATO strategy of 1999.[113] For example, the Bundestag supported German involvement in the EU mission 'Artemis' in the Democratic Republic of Congo (DRC, June 2003).[114] The CSU–SPD 'Grand Coalition' led by Merkel, provided military support to the EUFOR mission in 2006 to assist the UN operation in the DRC during the general elections. While the Bundestag supported the mission with a large majority, a very restricted mandate was voted to minimise risks and the leadership of the operation was avoided.[115]

Thus, Germany provided its contribution to international security within multilateral frameworks, but the political context – where coalition parties are sensitive to the survival of the coalition in the face of a reluctant parliament and public opinion – posed severe constraints on the type of deployment.[116] In Lebanon also, after the war between Israel and Hezbollah (2006), Berlin participated in the UN mission but avoided sending in ground troops in a post-conflict scenario. The multilateral frameworks of the missions in DRC and Lebanon fitted well with the German 'civilian narrative', while for the unilateral US interventions the degree of consistency with such a scheme was minimal.[117]

The decision to intervene in Afghanistan was complex. Many observers argue that German involvement in Afghanistan was specifically focused on 'solidarity' (with the US fear of abandonment in the background).[118] Thanks to its participation in Afghanistan, Germany presented itself as an 'affordable ally'.[119] Schröder affirmed that the lack of intervention in Afghanistan would have resulted in a 'severe loss of credibility for Germany policy'[120] and that 'the period of "cheque-book diplomacy" and "secondary assistance" had "irrevocably passed"'.[121] The Social Democrats and the Greens, who supported Schröder's government, did not enthusiastically embrace the mission. A vote of confidence was needed to reinforce party discipline, guaranteeing parliamentary approval (336 to 326 votes in favour) for the operation. The centre-right, while supporting involvement in Afghanistan, aimed to obtain a clear framework and mandate (time-limited) for the mission.[122] The small part of the parliamentary majority on the mission, as well as divided public opinion on the intervention, well emphasises the persistent significant opposition towards military operations aboard.[123]

Germany took part both in Operation Enduring Freedom, aimed at defeating the Taliban and eradicating the presence of Al Qaeda in Afghanistan with a small contingent of Special Forces, and in the NATO-led ISAF mission. This was the first time since the Second World War that German forces were involved in combat operations on the ground. However, the general contribution was still limited in comparison with other allies and the main focus of Berlin was still on aid and diplomacy, hosting, for instance, the Bonn conference on the post-Taliban future of Afghanistan. Little by little, Germany began to take on greater responsibility on the ground, such as the ISAF command for the Kabul region, increasing the number of troops deployed (with up to 5,350 soldiers in 2010).[124]

The Afghanistan intervention combined traditional aspects with elements of change, for which the Kosovo mission had provided an important input. First, the narratives adopted by German leaders gradually changed over time, but the overall anti-militarist sentiments still dominated the debate. On the one hand, the German executives defined the mission in Afghanistan 'as one that resonated with Germany's Civilian Power narrative'.[125] Schröder emphasised, for example, that the Bundeswehr deployment was not a war of aggression but a way to bring peace to Afghanistan, within a broader political and humanitarian intervention.[126] On the other hand, the speech by the Federal Minister of Defence Struck on the defence of Germany 'at the Hindu Kush' was viewed as 'the end of the era of abstention', finally pushing Berlin to be a 'security provider'.[127] However, despite years of post-Cold War military involvement, anti-militarist attitudes did not evaporate. The speech by Defence Minister Struck, in fact, was strongly contested, while the non-military component of the operation (such as development aid, nation-building and so on) dominated public communication on the mission. The German anti-militarist culture 'had evolved but not disappeared'.[128] In fact, then President Horst Köhler, who affirmed that Germany had to consider the use of force also to protect its economic interests, was forced to resign.[129]

In 2003, Germany took command of ISAF Regional Command North. The German military leadership interpreted the ISAF mission as a reconstruction operation: according to a German general, the area of Kunduz was stable, 'without war'.[130] The German 'civilian narrative' faced considerable challenges when ISAF forces moved into southern Afghanistan, since this mission – which involved combat operations – did not fit within the schemas of 'aid and reconstruction'.

The Merkel government rejected the request by allies to be actively involved in combat operations on the ground, prompting criticism from Washington and London and demands for burden-sharing.[131] With the intensification of pressure from the allies to increase the German military commitment in line with NATO's growing need to effectively address the challenges posed by the Taliban, the Bundestag finally extended the mandate of the mission in Afghanistan in 2008 by a large majority (442 to 570). A turning point for German military involvement in Afghanistan was the air strike in Kunduz on fuel tankers that killed around a hundred Afghan civilians (4 September 2009), which led to the resignation of the then Minister of Defence Franz Josef Jung. German leadership recognised 'that the mission in Afghanistan could be termed a "warlike situation"'.[132] Thus, the 'civilian narrative' lacked coherence with the context on the ground, while Berlin aimed to addresses the shortfalls in military capabilities that emerged over the years, allowing the use of force beyond immediate self-defence.[133]

The deteriorating security situation in Afghanistan forced Berlin to adjust its narratives and approaches. Defence ministers zu Guttenberg and de Maiziere both introduced changes in communication.[134] However, the mission, and the Bundeswehr in general, were given little coverage by the German media, and over time German public opinion's support for the intervention also declined. Until 2009, German support for ISAF exceeded 50 per cent,[135] while in a 2010 poll 51 per cent of Germans disapproved of national involvement in the Afghan mission, and in 2014 60 per cent opposed the general deployment of armed forces abroad.[136]

Secondly, institutional constraints limited the actual military involvement of the Bundeswehr in Afghanistan. The Bundestag constantly monitored compliance with the strict rules of engagement that dictated German deployment on the ground. Different from the case of Italy (see below), the Bundestag Defence Commission – which had considerable investigative power – met regularly with the Minister of Defence, monitoring the executive and the activities of the Bundeswehr, together with the Parliamentary Commissioner of Armed Forces. Moreover, as of 2001 any changes in mission (such as moving into another region, expanding commitment, deploying new weapons and so on) had to be formally approved by parliament. This was the case, for example, in 2003 when the Bundeswehr deployment extended beyond the capital,[137] or in 2007 when Germany expanded its military presence (meaning new tasks and risks for the Regional Command Nord) with the addition of new Tornados, and in 2008 when the mandate was extended. Such constant involvement of the Bundestag meant higher audience costs for the executive, allowing space for veto players to manoeuvre. As reported by a German officer, the Minister of Defence created 'specific instructions for troops on the ground in anticipation' of the parliamentary debate.[138] These mechanisms represented obstacles for those interested in moving away from the trajectory of the reluctant defence policy, increasing the costs associated with such choices in the face of a still cautious German society. Moreover, Germany redefined the role of the Bundestag on the basis of a new court ruling in 2008 regarding the presence of NATO AWACS in Turkey and a new Parliamentary Participation Act, which more clearly defined the type of 'deployment' that required the authorisation of the Bundestag.[139] As stated by a former member of the German Parliamentary Commission on defence reform, the Bundestag has also been 'crucial in legitimising' German military operations.[140]

A third element that made it possible to confirm the existing trajectory in German defence involves the limitations in the structure of the armed forces, and the consequences of a lack of operational experience. Timing and sequencing are again fundamental aspects to be considered. Offensive military actions revealed the Bundeswehr's weak points in undertaking COIN, especially with regard to the integration of low- and high-intensity tasks.[141] In fact, the Bundeswehr participated in higher-intensity operations in Taliban-dominated provinces, such as Operation 'Harekate Yolo II' (October 2007).[142] These operations revealed shortfalls in terms of resources and capabilities, but the legacies of the past help us to understand the German doctrinal confusion on 'insurgency versus stabilisation'.[143] The slow adaptation of the German operational strategy to the (US and British) counterinsurgency model ('shape, clear, hold and build') was clearly related to legal and material constraints, but also to a lack of attention to the requirements of expeditionary warfare. In fact, historical experience in aspects other than high-intensity warfare (mainly related to the Second World War context) had been constantly neglected.[144] The Afghan context was conceived as part of these operations, while the combat dimension was still left out.

An actual COIN doctrine did not emerge in the public debate. Because of the slow-starting process transformation, with limited operational experience 'soldiers trained for high-intensity conventional conflict scenarios during the Cold War',[145] and the German military suffered a disadvantage in doctrinal development. In a public context marked by the removal of war, and with the forces focusing on their 'lessons' in mechanised infantry, from the Eastern front in the Second World War to the Cold War against the Warsaw Pact, COIN tactics 'did not feature in Bundeswehr planning'.[146] The strategic reflection and the attempts to reform at the beginning of the century did not resolve the tension between the different concepts, despite the operations on the ground. The Bundeswehr's approach was outlined in the *'Heeresdienstvorschrift (HDv) Truppenführung von Landstreitkraeften (HDv) 100/100'* 82007 (Army Service Regulations: Army Field Manual). The document is extremely relevant with regard to the doctrine followed by German land forces. While other countries' armies, such as those of Britain and France, began to prepare for operations characterised by a 'continuum of conflict' after the experiences in the Balkans, German doctrine separated fighting, peace support and humanitarian aid into different categories in conflict situations. COIN never really featured even in new versions of the HDv 100/100.[147] The *Einsatzkonzept Operationen gegen Irregulaere Kraefte* (Einsatzkonzept OplK – Guidelines for Operations against Irregular Forces, 2005) dealt with irregular forces, offering guidance on the kinetic dimensions of conflicts, but never really integrating all elements of COIN together. The German approach to COIN, therefore, differed from the Allies' counterinsurgency doctrines, which were focused mainly on population security.[148] In Germany, the perceived need to simultaneously apply kinetic and non-kinetic actions was gradually conveyed in strategic documents, while the *'Denkverbot'* on COIN persisted in public discourse, which for years portrayed the operations in Afghanistan as stabilisation missions.

In short, the Bundeswehr deployments in 1990s (in the Balkans, for example) shaped the German military strategy that was later adopted in Afghanistan, but the overall historical post-Second World War experience of the German armed forces was extremely limited, or even completely absent regarding specific combat-like tasks, such as counterinsurgency.[149]

The evolution of German doctrine can be described as a balance between the 'traditional' concept of territorial defence and a 'crisis management approach'. After the war in Kosovo, two SPD ministers of defence (Rudolf Scharping and Peter Stuck) were instrumental in an attempt to promote the transformation of the Bundeswehr from a *Verteidigungsarmee* (territorial defence army) into an *Einsatzarmee* (for missions abroad). In 2000, the executive presented the 'Comprehensive Concept on Civilian Crisis Prevention, Conflict Resolution and Post-Conflict Peace-Building' (2000), defining civilian crisis prevention and management as a 'cornerstone of German foreign and security policy'.[150] Moreover, Defence Minister Struck gradually introduced elements of the RMA into the

Bundeswehr, developing concepts such as the *Infanterist der Zukunft* (infantrymen of the future).[151] The most important post-2001 German official defence publications (the 2004 'Conception of the Bundeswehr', the 2006 White Paper and the 2011 Defence Policy Guidelines) shared the need for transformation, with a focus on network-based operations (*Vernetzte Operationsführung* or *NetOpFu*).[152] However, this US-led concept was introduced very slowly in Germany, which lacked an implementation strategy and governance for NetOpFu, while the armed force structure still focused on territorial defence as a core task.[153] The first actual exercise with NetOpFu, introduced in 2004, only took place in 2013.

With reference to crisis management, German doctrine in the new century was shaped by the idea of the 'comprehensive approach'. In this sense, multilateral fora (mainly NATO) and previous missions on the ground (from the Balkans onwards) played a relevant role.[154] Attention to the concept (whose non-military dimension fitted well with the German strategic culture) increased considerably after the intervention in Kosovo. The lessons learned from the Kosovo intervention – and the clear need to address similar crises more effectively – defined the approach promoted by the Weiszäcker Commission. Despite changes, 'territorial and collective defence, rather than crisis management, remained the underlying rationale'.[155] A real shift to crisis management and full-spectrum operations occurred only in 2003, prompted by Afghanistan.[156] In fact, after 9/11 and the beginning of the intervention in Afghanistan, the Defence Policy Guidelines (VPR, 2003) outlined the ambition to develop the Bundeswehr into an expeditionary force beyond Europe also.[157] The VPR (which were issued by Defence Minister Peter Struck) represented the German approach to addressing the challenges of the post-9/11 era, finally identifying – thirteen years after the end of the Cold War – the notion of 'defence' as more than a reaction to a traditional conventional attack against Germany or its allies, thus paving the way to extending the role of the Bundeswehr to cover a wide spectrum of operations beyond NATO territory,[158] including conflict prevention, crisis management and counterterrorism.[159] According to the document, 'defence can no longer be narrowed down to geographical boundaries, but contributes to the safeguarding of our security wherever it is in jeopardy'.[160] In other words, the Bundeswehr gradually became a tool of German security policy. The VPR aimed to address both the capabilities gap (the lack of military capabilities for expeditionary missions) and the 'usability gap' (the fact that only a portion of the armed forces were deployable).[161]

However, despite these important new developments, the VPR were not formally approved by the government, and while the notion of territorial defence as the unique purpose of the Bundeswehr was dismissed by the document, the concept largely maintained its strategic relevance. In addition, the evolution of German doctrine occurred in strict conjunction with the debates underway in multilateral fora. For example, the Bundeswehr's conceptual development of the Effects-based Approach to Operations (EBAO) did not take off until 2006, partly because Germany awaited guidance from NATO for doctrinal development while other countries (the United Kingdom and France) had already developed their conceptual approach on the issue of net-centric warfare.[162]

The 2006 White Paper[163] focused on the concept of 'networked security' (*Vernetzte Sicherheit*), Germany's national approach to crisis management, which includes several phases of the conflict cycle, from mediation to intervention and post-conflict.[164] The White Paper was particularly ambitious with regard to adapting German defence to a changing security environment, conceiving the possibility of undertaking two operations of the size of ISAF and aiming to deploy 14,000 troops in up to five separate crisis management operations.

The trajectory of German doctrine is thus described as an attempt to strike a balance between new requirements and a consolidated legacy. First, despite the reorientation towards greater international military responsibility, the German culture of restraint – which also emphasises multilateralism, political solutions and humanitarianism – was still instrumental in shaping the national approach to Bundeswehr deployment.[165] The German approach to crisis management was characterised by a clear reluctance to the use of force and a preference for the EU as a supranational framework.[166] Despite activism in Kosovo and Afghanistan, continuity, rather than change, marked German defence policy.[167] The persisting German scepticism regarding the use of force, and the limited resources dedicated to the Bundeswehr, did not disappear. While to some, Kosovo, and later Afghanistan, represented critical junctures 'in the post-Cold War adaptation of German security policy', others regarded these deployments mainly as part of a slow process of evolution: the war in Kosovo was not a turning point in the recent history of German defence, but a milestone in a trajectory from which, after the air strikes in the Balkans, there was no 'turning back'.[168] Thus, the military involvement in Kosovo 'paved the way'[169] for further participation in ISAF.

Indeed there is not one single event that fostered change but 'a series of junctures' that led to a more active German military presence in the post-2001 era.[170] This shift towards a crisis management paradigm was extremely slow, as change was hampered by weak expeditionary capabilities (a legacy of the past) and the ever-present domestic constraints. Thus, the pattern reproduced itself over time, in some measure balancing the growing importance of crisis management consistently defined in humanitarian and moral terms, hence, in line with the national 'civilian narrative' with the enduring centrality of territorial and collective defence.[171] In fact, the ambitious VPR and the White Paper represented failed attempts to decisively move along a different trajectory, partly because of the incompatibility between emerging 'optimistic' doctrines and the realities illustrated by the inadequacy of Bundeswehr capabilities in northern Afghanistan.[172] The dramatic events of Kunduz in 2009 merely confirmed these inadequacies, and German defence policy quickly opted for 'narrowing the aspiring tasks' illustrated in the previous document.[173] Paradoxically, as a result of deployment abroad (primarily in Afghanistan) 'a new sense of realism about the deficiencies in processes and structures that constrained the force has set in'.[174]

In short, along with the first exigent combat missions undertaken by the Bundeswehr (Kosovo and Afghanistan) came the possibility of switching to another trajectory. However, due to the huge incentives to carry on along the same path, maintaining the balance that kept territorial defence at the centre of the strategic reflection, and the high costs involved in changing direction due to cultural, institutional and organisational constraints, German defence chose to go on with the same traditional dynamics. The doctrines elaborated in the post-2011 era well highlight the continuity of German defence policy and the significance of path-dependence processes.

4.2.3 Interlude: steps to redesigning German force structure in the 2000s

The war in Kosovo revealed the limited operational capabilities of the Bundeswehr, from Tornados to C2ISR and 'World War II-vintage' air-to-ground armaments.[175] The conflict highlighted the 'drastic need' for the German armed forces to 'modernise and adapt to the challenges of a real war'.[176] Consequently, institutional reforms aimed to accelerate military transformation. Special attention was given to the principles of interoperability with partners[177] and among services, such as logistics and procurement.[178] Indeed, jointness became crucial in the new century, as illustrated by the creation of the 'Operations Command' and the 'Response Force Operations Command' in 2001. Also in this sense, the lessons learned in Kosovo were vital: the Bundeswehr understood that such complex operations could not be adequately overseen by a single service command, but rather required support from all services.[179] In short, at the beginning of the new century Germany was in need of 'fundamental reforms'.[180]

However, the role of legacies remained crucial in maintaining the path of German defence policy. From the beginning of the 1990s, the forces continued to be reduced, but the 'taboo of conscription' was not directly dealt with for years.[181] The division between 'usable forces' and a large component (mainly conscripts) allocated to territorial defence still characterised the Bundeswehr.[182] However, after the war in Kosovo and the operations beyond the borders undertaken in the 1990s, the role of the armed forces was extended and, consequently, 'the strategic rationale of conscription' dwindled.[183] While some political parties (such as the Greens, in government since 1998) openly advocated a smaller all-volunteer force, mainly equipped for peace support and humanitarian missions, Germany maintained conscription until 2011, when it was suspended. Even at the beginning of the new century, in fact, conscription still attracted political consensus, consistent both with the perennial importance of territorial defence and the post-Second World War concern for creating a body of professional soldiers as a 'state within a state'.

An analysis of the reforms and the evolution of the forces illustrates the ways in which new operational and international pressures interacted with domestic constraints in shaping the trajectory of German defence policy. After the war in Kosovo, the Weizsäcker Commission's recommendations (2000) and the review by Chief of Staff Hans-Peter von Kirchbach, as well as Scharping's programme of defence reforms, pushed for the development of the expeditionary capabilities of the German armed forces and the redesigning of their structures.[184] While not advocating the end of conscription, the Commission proposed reducing the total size of the Bundeswehr from around 320,000 to 240,000 by 2006, bringing the *Generalinspecteur* (Inspector General of the Bundeswehr) more centrally into the chain of command, and requested more funding for R&D.[185] Scharping, whose programme of reforms was titled *The Bundeswehr: Advancing Steadily into the 21st Century, Cornerstones of a Fundamental Renewal*, aimed at equipping the armed forces with technologically up-to-date armaments.

However, the 1998–2002 reforms 'did not meet the operational demands emerging in Kosovo' (and later in Afghanistan).[186] Indeed, despite the willingness to modernise the Bundeswehr, the programme of reforms was carried out 'in the context of an ever-decreasing defence budget, which in real terms has been reduced by around 25 per cent since 1990'.[187] Thus, radical changes were hindered by severe financial restraints,[188] as well as increasing interservice competition aimed at getting the most out of shrinking resources.[189] Moreover, the learning process deriving from operational experience in missions abroad in the 1990s was limited (especially in comparison with other countries), and consequently the urgency of a speedy military transformation was not widely shared.[190]

Thus, after the 1990s reforms aimed at designing a new role for the Bundeswehr and the efforts made by the Red–Green coalition, the main attempt by German leaders at the beginning of the new century was that of 'reforming the reform'.[191] Germany aimed to provide additional funds for the new tasks of the German armed forces by cutting certain large procurement programmes, but the 'unfaltering commitment to retaining conscription' and the strong opposition by the *Länder* to the base closures represented considerable obstacles.[192]

The official documents approved in the first decade of the century – from the Defence Policy Guidelines (VPR 2003) and the *Konzeption der Bundeswehr* to the White Paper 2006 – attempted to further reinforce the ambition of effectively reforming the structure of the German armed forces. These documents promoted the modularisation of the Bundeswehr. Since 2004, in order to maximise readiness, efficiency and effectiveness, the German armed forces were functionally divided into rapid reaction forces (35,000), stabilisation forces (70,000) and support forces (147,500).[193] This three-tiered force structure had 'the aim of building a mission-oriented force that would cover the whole spectrum of operations'.[194] In 2007, Minister of Defence Jung also established a command staff for expeditionary operations within the ministry. Interoperability with allies, a new operational spectrum and financial considerations have been described as major drivers of the new reforms.[195]

Once again, despite the changes, Cold War legacies still carried weight: personnel expenses counted for almost half the budget, and in 2009 only 7 per cent of investment funds were available to be spent on new projects.[196] The 2005 annual report by the parliamentary ombudsman responsible for the German armed forces reported 'long-term under-financing of the German Armed Forces'.[197] Despite international pressure, Germany's defence budget remained stable at below 1.5 per cent of the GDP (see Graph 4.2) in the first decade of the century. Moreover, the gap between ambition and reality continued to be considerable for the armed forces, which had to transform drastically in order to meet new requirements. For instance, while the 2006 White Paper set the goal of deploying 14,000 troops in up to five separate crisis management operations (out of a total force of 252,500), in 2010, the Bundeswehr was still only capable of deploying 8,300.[198]

With reference to equipment, despite certain areas of progress (such as acquisitions of Puma infantry fighting vehicles, Tiger multi-role combat support helicopters, Airbus A-400M transport aircraft for strategic mobility, and NH-90 and CH-53 transport helicopters for tactical mobility), there were considerable delays in the actual delivery of assets on the ground. Germany faced significant operational problems, especially in Afghanistan, such as deficiencies in Command, Control, Intelligence Surveillance, Target Acquisition and Reconnaissance (C2-ISTAR) assets capabilities.[199] The 'Net-centric transformation' showed inadequacies in terms of actual implementation, partly due to the lack of a centralised institutional structure in the Ministry of Defence.[200] Consequently, while the forces were employed in Afghanistan, a very limited part of the equipment was 'network-ready'. ISAF also showed that the Bundeswehr suffered deficiencies in specialised units (for example, special forces) and platforms (mainly for air mobility) required for COIN.[201] At the same time, Germany remained committed to 'Cold War defence capability procurement programmes', such as submarines.[202] Legacies affected not only cultural and economic choices, but also the *timing* of procurement policy.

To overcome all these setbacks, the reforms adopted after 2009 by ministers Zu Guttemberg and De Meziere helped 'the re-structuring and the re-orientation of the German defence', by focusing specifically on budget procurement and personnel.[203] These reforms introduced important 'bureaucratic adjustments'[204] for the Bundeswehr, including the suspension of compulsory military service and the reduction in personnel.[205] After 2009, the need for a new round of German defence reforms became evident. New leadership (under Zu Guttenberg), a renewed sense of urgency relating to the realistic assessment of the Bundeswehr's deficiencies and deficits in expeditionary capabilities after years of missions abroad (and the dramatic incident in Kunduz), and the impending additional budget cuts due to widespread austerity measures called for changes to the organisational structure of the armed forces.[206]

Several analyses and reports, such as reviews by the Weise Commission in 2010 and by Inspector General, General Wieker, presented the idea of reconsidering conscription, the need to reduce the forces to a total of 180,000, the restructuring of procurement and the reinforcing of the joint organisation.[207] The idea of a voluntary conscription that would replace the draft overcame the opposition, and the Bundestag eventually approved the seminal reform. In December 2010, conscription was suspended, and the new force size was set at 185,000. Under Minister of Defence Karl Ernst Thomas De Maiziére (2011–2013), the Bundeswehr was effectively reduced to the proposed size of 180,000, with around 10,000 readily deployable abroad.[208]

Gradually, German defence also endeavoured to adapt to the challenges of its complex operational environment. For example, mainly due to its involvement in ISAF, Germany took major steps to improve the 'lessons-learned' process, addressing the former lack of coordination and increasing the efficiency of data collection and training.[209] Furthermore, the *Einsatzsofortbedarf* (Urgent Operational Requirements) 'enhanced the Bundeswehr's capacity to adapt to the operational environment by permitting the Services to meet vital capability requirements as operations evolve'.[210] The UOR scheme allowed the Services to procure equipment 'off the shelf' (such as unmanned aerial vehicles).[211] However, the Bundeswehr continued to suffer from various deficiencies (from protective vests to armoured vehicles),[212] and the lessons-learned process was unable to cope with 'all the expectations at tactical level'.[213] Consequently, De Maiziére established a new Equipment, Information Technology and In-Service Support Directorate (AIN) responsible for planning and acquisition, with the aim of bypassing individual services, including through the reinforcement of the role of the *Generalinspekteur* (Chief of Staff), thanks partly to the support of the *Planungsamt* (Planning Office).[214]

In conclusion, several innovations were introduced by the reforms adopted in the first decade of the century. Even in the new century, however, the established trajectory adopted by the post-bipolar 'restrained' German defence was not so radically different, while Berlin still struggled to move 'beyond legacy'.[215] In the 1990s, the Bundeswehr began to redefine its international role, but 'policymakers continue to act within the framework and authority of the German political system and strategic culture'.[216] The old 'culture of restraint' associated with the Bonn years no longer appeared to be so compatible with the new increased responsibility in foreign policy.[217] The German deployments abroad paved the way for developing the Bundeswehr into 'a globally deployable force'.[218] The Kosovo and Afghanistan wars combined were critical for the German armed forces. These experiences led to a growing reaction that prompted a gradual move away from the traditional path of German defence. The status of 'active player in crisis management operations'[219] was formally enshrined in the 2006 German defence White Paper.[220] The operations on the ground (mainly ISAF) promoted considerable adaptations in terms of training and equipment. Notable changes occurred, such as the suspension of conscription, the downsizing of forces, the restructuring of the Ministry of Defence and its directorates (which were halved), the rising power of the *Generalinspekteur* and the enhancement of jointness and interoperability. However, in terms of force structure also a radical change did not come about quickly,[221] with financial constraints, the cultural opposition to a robust military posture[222] and the close scrutiny by parliament still affected German defence, placing major obstacles in the path of further transformation.[223] Military effectiveness was 'sacrificed' once again 'for the aim of maintaining the Armed Forces' societal legitimacy'.[224] Despite the developments taking place as a result of a new military engagement on the ground in missions abroad, territorial defence remained a priority of the Bundeswehr and cultural and economic constraints did not disappear.

4.3 German defence after 2011

4.3.1 German doctrine after 2011

The Merkel-led CDU/CSU–FDP coalition did not to support NATO's 'Operation Unified Protector' in Libya in 2011. Germany abstained in the 1973 UN resolution imposing the no-fly zone on Libya, despite the multilateral context and the humanitarian standards that (at least at the beginning) defined the intervention. Notwithstanding the increasing military expertise gained in the post-Cold War period, the use of military force in combat operations (such as air strikes) still represented a problem for Germany.[225] The German attitude was largely driven by a 'reluctant' strategic culture and a persistent regulatory dissonance with the idea of participating in combat operations, combined with a total lack of relative pressing interests and with domestic political calculations regarding incoming regional elections.[226]

This abstention led to tensions with the Allies.[227] Former German Foreign Minister Joseph Martin Fischer saw the government's approach in Libya as a 'scandalous mistake', because, by failing to address the expectations of its allies, Berlin damaged its international reputation.[228] Various analyses[229] focused on domestic politics and especially on the role played by Foreign Minister Guido Westerwelle (FDP) and his calculation before a local election with high levels of public opposition to German intervention in Libya.[230] The FDP was also generally sceptical towards the use of military force and Westerwelle was an advocate of the 'culture of restraint'.[231] The risks to the stability of the government coalition as a consequence of a vote in the Bundestag were significant.[232] Once again, domestic concerns took precedence over international pressures. Also in the case of Libya, political leaders were reluctant to openly request a mandate from the Bundestag just before regional elections. In other words, the institutional constraints firmly established by the Constitutional Court in 1994 on the 'parliamentary army'[233] still played a vital role in affecting decisions in German defence in 2011.[234] Without submitting a motion to parliament, Merkel avoided audience costs and political responsibility relating to controversial debate before parliament.[235]

German military reluctance persisted after Libya. Berlin provided limited support to the 2013 French intervention in Mali,[236] and it later contributed militarily to the international missions EU Training Mission (EUTM), EU Capacity Building Mission (EUCAP) and United Nations Multidimensional Integrated Stabilisation Mission in Mali (MINUSMA, where Germany had more than 1,000 soldiers after 2018).[237] In this case also, German interventions were characterised by such constant elements as a large parliamentary consensus (with the exception of the far-left Die Linke Party), the existence of a multilateral framework, a non-combat role for the troops and a humanitarian frame. The decision to send weapons to the Kurdish military, or *Peshmerga*, which contrasted the rising menace of ISIS in Iraq in September 2014, followed in 2015 by the training mission, were also important moves in terms of solidarity with allies and humanitarian efforts. The military mission against ISIS was primarily justified on the grounds of alliance solidarity by Chancellor Merkel and Foreign Minister Heiko Maas.[238] The humanitarian narratives and the reluctance over the use of force (the German Tornados were used exclusively for reconnaissance and not air strikes, as did by Italian forces, see below) still defined the German approach, despite the fact that the majority of Germans supported the intervention.[239]

The repercussions of Germany's abstention in the UN Security Council vote on Libya had an effect on the German government's re-evaluation of its strategy.[240] This re-evaluation occurred gradually after the 2013 change in the majority coalition (a CDU/CSU–SPD 'grand coalition', again led by Angela Merkel), and especially following the growing development of the so-called 'Munich consensus'. The 2014 Munich Security Conference was in fact actually considered by several scholars as a 'landmark' in the process of evolution of German defence.[241] In this context, German political leaders, beginning with Federal President Joachim Gauck, openly recommended a more substantial national military engagement in the global scenario, going beyond the national sentiment of historical guilt.[242] Minister of Defence Ursula von der Leyen also stressed the German security obligation to provide a solution to crises and conflicts,[243] and Minister of Foreign Affairs Frank-Walter Steinmeier called on Germany to take on greater 'international responsibility'.[244] This reflection also occurred in a context characterised by an 'increasingly positive attitude towards the Bundeswehr'.[245] A key driver in this 're-orientation' was represented by the growing regional and international instability. Russia's annexation of Crimea was a watershed, illustrating the challenges posed by a resurgent Russia,[246] as the (first) war in Ukraine shaped the public threat perception and favoured a push for higher defence spending.[247]

After 2014, 'geopolitical concern about Russia'[248] increased among German leaders. These changes were interpreted by the German defence establishment as the need to place 'territorial defence' once again at the centre of military doctrine.[249] The invasion of Crimea was 'ammunition for those who supported a more traditional homeland defence',[250] decisively shifting Germany back to territorial defence. The armed forces – after being involved for years in military missions abroad – came back to a quasi-Cold War threat, which would also have required 'more familiar' equipment and approaches.[251] The salience attributed to crisis management in the 2003 and 2006 strategic documents was therefore somewhat short-lived. The traditional trajectory of German defence, which had held firm in those years, quickly re-emerged and was reinforced by the events.

Post-2014 doctrine highlights the perpetual importance of territorial defence. After the war in Libya, Germany confirmed, through the 2012 strategy (*Globalisierung gestalten – Partnerschaften ausbauen: Verantwortung teilen' Konzept der Bundesregierung*),[252] the relevance of conflict prevention as a key (and apparently less demanding) part of crisis management.[253] In a complex and dynamic world of globalisation, the main goal was to simply 'assist in shaping processes' rather than taking a leading role.[254] However, the most important document produced after the crises in Libya (2011) and Ukraine (2014), and after the interventions in Sahel and the Middle East, was the most recent German White Paper (2016). In line with the 2012 *Konzept*, this document illustrated Germany's new responsibility and 'greater ability to shape' (*Gestaltungsfähigkeit*).[255] The document highlights significant new elements, openly referring to the 'national interest' and to the possibility of also operating abroad in ad hoc multinational coalitions, far-removed from the strict multilateralism that constantly dominated German defence.[256] A key concept of the paper is the 'Enable and Enhance Initiative', consisting of the deployment of arms and training to local actors.[257] In other words, the feedback received from Afghanistan served in this context to focus on increasing the capacity to develop local actors rather than sending boots on the ground for combat operations.[258]

In addition, the White Paper also encouraged a 'more flexible interpretation of the law to be able to act if necessary, but ad hoc military coalitions might well turn out to be incompatible with Germany's Basic Law, although the Constitutional Court has yet to be called upon to give a verdict.'[259] Thus, the relaxing of domestic legal constrains was openly considered a premise for greater military activism. More importantly, despite the focus on a 'new German responsibility' in a deteriorating security environment (in conformity with the 'Munich consensus'), the 2016 White Paper crucially argues that international crisis management, national and collective defence, homeland security, defence diplomacy and humanitarian assistance are 'of equal importance'.[260] After the years of crisis management, territorial and collective defence returned to the centre of German doctrine, perfectly compatible with the structure, organisation and approaches of the Bundeswehr, which had been designed and trained for decades to defend their territory against the Warsaw Pact, while never developing proper doctrines for COIN despite years of operational involvement. So, the heritage of collective defence continued to dominate the doctrine. Generally speaking, the problematic experience of years of missions abroad, the ever-present institutional and cultural domestic constraints and the recent international events (such as the war in Ukraine) were all dynamics that contributed to reinforcing and consolidating the path of German defence.

The change occurring in post-Cold War defence was characterised by continual adjustments while preserving continuity in key aspects of the German defence, such as multilateralism, the humanitarian narrative and reluctance in the use of force in offensive operations. Adaptation to the post-2011 security context (Arab Spring, Russian invasion of Crimea, instability in the Sahel and MENA regions, and increasing challenges from ISIS) has effectively been implemented, but it remains anchored to the main principles of German defence, such as restraint and multilateralism.[261] In 2021, Germany was involved in twelve international missions, deploying approximately 3,500 soldiers abroad. For comparison, in 2021 Italian forces were deployed in in forty-two operations, deploying almost 7,000 soldiers (see Chapter 5). The size of German deployments 'has varied with the ebb and flow of international crisis-management demands'.[262] Germany's international role gradually became more akin to that of a 'normal country', but domestic constraints continued to play an important role after 'having triumphed' over international opportunities for many years.[263]

Lastly, the case of Libya illustrates clearly, after two decades, the persistence of Germany's reluctance to use force. In 2020, Germany also drafted an Indo-Pacific Strategy,[264] which almost entirely excludes 'any discussion of military issues'.[265] On the one hand, the Bundeswehr participated in military drills in the area, sending also naval vessels, Eurofighters and soldiers to east Asia.[266] On the other hand, while China is increasingly considered by Berlin as a competitor (or even as a challenge), German leaders are still hesitant to embrace a more confrontational stance, as advocated by allies, also because of close trading and investment relations with Beijing.[267] On the whole, despite rising concern on the deteriorating security context in recent years, Angela Merkel continued to resist updating German defence policy to cater to today's threats.[268] Generally speaking, a 'paradigm shift'[269] in German defence policy was effectively still needed. The future will reveal if the Russian invasion of Ukraine finally represents an actual *Zeitenwende*, an historical turning point for German defence, or not.[270]

4.3.2 Back to conventional? The last decade of German forces

Although German 'reluctance' to use military troops abroad did not disappear, as is evident from the war in Libya, the post-2011 era promoted further transformation in the force structure of the Bundeswehr. Renewed attention was given to defence spending, especially after the war in Ukraine (2014) and the subsequent NATO Wales Summit, where the allies agreed to spend 'a minimum of 2% of their Gross Domestic Product (GDP) on defence [and] spend more than 20% of their defence budgets on major equipment, including related Research & Development'.[271] Unfortunately, Germany struggled unsuccessfully for years to reach this threshold. On the contrary, 'a temporary low was reached in 2014–2016 when it hovered at around 1.1%, although since then spending increased and reached just under 1.4 % of GDP in 2020'.[272] As illustrated in Graph 4.2, it was not until after 2018 that Germany's defence spending finally began to increase. In this context, the United States continued to criticise Berlin's limited military budget, especially under the Trump administration.[273]

This growing interest in German defence spending – boosted by the Russian invasion of Ukraine[274] – was also related to the significant deficiencies in military capabilities that emerged in the previous years, to increasing personnel costs and to delays in old programmes such as those for the construction of frigates or Puma infantry fighting vehicles.[275] In fact, the German procurement process remained 'slow and inefficient' after 2014, while the *Bundesrechnungshof* (the Federal auditing office) 'has repeatedly exposed waste and inefficiencies'.[276] There is a long list of procurement decisions (Tornado replacement, the updating of Boxer armoured vehicles, development of Tiger helicopters, air and missile defence, and so on) that were not financially support by the government budget.[277]

These persisting problems are in contrast to the abovementioned emerging 'Munich consensus'. On the one hand, there was a rising (mainly scholarly) debate on a 'more active German foreign policy'[278] and on Germany as a 'reluctant hegemon'.[279] Public threat perceptions began to shift and, as of 2015, after many years concerns about possible threats to Germany's national security increased.[280] On the other hand, the German public 'still appeared to be in denial about the implications' of adopting a new foreign policy.[281] Despite growing concerns over the challenges in the regional (and international) context (after Ukraine, but also aroused by the instability in the Middle East and by the EU's stunned reaction to Brexit and to its complex relationship with the Trump administration), reluctance to effectively change Germany's security posture remained.[282] In fact, there was still no common understanding among the parties as to what the assumption of 'more responsibility' should concretely mean for German ambitions.[283]

At the same time, the constant involvement in multinational missions continued to provide feedback to keep Germany interoperable with its allies, thus increasing pressure to invest in its own capabilities (such as drones). As we have said, the *Konzept* (2012) and the 2016 White Paper[284] focused also on multidimensional coalitions that require interoperability beyond multilateral frameworks. However, domestic constraints hindered specific developments (such as armed drones) in that they were 'too far from the traditional path' of German defence, although in the post-conscription era, after the reforms promoted during the Zu Guttenberg and de Maiziere years, the 'need for transformation was still acknowledged'.[285] The 'joint mentality'[286] was reinforced after 2011, when the structure of the chiefs of staff was modified in order to increase coordination. In line with the 'Dresden Directive' (21 March 2012), the Chief of Defence became the administrative superior of all military personnel, acquiring responsibility for the Directorate-General for Planning, the Directorate-General for Forces Policy and the Directorate-General for Strategy and Operations.[287] The Chief of Defence assumed control of Bundeswehr operations, while operational and tactical levels were moved from the ministry to the Joint Forces Operations Command. The Ministry of Defence was restructured, reducing size in terms of personnel (by 35 per cent) and directorates (from sixteen to nine).[288] Moreover, the reorientation of the Bundeswehr led to further adjustments to the force structure (for example, brigades were reduced and additional bases were closed), ending the distinction between the categories of 'stabilisation operations' and 'crisis response missions'. The Defence Policy Guidelines (2011), after years of missions abroad, aimed to reconfigure the army towards lighter and medium forces, reducing the armoured component, as well as battle tanks and heavy artillery, while increasing the light infantry battalion.[289]

However, apart from the persisting cultural, political and economic constraints, two problems emerged for the reforms of German defence. First, the legacy of years of 'neglecting modernisation' of the forces played a role in slowing the implementation phase, which could not be realised immediately.[290] Secondly, feedback from decades of missions abroad was finally able to shape the force structure of the Bundeswehr in accordance with the needs on the ground, but when they were finally 'incorporated' in reform projects, after years of pressing demands, the international scenario changed as a result of the war in Crimea: from crisis management and COIN operations to the 'return' of the threat of conventional warfare in Europe. The 'war on terror' was almost over, and new demands for defending Europe in a possible high-intensity war-fighting scenario emerged. While territorial defence never stopped being the priority for the German armed forces, the 'constrained' Bundeswehr did not have the capabilities[291] needed for an effective deterrence on the eastern flank.[292] The ambitious plans aimed at boosting the modernisation of German defence (such as that proposed by Minister of Defence von der Leyen)[293] were not fully implemented, and at the same time it continued to be affected by the 'dramatic problems' and shortfalls of the Bundeswehr, as reported also by its Defence Commission.[294]

Notes

1. White Paper 1994, p. 23.
2. For a review, see Sakaki et al., *Reluctant Warriors*.
3. S. Bulmer and W. E. Paterson (2013), 'Germany as the EU's Reluctant Hegemon? Of Economic Strength and Political Constraints', *Journal of European Public Policy* 20(10): 1387–1405.
4. D. Wilsford (1994), 'Path Dependency, or Why History Makes It Difficult but Not Impossible to Reform Health Care Systems in a Big Way', *Journal of Public Policy* 14(3): 251–83; K. Longhurst (2003), 'Why Aren't the Germans Debating the Draft? Path Dependency and the Persistence of Conscription', *German Politics* 12(2): 147–65.
5. Longhurst, 'Why Aren't the Germans Debating the Draft?' 151. On German 'power' after the collapse of the Berlin Wall, see J. Joffe (1990), 'Once More: The German Question', *Survival* 32(2): 129–40. For a broader foreign policy perspective, see T. Risse-Kappen (1994), 'Ideas Do Not Float Freely: Transnational Coalitions, Domestic Structures, and the End of the Cold War', *International Organization* 48(2): 185–214; V. Rittberger (2001), *German Foreign Policy since Unification: Theories and Case Studies*. Manchester: Manchester University Press.
6. Longhurst, 'Why Aren't the Germans Debating the Draft?' 154–5; B. Giegerich and M. Terhalle (2021), *The Responsibility to Defend: Rethinking Germany's Strategic Culture*. New York: Routledge, 51.
7. Authors' interview, German strategic adviser to European Union Training, Potsdam, ZMSBw, 28 November 2019; Authors' interview, researcher on German defence policy, Potsdam, ZMSBw, 26 November 2019; K. Longhurst (2005), 'Endeavours to Restructure the Bundeswehr: The Reform of the German Armed Forces 1990–2003', *Defence & Security Analysis* 21(1): 21.
8. Authors' interview, researcher on German defence policy, Potsdam, ZMSBw, 26 November 2019.
9. Z. Juhasz (2001), 'German Public Opinion and the Use of Force in the Early Nineties', in P. Iserni and P. Everts (eds), *Public Opinion and the International Use of Force*. London: Routledge, 57–85.
10. M. E. Sarotte (2001), 'German Military Reform and EU Security', *Adelphi Paper 340*.
11. The international treaties were also instrumental in limiting this room for manoeuvre for German defence. Authors' interview, researcher on German defence policy, Potsdam, ZMSBw, 26 November 2019.
12. J. S. Lantis (2002), *Strategic Dilemmas and the Evolution of German Foreign Policy Since Unification*. Santa Barbara, CA: Greenwood, 13.

13. Berenskoetter and Giegerich, 'From NATO to ESDP', 422.
14. Ibid. As Longhurst emphasises, 'at the time of the Gulf War there was resistance to a shift to a more participatory contribution that went beyond Germany's traditional role of paymaster'. Longhurst, *Germany and the Use of Force*, 148.
15. On these missions, see, for example, Sakaki et al., *Reluctant Warriors*; Coticchia, *Qualcosa è cambiato*.
16. Longhurst, 'Why Aren't the Germans Debating the Draft?' 154–5.
17. D. Klos, H. Möllers and D. Stockfish (2013), 'The Military Services', in I. Wiesner (ed.), *German Defence Politics*. Baden-Baden: Nomos, 127–62.
18. Longhurst, 'Endeavours to Restructure the Bundeswehr', 22.
19. Ibid.
20. Authors' interview, former General staff officer, Ministry of Defence, Berlin, SWP, 26 November 2019.
21. Authors' interview, researcher on German defence policy, Potsdam, ZMSBw, 26 November 2019.
22. Authors' interview, researcher on German military operation in Afghanistan, Potsdam, ZMSBw, 28 November 2019.
23. Authors' interview, former general staff officer, Ministry of Defence, Berlin, SWP, 26 November 2019.
24. Berenskoetter and Giegerich, 'From NATO to ESDP', 432.
25. See Maull, 'Germany and the Use of Force', 56–80.
26. Sakaki et al., *Reluctant Warriors*, 99.
27. Sarotte, 'German Military Reform and EU Security', p. 9.
28. S. Harnisch (2009), '"The Politics of Domestication": A New Paradigm in German Foreign Policy', *German Politics* 18(4): 462.
29. Ibid.
30. Noetzel and Schreer, 'All the Way?' 212.
31. U. E. Franke (2012), 'A Tale of Stumbling Blocks and Road Bumps: Germany's (non-)Revolution in Military Affairs', *Comparative Strategy* 31(4): 353–75.
32. Germany also participated in the Implementation Force (IFOR) and the Stabilisation Force (SFOR) in Bosnia, after the civil war.
33. Berenskoetter and Giegerich, 'From NATO to ESDP'.
34. Ibid., 436.
35. Authors' interview, former general staff officer, Ministry of Defence, Berlin, SWP, 26 November 2019.
36. Maull, 'Germany and the Use of Force', 56–80.
37. The 'constraints imposed on the use of some of the Luftwaffe Tornados with special equipment to suppress anti-aircraft defences deployed within the NATO operation to protect UNPROFOR were so severe as to render these aircraft almost useless'. Maull, 'Germany and the Use of Force', 64.
38. Berenskoetter and Giegerich, 'From NATO to ESDP', 437
39. The document refers to the WEU. For a detailed analysis see, for example, Longhurst, 'Endeavours to Restructure the Bundeswehr'. In the opinion of Berenskoetter and Giegerich, the 1994 White Paper emphasises how German security was deeply bound to the process of European integration. Berenskoetter and Giegerich, 'From NATO to ESDP'.
40. Authors' interview, researcher on German military operation in Afghanistan, Potsdam, ZMSBw, 28 November 2019.
41. Sarotte, 'German Military Reform and EU Security', 17.
42. Franke, 'A Tale of Stumbling Blocks and Road Bumps', 363.
43. Kümmel and Leonhard, 'Casualties and Civil–Military Relations', 519. It is worth pointing out that casualties among German soldiers in the 1990s were mainly unrelated to combat.

44. 'Low executive autonomy continues to incentivise an inappropriate level of political interference in doctrinal development and constrains the core executive's ability to overcome the impact of organisational politics between the individual Services on capability investment' (244–5). Dyson, 'Managing Convergence', 244.
45. Noetzel and Schreer, 'All the Way?' 212.
46. Seibert, 'A Quiet Revolution', 60.
47. Franke, 'A Tale of Stumbling Blocks and Road Bumps'; Kümmel, 'The Winds of Change', 13.
48. Authors' interview, researcher on German military operation in Afghanistan, Potsdam, ZMSBw, 28 November 2019. See also Longhurst, 'Endeavours to Restructure the Bundeswehr', 25.
49. From 3.5 per cent in 1985 to 1.6 per cent in 1999. Sarotte, 'German Military Reform and EU Security'. As Maull points out, 'German defence expenditure fell from US$50bn in 1985 to $32.4bn in 1998 (in constant 1997 US dollars)'. Maull, 'Germany and the Use of Force'.
50. Sarotte, 'German Military Reform and EU Security'.
51. For details, see S. Lungu (2004), 'Military Modernisation and Political Choice: Germany and the US-Promoted Military Technological Revolution during the 1990s', *Defence & Security Analysis* 20(3): 262. See also Franke, 'A Tale of Stumbling Blocks and Road Bumps'.
52. Bundesrat (Drucksacke 3330/19; 09.08.19) Gesetzentwurf der Bundesregierung – Entwurf eines Gesetzes über die Feststellung des Bundeshaushaltsplans für das Hausaltsjahr 2020 (Hausaltsgesetz 2020) – übersichten – Teil V: Personalübersichten
53. Lungu, 'Military Modernisation', 263.
54. International treaties also limited the available number of forces. Authors' interview, former general staff officer, Ministry of Defence, Berlin, SWP, 26 November 2019. As reported by Maull, during the 'Two Plus Four' negotiations Germany agreed to reduce the Bundeswehr to a maximum of 370,000. Maull, 'Germany and the Use of Force'.
55. See Graph 4.1. According to an interviewee, the German military leadership fought to preserve their positions. See authors' interview, researcher on German military operation in Afghanistan, Potsdam, ZMSBw, 28 November 2019.
56. T. Dyson (2007), *The Politics of German Defence and Security: Policy Leadership and Military Reform in the post-Cold War Era*. New York: Berghahn.
57. Longhurst, 'Endeavours to Restructure the Bundeswehr', 25.
58. Maull, 'Germany and the Use of Force'.
59. Longhurst, 'Why Aren't the Germans Debating the Draft?'
60. Dyson, 'Managing Convergence'.
61. On Kohl's support of the military service system, see Longhurst, 'Why Aren't the Germans Debating the Draft?' 155. The Liberals and the Greens, on the other hand, opposed military service, and the PDS, whose goal was to abolish the Bundeswehr, also sought to put an end to conscription.
62. Dyson, 'Managing Convergence', 249–50.
63. Authors' interview, researcher on German defence and public opinion, Potsdam, ZMSBw, 2 April 2015.
64. Dyson, *The Politics of German Defence and Security*.
65. On the RMA (the signs of which are generally related to an increased use of high-end technology), see T. Gongora and H. von Riekhoff (2000), *Toward a Revolution in Military Affairs: Defence and Security at Dawn of the Twenty-First Century*. Westport, CT: Greenwood. On military–technological superiority, and on how countries can (or cannot) imitate the United States' advanced weapon systems, see A. Gilli and M. Gilli (2019), 'Why China Has Not Caught Up Yet: Military–Technological Superiority and the Limits of Imitation, Reverse Engineering, and Cyber Espionage', *International Security* 43(3): 141–9.

66. According to Franke, the main problem regarded the limited resources allocated to R&D, rather than the general level of defence spending. Franke, 'A Tale of Stumbling Blocks and Road Bumps'.
67. Lungu, 'Military Modernisation', 265.
68. Franke, 'A Tale of Stumbling Blocks and Road Bumps', 365.
69. I. Wiesner (2011), *Importing the American Way of War? Network-centric Warfare in the UK and Germany*. Baden-Baden: Nomos Verlag.
70. Dyson, *The Politics of German Defence and Security*, 1.
71. A. Miskimmon (2007), *Germany and the Common Foreign and Security Policy of the European Union*. New York: Palgrave, 189.
72. Seibert, 'A Quiet Revolution', 60.
73. T. Rid (2007), 'The Bundeswehr's New Media Challenge', *Military Review* July/August, 105.
74. On Germany's NATO membership as a factor favouring German military transformation, see Franke, 'A Tale of Stumbling Blocks and Road Bumps'. To the author, free-riding remained an issue, 'as the United States is assuming the major military responsibilities of the alliance', while European defence budgets were shrinking.
75. Kümmel and Leonhard, 'Casualties and Civil–Military Relations'; Juhász, 'German Public Opinion and the Use of Force'.
76. Sakaki et al., *Reluctant Warriors*, 99–103.
77. K. Longhurst and A. Miskimmon (2007), 'Same Challenges, Diverging Responses: Germany, the UK and European Security', *German Politics* 16(1): 82.
78. Dyson, *The Politics of German Defence and Security*.
79. Dyson, 'Managing Convergence', 264.
80. Ibid.
81. Seibert, 'A Quiet Revolution', 60.
82. Longhurst, 'Endeavours to Restructure the Bundeswehr', 21–35
83. Berenskoetter and Giegerich, 'From NATO to ESDP', 440.
84. Noetzel and Schreer, 'All the Way? 211–21.
85. G. Breuer, (2006), 'Between Ambitions and Financial Constraints: The Reform of the German Armed Forces', *German Politics* 15(2): 210.
86. Authors' interview, German army officer, Potsdam, ZMSBw, 26 November 2019.
87. Mello, *Democratic Participation in Armed Conflict*.
88. Maull, 'Germany and the Use of Force'. Berlin also participated in humanitarian efforts to support refugees in Albania, as well as providing a relevant contribution to the KFOR mission after the end of the air strikes.
89. Authors' interview, German army officer, Potsdam, ZMSBw, 26 November 2019.
90. Mello, *Democratic Participation in Armed Conflict*.
91. Ibid. The pacifist opposition was well illustrated by the mobilisation of the traditional *Ostermärsche*, the Easter demonstrations of pacifist movements. Maull, 'Germany and the Use of Force'.
92. R. M. Allers (2016), 'Are We Doing Enough? Change and Continuity in the German Approach to Crisis Management', *German Politics* 25(4): 524. Conversely, the Party of Democratic Socialism (PDS) strongly opposed the NATO mission.
93. Sakaki et al., *Reluctant Warriors,* 53.
94. Peter Struck, Chairman of the SPD in the Bundestag, 26 March 1999.
95. Berenskoetter and Giegerich, 'From NATO to ESDP', 440.
96. Similarly, the Italian government used the expression 'advanced defence'. See the next chapter.
97. Authors' interview, former general staff officer, Ministry of Defence, Berlin, SWP, 26 November 2019.
98. Longhurst and Miskimmon, 'Same Challenges, Diverging Responses', 84.

99. Buras and Longhurst, 'The Berlin Republic, Iraq, and the Use of Force', 216–17; G. Hellmann (2011), 'Normatively Disarmed, But Self-Confident', *Internationale Politik Global Edition* 3: 45–51.

100. To Maull, the 'culture of restraint' and its effects as constraints in the use of force, in humanitarian concerns and narratives, largely persisted. Maull, 'Germany and the Use of Force'; A. Miskimmon (2009), 'Falling into Line: The Legacy of Operation Allied Force on German Foreign Policy', *International Affairs* 85(3): 561–73; Sakaki et al., *Reluctant Warriors*, 47.

101. Longhurst, *Germany and the Use of Force*, 59.

102. Ibid., 140.

103. On 'legalism', see U. Krotz (2015), *History and Foreign Policy in France and German*. Houndmills: Palgrave.

104. Miskimmon, 'Falling into Line', 570.

105. See especially the debates held on 16 October1998, 25–26 March 1999 and 15 April 1999. Both the SPD and the CDU voted in favour.

106. Buras and Longhurst, 'The Berlin Republic, Iraq, and the Use of Force'.

107. For details, see 'Redefining German Security: Prospects for Bundeswehr Reform', AICGS 2001, *German Issues* 25, available at: https://www.aicgs.org/site/wp-content /uploads/2011/11/securitygroup.pdf.

108. Quoted in Longhurst, 'Endeavours to Restructure the Bundeswehr', 25.

109. '*Die Bundeswehr sicher ins 21. Jahrundert*' (2000). On this point, see Giegerich and Terhalle, *The Responsibility to Defend*, 13.

110. Dyson, *The Politics of German Defence and Security*, 1.

111. Allers, 'Are We Doing Enough?' 524.

112. For a detailed analysis of the German intervention in Afghanistan see, for example, P. Münch (2015), *Die Bundeswehr in Afghanistan: Militärische Handlungslogik in internationalen Interventionen*. Freiburg im Breisgau: Rombach Verlag.

113. See especially SPD's position in the paper on CFSP (*SPD, Die Zukunft der GASP*, November 2000). The document limited the role of the military, focusing on mediation, stabilisation and peace-building.

114. 'The mission had great symbolic value as it was the EU's first military operation launched independently from NATO'. Berenskoetter and Giegerich, 'From NATO to ESDP', 446.

115. K. Brummer (2013), 'The Reluctant Peacekeeper: Governmental Politics and Germany's Participation in EUFOR RD Congo', *Foreign Policy Analysis* 9(1): 1–20.

116. K. Brummer and K. Oppermann (2021), 'Poliheuristic Theory and Germany's (Non-)Participation in Multinational Military Interventions: The Non-compensatory Principle, Coalition Politics and Political Survival', *German Politics* 30(1): 106–21.

117. Schröder electorally exploited the public opposition against the war, still focusing on the efforts against terrorism in Afghanistan, where Germany aimed to reduce the rising tension with Washington by increasing its military presence in Central Asia.

118. Sakaki et al., *Reluctant Warriors*, 54. Germany's solidarity with Washington after 9/11 and its participation in the intervention in Afghanistan also gave more credibility to the position adopted by Berlin concerning the war in Iraq. Authors' interview, former general staff officer, Ministry of Defence, Berlin, SWP, 26 November 2019.

119. Authors' interview, German army officer, Potsdam, ZMSBw, 26 November 2019.

120. K. Becher (2004), 'German Forces in International Military Operations', *Orbis* 48(3): 402.

121. Allers, 'Are We Doing Enough?' 524.

122. Authors' interview, German army officer, Potsdam, ZMSBw, 26 November 2019.

123. According to a poll, 49 per cent of German citizens were against the mission. See Sakaki et al., *Reluctant Warriors*, 84.

124. Germany, which geographically shifted towards Kunduz and Faizabad, also provided Tornado aircraft and heavy artillery. Sakaki et al., *Reluctant Warriors*, 54.

125. Berenskoetter and Giegerich, 'From NATO to ESDP', 446.
126. Quoted in Buras and Longhurst, 'The Berlin Republic, Iraq, and the Use of Force'.
127. Becher, 'German Forces in International Military Operations', 403.
128. Sakaki et al., *Reluctant Warriors*, 68.
129. See Spiegel International (2010), 'German President Horst Köhler Resigns', 31 October, available at: http://www.spiegel.de/international/germany/controversy-over-afghanistan-remarks-german-president-horst-koehler-resigns-a-697785.html.
130. Quoted in E. Sangar (2015), 'The Weight of the Past(s): The Impact of the Bundeswehr's Use of Historical Experience on Strategy-Making in Afghanistan', *Journal of Strategic Studies* 8(4): 411–44, 414.
131. Berenskoetter and Giegerich, 'From NATO to ESDP'.
132. Sangar, 'The Weight of the Past(s)'.
133. In mid-2010, for example, the Ministry of Defence authorised the deployment of three *Panzerhaubitze 2000s*. See again Sangar, 'The Weight of the Past(s)'.
134. In keeping with this, Berlin reintroduced medals for bravery in combat, defining the soldiers deployed abroad as 'veterans'.
135. In 2002, on average support was 54 per cent in Italy and 56 per cent in Germany. Reported in Mello, *Democratic Participation in Armed Conflict*.
136. Quoted in Sakaki et al., *Reluctant Warriors*, 55.
137. It is worth noting that during 'Operation Enduring Freedom' German special operations played a 'limited role'. Authors' interview, former German general, Berlin, SWP, 9 April 2015.
138. Quoted in Auerswald and Saideman, *Nato in Afghanistan*, 145.
139. Relief operations and humanitarian aid do not require parliamentary consent. On this point, see H. Aust and M. Vashakmadze (2008), 'Parliamentary Consent to the Use of German Armed Forces Abroad: The 2008 Decision of the Federal Constitutional Court in the AWACS/Turkey Case', *German Law Journal* 9(12): 2233.
140. Interview with a former member of the Weizsäcker-Commission for Bundeswehr Reform, Berlin, 16 April 2015.
141. Dyson, 'Managing Convergence'.
142. Sangar, 'The Weight of the Past(s)'.
143. Sakaki et al., *Reluctant Warriors*, 55.
144. Sangar, 'The Weight of the Past(s)', 423.
145. Authors' interview, researcher on German defence policy, Potsdam, ZMSBw, 26 November 2019. See Dyson, 'Managing Convergence'.
146. Giegerich and Terhalle, *The Responsibility to Defend*, 13.
147. T. Noetzel, 'Germany', in T. Rid and T. Keneay (eds) (2010), *Understanding Counterinsurgency: Doctrine, Operations, and Challenges*. London: Routledge, 46–58.
148. Ibid. On German COIN. see especially J. Barbin (2015), *Imperialkriegführung im 21. Jahrhundert: Von Algier nach Bagdad. Die kolonialen Ursprünge der COIN-Doktrin.* Berlin: Miles-Verlag.
149. Sangar, 'The Weight of the Past(s)'.
150. Allers, 'Are We Doing Enough?'
151. Franke, 'A Tale of Stumbling Blocks and Road Bumps'.
152. The definition used by the Bundeswehr is 'a joint interoperable Bundeswehr communication and information system across all command levels, which connects all relevant individuals, locations, units, facilities and sensors and effectors with one another'. Quoted in Franke, 'A Tale of Stumbling Blocks and Road Bumps'. On NetOpFu, see Bundeswehr, *Vernetzte Operationsführung/Digitalisierung in der Bundeswehr (Modul 4024)*, available at: https://www.bundeswehr.de/de/organisation/weitere-bmvg-dienststellen/fuehrungsakademie-der-bundeswehr/zivile-und-militaerische-lehrgangsangebote/modul-4024-95992.
153. Wiesner, *Importing the American Way of War?*
154. Authors' interview, German army officer, Potsdam, ZMSBw, 26 November 2019.

155. Dyson, *The Politics of German Defence and Security*, 95.
156. Giegerich and Terhalle, *The Responsibility to Defend*, 52.
157. Noetzel and Schreer, 'All the Way?'
158. Longhurst, 'Endeavours to Restructure the Bundeswehr', 30.
159. Ibid., 32.
160. Breuer, 'Between Ambitions and Financial Constraints'.
161. Noetzel and Schreer, 'All the Way?'
162. Dyson, 'Condemned Forever to Becoming and Never to Being?' 553.
163. Federal Ministry of Defence (2006), *White Paper 2006 on German Security Policy and the Future of the Bundeswehr*. Berlin: Federal Ministry of Defence.
164. Allers, 'Are We Doing Enough?'
165. Breuer, 'Between Ambitions and Financial Constraints'.
166. Allers, 'Are We Doing Enough?' On the resonance between the European Security Strategy and the White Paper regarding the German approach to civilian crisis prevention, see also Berenskoetter and Giegerich, 'From NATO to ESDP'. However, the White Paper openly considered NATO as the foundation of German and European security.
167. Miskimmon, 'Falling into Line'.
168. Authors' interview, German army officer, Potsdam, ZMSBw, 26 November 2019.
169. Ibid.
170. Ibid.
171. Giegerich and Terhalle, *The Responsibility to Defend*, 52.
172. Such inadequacies regarded, for example, tactical transport aircraft, protected armed vehicles, surveillance and UAVs.
173. Interview with a ZMSBw researcher, Potsdam, 1 April 2015. With regard to these inadequacies, see also the Ministry of Defence 'Internal Deficit Review' (*Strukturkommission der Bendesweher*), 12 April 2010, and the review led by the Inspector General in August 2010.
174. Seibert, 'A Quiet Revolution', 60.
175. Lungu, 'Military Modernisation', 263.
176. Authors' interview, former member of the Weizsäcker Commission, Berlin, SWP, 16 April 2015.
177. Dyson, 'Managing Convergence', 256.
178. A. Seaboyer and I. Wiesner, I. (2011), 'Budgeting for Defence', *Internationale Politik* 12(2): 30–6.
179. Authors' interview, former German General, Berlin, SWP, 16 April 2015.
180. Authors' interview, former member of the Weizsäcker Commission, Berlin, SWP, 16 April 2015.
181. Ibid.
182. Longhurst, 'Why Aren't the Germans Debating the Draft?'
183. Ibid.
184. The 'red–green coalition' was responsible for introducing a change in defence policy, with regard also to the conceptualisation of civilian crisis management. Allers, 'Are We Doing Enough?' 523.
185. Longhurst, 'Endeavours to Restructure the Bundeswehr'.
186. Wiesner, *Importing the American Way of War*, 165.
187. Ibid.
188. Authors' interview, former member of the Weizsäcker Commission, Berlin, SWP, 16 April 2015.
189. Authors' interview, researcher on German defence policy, Berlin, SWP, 9 April 2015.
190. Interview with a senior SWP researcher, Berlin, 9 April 2015.
191. Longhurst, *Germany and the Use of Force*.
192. Longhurst, 'Endeavours to Restructure the Bundeswehr'. Minister Peter Struck, who still supported conscription, cut weapons programmes related to territorial defence and promoted base closure from 2002 to 2005. Seibert, 'A Quiet Revolution'.

193. Seaboyer and Wiesner, 'Budgeting for Defence', 31.
194. Noetzel and Schreer, 'All the Way?' 216.
195. These measures were aimed 'at reducing personnel costs in favour of new investments and adapting the personnel structure to the new operational parameters'. Breuer, 'Between Ambitions and Financial Constraints', 212.
196. Wiesner, *Importing the American Way of War?*.
197. Quoted in Longhurst and Miskimmon, 'Same Challenges, Diverging Responses', 82.
198. T. Dyson (2014), 'German Defence Policy under the Second Merkel Chancellorship', *German Politics* 23(4): 460–76.
199. Dyson, 'Managing Convergence', 247.
200. Wiesner, *Importing the American Way of War?*.
201. Noetzel and Schreer, 'All the Way?' 216.
202. Dyson, 'Managing Convergence'.
203. Interview with a ZMSBw researcher, Potsdam, 1 April 2015.
204. Interview with a former member of the Weiszäcker Commission, Berlin, 16 April 2015.
205. With the De Maziere reforms the Bundeswehr reduced its troops to 180,000.
206. Seibert, 'A Quiet Revolution'; Seaboyer and Wiesner, 'Budgeting for Defence'.
207. The Commission also proposed abolishing the separation between attack, stabilisation and support forces. Dyson, 'Managing Convergence'.
208. Dyson, 'German Defence Policy under the Second Merkel Chancellorship'.
209. 'In 2004 the InfoSysEEBw database was established at the *Einsatzfuehrungszentrum* (Bundeswehr Operations Command). At this stage, InfoSysEEBw developed a data collection tool for the storage of operational reports. The key step in the transformation of the lessons-learned process was the June 2008 creation of the *Einsatzfuehrungsstab* (Operations Staff) and section for *Einsatzauswertung*. The Army also profited from the increasing manpower allocated to the lessons-learned process, particularly in the German Army Forces Command, which is responsible for lessons learned.' Dyson, 'Managing Convergence', 257.
210. Ibid., 258.
211. A lack of responsiveness and incoherence in the weapons acquisition process was related to interservice competition and to the poor supervising skills of the Federal Auditing Office (BRH).
212. Dyson, 'Managing Convergence'. Even after ten years of mission in Afghanistan, 'strategic airlift needed to be completed'. Authors' interview, researcher on German military operation in Afghanistan, Potsdam, ZMSBw, 28 November 2019.
213. Authors' interview, former German general, Berlin, SWP, 16 April 2015.
214. Notwithstanding, the *Generalinspekteur* remained reliant upon the single services for information. Dyson, 'German Defence Policy under the Second Merkel Chancellorship'.
215. Authors' interview, researcher on German defence policy, Potsdam, ZMSBw, 26 November 2019.
216. Longhurst and Miskimmon, 'Same Challenges, Diverging Responses'.
217. Hellmann, 'Normatively Disarmed, But Self-Confident'.
218. Miskimmon, 'Falling into Line', 561.
219. Ibid.
220. Federal Ministry of Defence (2006), *White Paper 2006 on German Security Policy and the Future of the Bundeswehr*. Berlin: Federal Ministry of Defence.
221. Miskimmon, 'Falling into Line'.
222. Sakaki et al., *Reluctant Warriors*, 47.
223. Authors' interview, researcher on German defence policy, Potsdam, ZMSBw, 26 November 2019.
224. Seaboyer and Wiesner, 'Budgeting for Defence', 35.

225. Despite its abstention, Berlin allowed the use of (US) military bases and airspace for carrying out air strikes.
226. For a review, see A. Miskimmon (2012), 'German Foreign Policy and the Libya Crisis', *German Politics* 21(4): 392–410; Coticchia and F. N. Moro 'Peaceful Legislatures?', 482–503.
227. S. Brockmeier (2013), 'Germany and the Intervention in Libya', *Suvival* 55(6): 63.
228. Quoted in K. Oppermann (2012), 'National Role Conceptions, Domestic Constraints and the New "Normalcy" in German Foreign Policy: The Eurozone Crisis, Libya and Beyond', *German Politics* 21(4): 503. It is worth noting that Berlin increased the number of troops (as well as AWACS flights) in Afghanistan during the months of the intervention.
229. See Miskimmon, 'German Foreign Policy and the Libya Crisis'; Sakaki et al., *Reluctant Warriors*. For a broader analysis on the role of junior parties in German coalition government, see K. Oppermann and K. Brummer (2014), 'Patterns of Junior Partner Influence on the Foreign Policy of Coalition Governments', *British Journal of Politics and International Relations* 16(4): 555–71.
230. While generally supporting an international intervention in Libya, the German public opposed national participation (by 65 per cent). Bild poll, 20 March 2011, quoted in Miskimmon, 'German Foreign Policy and the Libya Crisis'.
231. As foreign minister, Westerwelle used his authority to openly emphasise his opposition to German intervention. See Brummer and Oppermann, 'Poliheuristic Theory'.
232. On the constant consensus-building on major foreign policy issues in German coalition government, see Noetzel and Schreer, 'All the Way?'
233. As was also defined by Westerwelle in his address to the Bundestag on 18 March 2011.
234. Authors' interview, journalist, expert on German defence, Berlin, 9 April 2015. For a different perspective, see M. Hansel and K. Oppermann (2016), 'Counterfactual Reasoning in Foreign Policy Analysis: The Case of German Nonparticipation in the Libya Intervention of 2011', *Foreign Policy Analysis* 12(2): 109–27.
235. Coticchia and Moro, 'Peaceful Legislatures?'
236. Allers, 'Are We Doing Enough?' 10.
237. Sakaki et al., *Reluctant Warriors*, 57.
238. J. Puglierin (2021), 'After Merkel: Why Germany Must End Its Inertia on Defence and Security', *European Council on Foreign Relations*, 15 January; F. Berenskötter and H. Stritzel (2021), '*Welche Macht darf es denn Sein?* Tracing "Power" in German Foreign Policy Discourse', *German Politics* 30(1): 31–50.
239. Almost 60 per cent according to Sakaki et al., *Reluctant Warriors*.
240. Sakaki et al., *Reluctant Warriors*, 57.
241. J. Eberle and A. Miskimmon (2021), 'International Theory and German Foreign Policy: Introduction to a Special Issue', *German Politics* 30(1): 1–13.
242. Quoted in Sakaki et al., *Reluctant Warriors*, 3. See also A. G. V. Hyde-Price (2015), 'The "Sleep-Walking Giant" Awakes: Resetting German Foreign and Security Policy', *European Security* 24(4): 600–16.
243. Quoted in F. Fogarty (2015), 'Backing the Bundeswehr: A Research Note Regarding the State of German Civil–Military Affairs', *Armed Forces & Society* 41(4): 742–55.
244. Quoted in Sakaki et al., *Reluctant Warriors*, 3.
245. Every year since 2005, some 75–83 per cent of Germans have shown a positive view towards the armed forces. Giegerich and Terhalle, *The Responsibility to Defend*, 45.
246. Sakaki et al., *Reluctant Warriors*, 57.
247. Of those polled in 2015, 30 per cent (against 6 per cent in 2014) perceived Germany's security situation as 'highly insecure'. Quoted in Sakaki et al., *Reluctant Warriors*, 49.
248. Authors' interview, former general staff officer, Ministry of Defence, Berlin, SWP, 26 November 2019.
249. Ibid.

250. Authors' interview, researcher on German military operation in Afghanistan, Potsdam, ZMSBw, 28 November 2019.
251. Authors' interview, German army officer, Potsdam, ZMSBw, 26 November 2019.
252. '*Globalisierung gestalten – Partnerschaften ausbauen – Verantwortung teilen*', *Konzept der Bundesregierung.*
253. Allers, 'Are We Doing Enough?'
254. Berenskötter and Stritzel, '*Welche Macht darf es denn Sein?*'
255. Quoted in Berenskötter and Stritzel, '*Welche Macht darf es denn Sein?*'
256. On the White Paper see, for example, D. Keohane (2016), *Constrained Leadership*, CSS ETH Zurich, available at: https://bit.ly/3QLtMGK.
257. In accordance with this concept, Merkel emphasised the need to enable partners, especially in Africa, to take security into their own hands. See Allers, 'Are We Doing Enough?'
258. The impact of what happened in Afghanistan is more clearly illustrated in the subsequent decision to provide support to local actors rather than being involved directly in military operations with boots on the ground. Authors' interview, German army officer, Potsdam, ZMSBw, 26 November 2019.
259. Keohane, *Constrained Leadership.*
260. Quoted in Giegerich and Terhalle, *The Responsibility to Defend*, 53.
261. Allers, 'Are We Doing Enough?'
262. Giegerich and Terhalle, *The Responsibility to Defend*, 47
263. Oppermann, 'National Role Conceptions', 503–4. See also K. Brummer and K. Opperman (2016), *Germany's Foreign Policy after the End of the Cold War: 'Becoming Normal?'* Oxford: Oxford Handbooks Online: Political Science, 1–30.
264. Policy Guidelines for the Indo Pacific (*Leilinien zum Indo-Pazifik*), 1 September 2020. It is interesting to note that a German national security strategy has never been drafted.
265. Giegerich and Terhalle, *The Responsibility to Defend*, 13.
266. The drill 'Pitch Black' occurred in August 2022, while the operation 'Rapid Pacific 2022' was the first mission by German air forces in the Pacific.
267. For a review of German foreign and defence policy towards China, see, among others, S. Biba (2021), 'Germany's Relations with the United States and China from a Strategic Triangle Perspective', *International Affairs* 97(6): 1905–24; R. Ulatowski (2022), 'Germany in the Indo-Pacific Region: Strengthening the Liberal Order and Regional Security', *International Affairs* 98(2): 383–402.
268. Puglierin, 'After Merkel'.
269. Giegerich and Terhalle, *The Responsibility to Defend*, 16.
270. On this point, see the Conclusions. As noted by Bunde: 'The puzzling question thus is not why the German government changed course so rapidly after the invasion but why it took it so long to acknowledge the changing contours of the European security environment. After all, critics point out, this watershed moment has been in the making for a long time.' Bunde, 'Lessons (to be) Learned?' 5. For a review of the debate, see also T. Bunde and S. Eisentraut (2022), *Zeitenwende for the G7: Insights from the Munich Security Index Special G7 Edition*, Munich Security Brief No. 3, Munich Security Conference; Mehrer, A. (2022) *Turn of phrase: Germany's Zeitenwende*, ECFR, available at: https://ecfr.eu/article/turn-of-phrase-germanys-zeitenwende/
271. Wales Summit Declaration, NATO (2014), available at: https://bit.ly/2QFyWVS.
272. Giegerich and Terhalle, *The Responsibility to Defend*, 52. Partly as a consequence of such national defence spending, the German defence industry focused especially on exports for generating returns.
273. D. Herszenhorn, (2019), 'Trump Threatens to Punish Germany over Military Spending', *Politico* 4 December, available at: https://politi.co/3Qv3J6Y.
274. On the recent debate on the war in Ukraine and German defence spending, see again the Conclusions. The next months and years will allow a proper assessment

of the impact of the war on German military spending. 'Europe's largest economy has committed to ramping up spending to meet the NATO-set target after years of neglect, going so far as to set up a €100 billion special fund to strengthen its military. [However] Government spending will continue to come just below target until 2027.' See C. Martuscelli (2022), 'Germany to Miss 2 percent NATO Defense Spending Target: Think Tank', 15 Augusti, *Politico Europe*, available at: https://www .politico.eu/article/germany-to-miss-2-percent-nato-defense-spending-target-think -tank.

275. Authors' interview, journalist, expert on German defence, Berlin, 9 April 2015.
276. Giegerich and Terhalle, *The Responsibility to Defend*, 61.
277. Ibid., 61. See also P. Carsten (2020), 'Die Bundeswehr hat problem, ihren ETAT richting zu investieren', *Frankfurter Allgemeine Zeitung*, 8 December.
278. Allers, 'Are We Doing Enough?'
279. For a review, see Eberle and Miskimmon, 'International Theory and German Foreign Policy'.
280. Sakaki et al., *Reluctant Warriors*, 3.
281. Ibid.
282. Sakaki et al. appropriately refer to the perpetual 'cordial indifference' (*freundliches Desinteresse*) – coined by former president Horst Köhler in 200 – to describe the German attitude towards security affairs. Sakaki et al., *Reluctant Warriors*, 49.
283. There were massive party-political disputes between the Conservatives and the Social Democrats right from the beginning of the legislative period, when the SPD decided to recall its tradition as Germany's true 'peace party'. Puglierin, 'After Merkel'.
284. The *Fähigkeitsprofil der Bundeswehr* planned the German armed forces after the White Paper.
285. Franke, 'A Tale of Stumbling Blocks and Road Bumps', 355.
286. Authors' interview, former German general, Berlin, SWP, 9 April 2015.
287. See Federal Minister of Defence, 'The directives on the top-level structure of the Bundeswehr', available at: https://www.bmvg.de/en/history/the-directives-on-the -top-level-structure-of-the-bundeswehr.
288. Seibert, 'A Quiet Revolution'.
289. Ibid. Air forces also suffered cuts, both in Tornados and Typhoons.
290. Sakaki et al., *Reluctant Warriors*, 3.
291. On this point, see the *Eckpuntke für die Bundeswehr der Zukunft* (2019), which recently illustrated the capabilities required by the Bundeswehr, available at: https:// bit.ly/3Qsc23o.
292. Authors' interview, former general staff officer, Ministry of Defence, Berlin, SWP, 26 November 2019.
293. For an updated and comprehensive analysis of the Germany's main military assets, see, among others, the official website of the Bundeswehr, available at: https://www .bundeswehr.de/de, and the annual report of the ISS Military Balancem available at: https://www.iiss.org/publications/the-military-balance.
294. The report was published by the parliamentary commissioner for the armed forces, Hans-Peter Bartels. 'The army's readiness to deploy has not improved in recent years, but instead has got even worse', Mr. Bartels told reporters at a press conference in Berlin. 'At the end of the year, six out of six submarines were not in use. At times, not one of the 14 Airbus A-400M could fly,' he said. In 'German army problems "dramatically bad", report says', BBC News, February 2018, available at https://www .bbc.com/news/world-europe-43134896.

Chapter 5

Italy: The Intervention–Transformation Loop

5.1 The 'brave' new world of Italian defence policy

5.1.1 Interventions and doctrinal change from the Gulf War to Kosovo

Since 1991, the Italian armed forces have been deployed in multiple contexts and with varying levels of intensity. Notwithstanding the interventions described in Chapter 2 showed Italy's interest in participating in multilateral peacekeeping initiatives, the change that started in the 1990s is relevant from a quantitative and qualitative point of view.[1] Before the collapse of the Berlin Wall, Italy deployed military personnel to ten UN missions. By 2021, Italian soldiers had been involved in more than forty missions concurrently. While in 2005 more than 10,000 troops were deployed abroad, the same figure was fewer than 100 in 1990, just before the beginning of operation Desert Storm in Iraq.[2] As occurred in recent decades, also in 2022 Italy is the leading contributor of the Global North to UN peacekeeping operations.[3]

The beginning of this new phase is marked by the military intervention against Saddam Hussein in 1991. Indeed, Desert Storm represents a critical juncture in the history of Italian defence, which following the disappearance of bipolar constraints started to become constantly involved in military operations abroad in the following decades.[4] The path was taken in 1991, when alternative trajectories (that is, limiting Italy's contribution to missions abroad) were still possible. That moment shaped the main features of the Italian approach to military interventions, as well as for national defence as a whole. Military doctrine was deeply reshaped by – and in turn contributed to frame – these interventions, so much so that any analysis of these two elements should consider them closely. And nowhere this is more important than in the case of the (second) Gulf War, which effectively ushered this new era of interventionism.

Understanding the impact of the Gulf War on military – and, in particular, doctrinal – transformation, requires first that the stage is set in which the intervention occurred. The end of the Cold War certainly opened up a space for military activism, yet, as Germany proves, new margins of manoeuvre accompanied by pressure from the major ally were not per se sufficient to bring countries to active military deployment. Domestic aspects played a key role here together with past experiences. In this sense, the first juncture in Italian defence policy was the result of external and internal factors, whose combination created a context in which change could effectively occur and set a new trajectory for Italian defence policy, that is, a doctrine geared towards the need to maximise the effectiveness of out-of-area (that is, beyond the defence of national terri-tory) military operations. An era of an 'Italian approach to military opera-tions abroad' started. Thus, it is worth examining how such a path began, as well as its contents and consequences for the transformation of Italian defence and its doctrine.

In terms of domestic politics, the decision to intervene militarily as a part of the international coalition against Saddam Hussein was not pre-ordained, with divisions within the Italian cabinet and the disapproval of the parliamentary opposition. The result of rather complex negotia-tions led to embracing a 'humanitarian narrative' that mainly focused on 'diplomatic and peace frames'.[5] Such a storyline avoided additional criticism by the opposition by restraining the 'military exposure' of the operation to public opinion that opposed the intervention.[6] The rather limited tools available to the Italian parliament to monitor activities in the defence domain – again, a result of practices that emerged during the Cold War – allowed the cabinet to adopt important measures, such as the concession that military bases could be used by the United States for their operations, bypassing parliamentary scrutiny and the connected audience costs.[7] More broadly, in the fluid context characterised by the end of the Cold War – which would soon produce a radical reshaping of the political landscape in Italy with the transformation of the party system – there was conceptual space to create a new political lexicon where military interven-tions were labelled as 'police operations'.[8] This, on the one hand, allowed the reconciliation of Italian domestic preferences with international pres-sures by making interventions possible – and legitimate – under the Italian constitution. Article 11, in fact, 'prohibits war', but nevertheless contains a specific clause for 'limitations of sovereignty that may be necessary to support a world order to ensure peace and justice among the Nations'.[9] On the other hand, this move sidestepped the problematic implications of formally declaring a 'state of war', as required by the constitution.[10] Such 'juridical fiction'[11] – which allowed the executive to elude parliamentary discussion (also on the concession of bases) became a constant reference made by the Italian executive since Desert Storm onwards, and it was often connected to the common criticism of 'backing decisions already taken at international level',[12] a move aimed also at reducing attribution of responsibility for the national executive. In sum, the 'peace and humanitarian narrative' excluded the military dimension from public debate and limited parliamentary oversight, so fostering executive autonomy in addressing requests by allies, as well as threats and opportunities related to a new international scenario. Thus, Desert Storm can be viewed as a 'formative moment of juncture'[13] for Italian defence, which started to play the role of 'international peacekeeper',[14] sending troops almost everywhere. As we will see, the initial patterns of institutionalisation that followed these critical junctures are crucial to understanding the evolution of Italian defence in the 1990s and the new century.

Path dependence, by generating positive feedback of self-reinforcement, explains how the reverse of the trajectory would have been inherently difficult in the case of Italy. But before illustrating the mechanisms that reinforced the particular path we should also look at the legacies that contributed to the start and the trajectory of Italian post-Cold War military activism. Indeed, rather than affecting whether Italy intervened, legacies give insights on *how* (limited) previous military engagements – in particular, Lebanon – and the 1985 *Libro Bianco* (White Paper) contributed to reshaping military doctrine after the crucial war in Iraq. The operations undertaken in the 1980s, from Beirut to Hormuz, represented an important 'advantage' for Italy despite the bipolar constraints.[15] Some of the tenets that emerged from Lebanon were confirmed – and very much reinforced – by the operational experience in the Gulf War, notwithstanding the diversity of the environments. The 1985 White Paper had already highlighted that deployability and jointness were key features for military operations. The Gulf War confirmed the centrality of requirements such as intense logistical coordination among the services for effective 'power projection'. The inability to deploy the Italian navy carrier the *Garibaldi* in the operation – allegedly due to its inability to deploy in a short timeframe – showed how preparedness to rapidly deploy had become an essential tool for modern military forces. While use of land forces in combat (and combat-support operations) did not occur mostly for political reasons, army leaders at the time also understood how the very design of a conscription-based force was ill-suited to new operational requirements. This was especially the case if a rather large contingent had to be deployed, as the Italian armed forces had – from the 1970s – invested in creating relatively small special forces-like units with capabilities for extensive deployment (used in Lebanon) and left untouched the overall structure of the conscription-based land forces.[16]

The service least affected by legacies was the air force, as its aircraft were used in combat for the first time since the Second World War, with 226 raids undertaken in forty-two days. Here, the early operational experience had a key role in shaping the perception of the requirements necessary to operate in the new security environment. The major problem identified was a lack of resources. First, the fleet – composed mostly of Tornadoes – was different than that of the United States and other allies, which limited joint exercises and, thus, operations.[17] Secondly, notwithstanding the relatively limited contribution in the overall effort, the mission pretty much exhausted available stockpiles. Finally, and most importantly from a doctrinal perspective, the air force undertook a mission in a large multinational operation that required profound redesign of some of the key tenets of air operations, which had been mostly designed in the context of fighting an enemy with peer capabilities and geared towards air defence.

The 1991 document titled *New Defence Model* represents the first to embody this new course. The premise, as illustrated also by the events in the Gulf, was that threat dynamics had radically changed, with the armed forces now required to undertake different types of mission – ranging from peacekeeping to 'combat', although such a notion is not explicitly mentioned – in different areas of the world. While in 1991 peacekeeping was not yet as developed as it would become in the coming years, the window of opportunity was there for military leadership to try and condense in the document as well as the lessons of the 1980s. As we have seen in Chapter 2, Italy gradually started to deploy troops abroad in the Mediterranean in the 1980s, from Malta to Sinai, from the Red Sea to Lebanon. As was already clear in the 1985 White Paper, in 1991 the ability to rapidly – and effectively – deploy became the paramount requirement for the new armed forces, whatever the type of mission. The *New Defence Model* clearly connected the deployment of troops abroad to the need of 'maintaining stability'[18] in a new regional and international context marked by 'instability'.[19] Also the document embraced the 'peace narrative', emphasising the willingness to bring 'peace and stability'.[20] The Italian defence strategy started to be based on the concept of 'active prevention', thanks to the constant use of armed forces to address crises.

The implications of such a path were both doctrinal and, perhaps most importantly, related to force structure (see below). The notion of jointness, which intersects both dimensions, is evident in the *New Defence Model* with regard to the 'functions'[21] that armed forces should perform (mostly, deploying and operating together) and away from single service requirements. Of course, such a shift is harder to achieve in practice, but jointness is clearly becoming the new mantra of the Italian armed forces. In sum, Desert Storm illustrated needs already (at least partially) stated in the 1985 White Paper.[22] Thus, the *New Defence Model* selected a specific path for the evolution of Italian doctrine, focusing on 'deployability' and moving away from the static Cold War approach.[23] The Gulf War profoundly altered, then, the course of Italian armed forces' evolution.

The path taken was reinforced by interventions in Somalia and, even more, in the Balkans. This was made possible – differently from the Cold War – by the emergence of a bipartisan consensus on the use of the armed forces in missions devoted to restoring or maintaining peace undertaken within a multilateral framework. The largest political party that emerged from the demise of the PCI – the PDS (Democratic Party of Left) – abandoned its predecessor's scepticism towards military commitments and swiftly moved towards a liberal internationalist approach in which military missions were the cornerstone of the country's contribution to a more peaceful world.[24] In this political environment, and with parliamentary institutions rarely able to meaningfully affect discussion over missions as long as they could be framed as 'peace' operations, the trajectory in the direction of deployability and jointness moved relatively fast, with each mission giving substantial positive feedback on the chosen path. Indeed, the widespread use of the 'peace and humanitarian narratives' was established in the 1990s by all the governments and by the main parties that supported deployment abroad,[25] reinforcing the path that started with the 'police operation' in Iraq, and its 'patterns of social practices'.[26]

Somalia represents an important moment of Italian deployment. The Italian mission 'IBIS' – part of the United Nations Operation in Somalia (UNSOM, 1992–1994) – was in fact an early test for the armed forces in their attempt to recast their role. Deployment in Somalia was clearly linked to new post-Cold War objectives and was based on (some of) the tenets of the new doctrine espoused in *New Defence Model*: the ability to deploy rapidly in an ongoing severe civil conflict and manage a dramatic crisis that had a large humanitarian dimension deeply involving civilian population management, delivering aid within a complex, multilateral framework.[27]

Security and development were problematically interlinked in this operation. Thus, Italy fostered cooperation between the armed forces and diplomats to better understand the features of local scenarios.[28] In Somalia, Italy suffered its first casualties in combat operations since the Second World War.[29] After the United States decided to withdraw its forces, the Italian (and the international) operation – which experienced 'mission creep' towards peace enforcement due to rising violence on the ground – ended, representing a considerable failure for the United Nations and the whole international community. Regarding IBIS and its role in the development of post-Cold War Italian defence policy, four elements should be emphasised.

First, the Italian military contribution was not symbolic, but rather significant (especially for the army) in terms of responsibilities on the ground and even in combat operations, where Italy suffered causalities against local militias. Italian armed forces definitely entered into the post-bipolar scenario of the 'war amongst the people',[30] but the overall structure of national forces and their suitability for the new theatres of intervention appeared to be lacking, similar to what happened in 1991 in Iraq.[31] Secondly, the Italian mission focused particularly on specific tasks, such as training of local forces and civil–military cooperation to enable effective deployment of aid. These aspects – along with a considerable restraint in the use of force – would have shaped the 'Italian way to missions abroad' also in the next decades.[32] Thirdly, such activities – and the overall military low profile – were consistent with the humanitarian narrative adopted by political leaders. Indeed, despite the violence on the ground,[33] the 'peace storyline' framed again the national debate while the parliament played a very limited role, formally approving the operation at its conclusion. Finally, the clashes with allies on how to better deal with local militias revealed a sort of national approach to 'counter-insurgency' that rejected the open military confrontation with insurgents advocated by Washington. Although the devastating failure of the US approach and the somewhat positive results obtained by the Italian more comprehensive perspective, any strategic reflection, or manual or documents, were elaborated and systematised after the intervention. The removal of any military dimensions from the 'peace mission' public narrative persisted.

On the whole, the mission contributed to underpinning the trajectory taken since Desert Storm and fostered further development of a national way to use armed forces in contexts of conflict. The interventions in the Balkans in the 1990s provided additional reinforcing feedback for the path adopted by the new Italian defence policy. Those missions were – again – framed as international missions to restore and preserve peace.[34] Italy was extremely active in the region, deploying troops for the peacekeeping mission in Bosnia after the war and for addressing crises (in 1991 and especially in 1997 with operation 'Alba') in Albania, leading a successful multinational force there that contributed to halting the surge of the civil war.[35] The missions involved thousands of Italian soldiers on the ground, fostering the New Defence Model along the way of 'deployability', representing relevant challenges for the armed forces but also confirming the new defence goals set by the strategic document in 1991: providing peace and security in the regional context. The multilateral framework of the missions, their 'humanitarian purposes', and the limited violence against Italian troops sustained the 'peace' narrative along the 1990s in the Balkans.

However, while this storyline guaranteed relatively wide consensus among political parties and the public, the use of the air force in combat operations in Kosovo represented a very different context. Italian public opinion did not sustain the air strikes while street protests occurred.[36] These were, in any case, unable to avoid or stop the intervention, although they contributed to further solidify the need to frame interventions as 'peace missions', almost always excluding the word 'war' from the political – and military – lexicon, similarly to what happened in Germany.[37] At the same time, the parliament (differently from the Bundestag) was again excluded from its oversight, voting the intervention only after some months. In the case of the Kosovo mission, the government crafted the term 'advanced defence'.[38] Once again, the 'peace narrative' was instrumental in avoiding closer scrutiny by the parliament, evading possible audience costs and opposition by junior parties (Greens and Communists) that supported the centre-left government but did not sustain the military intervention. Thus, narrative and limited if not absent parliamentary oversight allowed executive autonomy in defence policy. Yet, war was definitely there, at least in the early phases, as airpower played a relevant role in the missions in Kosovo, as it did previously in Bosnia. In fact, Italy's contribution to Operation 'Deliberate Force' in Bosnia – with the objective of limiting the ability of Bosnian Serb forces to operate and launch attacks on other safe areas – involved a limited number of sorties (thirty-two, about 1 per cent of the total NATO sorties from 30 August to 14 September 1995).

Clearly, Operation Allied Force represented a spearhead in air force involvement, with over 1,000 sorties, including combat missions (representing less than 4 per cent of NATO sorties from March to June 1999).[39] In this context, operational realities are decoupled from narratives and – in turn – there is a constraint in doctrinal development as 'combat' missions remain marginal in any public document or declaration.[40] Often, the effect is to severely limit the ability to elaborate autonomous national doctrine. Downloading of existing doctrine at the NATO level – for instance – largely characterises the experience of the Italian air force. In a survey conducted over hundreds of air force officers, responders argue that NATO doctrine and interactions with allies are far more relevant than national doctrine in shaping learning.[41] Quite interestingly, most of the learning that occurs on the ground or in the air seems to be encapsulated in the 'memories' of the units that operate, and they affect their internal reflections and training more than is being shared and constitute the basis of national doctrinal development.[42] This tendency is less evident – yet not absent – in land operations, from Somalia to the Balkans. However, Italy published a strategic document (*New Forces for a New Century*) only in 2001 (before 9/11), ten years after the *New Defence Model*, thus confirming again a (very) limited national reflection on defence issues.

New Forces for a New Century (2001), which represents the culmination of reflections over the eventful decade that had just ended, illustrates the trajectory taken by Italian defence after Desert Storm and reinforced by the missions undertaken in the 1990s as well as by the reforms adopted, (see below). The document acknowledges the 'new role'[43] of Italy in the post-bipolar era, corroborating the relevant of multilateral frameworks to provide international missions with 'peace, security and protection of human rights'.[44] Above all, *New Forces* emphasised the need for 'deployability',[45] mobility, and protection and force. The strategic document, which identifies the features of the 'national way to peace operations',[46] distinguishes between traditional peacekeeping operations, police missions, peace-building operations and humanitarian aid. In other words, far from the bipolar era, the doctrine – within ten years – has fully embraced a new military role for Italy thanks to its 'multinational peace interventions'. [47]

To sum up, the decade that followed the end of the Cold War witnessed an extraordinary transformation in the Italian armed forces. The way doctrine evolved throughout this decade was shaped by several factors. A rather permissive institutional setting at the beginning was followed by the emergence of a consensus on the overall objectives and narratives among major Italian parties that pushed for active multilateral engagement under the banner of 'peace' operations. Every mission had the effect of reinforcing the doctrine that underpinned them: objectives and *modi operandi* (presented in the 1991 *New Defence Model* document) were redefined along a trajectory that eventually led to *New Forces for a New Century*. However, narratives also constrained the space for learning as an essential tool of doctrinal development as well as imposing specific caveats or RoE for adopting a military low profile, leading to a partial decoupling of operational realities from doctrinal evolution. After the juncture occurred along the collapse of the bipolar era, the trajectory of Italian defence has been reinforced through the feedback derived by the constant military activism of the 1990s, limiting the space for alternative paths.

5.1.2 Towards a 'New Defence Model': Italian reforms in the 1990s

The abovementioned national doctrines and military operations abroad illustrate the stunning transformation of Italian defence policy in the 1990s, following the path of 'deployability'. But how and to what extent did Italian military organisation evolve and adapt along the new path? Leaving behind the Cold War approach was not easy, after decades of a 'static' defence approach. However, in the words of a former minister, Italian defence 'changed a lot' while the level of adaptation of its whole structure has been 'considerable' in recent decades.[48] The literature has identified, along the 'power projection', three main elements through which it is possible to assess the degree of variation that occurred in the organisation of Italian defence: professionalisation of forces and the end of conscription, jointness among services, and 'the search for a post-Cold War equilibrium' in defence budgets and force structure.[49]

Also for force structure and the organisational dimension, the analysis of such transformation should start from the critical juncture of 1991. Indeed, operation Desert Storm 'paved the way for the beginning of reforms in Italian defence'.[50] The mission revealed the extent of evolution required to properly follow the selected path on the need for greater coordination among the services for effective 'power projection'. The interventions by members of the armed forces before the parliamentary commissions after the war well illustrate such necessity.[51] On the whole, 'Desert Storm highlighted the need to professionalise forces, enhancing the expeditionary capabilities'.[52]

The national strategic debate started from such considerations. Indeed, the *New Defence Model*[53] deeply focused on power-projection capabilities as a main trait of the new Italian defence policy. To sustain the deployment of troops in military missions aimed at guaranteeing stability in the changed international scenario, the document pleaded for structural changes in the Italian armed forces: a reduction in personnel, qualitative improvements, readiness and jointness. Above all, the document developed a new defence model that was considerably different from the approach adopted during the Cold War. In fact, the document released in 1991 paved the way for the process of suspension of conscription, thus moving towards a professional model. In other words, jut few months after the end of the Cold War, Italy decided to deeply renovate its defence model, abandoning the draft. Once again, path dependent mechanisms are vital to understand such a process.

As stated in Chapter 2, the 1985 White Paper (elaborated after the intervention in Lebanon) already considered mass mobilisation to be inadequate for the new strategic needs. Thus, Italian doctrine in the 1980s focused on the possibility of changing the structure of forces, with smaller units composed of volunteers capable of rapid deployment. In other words, the text had already conceptually opened the door to the likelihood of the end of conscription. On this path, after the juncture of Desert Storm and the collapse of the bipolar era, Italy was able to start on significant change. Initially, a mixed system – between volunteers and conscripts – was considered. The *New Defence Model* distinguished the forces among units (mainly volunteers) as quickly deployable aboard, conscripts as 'second forces', and a reserve for a general mobilisation. In 1995, law No. 549 created the mixed system of conscripts and volunteers.

With Law Decree No. 196 of 12 May 1995,[54] Italy aimed to transform the armed forces' recruitment and promotion system, moving towards an all-volunteer force (see Graph 5.1). But, following the publication of the *New Defence Model*, the aim was that of converting Italian forces into all-volunteer services. Only in the new century would Italy have been formally able to reach such goal (see below). The role of '*volontari in serivizio permamente*' (VSP, volunteers in permanent service) was created. The VSP was a career soldier who, after five or six years of non-permanent service in the armed forces, was then offered a permanent contract. The number of VSPs in the armed forces was fixed at 23,586 by law No. 196.[55] The number of VSPs has increased across time, exceeding the number of non-permanent volunteers in 2010.[56] This would have deeply affected the problem of aging in the Italian armed forces, especially in the army (see below). [57]

In the 1990s the process of reforms continued, with the main purpose of reducing quantity while enhancing the overall level of quality of forces. Clearly, the constant military involvement in missions abroad, from Somalia to the Balkans, 'pushed for a more efficient organization'[58] of the Italian armed forces, which was still lacking in terms of assets and required an 'organizational re-structuring of forces' to properly sustain a trajectory of 'deployability'. For this reason, Italian policymakers adopted manifold reforms in the first decade of the post-Cold War era. The *Carabinieri* became a new 'armed force' (Law No. 78, 2000) along with the navy, air force and army. Such mixed military–police units played a crucial role in the missions, especially in the Balkans with the MSU, the multinational specialised unit constantly engaged in peacekeeping and humanitarian operations. The Carabinieri became a central asset for Italian military deployability and the structure of forces changed accordingly.[59] Within such a process of evolution, and modernisation, specific attention should also be devoted to the formal admission of women into the armed forces (Law No. 380, 1999).

In sum, the reforms purposely modified the composition and the organisation of the forces to sustain the new active national defence policy, which required a rapid evolution to address the growing needs from the ground. Thus, the military involvement in multinational operations pushed for change, giving reinforcing feedback to the trajectory followed after 1991, while the public and parliamentary debates on significant reforms – such as the end of conscription – remained paradoxically limited,[60] in line with the scarce oversight that the assembly played in the case of Italy. Timing also played a role, because specific circumstances following the 1985 White Paper opened the door to the process that led to all-volunteer forces, while the path – after Desert Storm, the *New Defence Model* and the military operations of the 1990s – became difficult to reverse.

However, the legacy of the past is also crucial in understanding the obstacles that Italy addressed in such process, which indeed can be considered as 'incomplete'.[61] In fact, both the aims of jointness among services and the expected equilibrium in terms of budget and forces were not (completely or even partially) reached. Overcoming the heritage of the Cold War was complex, from swiftly reducing the number of troops, restructuring the composition of forces (for example, by reducing officials), to fostering a balanced budget (mainly through a drastic reduction in the costs connected to personnel).[62]

As illustrated in Chapter 2, the 'defensive posture'[63] of Italian defence adopted in the post-Second World War era clearly shaped the structure of forces mainly directed to confront the menace of the Warsaw Pact in the northeast of the country. Chapter 2 has already mentioned the failed attempts to (a) modify the unbalanced budget, connected to a never-ending gap between force size and financial resources[64]; and (b) a more effective interservice integration.

On this last point, some results were achieved in the 1990s. In 1997, under the pressure from Minister of Defence Andreatta, and just before the Italian-led mission in Albania ('Alba'), Italy approved Law No. 25 that reformed the chiefs of staff (*Stato Maggiore della Difesa*), with the aim of fostering synergy cooperation among forces while enhancing power in the hands of the chairman of the joint chiefs of staff, who was formerly just *primus inter pares*. The *Comando Operativo di Vertice Interforze* (COI, Joint Operational Command) was designed in 1997 as the main framework to manage missions abroad, aiming also to foster jointness in the process of collection and analysis of lessons learned.

However, beyond the 1997 reform, the level of actual interoperability remained limited, as in personnel management with each service reluctant to concede their autonomy. Since the 1980s, the Italian defence policy pleaded for greater interservice planning and coordination, also to avoid waste and duplication, but the results were still negligible. The transformation of Italian defence in the 1990s along the path of deployability introduced – as seen – some novelties, but the opposition to enhancing the '*interforzizzazione*' persisted.[65] Also from the perspective of military culture, the adoption of a different mind-set that embraces jointness was a task that would require time.[66] In sum, there was a stiff bureaucratic resistance across the services that hindered such innovations.

The same occurred in the search for equilibrium, in terms of composition of forces and defence budget. Italy slowly started to reduce the overall number of troops, transforming in few years the Cold War structure. Nevertheless, the kind of decrease that actually occurred was gradual especially in comparison with other European countries that undergone the same process,[67] with notable differences among the different components of personnel (Graph 5.1). While overall numbers were more than halved (by 56 per cent), troops (67 per cent) and NCOs (63 per cent) decreased far more than officers (40 per cent) in three decades since 1990. This asymmetry in the process of downsizing started immediately: all services tried to carefully balance size reduction by cuts that were deemed more sustainable in light of their internal political arrangements, besides specific force requirements, with officers being more able to hold on to previous levels. This was due to better positioning of officers in lobbying, but also to the nature of their longer-term tenure in office, which made redundancy very difficult to address.

Also, the defence budget (see Graph 5.2) decreased until the middle of the 1990s, but besides overall expenditures what was more problematic was that the lack of internal balance. More than two-thirds of the expenses were in most years devoted exclusively to personnel, despite the abovementioned cuts to the number of troops, and this left limited room of manoeuvre and flexibility in managing economic resources.[68] Restraint in the possibility of allocating resources towards the construction of the more deployable force envisioned in doctrinal documents is largely due to this stickiness of resource distribution. In the early 1990s, a path was taken on defence expenditures that would have then continued in the following decades.

It is worth noting that Italy tried to adapt (also under resource constraints) while addressing the complex legacy of the Cold War structure, especially concerning the composition of forces. But – differently from the military activism that quickly became the main trait of the new path of deployability – the overall restructuring of forces was much slower and a suitable equilibrium in terms of resource allocation was not reached. Thus, changes occurred in the 1990s but the legacy of the Cold War – along with opposition by the military – imposed a very slow process of organisational evolution in the first decade of the post-bipolar era. However, as illustrate above, the reforms adopted since 1991 were manifold and relevant. At the end of the 1990s, the document *New Forces for a New Century* (2001)[69] conceived all these reforms as the premise to address the challenges of the new century. Still, greater 'synergy' and interoperability[70] among services and a better equilibrium in terms of force composition and budget were strongly suggested.[71]

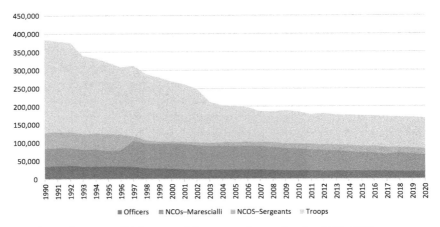

Graph 5.1 Structure of Italian armed forces: numbers and ranks, 1990–2020
Source: Authors' elaboration based on Italian official documents.[72]

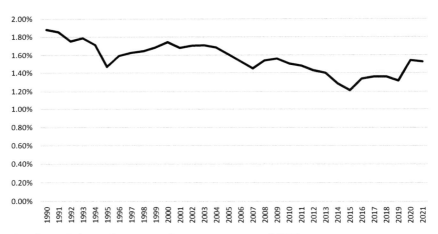

Graph 5.2 Italian military expenditure as percentage of GDP, 1990–2020
Source: Authors' elaboration based on SIPRI yearbook data.

5.2 Italian defence and the war on terror

5.2.1 Italian doctrinal change in the new century

The attacks of 11 September 2001, altered the global security environ-ment. External factors, the terrorist threats and – most decisively – the American response in the following years, are the primary factors that cre-ated a juncture ripe for change. In terms of doctrinal change, US-led poli-cies that evolved as a response to these attacks redefined the very objectives that armed forces should achieve with their operations, by expanding them to include radical reshaping of political and socioeconomic settings. As we have seen, Italy arrived at this juncture with the large baggage of experiences accumulated in the 1990s. Assessing the trajectory of change in this decade, characterised by the three among the largest, most dramatic and complex operations undertaken by the Italian armed forces since the Second World War (that is, Iraq, Lebanon and, especially, Afghanistan),[73] requires careful consideration– besides the role of allies – of how strategic narratives crafted in the previous decade and the lessons accumulated in missions had reshaped the Italian trajectory of military doctrine. These factors – and constraints – led throughout the decade to the development of a doctrinal blend that is composed by a national re-elaboration of the new strategic and operational environment. As for the whole period of analysis, clear identification of the doctrinal developments is partially hindered by the lack of documents, which per se represents an interesting feature of how policies related to armed forces rarely become a matter of debate beyond very small circles.

How and to what extent did the change in international context after 9/11 and the war on terror shape the trajectory adopted by the post-bipolar Italian defence? Once again, path dependent mechanisms allow the illustration of such processes. External and domestic drivers, along with the crucial operational experience collected in the pre-2001 years, affected the path. The impact of strategic narratives on doctrine, as we observed above, is to delimit and constrain the space for elaboration of doctrine by placing normative boundaries. The exclusion of the concept of 'war' – and more operationally, even the explicit recognition of the centrality of 'combat' – in contemporary use of armed forces constrains development of doctrine that includes reflections on the full range of operations that the armed forces are likely to undertake. The case of COIN doctrine is exemplary: while Italy found itself operating in a context characterised, at least in some phases, by intense violence and by harsh contrast with insurgents, the kinetic dimension has always been underestimated or removed from the debate.[74] Quite remarkably, this 'omission' occurred also in the highly intense and bloody post-2001 missions: the peace narrative that was crafted after Desert Storm continued to shape the debate over Italian missions even in the combat scenarios of Afghanistan and Iraq. As widely illustrated by the literature,[75] the narratives – while instrumental in collecting public and parliamentary support (thus avoiding scrutiny) – influenced formal goals, but also structures and assets of the missions, which often suffered the consequences of the gap between the 'humanitarian' and light composition of the operation and the level of violence on the ground. For instance, the absence of armoured vehicles and helicopters, as well as the protection of bases from external attacks, were the direct causes of casualties among Italian soldiers in Iraq. The case of the devastating attack in Nasiriya (12 November 2003),[76] which killed nineteen Italians (of twenty-eight victims), dramatically highlights the effects of such a gap between 'peace narrative' and the actual context on the ground.

Therefore, the Italian narrative, despite the features of the missions undertaken during the 'war on terror', was *not* altered. But the trajectory of Italian military doctrine in this phase is represented by how legacies from the previous decade were reinterpreted to fit with the master frame. In general terms, there is a remarkable degree of continuity in doctrinal development that seems at least partly in contrast to the new threat environment, the demands coming from the major ally, and operational requirements. Again, the example of the development of a COIN strategy is illustrative of this trend. Starting in 2006–2007, the American armed forces, starting with the army and marines that provided the bulk of troops in Iraq and Afghanistan, underwent a thorough recalibration of their approach to what was then growing violence and a strengthened insurgency by adopting two connected changes to existing strategy. The new focus was on increasing troop numbers on the ground (the so-called 'boots on the ground') to guarantee more security to the local population. Provision of such security was intended in broad terms as including, besides training and support of local security forces, also basic means of livelihood and access to services such as health and education. This would have provided support for US troops and their local allies, while reducing the backing for insurgents.[77] Undertaking such large-scale operations required combining combat operations to degrade insurgent capabilities – which maintained a central place in American activities both in Iraq and Afghanistan – with 'non-kinetic' activities that include a variety of actors (from civilian government agencies to IOs and NGOs) and practices.

In this context, the evolving Italian doctrine is based on a re-adaptation of the American one.[78] COIN is often *not* mentioned as a key activity undertaken by the army in this phase, rather the focus is on how Italian units adopted a population-centric approach. Some essential traits of this approach are 'understanding of human conditions, humbleness, courtesy and attention towards the local population', representing 'the true distinctive traits in the behaviour of every Italian soldier'.[79] Continuity with previous experiences was also explicitly stressed: there is a direct thread that connects the Balkans with Lebanon and Afghanistan where the nature of the Italian approach is unchanged. At the same time, missions also fostered the transformation of Italian defence in terms of the public image of the armed forces, thanks to 'compelling narratives' on 'good Italians'.[80] Actually, on the ground, civilian–military cooperation (CIMIC) is the prescribed tool for achieving the key objectives of missions whose objective is to implement 'peace plan(s)' as it allows the effective coordination of several activities (starting with the provision of humanitarian aid and going through different reconstruction phases and projects) under a security umbrella guaranteed by the military forces on the ground.

The UN mission in Lebanon (UNIFIL) is a relevant example for the Italian CIMIC.[81] Indeed, in southern Lebanon, where Italian forces guided the international operation after the 2006 war between Israel and Hezbollah, the civil–military cooperation represented a core task of the intervention, involving both military units but also where dozens of NGOs active on the ground.[82] There was a huge difference with the previous more contested and controversial mission in Iraq, where the vast majority of Italian NGOs, in line with widespread public opposition to the operation, were not present, avoiding in any case a strict cooperation with the military during the occupation. More interestingly, the lessons learnt from the Iraqi mission – in terms of force protection in high-intensity scenarios – were carefully considered before sending additional troops in Lebanon in 2006, providing all the adequate military assets in a very robust operation.[83] In other words, the constant military involvement on the ground helped Italian defence to adjust and adapt approaches and tools, even despite a limited level of public strategic reflection, which was generally focused – in line with the main peace narrative – on non-kinetic aspects.

Indeed, contrary to COIN (notwithstanding the relevant experience in Somalia), the centrality of CIMIC in Italian doctrine is highly institutionalised: in 2002, the army started a Joint Multinational CIMIC HQ to be commanded by Italy, which in 2004 became the CIMIC Group South (CGS), a NATO structure in which five other southern and eastern European countries participate. As seen, the peculiar role of the Carabinieri also assumed centrality, both in doctrine and in military missions, for guaranteeing local security and for training and mentoring of local forces (which also represents a central asset for any successful COIN operations).

On the whole, the post-2001 era emphasised how missions represented – in the words of a former Minister of Defence – 'a driver for change'. [84] The deployment in high-intensity scenarios – such as Iraq and especially Afghanistan – has been defined as a 'gym for generations of Italian soldiers' and for the whole national defence, in terms of assets, approaches and communication: 'all changed in 20 years because (the US to begin with)[of] the out of area missions'.[85] Clearly, alliances and international events and pressures played a crucial role in the new century in fostering further the Italian military activism started in 1991, while the 'good performance of armed forces abroad aligned such process' as well as the international demands.[86]

Thus, missions have been crucial for the transformation of Italian armed forces. Moreover, differently from other European countries, the latest Italian chiefs of armed forces have had years experience of missions, starting in the 1990s and developed – with more demanding tasks – in the new century. [87] Constant operational activities in complex scenarios promoted a process of change, from training to technology. An interesting example is the evolution of recognition on the ground in Afghanistan: initially on foot, then with armoured vehicles and, finally, with drones.[88] Also the tactical deployment of armoured vehicles and the 'battle against IED' well illustrates the lessons learnt derived from experience on the ground, from the need to develop new vehicles to their disposition (for example, at the beginning and at the end of the convoy).[89]

Following such evolution, doctrine was also modified, but still along the path started after the critical juncture of Desert Storm. In the post-9/11 period, Italy drafted a White Paper (2002) and other relevant documents that allow understanding of the evolution of Italian doctrine in the first decade of the new century. As mentioned above, CIMIC and training played a crucial role in the 'national way' to peace missions described by the documents. More importantly, the 'deployability' of forces confirms its centrality also in the new century. The 'awareness of the new international responsibility' of Italy is the premise of the 2002 White Paper, which focuses especially on the management of international crises through multilateral frameworks as main characteristic of Italian defence.[90] 'Expeditionary' capabilities are then illustrated by following documents as the vital need for better contrast with the multidimensional menaces to Italian and international security.[91] Specific attention is also devoted to information technology and net centric capabilities to enhance 'situational awareness' and provide 'information superiority'.[92] Finally, the description of 'high-intensity operations' that also require 'combat capabilities',[93] emphasises the impact of the collected experience in the first years of the century, from Bagdad to Kabul, breaking (at least verbally, because on the ground Italian soldiers have been fighting enemies since 1991) the taboo of 'combat' interventions. While the public debate remained fully connected within the storyline of the peace missions, the national doctrine gradually reflected in depth along the lessons learnt collected for almost two decades, pushing for the development of all possible 'expeditionary' capabilities in a new security context.

In conclusion, the path developed in the 1990s by Italian defence policy consolidated across time, moving definitely away from the static Cold War approach. In the new century, the trajectory of Italian defence has been developed ahead of pressing requests for solidarity made by allies (Afghanistan and Iraq) and international organisations (Lebanon). Despite involvement in the most complex, dangerous and bloodiest missions under-taken since the Second World War, the 'peace narrative' persisted,[94] while parliamentary oversight remained absolutely limited. Italian soldiers fought in southern Iraq and western Afghanistan, carrying out very different tasks, but the Italian parliament rarely monitored in detail the operations on the ground, leaving again huge executive autonomy. Finally, the collected expe-riences in the 1990s, from Somalia to Kosovo, allowed Italy to promote further 'expeditionary capabilities' to address major threats.

5.2.2 Italian armed forces Italy in the new century

The first decade of the new century strongly reinforced the trajectory of Italian defence policy along deployability and power projection lines. At the same, the variation that occurred in the organisation of Italian defence did not proceed in same way. While the professionalisation of forces was a significant result obtained at the end of a process starting with the *New Defence Model*, jointness among services and the wished equilibrium in defence budget and force structure were far from being obtained.

Laws Nos. 331/2000 and 226/2004 formally suspended conscription and Italy has finally had all-volunteer armed forces since 2005. Law No. 226/2004 amended the previous Acts, such as Law No. l. 549 that cre-ated a mixed system of conscripts and volunteers, modifying the selected categories of volunteers by introducing volunteers for one year or four years. The overall number of forces has been further reduced, designing models at 230,000/250,000 units (Legislative Decree No. 215/2001, then 190,000 – and 30,000 civilians – to be reached before 2021). Nonetheless, as highlighted by Graph 5.1, while the number of troops decreased signifi-cantly in the first years of the century, the reduction was almost halted and it did not actually occur, thus not solving the imbalance in the composi-tion of forces. Only the reform later adopted by the Monti's government in 2012 – which pushed for a model based on 150,000 units (see below) – revealed the urgent need to achieve the original goal of restructuring pro-fessional forces the post-Cold War. Relatedly, due to the heavy burden of personnel-related costs within the Italian budget this has never been properly addressed.

All the documents published in this decade well illustrate how the organisational evolution of Italian defence policy still suffered obstacles that are yet to be overcame. For instance, the 2002 White Paper empha-sises the gap between the manifold military operations undertaken by Italian forces abroad and a shrinking and unbalanced budget, with a preponderance of costs dedicated to personnel. The *Chief of the Italian*

Defence Staff Strategic Concept (2005) asked for greater interoperability, while the document *Investire in Sicurezza* (Investing in Security, 2005), stressed the risks of the 'usability' of the military instrument due to the abovementioned never-ending problems in the organisation.

The post-2006 downsizing of resources devoted to Italian defence worsened (due to the different elasticity of the items) the asymmetric structure of the Italian budget and the costs related to personnel reached a peak of 70 per cent of the overall figure. Such disproportionateness was later accentuated by the financial crisis. At the end of the decade the item '*esercizio*' (functioning/operations, which, for instance, was crucial to sustain training activities and maintenance) represented only 10 per cent of the whole budget. Clearly, the sustainability of the entire Italian defence, and especially of its capability to effectively send troops abroad, was at risk with such figures. However, the trajectory of deployability, was marked by self-enforcing mechanisms: 'extra-budget was specifically devoted to missions and industrial investments constituted at least a partial remedy as in recent years it funded respectively essential operational requirements (with deployments representing a key moment for "testing" as well as actual use) and innovation in equipment.'[95] In other words, a specific budget devoted to the missions abroad allowed the gaps suffered in the maintenance and other expenditures directly connected with the need to prepare and maintain operational readiness to be addressed. Thus, operations became crucial by themselves to guarantee the sustainability of Italian armed forces.

On the one hand, the 'expeditionary approach' remained the main asset of military transformation, fostering also the advancement of military technology (for example, moving from the F-104 to the Eurofighter) and digitalisation of forces,[96] pushing Rome to develop its procurement to support the engagement on the ground that required new and adequate assets.[97] On the other hand, the organisational problems remained, and the Cold War legacy, along with internal opposition to reforms in the field of force composition, budget and jointness, hindered the 'complete' realisation of the *New Defence Model*. At the same time, some relevant changes occurred. For instance, the Centre for Defence Innovation (*Centro Innovazione Difesa*, CID) was created in 2009 to develop doctrine and lessons learnt at the joint level. The demanding operations undertaken at the beginning of the new century also shaped the COI that involve a growing number of personnel who have acquired experience on the ground.[98]

On the whole, the most challenging period for post-Second World War Italian defence highlighted how the process of transformation of Italian force structure and budget still suffered pitfalls. The stunning evolution of deployability and the development of the path adopted since 1991 was only partially supported by the reorganisation of forces at domestic level.

However, the missions (that is, with extra budget) contributed to maintaining the sustainability of the Italian military instrument, in a context constantly marked by scant public and parliamentary debate on reforms in the defence sector.

5.3 Italian defence after Libya

5.3.1 Re-assessing objectives and approaches: Italian doctrine after 2011

External and domestic factors contributed to radically reshaping the environment of Italian defence policy in 2011. The Arab uprisings contributed to create a situation of instability in the Mediterranean that affected Italian security in multiple ways. The controversial intervention in Libya,[99] and the enduring conflict that followed, created a new central front for Italy, increasing also scepticism among political leaders and public opinion on the effectiveness of military interventions.[100] Moreover, the end of the operations in Iraq and Afghanistan (and their substantial and dramatic failures) enhanced such views, also promoting a strategic reflection on Italian foreign and defence policy after decades of military interventions abroad.[101] Subsequently to Italian military involvement in Iraq against ISIL (2014),[102] Italian policymakers identified the need to 'pivot to Africa', as the region most directly affecting Italian security, fostering re-location of troops towards Sahel and North Africa.[103]

The domestic political landscape also changed radically in 2011. First, the economic crisis hit the country very hard,[104] leading to a 'technocratic' government (the Monti cabinet) that enacted profound budget cuts and a large-scale defence reform (see below) targeting a cost-effective allocation of resources. Secondly, the main national security concerns – still focused on terrorism (especially after the rise of ISIL and the dozens of attacks on European soil) – pertain to the issue of migration, which became dominant in Italian public debate, even supporting the use of armed force to reduce instability in the region and to directly stop flows of migrants in the Mediterranean Sea.[105] Thirdly, after the 'populist storm' of the 2018 elections,[106] the Five Star Movement (M5S) and the Northern League (LN) created the 'Yellow–Green government': the first executive in western Europe without mainstream parties. Therefore, 'populist and anti-establishment forces' guided Italian foreign and defence policy.[107]

Despite these transformations that occurred at international and domestic level, the trajectory of Italian defence was *not* altered and path-dependence mechanisms still played a role in shaping its main contents.

Before looking at the evolution of doctrine in the post-2011 era, we should emphasise four crucial aspects that emerge from analysis of post-2011 Italian defence.

First, the perceived Italian military retrenchment – after the reduction in troops deployed with the end of the missions related to the 'war on terror' (particularly Afghanistan) and questions over the prudence of committing forces in other contexts (that is, Syria and Libya)[108] despite international requests by allies – encouraged a debate over a possible significant change in Italian defence policy after decades of 'activism'.[109] However, recent research has empirically shown that despite a period of reduction in the military presence abroad, 'the number of missions per year has continued to rise, and both the number of troops and the funds dedicated to deployment have not decreased significantly', while the growing emphasis on military interventions in the *Mediterraneo allargato* ('Enlarged Mediterranean') compensated 'for a progressive disengagement from other areas such as the Balkans, Middle East, and Asia (Afghanistan).'[110] Thus, we cannot talk about an inversion in the trend of Italian military engagement abroad, and the path of Italian 'deployability' remains solid.

Secondly, and relatedly, the missions undertaken in these years, from Libya to northern Iraq, from naval operations in the Mediterranean to the new interventions in Sahel, did not diverge from the traditional trajectory adopted decades ago. On the contrary, those missions again reinforced the path, consolidating it despite relevant international and domestic changes. In fact, even after decades of combat operations, the 'peace narrative' has still shaped public debate. Nonetheless, air strikes against a former colony, the frames of humanitarianism and multilateralism deeply affected Italian political debate over the mission in Libya, paradoxically removing the military dimension from the discussion.[111] Both the government[112] and the opposition[113] fully shared the 'humanitarian narrative' while – as later revealed by the air force chief of staff – an overall 'blanket of silence' affected public communication during the mission.[114] In the years following the end of Gadhafi's regime, while violence and instability erupted, Italy maintained a military presence on the ground, but avoided a large-scale operation, because, in the words of the then Undersecretary of Defence Rossi, Italian 'humanitarian concern and solidarity were better illustrated by a field hospital deployed in Misrata'.[115] The post-2011 'military prudence'[116] has not hindered Rome in deploying thousands of troops in Iraq since 2014 to support local actors – still with the main intent of training and mentoring – against ISIL. Here, Italian military aircraft carried out surveillance and recognition missions but avoided air strikes, because of what then Minister of Defence Pinotti called an Italian 'cultural concern'.[117] Once again, the peace narrative also affected – through caveat and RoE – operations on the ground, removing the military dimension from a debate featured in public opposition to combat interventions. Moreover, the 'multilateral and humanitarian narrative' was also supported by the lack of military operations in the Syrian civil war.[118] The absence of parliamentary oversight still granted autonomy to the executive, avoiding discussion by new opposition parties (for example, the Five Star Movement) that at that time openly opposed Italian military activism. Only in December 2016 did Italy adopt a new comprehensive law (No. 145/2016) on missions abroad, finally detailing – after almost thirty years of interventions – the monitoring power of parliament to discuss the specific goals, resources and assets of each mission.[119] Yet, in 2021, the implementation of the law suffered several problems, with formal approval occurring months after the beginning of the year and very limited discussion on each intervention.

Thirdly, as in the previous two decades, the Italian armed forces continued to develop military capabilities on the ground, fostering military adaptation and lessons learnt thanks to the former operational experience. Apart from the already-mentioned centrality acquired by the training of local security actors, it is worth noting also how naval operations such as those launched in the Mediterranean ('Mare Nostrum', 2013–2014 and the following EU missions EunavforMed 'Sophia' and then 'Irini') benefited from previous naval interventions in complex scenarios, such as the long and successful anti-piracy mission 'Atalanta'.[120]

Fourthly, the success of parties (that is, the M5S) that expressed harsh criticism towards Italian military operations,[121] as well as the experiment of the 'full-populist' Yellow–Green government, questioned possible discontinuities in Italian defence, especially concerning its missions abroad. However, recent studies[122] have highlighted a substantial continuity in Italian foreign and defence policy. Except for some vocal and symbolic policies, the main traits of Italian defence have been fully confirmed, as occurred for all the military missions approved by previous governments. In July 2021, more than 90 per cent of MPs approved the resolutions that authorised military interventions, confirming the large bipartisan consensus that has sustained post-bipolar Italian defence.[123]

In sum, neither the abovementioned domestic nor international change altered the trajectory of the Italian defence, while the never-ending deployability provided additional positive feedbacks to the path. The analysis of Italian doctrine confirms such claims. The Ministerial Directive 2013,[124] despite its main aim being to review the defence sector after the financial crisis (on reforms, see Chapter 5), fully endorses the Italian commitment to multilateral operations, supporting the use of expeditionary capabilities to address regional and global instability.

The then Minister of Foreign Affairs Giulio Terzi defined Italy as a 'global power, with global interests'.[125]

More broadly, the 2015 White Paper[126] continued to support 'Italian deployability', identifying, however – after decades of military interventions worldwide – a key strategic region for Italy: the so-called 'Enlarged Mediterranean'.[127] Thus, Italy clearly focused on an area that is conceived as vital to its national interests, a geographical context from which multidimensional threats can affect Italian and regional security.[128] In front of the evolution of the regional and international security scenario, 'the document, after paying lip service to the national defence function, stresses throughout the text – and most clearly in the lessons learnt section – almost exclusively non-conventional missions, like hybrid/asymmetric conflicts and, above all, stabilization operations'.[129]

The salience devoted to the Mediterranean by the 2015 White Paper is also consistent with the political battle fought by Italy, especially since the Russian invasion of Crimea in 2014, within NATO to enhance the Alliance's attention towards its 'southern front'.[130] Consequently, the document, which still focuses on the military instrument as expeditionary and interoperable with allies,[131] fostered a 're-modulation of the Italian defence towards the Mediterranean', addressing 'fragility in the Sahel'.[132] The White Paper contributed to the promotion of a strategic relocation of Italian armed forces, from other scenarios (for example, from Iraq in 2018) to Sahel (especially to Niger, where a bilateral mission started to support the capabilities of the state to combat menaces such as terrorism and illegal migration).[133]

In a bipartisan way, Italian political leaders, since 2015, have shared the priority given to Sahel and North Africa, approving new missions in the region, from the Gulf of Guinea to the involvement in the French-led Takuba mission, between Mali, Niger and Burkina. When the White Paper was published the Undersecretary of Defence Rossi affirmed that: 'The Mediterranean was the strategic goal of Italy.'[134] Years later, the M5S Minister Elisabetta Trenta also emphasised how missions are a national instrument 'to promote and defend its interests' in an area that is crucial for Italy.[135]

Despite the Russian invasion of Ukraine in 2022 raising growing concerns related to the 'eastern front' in Rome, and although Italy provided additional military forces within the NATO framework in eastern Europe, the strategic centrality of the Mediterranean has not (so far), diminished as is well-illustrated by a new strategic document specifically devoted to the region, the *Strategia di sicurezza e difesa per il Mediterraneo* (June 2022).[136]

For some authors, the White Paper's language and concepts represent a cultural departure from dominant traditions in Italian foreign and defence policy by, for instance, 'assigning a central role to national interests'.[137] However, despite such 'return of national interests', they have never been defined at political level, where a 'national security strategy' is still lacking.[138] Moreover, the fact that the 2015 White Paper was the first to be published in thirteen dense years testifies to the still limited national strategic reflection, along with public and political indifference towards military affairs.

In conclusion, the 2015 White Paper also conceives the military instrument as being an 'expeditionary, mission-oriented force: to that end, "jointness" and "interoperability" become central features in the design of force structure and posture'.[139] This is very much in line with main features of the trajectory adopted by Italian defence since 1991. After the end of the bipolar era, military activism has transformed the Cold War Italian static approach. In few years Italy has become a 'necessary and inescapable country in contemporary international affairs'.[140] Having once opted for the path started with Desert Storm, recovering an international military role by sharing the burden with allies, the armed forces pushed for a continuation of this trajectory, and the *New Defence Model* allowed Italian defence policy to fully adopt a new dynamic approach. More recent documents do not diverge from the established path, which has been consolidated across time in a path dependent process thanks to constant military engagement, allowed by domestic conditions (the 'peace narrative' along with limited parliamentary oversight) and international pressures (security threats, requests by allies).

5.3.2 New reforms for Italian forces?

The reforms and the official documents adopted in the post-2011 era well illustrate the attempt to finally overcome the obstacles that have hindered the transformation of the Italian armed forces. Still moving along the path of 'deployability', despite greater prudence in sending troops abroad after the dramatic years of the 'war on terror' and the financial crisis, Italian defence has attempted to address the never-ending problems in terms of equilibrium of budget, organisation and composition of the forces. However, while introducing a considerable element of novelty, the goals have not been fully reached.

In 2012, the Monti government adopted a reform that aimed to enhance parliamentary control of procurement. The purpose was to improve the very limited role played by parliamentary commissions in the oversight of military procurement, especially the long-term programmes with rising costs that have been rarely monitored by MPs apart from the initial assessment. Moreover, the technocratic executive led by Monti – who adopted a comprehensive spending review in the public sector – approved other reforms with the goal of restructuring the unbalanced composition of the armed forces and the defence budget.[141]

With Law No. 244/2012 (which is generally known as the 'Di Paola law', from the name of the then Minister of Defence), the government set a target of 150,000 troops (plus 20,000 civilians) for Italian armed forces to be reached before the 2024. 'Preferring quality to quantity'[142] has been the long-term object of Italian post-Cold War defence policy since 1991. Also at NATO level, after the financial crisis, the 'Smart Defence' and 'Pooling&Sharing' approaches were developed to avoid wasting resources. Relatedly, the law established the following distribution among items to promote a more balanced budget: 50 per cent for personnel, 25 per cent for investments and 25 per cent for operations/maintenance. However, the asymmetry of the Italian budget persisted, with the costs related to personnel reaching almost 75 per cent in 2017 (with less than 10 per cent devoted to maintenance in the same year).[143] The overall defence budget did not move towards the benchmark of 2 per cent, but in recent years there has been a significant increase in resources. This has allowed Italy to sustain large-scale commitments such as the new multi-role fighter Tempest, new aerial drones, new destroyers and frigates and armoured vehicles. Furthermore, after 2011, the specific fund for missions (*Fondo per il finanziamento delle missioni internazionali*) also continued to provide resources for training and maintenance, partially addressing the lack of resources devoted to these in the defence budget.[144] This aspect is vital to understanding the incremental process of transformation of the Italian forces with regard to their organisation: extra resources allowed obstacles to be overcome, thus augmenting the evolution of the adopted defence trajectory.

At the same time, while the reduction in the armed forces actually occurred (around 170,000 in 2017 and 165,000 in 2021), the process of decreasing numbers was not as rapid as expected, and the composition of the forces was still unbalanced, with a considerably larger number of officials than planned. Such lack of equilibrium clearly exacerbated the problematic imbalance in the budget with rising costs for personnel. The legacy of the 'static' Cold War armed forces was very complex to overcome after three decades. In addition, the armed forces openly opposed the reforms by the Monti's government, having also recently asked for changes that would enhance (and not reduced) troop numbers.[145] The chiefs of the armed forces have regularly expressed their support for the idea of eschewing the 'Di Paola law', stopping the planned process of reduction in personnel. The Russian invasion of Crimea and the attack following on

Ukraine in 2022 were exploited as proof of the need for new investment in military assets,[146] as well as to reverse the cutbacks in troop numbers to better address the possible return of traditional menaces after years of counterinsurgency, peace-building and light infantry on the ground. More recently, a proposal to reform the whole model to overcome Law No. 244/2012 was also debated in parliament, testifying to the never-ending resistance to the decline in personnel.[147]

The 'internal' opposition to the reforms of the organisation was also evident in the attempt to finally promote jointness. The 2015 White Paper devoted specific emphasis to the need to enhance interoperability among the services. As stated by former Minister of Defence Roberta Pinotti, who drafted the White Paper,[148] the reforms advocated on interoperability – regarding, for instance, the promotion of jointness in logistics and in career advancements – were strongly opposed by the armed forces. Indeed, each service remained jealous of its autonomy, despite the duplication and waste that this has caused across time (for example, the maintenance of helicopters was managed by each service independently). The document aimed to improve coordination, but armed forces 'acted as a trade union'[149] and the reforms were not actually implemented, as has often occurred in recent decades when political willingness to restructure the armed forces was effectively in conflict with the preference of the services for the status quo.[150] At the same time, some innovations were slowly introduced. For instance, only in 2021, the COI was re-named as *Comando operativo di vertice interforze* (COVI), acquiring additional functions (for example, in the cyber domain) and promoting better coordination of forces, in line with the aims expressed by the most recent Strategic Concept of the Chief of the Staff.[151]

On the whole, while the path of deployability was fully embraced by Italian defence, as testified by the operations abroad carried out even after the end of the 'war on terror' era, muddling through and incremental change still affected the organisation of Italian armed forces. As reported by an anonymous high-level member of the Ministry of Defence, the leadership of the armed forces had generally engaged in 'massive resistance' to the political attempts – which are sometimes viewed as 'interference' – to reform of the military organisation.[152] In sum, 'the evolution has been significant since the collapse of the Berlin Wall, but recent years illustrate a diverse path, where Italy has managed to *muddle through* towards limited incremental changes in a context of severe financial crisis'.[153] Financial constraints, especially after the 2008 crisis, played a crucial role in hindering the planned re-structuring of the forces and budget. But all these problems – as well as the lack of capabilities to address them – are strictly related to Cold War legacies. As stressed by a former Minister of Defence, the bipolar logic still shapes the imbalanced structure of the forces, which are indeed deployed mainly in bases in the north of Italy exactly as they were when the aim was to defend against a possible attack by the Warsaw Pact, despite the fact that thirty years later the main 'menaces' for Italy derive from the southern 'front'.[154]

Notes

1. E. Brighi (2013), *Foreign Policy, Domestic Politics and International Relations: The Case of Italy*. New York: Routledge; Ignazi et al., *Italian Military Operations Abroad*.
2. For a comprehensive and updated analysis of the data regarding the evolution of Italian missions, see Vignoli and Coticchia, 'Italy's Military Operations Abroad', 436–62.
3. See the official website of the UN Peacekeeping Operations, available at: https://peacekeeping.un.org/en/troop-and-police-contributors. See also G. Abbondanza (2020), 'The West's Policeman? Assessing Italy's Status in Global Peacekeeping', *International Spectator* 55(2): 127–41; Vignoli and Coticchia, 'Italy's Military Operations Abroad'.
4. N. Labanca (ed.) (2009), *Le armi della Repubblica: dalla Liberazione ad oggi*. Turin: UTET.
5. See, for instance, the speeches by the ministers De Michelis and Rognoni on the 'pacific nature' of the Italian military means. Chamber of Deputies, 20 September 1990 and 9 December 1990.
6. P. Everts and P. Isernia (eds) (2015), *Public Opinion, Transatlantic Relations and the Use of Force*. Houndmills: Palgrave.
7. Coticchia and Moro, 'Peaceful legislatures?' 482–503.
8. Prime Minister Giulio Andreotti, 16 January 1991, Chamber of Deputies. For a detailed analysis of the debate, see Ignazi et al., *Italian Military Operations Abroad*.
9. Andreotti affirmed that the main concern of the government was respect of international law, focusing on 'the second part of article 11 of the Constitution, and in line with that we do not invoke a state of war (art 72)'. Andreotti, 16 January 1991, Chamber of Deputies.
10. The opposition strongly emphasised this point, constantly referring to the constitution (Article 11, but also Articles 52, 78 and 87 on 'the state of war'). See Arnaboldi et al. (PCI), 16 January 1991, Chamber of Deputies.
11. Guerzoni (PCI), 16 January 1991, Chamber of Deputies
12. Russo Spena (PCI), 23 August 1990, Chamber of Deputies.
13. Pierson, *Politics in Time*.
14. F. Coticchia and A. Ruggeri (2022), 'An International Peacekeeper: The Evolution of Italian Foreign and Defence Policy', *IAI Policy Paper*, 22/06, Osservatorio IAI-ISPI sulla Politica Estera italiana.
15. Authors' interview with a former staff member at the Ministry of Defence (2018–2019), Rome, 7 November 2019.
16. See again Chapter 2, especially on the FIR (*Forza di Intervento Rapido*).
17. On the relationship between the lack of joint training and the narrative of 'police operation' that attempted to remove the military dimension from the debate, see Coticchia, *Qualcosa è cambiato*.
18. Ministry of Defence (1991), *Modello di difesa: Lineamenti di sviluppo delle FFAA negli anni 90*. Rome: Stato Maggiore della Difesa, 13
19. Ibid., 20.

20. Ibid., 33.

21. The document identifies three main functions of the armed forces: (1) protecting institutions (and intervening in natural disasters); (2) contributing to internationals security, fostering peace and defending Italian interests; and (3) defending national integrity. For a detailed discussion, see Coticchia, *Qualcosa è cambiato* , especially 76–81.

22. For a broader analysis on links between the New Defence Model and the White Book 1985 see also Santoro, C. M. (ed.) (1992). *L'Elmo di Scipio. Studi sul modello di difesa italiano*. Bologna: Il Mulino

23. Also for this reason, peace movements criticized the document. For a similar cricitism see, among others, Peyretti, E. (1998) *La politica è pace*. Assisi: Cittadella.

24. Coticchia and Vignoli, 'Italian Political Parties and Military Operations'.

25. See especially Ignazi et al., *Italian Military Operations Abroad*.

26. Sydow et al., 'Organizational Path Dependence', 696.

27. On the Italian mission in Somalia, see, among others, B. Loi (2004), *Peacekeeping: pace o guerra?* Firenze: Vallecchi; Coticchia, *Qualcosa è cambiato*.

28. Authors' interview, anonymous high-level diplomat at the Ministry of Foreign Affairs involved in the Italian operation in Somalia in 1992 and 1993, 31 October 2019, Rome.

29. Eleven Italian soldiers died during the operation. Three Italian soldiers died and dozens were wounded in the fierce battle of the 'checkpoint pasta' against the local militias (2 July 1993).

30. R. Smith (2006), *The Utility of Force: The Art of World in the Modern World*. New York: Penguin.

31. For a detailed analysis of the lacks of Italian contingent (especially in terms of military assets as helicopters or tanks, which were planned for a completely different context), see the former commander of IBIS, Loi, *Peacekeeping*.

32. Coticchia and Moro, *The Transformation of Italian Armed Forces in Comparative Perspective*.

33. In 1997, three years after the end of the mission, the IBIS mission came back into Italian public debate because of the scandal revealed by the newspaper *Panorama* that printed pictures of torture carried out by Italian soldiers. Investigations later found only 'personal responsibilities' along with lacks in the chain of command. Coticchia, *Qualcosa è cambiato*, 137–8.

34. Ignazi et al., *Italian Military Operations Abroad*.

35. On 'Alba' see, among others, E. Greco (1998), 'New Trends in Peacekeeping: The Operation Alba', *Security Dialogue* 29(2): 35–57. On the lively domestic political debate within the centre-left Prodi government (*Rifondazione Comunista* did not support the mission, which was approved only thanks to the votes of the centre-right), see Coticchia and Davidson, 'The Limits of Radical Parties in Coalition Foreign Policy'.

36. See Battistelli, *Gli italiani e la guerra*.

37. See again Coticchia and Davidson, 'The Limits of Radical Parties in Coalition Foreign Policy'.

38. Prime Minister Massimo D'Alema, quoted in Ignazi et al., *Italian Military Operations Abroad*.

39. A. H. Cordesman (2001), *The Lessons and Non-Lessons of the Air and Missile Campaign over Kosovo*. Westport, CT: Prager.

40. At the same time, Italy maintained caveats and rules of engagement that allowed it to preserve such 'peace narrative', and a military 'low profile'. M. D'Alema (1999), *Kosovo, gli italiani e la guerra*. Milano: Mondadori.

41. F. N. Moro, L. Cicchi and F. Coticchia (2018), 'Through Military Lenses: Perception of Security Threats and Jointness in the Italian Air Force', *Defence Studies* 18(2): 207–28

42. Moro, Cicchi and Coticchia, 'Through Military Lenses'; Coticchia and Moro, 'Learning from Others?'
43. Ministry of Defence (2011), *Nuove Forze per un Nuovo Secolo*. Rome: Stato Maggiore della Difesa, 37.
44. Ibid., 8. The document, which emphasises the legitimacy of 'multinational peace interventions', fully embraces the national 'peace and humanitarian narrative'. See esp., 50.
45. Ibid., 11.
46. Ibid.. 49. By examining the interventions undertaken in the 1990s, the document focuses on the following features: combined use of diplomacy, force and intelligence, along with reconstruction and development; a proportional use of force, the role of the Carabinieri (a military police force) as a key-asset.
47. Ibid., 50
48. Author's interview, Elisabetta Trenta, former Minister of Defence (2018–2019), Rome, 31 October 2019.
49. F. Coticchia (2020), 'La Politica di Difesa', in G. Capano and A. Natalini (eds), *Le politiche pubbliche in Italia*. Bologna: Il Mulino, 77–94.
50. Author's anonymous interview with former staff member at the Ministry of Defence (2018–2019), Rome, 7 November 2019.
51. Ignazi et al., *Italian Military Operations Abroad.*
52. Authors anonymous interview with former staff member at the Ministry of Defence (2018–2019).
53. Ministry of Defence, *Modello di difesa*.
54. Law Decree 12 May 1995, No. 196, *Attuazione dell'art. 3 della legge 6 marzo 1992, n. 216, in materia di riordino dei ruoli, modifica alle norme di reclutamento, stato ed avanzamento del personale non direttivo delle Forze armate*.
55. Ibid., 14.
56. Ministry of Defence (2020), *Documento Programmatico Pluriennale della Difesa per il Triennio 2020–2022*. Rome: Stato Maggiore della Difesa, E-II. In 2022, VPS were 55,935, while the number of non-permanent volunteers in the ranks was 26,221. See also Senato della Repubblica (2018), *In Difesa della Patria: Dai soldati di leva ai militari professionisti: come sta funzionando il nuovo modello delle Forze armate italiane?* Focus, Impact Assessment Office, available at: https://www.senato.it/service/PDF/PDFServer/BGT/01077449.pdf). The authors wish to thank Matteo Mazziotti di Cieslo on this point.
57. Office of the Deputy Chief of Staff of the Army (2021), *Rapporto Esercito 2020*. Rome: Stato Maggiore dell'Esercito, 46. In 2020, the average age in the Italian army was around 38, while in Germany it was 23.8 years, German Bundestag (2020), Annual Report 2020. Information from the Parliamentary Commissioner for the Armed Forces, available at: https://www.bundestag.de/resource/blob/839328/e1a86 4120697c27057534944ceb20111/annual_report_2020_62nd_report-data.pdf.
58. Authors' telephone interview, journalist, expert on Italian defence, 30 October 2019.
59. On the role of Carabinieri in Italian missions, see Coticchia, *Qualcosa è cambiato*; P. Foradori (2018), 'Cops in Foreign Lands: Italy's Role in International Policing', *International Peacekeeping* 25(4): 497–527; Abbondanza, 'The West's Policeman?'; E. Braw (2021), 'Italy's Carabinieri Were the Perfect Force for the Kabul Evacuation', *Defense One*, 3 September. On their 'new tasks', see also L. Rush and L. B. Millington (2019), *The Carabinieri Command for the Protection of Cultural Property: Saving the World's Heritage*. Suffolk: Boydell Press.
60. D'Amore, *Governare la difesa*; Ertola, *Democrazia e difesa*.
61. F. Coticchia (2019), 'Italy', in H. Meijer and M. Wyss (eds), *The Handbook of European Defence Policies and Armed Forces*. Oxford: Oxford University Press, 109–24.
62. For a detailed cross-time analysis on defence budgets, see Coticchia and Moro, 'Learning from Others?'
63. White Book, 1977.

64. See Ilari, 'The New Model of Italian Defence', 80–7.
65. Authors' interview, researcher at Italian Institute of International Affairs, Rome, 21 October 2019.
66. Interview with former staff member at the Ministry of Defence (2018–2019), Rome, 7 November 2019.
67. For a detailed comparison with France and the United Kingdom, see esp. Coticchia and Moro, *Adapt, Improvise, Overcome?*
68. Among services, the army has constantly the main recipient of resources, specifically because of personnel costs.
69. Ministry of Defence, *Nuove Forze per un Nuovo Secolo.*
70. Ibid., 46.
71. The document called also for a greater economic effort, moving the budget towards NATO's benchmark of 2 per cent GDP.
72. The documents are: *Nota aggiuntiva allo stato di previsione della difesa*; *Bilancio di Previsione dello Stato*; *Documento Programmatico Pluriennale.*
73. The literature, despite a very limited national debate on Italian defence, has gradually focused on these post-2001 intense missions. For comprehensive analyses, see, among others, Battistelli, *Gli italiani e la guerra*; L. Petrilli and V. Sinapi (2007), *Nassiriya, la vera storia*. Torino: Lindau; Davidson, *America's Allies and War*; Ignazi et al., *Italian Military Operations Abroad*; F. Battistelli, M. G. Galantino, L. F. Lucianetti and L. Striuli (2012), *Opinioni sulla guerra: L'opinione pubblica italiana e internazionale di fronte all'uso della forza*. Milano: Franco Angeli; Coticchia, *Qualcosa è cambiato*; Coticchia and Moro, *Adapt, Improvise, Overcome?*; A. Carati and A. Locatelli (2017), 'Cui prodest? Italy's Questionable Involvement in Multilateral Military Operations amid Ethical Concerns and National Interest', *International Peacekeeping* 24(1): 86–107.
74. A partial exception is: Stato Maggiore dell'Esercito (2008). *Le Operazioni Contro-insurrezionali*. SME III RIF-COE. Yearly reports published by the army also provide insights on how operations are assessed and how this can affect doctrine (as well as training, structure and equipment), yet these exclude COIN from the discussion in the years 2007–2010.
75. Ignazi et al., *Italian Military Operations Abroad.*
76. Since 2009, 12 November has been the 'remembrance day for the civilian and military victims in missions abroad'.
77. The key document here is the famous US Army and Marine Corps Field Manual 3-24. The debate that led to such document and to adoption of related strategies as well as on their effectiveness is immense. For a short review, see E. Berman and A. M. Matanock (2015), 'The Empiricists' Insurgency', *Annual Review of Political Science* 18: 443–64; J. Rovner (2014), 'Questions about COIN after Iraq and Afghanistan', in C. W, Gventer, D. M. Jones and M. L. R. Smith (eds), *The New Counter-insurgency Era in Critical Perspective*. London: Palgrave Macmillan, 299–318.
78. The theme is discussed more thoroughly in Coticchia and Moro, 'Learning from Others?'
79. Stato Maggiore dell'Esercito (2008), *Army Report 2008*. Rome, 140.
80. Authors' telephone interview, Coordinator Italian Disarmament Network, 5 November 2019.
81. See Ignazi et al., *Italian Military Operations Abroad*; L. Cladi and A. Locatelli (2019), 'Why did Italy Contribute to UNIFIL II? An Analytical Eclectic Analysis', *Italian Political Science Review* 49(1): 85–97.
82. 'The Italian armed forces strongly improved across time in properly understanding local scenarios, interacting with local actors' fostering cooperation with diplomats and NGOs. Afghanistan, despite the complex relationship between security and development 'improved such interaction.' Authors interview, high-level diplomat of the Ministry of Foreign Affairs.

83. Ignazi et al., *Italian Military Operations Abroad*.
84. Authors' interview, Elisabetta Trenta, former Minister of Defence (2018–2019). Rome, 31 October 2019.
85. Authors' interview, former counter-intelligence section chief and security officer at RC-C HQ, ISAF, 23 October 2019.
86. Authors' telephone interview, journalist, expert on Italian defence, 30 October 2019. The literature has illustrated how the international requests for Italian military involvement were also referred to peculiar features of Italian armed forces, such as training of local police and security actor through the Carabinieri. See Coticchia, *Qualcosa è cambiato*.
87. Authors' interview, researcher, Rome, Italian Institute of International Affairs, 21 October 2019.
88. Authors' interview, former counter-intelligence section chief and security officer at RC-C HQ, ISAF, 23 October 2019.
89. At the beginning of the mission the VM vehicles were not properly armoured against IEDs. Also the type of bulletproof vests were changed across time. Authors' interview, former counter intelligence section chief and security officer at RC-C HQ, ISAF, 23 October 2019.
90. Ministero della Difesa (2002), *Il Libro Bianco della Difesa*. Rome: Stato Maggiore della Difesa, 13.
91. See, for instance, Ministero della Difesa (2005), *Il concetto strategico del Capo di Stato Maggiore*. Rome: Stato Maggiore della Difesa, 11.
92. Stato Maggiore della Difesa (2005), *La Trasformazione net-centrica*. Rome: Stato Maggiore della Difesa, 6.
93. Ibid., 18. Also the document '*Investire in Sicurezza*' (2005) considers the possibility of engagement in 'short and limited combat interventions' (16), distinguishing between post-conflict and combat phases.
94. The 'peace narrative' was consolidated in public debate, as illustrated by the fact that it was shared also by public opposition in the case of the Italian mission 'Antica Babilonia' in Iraq in 2003, which was largely opposed by public opinion. Battistelli, *Gli Italiani e la Guerra*; Coticchia, *La Guerra che non c'era*.
95. Coticchia and Moro, *Adapt, Improvise, Overcome?*
96. On this point, see M. Nones and A. Marrone (2011), *La trasformazione delle Forze armate: il programma Forza NEC*. Roma: Carocci Army Report (2012).
97. Also international cooperation on procurement benefited from involvement in military operations abroad. Authors' telephone interview, journalist, expert on Italian defence, 30 October 2019.
98. Authors' interview, former counter-intelligence section chief and security officer at RC-C HQ, ISAF, 23 October 2019.
99. B. Lombardi (2011), 'The Berlusconi Government and Intervention in Libya', *International Spectator* 46(4): 31–44; O. Croci and M. Valigi (2013), 'Continuity and Change in Italian Foreign Policy: The Case of the International Intervention in Libya', *Contemporary Italian Politics* 5(1): 38–54; M. Ceccorulli and F. Coticchia (2015), 'Multidimensional Threats and Military Engagement: The Case of the Italian Intervention in Libya', *Mediterranean Politics* 20(3): 303–21; Carati and Locatelli, 'Cui prodest?' For a recent review, see E. Diodato and F. Niglia (2017), *Italy in International Relations: The Foreign Policy Conundrum*. Basingstoke: Palgrave Macmillan; C. Monteleone (2019), *Italy in Uncertain Times: Europeanizing Foreign Policy in the Declining Process of the American Hegemony*. London:Lexington Books.
100. F. Coticchia and J. Davidson (2019), *Italian Foreign Policy during Matteo Renzi's Government: A Domestically-Focused Outsider and the World*. Lanham, MD: Lexington Books. On public opinion, see IAI-LASP (2017), *Gli Italiani e la politica estera*, available at: https://www.iai.it/sites/de- fault/files/laps-iai_2017.pdf.

101. P. Isernia and F. Longo (2017), 'The Italian Foreign Policy: Challenges and Continuities', *Italian Political Science Review* 47(2): 107–24.
102. A. Dessì and F. Olmastroni (2017), 'Foreign Posture in Comparative Perspective: A Quantitative and Qualitative Appraisal of Italian Foreign and Defence Policy during the Renzi Government', *Contemporary Italian Politics* 9(2): 201–18; F. Coticchia (2019), 'Unheard Voices: International Relations Theory and Italian Defence Policy', in R. Belloni, V. Della Sala and P. Viotti (eds), *Fear and Uncertainty in Europe: The Return to Realism?* Houndmills: Palgrave, 131–50.
103. M. Ceccorulli and F. Coticchia (2020), '"I'll Take Two": Migration, Terrorism, and the Italian Military Engagement in Niger and Libya', *Journal of Modern Italian Studies* 25(2): 174–96; G. Dentice and F. Donelli (2021), 'Reasserting (Middle) Power by Looking Southwards: Italy's Policy towards Africa', *Contemporary Italian Politics* 12(3): 331–51.
104. M. Evangelista (ed.) (2018), *Italy from Crisis to Crisis*. London: Routledge.
105. Also in this case, the lessons learnt of previous operations (e.g., the naval component of Alba that in 1997 addressed the flows of migrants in the Adriatic Sea) were (controversially) adopted. On migration and Italian foreign policy, see the polls collected by IAI-LAPS (2017–2021). On the refugee crisis and European and Italian foreign and defence policy, see S. Panebianco (ed.) (2016), *Sulle onde del Mediterraneo: Cambiamenti globali e risposte alle crisi migratorie*. Milano: Egea; Coticchia and Davidson, *Italian Foreign Policy during Matteo Renzi's Government*; F. Attinà (2019), 'L'Italia e la crisi migratoria dell'Europa', in P. Isernia and F. Longo (eds), *La politica estera italiana nel nuovo millennio*. Bologna: Il Mulino, 181–202; E. Cusumano and M. Villa (2021), 'From "Angels" to "Vice Smugglers": The Criminalization of Sea Rescue NGOs in Italy', *European Journal on Criminal Policy and Research* 27(1): 23–40.
106. G. Baldini amd M. F. N. Giglioli (2019), 'Italy 2018: The Perfect Populist Storm?' *Parliamentary Affairs* 73(2): 365.
107. E. Jones (2018), 'Italy, Its Populists and the EU', *Survival* 60(4): 113–22; P. Giurlando (2020), 'Populist Foreign Policy: The Case of Italy', *Canadian Foreign Policy Journal* 27(2): 1–18; F. Coticchia (2021), 'A "Sovereignist Revolution"? Italy's Foreign Policy under the "Yellow–Green" Government', *Comparative European Politics* 19(6): 739–59.
108. The requests have been made by France and the United States. On this point, see esp. Coticchia Davidson, *Italian Foreign Policy under Matteo Renzi's Goverment*.
109. On this debate, see A. Marrone and M. Nones (eds) (2016), *Italy and the Security in the Mediterranean*. Roma: Nuova Cultura; Coticchia and Moro, 'From Enthusiasm to Retreat'.
110. Vignoli and Coticchia, 'Italy's Military Operations Abroad'.
111. Italian public opinion has never supported the mission in Libya. See Coticchia, *La guerra che non c'era*.
112. See especially the interventions by Minister of Foreign Affairs Franco Frattini and by Minister of Defence Ignazio La Russa. For instance, A. Gentili (2011), 'La Russa: l'azione sta andando bene, ora avanti la politica e la diplomazia', *Il Messaggero*, 11 May.
113. See, for instance, the speech by the MP Massimo Livi Bacci. (Democratic Party), Senate, 23 March 2011.
114. Quoted in F. Biloslavo (2012), 'Solo ora lo ammettiamo: sulla Libia una pioggia di bombe', *Panorama*, 12 December.
115. Authors' telephone interview, Domenico Rossi, former undersecretary of defence (2014–2018), June 2017.
116. Several Italian leaders believed that 'after years of mission, air strikes and military focus would have created more problems rather than solving them', sharing a 'broader approach against terrorism'. Authors' interview with Andrea Manciulli,

Vice-President of the Foreign Affairs Committee in the Chamber of Deputies, Florence, February 2016.

117. Authors' interview, Roberta Pinotti, former Minister of Defence (2014–2018), Genova, May 2018.

118. Authors' telephone interview, European Council of Foreign Relations expert on Italian foreign policy, North Africa and Middle East, February 2017.

119. On the law, see N. Ronzitti (2017), 'La legge italiana sulle missioni internazionali', *Rivista di diritto internazionale* 100(2): 474–95.

120. Authors' interview with EU-Navfor Med – Sophia Command, Rome, 10 July 2017.

121. For additional details on the M5S's views on defence policy, see Coticchia and Vignoli, 'Populist Parties and Foreign Policy'.

122. C. Lequesne (2021), 'Populist Governments and Career Diplomats in the EU: The Challenge of Political Capture', *Comparative European Politics* 19(6): 779–95; Coticchia, 'A "Sovereignist Revolution"?'

123. See Chamber of Deputies, 15 July 2021, available at: https://www.camera.it/leg18/410?idSeduta=0541&tipo=alfabetico_stenografico.

124. Ministry of Defence (2013), *Direttiva Ministeriale in merito alla politica militare per l'anno 2013*. Rome: Stato Maggiore della Difesa.

125. Chamber of Deputies, Foreign Affairs Commission, 30 November 2011

126. Ministry of Defence (2015), *Libro Bianco della Difesa e della Sicurezza*. Rome: Stato Maggiore della Difesa. On the White Paper, see A. Gilli, A. R. Ungaro and A. Marrone (2015), 'The Italian White Paper for International Security and Defence', *RUSI Journal* 160(6): 34–41; A. Locatelli, F. N. Moro and F. Coticchia (2016), 'Renew or Reload? Continuity and Change in Italian Defence Policy', *EUI Working Papers Series*, EUI RSCAS 1.

127. In the document such region covers a broad area, from Sahel to MENA. More accurately, Minister of Defence Lorenzo Guerini (2019–2022) – who has constantly repeated the saliency of the *Mediterraneo Allargato* – has provided a useful definition of the geographical priority of Italian defence: a triangle (whose angles are: Libya and Mediterranean Sea, the Gulf of Guinea and the Horn of Africa) with the Sahel in the centre. See Minister Lorenzo Guerini, Chamber of Deputies, 7 July2021.

128. 'The White Paper represents a fundamental turning point as it clearly rebalances Italian defence policy towards the "Euro-Mediterranean region", henceforth considered the "scenario for national interventions.' Gilli, Ungaro and Marrone, 'The Italian White Paper 37.

129. Locatelli, Moro and Coticchia, 'Renew or Reload?', 6

130. Clearly, the same occurred within the EU, especially concerning the migration issue. Authors' interview, Andrea Manciulli.

131. Locatelli, Moro and Coticchia, 'Renew or Reload?'

132. Authors' interview, Roberta Pinotti.

133. Chamber of Deputies, 17 January 2018.

134. Authors' interview, Undersecretary of Defence Domenico Rossi, 26 June 2017.

135. Authors interview, Elisabetta Trenta, former Minister of Defence (2018–2019), Rome, 31 October 2019.

136. Italian Ministry of Defence (2022), *Strategia di Sicurezza e Difesa per il Mediterraneo*. Rome: Stato Maggiore della Difesa.

137. Gilli, Ungaro and Marrone, 'The Italian White Paper', 36.

138. There is not a definition of national interests in strategic documents. Authors anonymous interview with former staff member at the Ministry of Defence (2018–2019), Rome, 7 November 2019.

139. Locatelli, Moro and Coticchia, 'Renew or Reload?' 11.

140. Brighi, *Foreign Policy, Domestic Politics and International Relations*, 6.

141. Law Nos 135/2012, 244/2012 and 8/2014. For a review, see again the Ministerial Directive (2013).

142. Ministry of Defence *Direttiva Ministeriale in merito alla politica militare per l'anno 2013*, 9.
143. See DPP 2017–2019, available at: https://www.difesa.it/Content/Documents/DPP/DPP_2017_2019_Approvato_light.pdf.
144. Authors' anonymous interview with former staff member at the Ministry of Defence (2018–2019), Rome, 7 November 2019.
145. For details, see P. Batacchi (2020), 'Una nuova riforma per la Difesa?' *Rivista Italiana Difesa* 12/2021.
146. For an updated and comprehensive analysis of Italy's main military assets, see, among others, the annual report of the ISS Military Balance, available at: https://www.iiss.org/publications/the-military-balance.
147. See the proposal, '*Disposizioni di revisione del modello di Forze armate interamente professionali*', at: https://documenti.camera.it/leg18/pdl/pdf/leg.18.pdl.camera.18 70_A.18PDL0170560.pdf. At the time of writing, the proposed reform, substantially aimed at delaying the degree of reduction in forces advocated by Monti's reform, is still being discussed in the parliament. For details (along a critical perspective), see at: https://www.analisidifesa.it/2022/05/il-punto-sulla-revisione-del-modello-delle-for ze-armate-italiane.
148. Authors' interview, Roberta Pinotti, former Minister of Defence.
149. Ibid.
150. Authors' telephone interview, Coordinator Italian Disarmament Network, 5 November 2019.
151. Italian Ministry of Defence (2022), *The Chief of Defence Strategic Concept*. Rome: Stato Maggiore della Difesa.
152. Author's interview, anonymous high-level member of the Ministry of Defence, Rome, October 2019.
153. F. Coticchia (2017), 'Running in Chains: The Transformation of Italian Defence Policy, in M. Evangelista (ed.), *Italy from Crisis to Crisis*. London: Routledge, 119–35.
154. Authors' interview, Elisabetta Trenta, former Minister of Defence (2018–2019), Rome, 31 October 2019.

Chapter 6

Japan: From Defensive Defence to Proactive Contributions to Peace

6.1 Japanese defence policies after the Cold War

6.1.1 Japanese military doctrine in the 1990s

In the post-Cold War period, Japanese security policy underwent a fundamental redefinition, shaped by the interplay of external and domestic factors. Cultural, political and organisational legacies influenced how the Japanese leadership responded to these long-term trends. The rise of China completely redefined the regional balance of power in East Asia. The emergence of the North Korean nuclear and ballistic threat added urgency to the need to promote a military doctrine and a force structure that would be equal to the task of preserving Japan's security and regional stability. The alliance with the United States substantially strengthened the country's security, but it also increased external pressure and the fear of entrapment (especially during the 'War on Terror') and abandonment (notably during the Trump years).

The policies put in place by the Japanese leadership were also influenced by long-term trends affecting the country's domestic politics. On the Left, the steep decline in the influence of the Japanese Socialist Party (*Nihon Shakai-Tō*) after its short-lived experience in government between 1993 and 1996 eroded political support for radical pacifism and anti-militarism.[1] The Democratic Party of Japan (DPJ or *Minshutō*), the new political alternative to the hegemony of the LDP (*Jimintō*), embraced the idea of an active security policy and recognised the legitimacy of the JSDF, even though it sought greater autonomy from the United States. During the 2000s and the 2010s the LDP, especially under the leadership of Koizumi Junichiro and Abe Shinzo, endeavoured to overcome most post-war institutional constraints and promote a greater security role for Japan.

In addition to the key critical juncture represented by the end of the Cold War, two others can be identified in the late 1990s and early 2010s. In these cases, the pivotal choices made over the following years were to produce a series of self-reinforcing mechanisms and legacy effects which would make it very difficult for policymakers to significantly deviate from the established trajectory. Both cases are defined by a perception of deterioration in the external environment, with the increasing threat posed by China and North Korea. In the 1990s, external threats took the form of the Third Taiwan Strait Crisis and the so-called 'Taepodong Shock', and in the early 2010s that of the emergence of Beijing's coercive strategy in the East China Sea and the maturation of the North Korean nuclear and ballistic programme. In both cases, external elements interacted with the demise of alternative domestic coalitions that had sought to formulate a different approach to foreign and security policies from that promoted by the LDP hegemony. Leaders who sought to promote alternative choices, such as Murayama, Hatoyama and, to a lesser extent, Kan and Noda, faced both internal organisational and institutional resistance and opposition from Washington. Overall, their inability to recalibrate Japan's foreign and defence policies shows how path dependence and lock-in effects have a significant impact on policy outcomes. The substantial failure of the political projects promoted by the JSP up to 1996 and by the DPJ up to 2012 established the LDP's control of the government and allowed it to shape and later consolidate the path preferred by its leadership. On both occasions, conservative leaders such as Hashimoto, Koizumi and especially Abe responded by doubling down on the consolidated path represented by the consolidation of the alliance and the expansion of Japan's security role.

These choices generated two long-term trends that affected both Japan's security narrative and its strategic role in the region. Japan gradually overcame several post-war institutional constraints that had defined the Cold War era. This trend has been defined by scholars as 'normalisation': Japan has been slowly abandoning its identity as a peace-loving nation (*heiwa kokka*) to become a 'normal nation' (*futsū no kuni*).[2] This evolution does not necessarily entail a complete departure from a pacifist narrative, but rather a significant re-elaboration. During the Cold War period, radical pacifism and anti-militarism translated into a strict political and bureaucratic control over the self-defence forces and into mechanisms aimed at preventing Japanese involvement in conflicts generated by the Cold War rivalry. In the post-Cold War period, the continuing influence of the pacifist legacy led Japan to embrace the idea of promoting 'proactive contributions to peace' (*Sekkyokuteki heiwa shugi*). This long-term trend combines the need to reaffirm Japan's status in Asia with the desire to embrace a role as defender of the regional order and its strategic and normative pillars. In this context, 'peace' must be actively promoted and associated with the promotion of liberal values.[3]

In the last three decades, Japan's military doctrine and force structure has changed profoundly since the end of the Cold War in several related ways. Japan embarked on a process of normalisation, overcoming many, though not all, of the institutional constraints that defined post-war pacifism and anti-militarism. Basic rules and restrictions still hold their ground, appearing resilient to change: Article 9 of the constitution, first and foremost, but also the Three Non-Nuclear Principles. Moreover, as public opinion has extensively demonstrated, throughout the post-Cold War era, pacifism and anti-militarism have remained deeply ingrained in Japanese political culture and society.

These developments were very difficult for any observer to predict in the early 1990s. In the aftermath of the Cold War, the security environment surrounding Japan was profoundly different from that of today. The demise of the Soviet Union drastically reduced the level of external threat as well as the possibility of being unwillingly involved in a conflict created by superpower rivalries. The early 1990s represented the peak of Japanese influence and power, in economic, political and security terms. Consequently, the long-standing value of the US–Japan alliance was called into question in both countries. In Japan, conservative 'neo-autonomists' argued in favour of an independent major power role for Japan. Progressives considered the alliance as a betrayal of the country's pacifist identity and an obstacle to reconciliation with the rest of Asia. Most mainstream policymakers favoured maintaining the alliance, but also advocated the diversification of the country's foreign and security policy, with participation in regional security institutions such as the East Asia Summit, or, more actively, in UN-led activities.[4]

In Washington, the early 1990s were characterised by the rise of the 'Japan threat'. Due to its economic competitiveness and its technological prowess, several scholars and analysts regarded Japan more as an economic rival rather than an ally and a partner.[5] The first Clinton administration considered the possibility of gradual disengagement from the alliance and a much more adversarial approach in economic and diplomatic terms.[6]

In the aftermath of the Cold War, Japan's military doctrine was still largely defined by the concept of an exclusively 'defensive defence', or defence-oriented defence (*senshu bōei*). This entailed maintaining a hedgehog-like posture, focused only on self-defence, and eschewed the development of abilities aimed at power projection, deterrence by punishment and other 'offensive capabilities', which were considered illegal under

Article 9. After the Gulf War this concept, and the Japanese security policy as a whole, came under strong criticism. The government in Tokyo found itself caught between competing pressures; on the one hand, the United States was pushing for a substantial contribution to be made to the war, while on the other, the institutional constraints on the use of force and the JSDF that had characterised the post-war era were still fully in place. Consequently, there were no legal grounds for deploying the JSDF abroad, which was also barred from defending the military personnel of other countries. Part of the LDP supported a potential deployment of the JSDF under the UN mandate, but Prime Minister Kaifu failed to find a majority in the Diet for an active Japanese involvement. Therefore, as in Germany, Japan opted for so-called 'cheque-book diplomacy', contributing financially to the war effort, and sending a mine-sweeping mission after the end of the conflict.[7] Together with the demise of the USSR, cheque-book diplomacy represents a fundamental critical juncture in Japanese military doctrine and, more generally, its security policy, even though the impact of both differs with respect to the Italian and the German cases. The debate on the possibility of contributing to the Gulf War highlighted the contrast between Japan's desire to be recognised as a great power internationally, its capacity to play a meaningful security role in the post-Cold War environment, and the continuing pacifist orientation of public opinion.

In 1992, partly as a reaction to the perceived debacle of the cheque-book diplomacy, the Diet approved the law on peacekeeping operations (PKOs). Under this law the JSDF was allowed, for the first time, to be deployed abroad, although its activities were strictly limited. Japan's participation in PKOs was restricted to situations in which the parties had agreed on a ceasefire and the mission had obtained the consent of the UN and the parties involved. Moreover, the use of weapons had to be kept to a minimum and Japan had to maintain neutrality in the disputes. This law implied that the authorisation to deploy the JSDF on missions not approved by the UN required an ad hoc provisional law. This principle was not revised until 2015, after which the peace and security reforms adopted by the Abe government required only the authorisation of the Diet.[8] Despite the restrictions, the PKO law allowed the JSDF to participate in several UN-sponsored peacekeeping missions, including those in Cambodia (1992–1993), Lebanon (1996–2013), Mozambique (1992–1994), East Timor (2002–2004, 2010–2012), Haiti (2010–2013) and South Sudan (2011–2017).[9]

These experiences with PKOs had several, and often unintentional, consequences. On the whole, unlike Italy, Japan never considered PKOs or military interventions abroad as the primary function of its armed forces.

On the contrary, they served other significant purposes. First, in terms of domestic politics, over time they helped to break the taboo of the deployment of the JSDF abroad and convince part of Japanese public opinion that Japan could make a positive contribution to global security without threatening its neighbours or basically deviating from its peace-oriented identity. This acceptance was facilitated by domestic factors, such as the decline of the Japanese Socialist Party, the principal guardian of radical pacifism, and the emergence of the Democratic Party of Japan (DPJ) as a main alternative to the LDP. The DPJ basically accepted the process of normalisation of the country's defence policies, while advocating a degree of autonomy from the United States and closer relations with China and the rest of East Asia.[10]

On the side of the conservatives, many political leaders considered the Japanese role in PKOs to be a matter of prestige for the country and a small but significant step in the process of emerging from the post-war pacifist constraints. PKOs also served to ease the external pressure (*gaiatsu*) from the United States, which, especially during the 'War on Terror', urged Japan to take on greater global commitments. With the participation in PKOs, despite the small number of personnel involved, the JSDF was forced to deal with its own limitations in terms of its ability to operate with other militaries and in a distant theatre, by performing functions such as logistics, transportation and intelligence. Internationally, reactions to Japan's role were mixed. While most partners welcomed Tokyo's contribution, the activities of the JSDF were substantially limited by the 1992 law, leading most of the partners to suspect that Japan was not actually sharing the costs and risks associated with the missions.

The evolution of the Japanese military doctrine was influenced not so much by the need to adapt to a new purpose as by the interaction between domestic politics and external factors, such as emerging threats from China and North Korea and the climate within the alliance with the United States.

In 1995, the Japanese Defence Agency[11] published the new National Defence Programme Outline (NDPO), which described the Japanese defence doctrine and force structure. The first version of the NDPO had been published in 1976, ending the series of Buildup Plans. Since 2004, the editions have been labelled National Defence Plan Guidelines (NDPG). The 2019 White Paper *Defence of Japan* defines the NDPG as a 'grand design' to ensure the peace and security of Japan, which establishes the posture of Japan's defence capability and the level to achieve. As explained by the Ministry of Defence in 2022, the document 'sets forth the basic policy for Japan's defence, the significance and role of defence capabilities, and the basic guidelines for future defence capabilities, which include matters such as the specific structures of the SDF and the target for the procurement of major equipment'.[12] The NDPO 1995 was approved by the government led by Socialist Murayama Tomiichi and supported by a 'grand coalition' that included JSP and LDP. It marked the beginning of a process of evolution of the Japanese military doctrine that was to become much more manifest in the following decades. The new NDPO was preceded by a report compiled by a panel of external experts, the Hinoguchi Commission, which stressed both the role of the alliance and the need for Japan to invest in multilateral security arrangements.[13] While confirming the centrality of the principle of 'defensive defence', it also introduced several relevant, yet incremental, changes. First, it underlined how preserving stability in the areas surrounding Japan represented a new key mission for the JSDF. Moreover, it confirmed the need to expand the country's role in multilateral PKOs. Secondly, Japan needed to retain the capacity to autonomously repel possible direct aggressions without having to rely on US assistance. These changes reflected the perception of a less severe threat environment compared with the Cold War years, but also the emergence of sources of instability relating to North Korea, China, and maritime and territorial disputes. The document also anticipated some of the changes later institutionalised by the 1997 Alliance Guidelines, in terms of peacetime cooperation in the alliance and the sharing of responsibility in terms of promoting regional stability. This would help to consolidate the role of the JMSDF, both in terms of the defence of territorial waters and the protection of SLOCs in the region.[14] The NDPO also requested that the JSDF be given a greater role in disaster relief operations. In 1995, the Kobe earthquake exposed how a lack of coordination between military and civilian units could inhibit the deployment of the JSDF even within Japanese territory, encumbering the effectiveness of operations aimed at containing damage caused by natural disasters. In the following months, the Diet approved the Disaster Countermeasures Law, which granted the JSDF a broader scope of action, enabling greater coordination logistically and with local civilian authorities.[15]

The first signs of key long-term trends such as China's military modernisation and the emergence of the North Korean nuclear and ballistic threat, as well as the Japanese economic stagnation during the 'lost decade' of the 1990s, contributed to changing both the dynamics of the alliance and Japan's own doctrine. The Third Taiwan Crisis in 1995–1996 and the 'Taepodong Shock' in 1998, when North Korea launched an intermediate-range ballistic missile across the Sea of Japan, jointly represent a key critical juncture. This brought the post-Cold War period to a close and introduced an era characterised both by the 'normalisation' of security policies and the developing of the US–Japan alliance.

The emergence of new threats in the region prompted both parties to significantly review their defence policies. In Washington, Joseph Nye, then Assistant Secretary of Defense, promoted the so-called Nye Initiative, which reaffirmed the centrality of the alliance for regional stability, and the need to rationalise and consolidate the US presence in the region in order to face future challenges.[16] At the same time, in Japan the election of Hashimoto and the consequent return to power of the LDP facilitated cooperation in the alliance, while undermining the possibility of a more autonomist and 'Asia-centred' foreign policy in Tokyo. This convergence resulted in a period of major redefinition for the alliance, culminating in the Clinton–Hashimoto Summit of 1996 and the approval of the new guidelines for the alliance in 1997, which re-established the role and the commitments of the two countries both in peacetime and in time of war. The document introduced a role for the JSDF in rear area support in case of contingencies, expanded the areas of cooperation in peacetime and institutionalised a 2+2 meeting between the ministers of defence and foreign affairs.[17] Moreover, the guidelines provided a framework for cooperation on issues not previously covered by existing agreements, such as emergency relief operations and cooperation in UN peacekeeping activities. These guidelines were crucial in plotting a path that would determine the choices to come and generate self-reinforcing mechanisms geared to the consolidation of the alliance and the normalisation of the Japanese security doctrine during the early 2000s. On the whole, the period between 1996 and 1998 represents a critical juncture for the post-Cold War era, which crucially contributed to defining future trajectories in the evolution of Japan's military doctrine and force structure. The cumulative effects of emerging external threats embodied by the Third Taiwan Strait Crisis and the Taepodong Shock and the return to power of the LDP after the instability of the years 1993–1996 led to the forging of a path that would be reinforced considerably in the following decades. On the one hand, Japan would seek to encapsulate its growing role and responsibilities within a process of consolidation of the alliance, which would later be integrated with new minilateral partnerships. On the other hand, it would attempt to reconcile this evolving role with a still very influential pacifist narrative, thus presenting its expanding security activities in the region as an active contribution to regional and global peace. Even more importantly, these choices created effects of path dependence, substantially foreclosing possible 'alternative futures' based either on neutralism and pacifism, forms of multilateralism without the alliance centred on the UN role or on emerging institutions such as the ASEAN Regional Forum, or an autonomous 'Great Power' role.[18] As became clear during the period 2009–2012, when the LDP briefly lost control of the government, the path established in this phase became extremely resistant to change, despite attempts by the DPJ to promote a defence policy less centred on the alliance with the US.

6.1.2 Japanese force structure in the 1990s

In the early 1990s, the demise of the Soviet Union and the end of the Cold War generated a relatively benign environment. Moreover, the regional balance of power at the time was overwhelmingly in favour of Japan. The threats from China and North Korea only fully materialised in the following years. In 1991, Japanese GDP was higher than those of China, India, Russia and South Korea combined. Its military budget was three times greater than that of China. In the following decades, the economic and military rise of China completely reversed the regional balance of power. China overtook Japan in terms of GDP in 2010 and in terms of military spending in 2001. In 2020, China spent around US$252 billion on defence, while Japan spent US$49 billion.[19] On top of this massive change in the balance of power, the emergence of the North Korean threat, coupled with the threats posed by new technologies in the field of ballistic missiles, anti-access capabilities and cybersecurity, led to new requirements for the JSDF that contributed to the significant evolution in Japan's force structure.

During the 1980s, despite the 1 per cent ceiling and the persisting legacy of other anti-militarist limits, the JSDF had developed into a highly sophisticated, capable and well-funded force. The NDPO released in 1995 described this situation in detail. The document re-affirmed the concept of 'basic and standard capability' previously introduced in the 1976 document. Japan needed to possess 'the minimum necessary defence capability for an independent nation so that it would not become a source of instability in the surrounding region by creating a vacuum of power rather than building a military capability directly related to a threat to the country'.[20]

The 1995 NDPO introduced several significant changes compared with the 1976 version. It called for investments in capacities to repel forms of direct aggression without the assistance of the United States. More than merely a reaction to external threats, this reflected both the legacy of the tensions with Washington in the early 1990s and the cutback in US troops deployed in Japan from 100,000 to 44,000, in the late 1990s. The NDPO also stressed the need to adopt capabilities functional to the expansion of the JSDF requirement, including PKOs and disaster relief. Ultimately, the JSDF needed to become 'streamlined, effective and flexible', performing more duties with the same or less resources and budget.

The 1995 NDPO led to a reduction in overall personnel numbers and resources. This had different consequences for each service. The GSDF became the primary victim of budget and personnel cuts since the 1990s, but also the service that resisted most actively the changes deriving from the need for the JSDF to adapt to new requirements and new threats. Between 1995 and 2001 the GSDF lost 20 per cent of their personnel and 25 per cent of their battle tanks. The GSDF, despite the cuts, was forced to redirect its main mission from territorial defence, focusing on Hokkaido, to PKOs and HR/DR activities. At this time, however, the GSDF sought more to retain its territorial defence capabilities than to invest in the resources (such as strategic lift, logistics and transportation) that would have been necessary if it were to be fully prepared to embrace both peacekeeping and disaster relief as its core missions.[21] This had significant consequences for the disaster-relief operation following the 1995 Kobe earthquake. The efforts of the JSDF proved to be inefficient due both to a lack of capabilities and to institutional constraints that hindered both the deployment of the forces and coordination between military and civilian authorities. After 1995, the JSDF developed significant capabilities in the fields of water purification and logistical and medical assistance, which were to prove essential during HR/DR operations in the following decades, especially the Fukushima disaster of March 2011.

The 1995 NDPO also had a significant impact on the MSDF, whose total assets underwent cuts amounting to 17 per cent of the total surface fleet compared with the original 1976 'basic defence concept'. As pointed out by Patalano, however, in the medium term this did not necessarily represent a loss from the point of view of capabilities, but rather a process of evolution.[22] In the 1980s, the MSDF had benefited from substantial investments which had considerably increased its anti-submarine warfare capabilities and its capacity to protect SLOCs. Furthermore, the MSDF invested in new platforms, such as the Osumi class tank-landing ship, with the aim of establishing new expeditionary capabilities functional to PKO missions in distant theatres. Overall, despite the budget cuts the total tonnage of the MSDF continued to grow during this period, albeit at a slower rate than in the Cold War era. It also kept its number of diesel-propelled attack submarines at sixteen and in, the late 1990s, introduced a new class, the Oyashio.[23]

Likewise in the case of the ASDF, budget reductions did not necessarily compromise Japan's capabilities, though they did lead to the rethinking of certain procurement choices. In spite of the decreasing need for interception operations, the ASDF maintained its fleet of F-15s and introduced the F-2, a domestically modified version of the F-16. Due to budget cuts, the ASDF had to postpone plans for developing a completely indigenous fighter jet. Additionally, despite the political emphasis on the Japanese role in PKOs, the ASDF did not expand its capabilities in the sector of strategic airlift until the mid-2000s, continuing rather to rely on the C-130H of the Cold War era. This created several difficulties in the transportation of equipment and troops to distant theatres, like Cambodia, and demonstrated how the political importance of PKOs was not matched by the level of priority assigned to them by the JDA and the JSDF in terms of procurement and planning.[24]

6.2 Japanese defence policies from to 9/11 to 3/11

6.2.1 Japanese military doctrine in the 2000s

The process of evolution of Japanese military doctrine speeded up considerably in the aftermath of the terrorist attacks of 11 September 2001. However, rather than representing a critical juncture, this contributed to accelerating the general course adopted in the late 1990s and locking in the trajectory defined by the development of the alliance and the process of normalisation. The GWOT represented a new, more intense form of *gaiatsu* (external pressure) by the United States, which requested that all its main partners actively contribute to the military operations in Afghanistan and Iraq in the early 2000s. As a reaction to 9/11, in 2002, the Diet adopted a package that included laws regulating the response to an armed attack on Japanese soil or an imminent threat, allowing the JSDF to provide non-combatant support to US troops and to defend US facilities on Japanese soil. In 2003, the Diet approved the Special Measures on Humanitarian and Reconstruction Assistance, which authorised the JSDF to provide logistical support to the US-led coalition in Iraq and Afghanistan.[25] Significantly, these laws established a legal framework to bypass the exclusively defensive orientation of Japanese military doctrine and provide support for an international coalition outside the narrowly defined 'areas surrounding Japan' and beyond the limits defined by the law on UN PKOs. Despite considerable resistance from the opposition parties, these laws made it possible to deploy a small contingent in Iraq from 2004 to 2006 and a refuelling mission in the Indian Ocean in support of the war effort in Afghanistan. Unlike Italy, Japan did not have a major role in the COIN operations in the Middle East and terrorism never topped the list of perceived threats for Tokyo. The impact generated by 9/11 and the subsequent 'War on Terror' were different but substantial. First, they heightened Japan's perception of risk and instability associated with regional threats such as North Korea's nuclear and ballistic programme and China's military modernisation. The inclusion of North Korea in the 'Axis of Evil' in 2002 and the regime changes operated by the United

States in the Middle East strengthened North Korea's resolve to develop a nuclear deterrent.[26] The Six Party Talks held between 2003 and 2007 delayed but did not halt North Korea's progress.[27] The regime conducted its first nuclear weapon test in 2006.

The GWOT changed the dynamic of the alliance in several ways. On the one hand, Washington began to concentrate its attention and resources in other regional theatres, mainly in the Middle East and Central Asia, raising fears of abandonment in Japan. On the other hand, the Bush administration displayed an aggressive stance towards North Korea, threatening regime change in Pyongyang, causing Tokyo to fear being caught up in a conflict. In the same period, the Chinese military budget rose from US$28 billion to US$138 billion. This allowed the People's Liberation Army (PLA) to expand and modernise its air and naval forces, and begin building the key components of its Anti-Access/Area Denial (A2/AD) strategy in the First Island Chain.[28] These developments empowered a domestic leadership, led by Koizumi Junichiro and later by Abe Shinzo[29] and the so-called 'normal nationalist' conservatives in the LDP, who actively sought to accelerate the normalisation of the Japanese security policies and promote a much more active security role both in the region and globally.

The new NDPG, published in 2004, crystallised the impact of the new changing external environment as well as the initiatives of the new leadership in Japanese military doctrine. The document identified more clearly the threats emerging from North Korea and China, as well as the danger associated with the proliferation of weapons of mass destruction and missile technology. Previous documents had refrained from directly describing China as a security threat; all such inferences had been implicit, using such formulas as 'lack of transparency . . . that should be monitored'. The NDPG significantly expanded the geographical scope of Japan's security interests to include 'the arc of instability spreading from East Asia to the Middle East', somehow anticipating contemporary debates on the concept of Indo-Pacific. This meant that Japan needed to develop a force that could participate actively in UN-led or US-led coalitions and increase both its power projection capabilities and its level of interoperability with other militaries.[30]

Throughout the 'War on Terror', Washington urged its allies to actively support its military effort. This led to further steps towards consolidating the alliance, locking in choices and reinforcing the path chosen in the late 1990s. The most important development for the alliance was the approval of the *US–Japan Alliance: Transformation and Realignment for the Future*, signed in 2005. It allowed great progress to be made in the areas of interoperability, bilateral contingency planning and intelligence sharing, and brought about a gradual expansion of Japan's role in the region.

The alliance was increasingly regarded as effective in promoting stability in the wider region, paving the way for forms of cooperation well beyond the geographic boundaries of East Asia.[31]

The consolidation of the alliance momentarily stalled in 2009 when the Democratic Party of Japan (*Minshutō*) gained the majority in the Diet and elected Hatoyama Yukio as prime minister. Hatoyama's desire to promote a more autonomous foreign policy half-way between Washington and Beijing was perceived by the United States as a threat to the stability of the regional security architecture, rather than a legitimate recalibration of Japanese foreign policy. During Hatoyama's short tenure Japan's new course was opposed by the Obama administration, which assumed an uncompromising stance on important issues such as the relocation of the US base of Futenma in Okinawa.[32] It was also received with open scepticism by the organisational structure of country's foreign and security policies and, in particular, by the ministries of Foreign Affairs and Defence.[33] Despite the expectations of radical change sparked by the election of Hatoyama and the DPJ in 2009, the process of evolution of the Japanese military doctrine continued from 2010 to 2012 with the governments led by Kan and Noda.[34] Hatoyama's resignation in 2010, along with the re-emergence of territorial disputes with China over the Senkaku/Diaoyu Islands, led Tokyo to return to an alliance-centred security policy and accelerate the process of normalisation, as well as the geographic and functional expansion of the JSDF's activities, in keeping with the path established in the late 1990s and consolidated during the early 2000s. The 2010 NDPG shows clear signs in this direction. It mentions openly the threats posed by China and North Korea, and stresses for the first time the dangers represented by grey zone activities in the South and East China Sea, which would become central in the Abe period. Grey zone activities are coercive and aggressive in nature, but also deliberately designed to remain below the threshold of conventional military conflict and open interstate war. Their key features are gradualism, hybridity and deniability.[35]

To cope with these threats, the 2010 NDPG introduced the concept of 'dynamic deterrence', which significantly expanded the role of the JSDF beyond the traditional 'defensive defence'. Dynamic deterrence aims at closing so-called 'windows of deterrence' in order to block China's 'creeping expansion' and avoid any possible *fait accompli* in the East China Sea. To do this, the NDPG proposed investments in ISR capabilities and greater coordination between high levels of government, the Ministry of Defence[36] and the JSDF.[37]

Tokyo was already in the process of going back to defining its defence policy centred on the alliance when it was struck by the 'Triple Disaster' that hit the prefecture of Fukushima on 3 March 2011.[38] Apart from the enormous loss in human and economic terms that the 3/11 crisis caused, there were also other substantial consequences that contributed to further consolidating the path that emerged in the late 1990s and took form under Koizumi's leadership. First, the disaster relief operations led by the JSDF with the support of US forces led to renewed support from the public, both for the JSDF and the alliance.[39] For the JSDF and its perception in society, 3/11 constituted a real turning point. Japan's participation in PKOs had already helped the Japanese public to accept the legitimacy of the country's contribution to international peace and stability. Disaster relief operations after the Triple Disaster of 2011, considerably improved the public's perception of the JSDF, demonstrating its important role for the security of all the Japanese. This further undermined the support for those, such as the JSP, that supported radical pacifism and criticised the legitimacy of the JSDF.

Secondly, it was partly due to the difficulties in managing the aftermath of the disaster that the DPJ lost the chance to present itself as a viable alternative to the LDP political hegemony. All possibilities of recalibrating the country's security strategy with the partial downgrading of the centrality of the alliance and upgrading of the role of regional institutions, together with major attempts at reconciliation with China and South Korea, were definitively exhausted in 2012. The DPJ's experience in government demonstrated how difficult and costly it could be to break away from the path that was established in the late 1990s and developed in the early 2000s. The lock-in effects and the legacy of choices made in the previous periods led the Japanese government, the Ministry of Defence and the JSDF to expand the role of the alliance and foster interoperability and integration with US forces. Such a move not only increased US influence over Japan's policymaking but also fomented internal resistance to alternative strategies.

This ultimately paved the way for a decade of uninterrupted political hegemony by the LDP, coinciding with the premiership of Abe Shinzo (2012–2020), Suga Yoshihide (2020–2021) and Kishida Fumio (since 2021).

6.2.2 Force structure from 9/11 to 3/11

The 2000s were characterised by the emergence of multiple and often conflicting requirements for the JSDF, coupled with the continuing fiscal austerity determined by the 1 per cent ceiling. Due to the 'War on Terror', the country was under heavy external pressure to take part in the US-led coalitions and out-of-area missions, while the North Korean and Chinese threat contributed to significantly altering the regional environment. Consequently, key decisions in terms of force structure and procurement had to be reconciled with these conflicting priorities.[40]

The 2004 NDPG, together with the Mid-Term Defence Programme (MTDP), represented a compromise between these different needs. New platforms designed for power projection and out-of-area missions were introduced, while the bulk of new acquisitions was determined by the need to deal with new threats to Japanese security (such as ballistic missiles) and to increase the level of interoperability with US forces.

The deployment of the GSDF in Samawah, Iraq from 2004 to 2006 marked an important political step towards the normalisation of the country's defence policy and taught several valuable lessons in terms of procurement.[41] From the point of view of logistics and transportation, the capacity of the JSDF to project power into distant theatres was limited. The units deployed in Iraq could use force only for self-defence and had limited possibility to cooperate with armed forces in the coalition. In reaction to these limitations, the JSDF concentrated its activities in the areas of rebuilding infrastructure, providing medical care and provisioning water supplies. Nevertheless, the mission gave the JSDF the opportunity to create a Central Readiness Force, especially trained and equipped for out-of-area missions. In this period, moreover, procurement choices included weapons systems that could be used in out-of-area missions, such as CH-47JA transport helicopters and Boeing KC-767s, which were designed for both in-flight aerial refuelling and strategic transport. Similarly, the refuelling mission in the Indian Ocean supporting the coalition in Afghanistan (2001–2010) and the anti-piracy mission in the Gulf of Aden (since 2009) helped the MSDF to improve its ISR and gain experience in cooperating with allies and partners, and also to justify certain of its procurement choices, such as the Osumi class tank-landing ships.[42]

The limited impact of the mission in Iraq and other contributions to out-of-area missions is attributable both to sequencing and to the legacy of previous decisions. Indeed, in the 1990s, when external threats were less significant, the JSDF could have been transformed into an expeditionary force, like the Italian armed forces before them, but due to institutional and cultural legacies and domestic opposition this never took place. In the 2000s, the international and domestic environment created favourable conditions for a greater contribution to the 'War on Terror'. However, the emergence of new threats from China and North Korea induced Japan to prioritise the development of capabilities and strategies geared to territorial defence and deterrence, rather than deployment in distant theatres or counterinsurgency.

In this context, Japan's participation in the US-led ballistic defence system was a key development. In 2003, the Koizumi government approved participation in the BMD system. This decision helped to erode several previous norms and practices. The system itself de facto breached the principle of the peaceful use of space,[43] included forms of collective self-defence which were then illegal under Article 9, and led to the acquisition of potentially offensive capabilities. Moreover, it extended the boundaries defined by the Three Principles on Arms Export to include intense cooperation in the designing and operating of satellites and missile systems.[44] This decision led to investment in sophisticated, complex and expensive new capabilities, such as PAC-3 terminal phase interceptors, SM-3 mid-phase interceptors, early warning radars and, especially, Kongo and Atago class Aegis-equipped destroyers, the introduction of X-band radars and the modernisation of the Japan Air Defence Ground Environment (JADGE).[45] Since the GDP ceiling remained at 1 per cent, these procurement choices resulted in new restrictions for all services and, in particular, for the GSDF. Moreover, the extremely expensive and complex weapons system that would be developed and integrated in the following decades generated a self-reinforcing mechanism geared to increasing interoperability and industrial cooperation with the US defence industrial sector.

During the 2000s, other decisions reflected the need to strengthen the defence of the Southwest Islands, such as the introduction of Sōryū attack submarines (the first to feature an air-independent propulsion system), the Hyūga class helicopter carriers,[46] C-130H tankers, and F-2 fighters and the extension of F-15s. These decisions marked the beginning of a geographical re-orientation, from north to southwest, which would be reinforced in the following decade to counter the mounting threat posed by China to remote Japanese islands. Lastly, Japanese policymakers understood that due to the multiple requirements that had to be met, along with the increasingly severe budget constraints, it had become necessary to abandon the policy of *kokusanka* (the aim of which was to maximise the country's technological and industrial self-reliance) and made the decision to purchase American equipment or to co-produce weapons systems.[47]

The 2010 NDPG published by the Kan government appeared to ease the tensions of the previous period, reflecting more clearly the deterioration of the security environment and the centrality of the threat posed by China, particularly in terms of its grey zone activities.[48] Although the document was published by a DPJ-led government, it signalled an important step in the evolution of Japanese force structure, since it clearly identified as a main priority the need to equip the JSDF with capabilities that could stand up to the Chinese threat to the country's southeast, marginalising the requirements associated with PKOs. This trend would then be

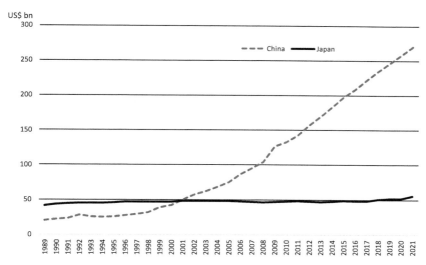

Graph 6.1 Japanese (and Chinese) military expenditures, 1989–2021 (US$ 2020)
Source: SIPRI military expenditures database.

confirmed and consolidated with the successive NDPGs, especially during the Abe period.

The 2010 NDPG marked a key change for the force structure of the JSDF in that it abandoned the 'basic defence force concept' in favour of a 'dynamic defence force' (*doteki boeiryoku*), in keeping with the new objective of providing 'dynamic deterrence'. This meant that Japan's defence forces would retain autonomous capabilities geared not only to repelling an invasion, but also to exercising active deterrence and contributing to stability and deterrence in the region.[49]

The document also reinforces the trend towards jointness and inter-operability with US forces, and stresses the central importance of anti-submarine warfare, ballistic defence and the need to improve ISR capabilities. Together with the 'Mid-Term Defence Programme (MTDP) for FY2011–FY2015', the document led to key decisions for the future of the JSDF, including significant investments in the submarine fleet, with the expansion of the fleet of Sōryū submarines, and in ISR with the procurement of P-3 aircraft, and the expansion of the BMD system. Moreover, the government led by Noda decided to procure the F-35 as future multi-role jet fighter, rather than the Eurofighter, the F-18 Superhornet or choosing to develop an indigenous fighter such as the Mitsubishi X-2 Shinshin.[50]

Consistent with the long-term trend of budget austerity, these changes did not coincide with an increase in the total military budget. Consequently, the JSDF was forced to make cuts in other areas, especially GSDF resources and personnel. In addition, the 2010 NDPG clearly accelerated the trend, already underway in the previous year, of geographically rebalancing JSDF presence from north to south in order to exercise deterrence against China's grey zone tactics.[51]

Lastly, the evolution of the JSDF force structure and capabilities was influenced by 3/11 and the subsequent disaster relief operations. In the aftermath of the disaster, the JSDF deployed 76,000 troops to provide assistance in the areas affected and mobilised another 100,000 reserves. The mission showed how greatly disaster relief operations had improved since those of the 1995 Kobe earthquake, but also what further progress had to be made in terms of integration between services and with US forces. Moreover, disaster relief operations revealed the need to upgrade command and control structures, ISR capabilities, logistics and heavy lifting, and survivability of communications and transportation networks.[52]

6.3 The Abe era and Great Power competition

6.3.1 Japanese military doctrine during the Abe era

Abe returned to power in December 2012 determined to promote a narrative of national rebirth after the 3/11 disaster and to reassert Japan's status as a 'first-tier' nation capable of offering a 'proactive contribution to peace' by enhancing the stability of the regional order.[53] This vision has been associated with a particular redefinition of the region in geographical terms. Throughout the post-Cold War period, the image presented by Tokyo was of a region open to US influence. Since the mid-2000s, it has advocated further expansion of the region's borders to include other democratic powers, such as India and Australia. This vision had already emerged in 2007 when Abe proposed the idea of the 'Confluence of the Two Seas', which envisaged how India and Japan could aspire to an active role in promoting a regional order based not only on security and stability and shared values. The return to power of Abe and the LDP in 2012 helped to consolidate this path through concepts such as the 'Security Diamond' and, especially, the 'Free and Open Indo Pacific'.[54] This latter concept would give the democratic powers of the region an active role in limiting the revisionist aspects of China's rise, reaffirming the standards and values that were central to the regional order, such as freedom of navigation, international law and the peaceful settlement of disputes, in the wide area that extended from the Indian Ocean to Hawaii.[55] This role became even more explicit with the adoption of the Free and Open Indo-Pacific vision, which assigned Tokyo a central role in the promotion of a rules-based regional order.[56]

The expansion of the Japanese security role was accompanied by a reworking of the Japanese pacifist narrative. The concept of peace remains central. Post-war Japan focused on avoiding being dragged into another war, minimising the risk of being caught up in Cold War rivalry and keeping its own military under strict control. Contemporary Japan presents itself as a country capable of making a 'proactive contribution to peace' by helping to uphold the regional order and its main normative pillars. This idea is functional to the geographic expansion of the Japanese strategic horizon promoted with the Free and Open Indo Pacific vision, which envisages a role for Tokyo as a main partner of the United States and a 'first-tier' nation in the wider region extending from the Indian Ocean to Hawaii.

Abe also promoted the idea of 'ending the post-war', which entailed an effort to transcend post-war pacifist constraints and reform Article 9. This concept was also associated with a renewed sense of pride in the country's history and a desire to overcome the sense of guilt deriving from Japan's wartime conduct.[57]

During the period 2012–2022, there was a sharp deterioration in the Japanese security environment.[58] As highlighted in the 2022 White Paper *Defence of Japan* and previous official documents of the Japanese Ministry of Defence, the Chinese threat intensified along the entire spectrum of military intensity.[59] The National Security Strategy published in 2022 defines China as it 'presents an unprecedented and the greatest strategic challenge in ensuring the peace and security of Japan and the peace and stability of the international community', adding that 'Japan should respond with its comprehensive national power and in cooperation with its ally, like-minded countries and others'.[60]

At the high end of the spectrum, China's Anti-Access/Area Denial (A2/AD) strategy has been posing a formidable challenge. The capabilities developed by the PLA to promote this strategy, such as middle- and long-range ballistic missiles, fourth and fifth generation fighters, UAVs and long-range bombers, and a vast fleet of submarine and surface warships, represent a direct threat to Japan's territory and its territorial waters, undermining the capacity of both Japan and the United States to exercise deterrence.[61] These capabilities have enabled China to use grey zone strategies, posing a threat to both Japan's control of the Senkaku Islands and its free access to the sea lines of communications that connect the country with Southeast Asia, the Middle East and Europe.[62]

Beyond the security challenges posed by China, Russia's invasion of Ukraine in 2022 contributed to further deteriorate Japan's threat perception in two ways: first, it was a reminder that war remains a concrete possibility and it could be triggered by an escalation in one of the many regional flash points. Secondly, Japan, throughout the 2000s and 2010s had tried to cultivate a positive relationship with Russia. The invasion of Ukraine led to a renewed alignment between Beijing and Moscow, a development entirely negative for Japan, which needs now to deal with two hostile great powers on the Asian mainland.[63]

During the 2010s and early 2020s, North Korea's nuclear and ballistic programme achieved several milestones, such as the testing of hydrogen bombs and the development of increasingly accurate and reliable short, intermediate and intercontinental ballistic missiles. Since 2017, the North Korean regime has had the capacity to threat both Japan and the United States with nuclear weapons, and also to inflict significant damage on neighbouring countries with conventional weapons in case of conflict.[64]

On his return to power, Abe reacted to the deterioration in the security environment by promoting a large array of reforms, thereby accelerating the agenda adopted in the previous periods. The most consequential of these reforms regarded the re-interpretation of Article 9 of the constitution, which has allowed Japan to engage in 'collective self-defence'. This means that the use of force as legitimate only in defence of Japanese territory also includes cases 'when an armed attack against a foreign country that is in a close relationship with Japan occurs and as a result threatens Japan's survival'.[65] This interpretation allows Japan to protect the US forces deployed in East Asia, to intercept missiles directed at the United States and to exercise deterrence autonomously or jointly with US forces against both China and North Korea.

Other fundamental reforms promoted by Abe were: the approval of a state secrecy law geared to developing intelligence-sharing with the United States and other partners; the creation of a National Security Council, which, based on the American model, would strengthen coordination between ministries and agencies; the reform of the principles of arms export, which would legalise the joint development of weapon systems with friendly nations; and the issuing of the country's first National Security Strategy (NSS).[66]

The path promoted by Abe was reinforced by his successors, especially by Kishida Fumio. In December 2022, his government adopted a new NSS and a new National Defence Strategy (NDS) that deepened Abe's efforts to embrace a proactive security role in the Indo-Pacific, bolstering the country's security posture and exercising deterrence towards China and North Korea, also through the acquisition of counter-strike capabilities.

The Abe era has also been characterised by a significant consolidation of the alliance. The most important development was the adoption of the 2015 Guidelines, which further redefined the division of roles and significantly improved the levels of interoperability, intelligence-sharing and coordination. The 2015 Guidelines focused largely on the need for the alliance to adapt to the emergence of grey zone threats, implementing the concept of seamless cooperation. This concern had already appeared central in the 2013 NDPG, which underlined the need to deter *fait accompli* and emphasise the resolve and credibility of deterrence through upgrades in ISR, readiness, rapid deployments and military exercises.[67] The 2013 NDPG introduced the idea of using escalation management and the Flexible Deterrent Options (FDOs) to face these challenges. FDOs are defined as 'preplanned, deterrence-oriented actions carefully tailored to send the right signal and influence an adversary's actions'. Examples include increasing levels of readiness, posture of forces, deployments in potential areas of conflict, increasing training and exercise activities. Essentially, the 2015 Guidelines introduced the concept of 'seamless coordination', completing a long-term trend of coordination and jointness with US forces which began in the late 1990s. Originally, the alliance was to be 'activated' only in case of conflict, but with the 1997 Guidelines forms of peacetime collaboration were introduced. The 2015 document abolished this distinction, with the purpose of responding to the use of grey zone strategies by the Chinese armed forces through efforts to boost intelligence-sharing, surveillance and reconnaissance, joint maritime patrolling, and coordination in the fields of missile defence, outer space and cyberspace.[68]

The process of consolidation of the alliance slowed down during the Trump administration. Especially during the first two years, Trump's transactional approach to alliance relations generated fears of abandonment in Japan. Trump did not consider the US commitment to Japan's security as unconditional and absolute, but dependent on Tokyo's willingness to contribute in terms of burden-sharing or economic and commercial concessions. Japan's fears were further exacerbated by the president's approach to the negotiations with North Korea, during which he seemed to be willing to sacrifice the allies' security concerns in order to achieve a breakthrough with Kim Jong Un.[69] In the second half of the Trump presidency, the emergence of the 'Great Power competition'[70] with China led the administration to stress the importance of alliance and develop personal relations between Trump and Abe. Despite the rhetoric on an allegedly 'stronger than ever' alliance, significant frictions persisted regarding issues such as North Korea, China and host-nation support. The first years of the Biden presidency have led to efforts towards further strengthening the alliance. Suga, who succeeded Abe in September 2020, was the first ally to pay a state visit to Washington in April 2021. The visit gave emphasis to the renewed alignment and the efforts to promote a coherent approach to the major regional security challenges. This trend continued with Prime Minister Kishida, who succeeded Suga in October 2021.

The bilateral summit between Biden and Kishida held in Washington in January 2023, signalled the alignment on a common vision for a Free and Open Indo-Pacific as well as the appreciation of the Biden administration for steps undertaken by Kishida with the NSS and the NDS.[71]

The aim of upholding the stability of the regional order in the Indo-Pacific area has prompted Japan to also invest considerably in new forms of defence cooperation with regional partners. The JSDF has been increasingly involved in bilateral, minilateral and multilateral initiatives. The most significant progress has been made in the bilateral relationship with Australia. Under the Special Strategic Partnership (2014) and the 'reinforced' Acquisition and Cross-Servicing Agreement (2017) the two countries carried out joint training and exercises, personnel exchanges, cooperation in the realm of HA/DR, intelligence and maritime security.[72] Since 2020, the Reciprocal Access Agreement has authorised the temporary deployment of Japanese and Australian militaries in each other's territory. This also means that the JSDF, under the new interpretation of Article 9, is allowed to protect Australian troops.

The most important minilateral is the Quadrilateral Security Dialogue (or Quad). Politically, it signals the intent of the United States, Japan, Australia and India to uphold the regional order in the face of the Chinese challenge. Militarily, the Quad has led the JSDF to participate in several military exercises, such as Malabar and Talisman Sabre, with the aim of improving interoperability and coordination. The most significant multilateral initiative is the Vientiane Vision, through which the JSDF has supported ASEAN countries in their efforts to preserve the principles of international law, focusing particularly on maritime and navigation law, and to counter China's hybrid coercive activities. This has entailed cooperation in the realm of maritime security, ISR, cybersecurity, peacekeeping, humanitarian assistance and disaster relief, and the planning and organisation of exercises.[73]

In conclusion, in the evolution of Japanese military doctrine the Abe period significantly reinforced the previous trajectories in all major areas: the overcoming of anti-militarist rules and standards; the consolidation of the alliance; and cooperation with regional partners in an effort to uphold the regional order, while expanding Japan's role within it.[74] This has represented more than just an effort to counteract China's power or the threat posed by North Korea. On the contrary, in fact, the Japanese leadership's determination to play an active part in consolidating the regional order, strengthening the alliance and expanding Japan's security role have been central in shaping Tokyo's security choices.[75] Moreover, domestic politics constituted a fundamental permissive condition. Abe governed Japan from December 2012 until his resignation in September

2020, becoming the longest-serving prime minister in the country's history.[76] Through his control over the Diet and the LDP, Abe left a very deep mark on the evolution of Japanese security policies and military doctrine. Despite this, however, even Abe did not manage to achieve one of his most treasured ideological objectives – the amendment of Article 9 of the constitution – due partly to unfavourable public opinion and partly to the complexities of the process of constitutional revision. Abe's resignation marked the beginning of a new period of leadership instability, caused more by a renewed influence of factions in the LDP than the emergence of a real political alternative. His successors Suga and Kishida, have been following the path established during the Abe era. Because of their ideological and political proximity with Abe, in fact, coupled with a lesser degree of control over the LDP and its factions, neither Kishida nor Suga before him have offered any significant alternative in terms of security strategy.[77] On the other hand, the legacy of the options available to Abe's successors is conditioned by the path that was consolidated during the 2010s.

6.3.2 Japanese force structure and great power competition

The drastic evolution of the balance of power determined by China's fast-paced military modernisation and the emergence of major threats posed by the North Korean nuclear and ballistic programmes represented a key driver of change for Japan's military doctrine and force structure. Decisive choices in terms of procurement and organisation were primarily made in response to threats such as Beijing's A2AD strategy or its use of hybrid strategies in the East China Sea, or Pyongyang's development in the nuclear and ballistic field.

After his return to power in late 2012, Abe Shinzo had to face a rapidly deteriorating security environment, determined by the expansion of China's capabilities and by Beijing's rapidly growing use of hybrid tactics against Japan's remote Southwest Islands. As reported by the Japanese Ministry of Defence (Table 6.1), after 2012, China's air forces navy and maritime militias began to repeatedly intrude Japan's airspace and maritime space.[78]

The need to tackle the threat posed by China and North Korea, but also the process of consolidation of the alliance and the expansion of Japan's regional role, meant a series of new missions and tasks for the JSDF. The response in terms of force structure and military planning was largely the result of Abe's activism in promoting several important reforms enabling a reaction to the Chinese and North Korean threats that was not possible in previous years.[79]

Table 6.1 Data on intrusions of Chinese government naval units in Japanese territorial waters

Year	Number of days with intrusions	Number of vessels identified per year
2012	79	407
2013	232	819
2014	243	729
2015	240	709
2016	211	752
2017	171	696
2018	158	607
2019	282	1097
2020	83	289

Source: Defence of Japan, 2020.

Many of the key choices in terms of procurement and force structure were favoured by political decisions that led to abolishing or working around some of the pillars of Japanese post-war pacifism. The 2014 reinterpretation of Article 9 allowed for 'collective self-defence', significantly moving away from the original idea of banning any form of collective defence agreements. The decision to participate in a ballistic defence system circumvented the ban on military use of space.[80] The reinterpretation of the Three Principles of Arms Export favoured both the export of defence systems to other countries and the participation of the Japanese defence industry in joint programmes.[81] Furthermore, it was instrumental in improving interoperability with the United States and cooperation with other states in multilateral initiatives such as the Quad or the Vientiane Vision.[82] The decision to acquire autonomous strike capabilities, undertaken with the NSS 2022, and the procurement of F-35s and Izumo class helicopter/aircraft carriers[83] further eroded the boundaries associated with the ban on offensive weapons and power projection capacities. Nevertheless, the legacy of post-war pacifism and relative institutional limits still lingers and continues to be an influence. Other restrictions have remained in place, such as the Three Non-Nuclear Principles, which forbids Japan from producing, storing and transporting nuclear weapons.

It is important to underline that the expansion of the Japanese security role took place while facing considerable budget constraints. China's budget today is twenty-two times higher than in 1990, while Japan's budget has grown only marginally. The JSDF undertook a thorough revision of its doctrine and structure while facing budget austerity, caused by the adherence, up to 2023, to the 1 per cent GDP cap associated with the very low growth rates of post-Cold War Japan. These budget constraints became even more pressing after the decision to introduce very expensive weapons systems such as the BMD, F-35s and Aegis destroyers.

Abe repeatedly declared that he was in favour of increasing the military budget and funding to the JSDF. However, up to 2022, the Japanese government sought to work around the numbers either by spending slightly more than 1 per cent over several fiscal years or by moving budget items under non-defence related expenditures. The 1 per cent GDP ceiling on the military budget, coupled with Japan's relative decline in the region, represented a significant constraint and contributed to shaping and often to delaying Japan's responses to the changing security environment. Only in late 2022, did the Kishida government announce the decision to abolish the 1 per cent GDP cap, planning a substantial increase in the military budget that is projected to reach 2 per cent GDP by 2028.

Lastly, the reform of the Three Principles of Arms Export, which enabled the export and co-production of weapons systems, led to a reduction in the price tag of key platforms and a more effective use of the economic resources available.[84] The combination of an opening-up to defence cooperation after 2014 and the budget ceiling reinforced the trend towards further interoperability with US forces. This led to the acquisition of weapons systems geared to rationalising the resources needed for current and future defence requirements, as demonstrated by the procurement of platforms such as F-35s or Kongo class destroyers equipped with Aegis missile systems. The decision to open up the defence industry to international cooperation and foreign sales after the reform of the Three Principles of Arms Export and the abolition of the budget ceiling in 2022 only partially alleviated financial constraints determined by the need to procure increasingly sophisticated and expensive platforms.

The 2013 NDPG, published at the same time as the country's first National Security Strategy, sought to advance the process of transformation of the role and the structure of the JSDF by promoting the concept of Joint Dynamic Defence Force. This concept confirms the centrality of 'dynamic defence' as a key purpose and stresses the need to increase jointness between the three branches of the JSDF. The document presented the need to maintain both ISR and air superiority. This led to the procurement of P-1 surveillance aircraft and UAVs, such as the Global Hawk, while radars were reinforced and the capabilities of the ASDF were expanded with additional F-35 and F-2 jets.[85]

The evolution of the threat environment also led to the acceleration of the geographic reorientation of Japanese force structure. In recent years, most of the JSDF's attention and resources have been focused on protecting the Southwest Islands from changes in the territorial status quo by China's PLA. Consequently, the JSDF increased its amphibious assault capabilities for the defence and possible recapture of remote islands. This affected primarily the GSDF, which was obliged to speed up its transition towards an amphibious, rapid-response force. For these reasons, the NDPG established new rapid-deployment units, including an amphibious rapid-deployment brigade. The ASDF, meanwhile, acquired new air-refuelling capabilities and mobile combat vehicles. Furthermore, the JSDF continued to geographically relocate its structure, moving additional units of the ASDF and the GSDF to the Ryukyu Islands and expanding existing bases in southern and western Kyushu.[86]

The third key aspect is represented by capabilities in anti-submarine warfare. The 2013 NDPG brought about a significant improvement with the enlargement of the Sōryū submarine fleet and the deployment of the Izumo helicopter carrier used in anti-submarine warfare. A few years later, in 2018, the Izumo would be converted into a de facto aircraft carrier capable of carrying F-35B fighters.

In the 2013 NDPG significant emphasis was placed, for the first time, on cyber and space, pointing out that the entire Japanese military structure depended on free access to space and cyber communications. Consequently, the document called for a government-wide effort to increase the capacity to identify vulnerabilities, secure the networks and repair any damages.

The force structure of the JSDF was influenced also by the 2015 Guidelines, which emphasised the need for seamless coordination in dealing with grey zone threats. These guidelines led to the establishing of a permanent Alliance Coordination Mechanism for promoting a more flexible and 'whole of government' reaction to possible contingencies. They also furthered progress in terms of integration of the ISR networks between US forces and the JSDF.

The focus on China and North Korea did not lead to a complete withdrawal of out-of-area missions and PKOs from the front. The Abe government approved the Permanent International Peace Support Law, which established a procedure allowing the JSDF to provide logistical support to international missions without an ad hoc law.[87] The same law also approved the use of force to rescue Japanese nationals and clarified the conditions for the exercise of collective self-defence. Despite the new law, the involvement of the JSDF in PKOs all but ceased during Abe's tenure, with Japan withdrawing from the UN Mission in South Sudan in 2017.[88] These developments confirm the peculiar nature of the direction in which Japan had been moving since the early 1990s and the divergence from the trajectory of evolution that characterised Italy and (to a lesser extent) Germany. While PKOs were important from a political and normative point of view, they never became the 'core business' of the JSDF. Nor were they the most pre-eminent driver in the development of the JSDF force structure, which was shaped primarily by external threats and alliance dynamics. Tokyo's attitude towards missions abroad also demonstrates the importance of sequencing. When Japan was asked to provide a substantial contribution to military missions abroad, the influence of domestic constraints and unfavourable public opinion was still too great to allow the JSDF to fully embrace peacekeeping and out-of-area activities as its main mission. However, when the domestic situation was such that a more significant contribution could be considered, the JSDF was forced to give priority to threats that were closer to home. Moreover, the 2010s marked a general trend towards shifting the burden of manning UNPKOs onto the armed forces of developing countries, thereby decreasing the pressure not only on Japan but on many other major Western powers.[89]

The period between 2017 and 2020 significantly shaped Japan's choices in terms of military planning and force structure. The Trump administration further destabilised the security environment by introducing uncertainty in the alliance, fuelling security competition with China and generating fears of both entrapment and abandonment with its policies towards North Korea.[90]

In describing this trend, the 2019 NDPG states that the 'security environment surrounding Japan is changing at extremely high speeds'. The document portrays a situation in which political and strategic trends are heightened by the introduction of disruptive technologies. Space, cybersecurity and electromagnetic spectrum domains are described as central to the future of warfare. Artificial Intelligence (AI), hypersonic missiles and high-power energy technologies are presented as potential game changers.[91] For this reason, the JSDF is urged to become a 'Multi-domain Defence Force' capable of carrying out 'cross-domain operations organically fusing capabilities in all domains'.[92] Consequently, the document places great emphasis on the creation of systems for the new Space Operation Squadron, the procurement of Space Situational Awareness (SSA) satellites, the improvement of defensive and offensive electromagnetic capabilities, and the development of cyberwarfare capacities. Many of these new skills might be interpreted as 'offensive'. The aim of cyber capabilities, for example, is 'to disrupt the adversary's ability to employ cyber space to attack'. Likewise, counter-space systems are designed to gain 'the ability to disrupt adversary command, control and intelligence'.[93]

The renewed focus on jointness and multi-domain warfare allows the GSDF to resist the tendency to rebalance resources and personnel towards the MSDF and ASDF. On the one hand, most systems that are critical for Japan require interservice cooperation. On the other hand, integration and jointness are regarded as a tool for placating interservice rivalries between the GSDF and the other branches and reducing duplications due to interservice competition, particularly in expensive systems such as BMD.[94]

The document highlights an increased acceleration in previous trends in terms of the development of new capabilities geared to dealing with the threats posed by China and North Korea. To this end, Japan plans to invest more in defending the country's remote Southwest Islands, expanding the ISR system, and further consolidating BMD and submarine and surface naval units. The NDPG also stresses the need to cultivate amphibious capabilities, through the development of an Amphibious Rapid Deployment Brigade (ARDB), based in Ainoura in southwestern Kyushu, to recapture any remote islands that may be illegally occupied by enemy troops. It also highlights the need to increase resilience, such as the capacity to continue to operate after an attack, especially an attack on the Southwest Islands (such as the Senkaku Islands) or after major disruptions to the country's basic infrastructure. For this purpose, the document calls for major improvements in terms of mobility, heavy lift, logistics, redundancy and dispersion.[95]

Addressing an issue that emerged in the context of security policy, especially after 2017, the NDPG also recommended developing autonomous counter-strike capabilities through the acquisition of ground-based ballistic missiles and standoff weapons, geared to buttressing the credibility of Japanese deterrence.[96] This debate intensified after the cancellation of the Aegis Ashore programme and, more broadly, as a consequence of the increasingly high costs of BMD systems.[97] In 2018, Tokyo introduced a series of standoff missiles, such as the Joint Strike Missile (JSM), which can be launched from F-15s and has a range of up to 900 km, the Joint Air-to-Surface Standoff Missile (JASSM) and the Long-Range Anti-Ship Missile (LRASM), which can be launched from F-35s and has a range of 500 km.[98] With the release of the NSS and NDS 2022 the Japanese government put an end to the legal and strategic debate on counter-strike capabilities, stating that long range counter-strike capabilities are essential to deter China and North Korea. Therefore, the JSDF will initially procure US-made Tomahawk missiles, while looking to develop an indigenous alternative in the future.

The two documents released by the Kishida government in late 2022 further accelerate previous trajectories in terms of evolution of force structure, especially when it comes to emphasis on deterrence. Beyond the momentous decision to adopt counter-strike capabilities, the NDS, which replaces the NDPG, plans to capitalise on the abolition of the 1 per cent GDP ceiling by accelerating investment in cyber, space and intelligence capabilities. Further investments will also regard ballistic defence, and unmanned defence capabilities. Additionally, in 2022, Japan also embarked in a new ambitious project in the realm of the defence industry, creating a consortium with Italy and the United Kingdom to design and produce a 'sixth generation' fighter jet, the Tempest.[99] Ultimately, the decision to allow the budget to align to the NATO standard of 2 per cent GDP should make past budgetary trade-offs less constraining, speeding up the process of modernisation and facilitating the creation of a joint operational posture all the branches of the JSDF.[100]

In conclusion, during the Abe period the security threats posed by China and North Korea were instrumental in shaping the choices of the JSDF in terms of force structure and budget. The nature of the threat posed by China, and especially its constant use of grey zone tactics, was central in formulating Japan's response, influencing its military planning and procurement, placing major emphasis on ISR and amphibious forces, and highlighting the need to implement 'whole of government' coordination. Nevertheless, these threats were not the only drivers. Budgetary limits, as well as institutional and, more generally, domestic constraints, continued to impact decisions regarding procurement and budget, despite the fluidity of normative boundaries in this period.

Alliance politics played a significant role. The long-term effects of 'fear of abandonment' generated by the Trump administration, led the government and the JSDF to opt for such solutions as counter-strike capabilities, which would be compatible with the possibility of a declining US role, despite the renewed strategic alignment during the Biden administration. Technology represented another key driver in two respects. Essentially, it made it possible to overcome institutional constraints before they were accepted by public opinion and established with the approval of new laws. The main example of this is the role of the BMD system with regard to the military use of space, collective self-defence, cooperation in research and design, and intelligence-sharing. Ultimately, technology has had a very relevant impact on Japan's choices, both in terms of procurement and force structure, and of military doctrine. In the field of missile defence or counter-strike capabilities, in fact, decisions have been clearly influenced both by emerging threats in the cyber domain and the proliferation of ballistic and cruise missiles. Besides the need for new capabilities to match the adversary's advancements, technological factors also had a more indirect impact. Technologies such as ballistic defence, counter-strike capabilities, the use of satellites for military purposes, cyber-weapons and the emergence of grey zone strategies contributed to blurring the boundaries between offence and defence, thereby making it more difficult for Japan to maintain its original doctrine based on defensive defence and favoured the transition towards a doctrine centred around 'dynamic deterrence'.

Notes

1. In 1993, the LDP lost the majority of its seats in the Diet for the first time since it was formed in 1955. This led first to an 'anti-LDP' coalition led by Morihiro Hosokawa, which governed for ten months only, and then, from 1994 to 1996, to a grand coalition led by the Socialist Murayama Tomiichi.
2. Oros, *Normalizing Japan*; K. Gustafsson, L. Hagström and U. Hanssen (2018), 'Japan's Pacifism is Dead', *Survival* 60(6): 137–58; Samuels, *Securing Japan*.
3. M. Dian (2020), 'Japan, South Korea and the Rise of a Networked Security Architecture in East Asia', *International Politics* 57(2): 185–207.
4. Samuels, 'Securing Japan: The Current Discourse', 125–52.
5. M. Thorsten (2012), *Superhuman Japan: Knowledge, Nation and Culture in US–Japan Relations*. London: Routledge.
6. M. H. Armacost (1996). *Friends or Rivals? The Insider's Account of US–Japan Relations*. New York: Columbia University Press; R, M. Uriu (2009), *Clinton and Japan: The Impact of Revisionism on US Trade Policy*. Oxford: Oxford University Press.
7. Japan's financial contribution to the conflict was considerable, amounting to US$13 billion, the equivalent of more than a third of the country's defence budget at that time.
8. Fujishige, Uesugi and Honda, *Japan's Peacekeeping at a Crossroads*.
9. Smith, *Japan Rearmed*; Mulloy, G. (2021), *Defenders of Japan. Post Imperial Armed Forces, 1946-2016*. London: Hurst.
10. C. W. Hughes (2012), 'The Democratic Party of Japan's New (but Failing) Grand Security Strategy: From "Reluctant Realism" to "Resentful Realism"?' *Journal of Japanese Studies* 38(1): 109–40.
11. Until 2007 Japan did not have an autonomous Ministry of Defence, but a Defence Agency that answered directly to the prime minister.
12. Japanese Ministry of Defence (2022), *National Defence Program Guidelines (NDPG) and Medium Term Defence Program (MTDP)*, available at: https://www.mod.go.jp /en/d_policy/basis/guideline/index.html.
13. T. Yuzawa (2007), *Japan's Security Policy and the ASEAN Regional Forum: The Search for Multilateral Security in the Asia-Pacific*. London: Routledge.
14. Patalano, 'Shielding the "Hot Gates"', 859–95.
15. Smith, *Japan Rearmed*, 97.
16. J. S. Nye (2001), 'The "Nye Report": Six Years Later', *International Relations of the Asia-Pacific* 1(1): 95–103.
17. At the time Japan did not have an autonomous Ministry of Defence. The Japanese Defence Agency was under the direct control of the prime minister.
18. P. Midford (2018), 'Decentering from the US in Regional Security Multilateralism: Japan's 1991 Pivot', *Pacific Review* 31(4): 441–59; T. Yuzawa (2018), 'From a Decentering to Recentering Imperative: Japan's Approach to Asian Security Multilateralism', *Pacific Review* 31(4): 460–79.
19. SIPRI (2022), Military Expenditures Database, Stockholm, available at: https://www .sipri.org/databases/milex.
20. Japanese Ministry of Foreign Affairs (1995), National Defense Program Outline in and after FY 1996, Tokyo, available at: https://www.mofa.go.jp/policy/security/de fense96.
21. D. Hunter-Chester (2016), *Creating Japan's Ground Self-Defense Force, 1945–2015: A Sword Well Made*. Lanham, MD: Lexington Books.
22. Patalano, *Post-War Japan as a Sea Power*.
23. Ibid.
24. Mulloy, *Defenders of Japan*.

25. Y. Miyagi (2009), 'Foreign Policy-making under Koizumi: Norms and Japan's Role in the 2003 Iraq War', *Foreign Policy Analysis* 5(4): 349–66.
26. V. D. Cha and D. C. Kang (2018), *Nuclear North Korea: A Debate on Engagement Strategies*. New York: Columbia University Press.
27. L. Buszynski (2013), *Negotiating with North Korea: The Six Party Talks and the Nuclear Issue*. London: Routledge.
28. J. Johnson (2017), 'Washington's Perceptions and Misperceptions of Beijing's Anti-Access Area-Denial (A2-AD) "Strategy": Implications for Military Escalation Control and Strategic Stability', *Pacific Review* 30(3): 271–88; T. G. Mahnken (2011), 'China's anti-Access Strategy in Historical and Theoretical Perspective', *Journal of Strategic Studies* 34(3): 299–323.
29. Koizumi Junichiro served as prime minister between April 2001 and September 2006. Abe Shinzo was the longest-serving prime minister in Japan's history, serving from September 2006 to September 2007 and from December 2012 to September 2020.
30. Japanese Ministry of Defence, 'National Defense Program Guidelines, FY 2005 and after'.
31. Dian, *The Evolution of the US–Japan Alliance*.
32. M. Dian (2020), 'Obama and Japan: An Endangered Legacy', in I. Parmar and O. Turner (eds), *The United States in the Indo-Pacific*. Manchester: Manchester University Press, 63–78; M. J. Green (2010), 'Japan's Confused Revolution', *Washington Quarterly* 33(1): 3–19.
33. Interviews with officials of the Japanese Ministry of Defence (Strategic Planning Division), Japanese Ministry of Foreign Affairs (International Cooperation Bureau), November 2017, October 2018.
34. Hughes, 'The Democratic Party of Japan's New (but Failing) Grand Security Strategy', 109–40.
35. See M. J. Green, K. Hicks, Z. Cooper, J. Schaus and J. Douglas (2017), *Countering Coercion in Maritime Asia: the Theory and Practice of Gray Zone Deterrence*. New York: Rowman & Littlefield.
36. The Japanese Defence Agency was elevated to ministerial status in 2007.
37. D. Altman (2017), 'By Fait Accompli, Not Coercion: How States Wrest Territory from Their Adversaries', *International Studies Quarterly* 61(4): 881–8; S. Takahashi (2019), 'Development of Grey-Zone Deterrence: Concept Building and Lessons from Japan's Experience', *Pacific Review* 31(6): 787–810.
38. The massive earthquake that hit the northeast of the country also produced a giant tsunami which damaged the local nuclear power plant, resulting in a nuclear crisis.
39. R. J. Samuels (2013), *3.11: Disaster and Change in Japan*. Ithaca, NY: Cornell University Press; M. J. Green and N. Szechenyi (2012). 'US–Japan Relations: Back to Normal?' *Comparative Connections* 14(1): 1–10.
40. Oros, *Japan's Security Renaissance*; Samuels, *Securing Japan*.
41. Smith, *Japan Rearmed*.
42. Eldridge and Midford, *The Japanese Ground Self-defense Force*.
43. In 2008 the Basic Space Law amended the ban on the use of space technology for military purposes, restricting it to 'aggressive purposes', but allowing the functions of intelligence, surveillance and recognition (ISR).
44. S. Pekkanen and P. Kallender-Umezu (2010), *In Defense of Japan: From the Market to the Military in Space Policy*. Stanford, CA: Stanford University Press.
45. C. W. Hughes (2013), 'Japan, Ballistic Missile Defence and Remilitarisation', *Space Policy* 29(2): 128–34.
46. The Hyūga class helicopter carrier, after appropriate technical modification, would be able to deploy short take off and landing fighter jets such as the F-35B.
47. C. W. Hughes (2011), 'The Slow Death of Japanese Techno-Nationalism? Emerging Comparative Lessons for China's Defense Production', *Journal of Strategic Studies* 34(3): 451–79.

48. K. Jimbo (2012), 'Japan's National Defense Planning for the New Security Environment: The 2010 National Defense Program Guidelines', *DTP Policy Briefs, 2012*, Policy Brief 3; A. Berkofsky (2011), 'Japan's December 2010 "National Defense Program Guidelines (Ndpg)": The "Big Bang" of Japanese Security and Defense Policies?' *Korean Review of International Studies* 14(1): 33–52.

49. Takahashi, 'Development of Gray-Zone Deterrence', 787–810.

50. Japanese Ministry of Defence (2010), *National Defense Program Guidelines for FY2011*. Tokyo.

51. K. Jimbo, R. Sahashi, S. Takahashi, Y. Sakata, M. Masuda and T. Yuzawa (2011), *Japan's Security Strategy toward China: Integration, Balancing and Deterrence in the Era of Power Shift*. Tokyo: Tokyo Foundation.

52. Y. Tatsumi (2012), *Great Eastern Japan Earthquake: 'Lessons Learned' for Japanese Defense Policy*. Washigton, DC: Stimson Center.

53. Japanese Ministry of Defence (2013), *National Security Strategy*. Tokyo.

54. The concept of Free and Open Indo Pacific was coined by the Abe government. The United States began to use the same term in official documents and statements in 2017.

55. Y. Hosoya (2019), 'FOIP 2.0: The Evolution of Japan's Free and Open Indo-Pacific Strategy', *Asia-Pacific Review* 26(1): 18–28; A. Insisa and G. Pugliese (2022), 'The Free and Open Indo-Pacific versus the Belt and Road: Spheres of Influence and Sino-Japanese Relations', *Pacific Review* 35(3): 557–85.

56. Japanese Ministry of Defence (2021), *Development of the Free and Open Indo Pacific Vision*, Tokyo, available at: https://www.mod.go.jp/en/d_act/exc/india_pacific/indi a_pacific-en.html.

57. Dian, *Contested Memories in Chinese and Japanese Foreign Policy*.

58. For an updated and comprehensive analysis of the Japan's main military assets, see, among others, the annual report of the ISS Military Balance, available at: https://www.iiss.org/publications/the-military-balance.

59. Japanese Ministry of Defence (2022), *Defense of Japan 2022*. Tokyo.

60. Japanese Ministry of Foreign Affairs (2022), *The National Security Strategy of Japan*, Tokyo.

61. M. Dian (2015), 'The Pivot to Asia, Air–Sea Battle and Contested Commons in the Asia Pacific Region', *Pacific Review* 28(2): 237–57; Y. H. Lim (2017), 'Expanding the Dragon's Reach: The Rise of China's Anti-Access Naval Doctrine and Forces', *Journal of Strategic Studies* 40(1/2): 146–68; Defence Intelligence Agency (2019), *China's Military Power: Modernizing a Defense Force to Fight and Win*. Washington, DC; S. Biddle and I. Oelrich (2016), 'Future Warfare in the Western Pacific: Chinese Antiaccess/Area Denial, US Airsea Battle, and Command of the Commons in East Asia', *International Security* 41(1): 7–48.

62. Interviews with officials of the Japanese Ministry of Defence (Japan–US Defence Cooperation Division, Strategic Planning Division), November 2017; Japanese Ministry of Foreign Affairs (October 2018); and National Institute for Defence Studies (NIDS), November 2017.

63. M. Dian and A. Kireeva (2022), 'Wedge Strategies in Russia–Japan Relations', *Pacific Review* 35(5): 853–83.

64. A. Panda (2020), *Kim Jong Un and the Bomb: Survival and Deterrence in North Korea*. London: Hurst.

65. Japanese Ministry of Foreign Affairs (2014), 'Cabinet Decision on Development of Seamless Security Legislation to Ensure Japan's Survival and Protect its People', available at: https://www.mofa.go.jp/fp/nsp/page23e_000273.html.

66. C. W. Hughes (2015), *Japan's Foreign and Security Policy Under the 'Abe Doctrine': New Dynamism or New Dead End?* Basingstoke: Palgrave Macmillan.

67. Japanese Ministry of Defence (2014), *National Defense Program Guidelines for FY2014 and Beyond*. Tokyo.

68. S. W. Harold, Y. Nakagawa and J. Fukuda (2017), *The US–Japan Alliance and Deterring Gray Zone Coercion in the Maritime, Cyber, and Space Domains*. Santa Monica, CA: RAND Corp.; J. L. Schoff (2017), *Uncommon Alliance for the Common Good: The United States and Japan After the Cold War*. Washington, DC: Carnegie Endowment for International Peace; B. E. M. Grønning (2018), 'Operational and Industrial Military Integration: Extending the Frontiers of the Japan–US Alliance', *International Affairs* 94(4): 755–72.

69. P. O'Shea and S. Maslow (2021), '"Making the Alliance even Greater": (Mis-)managing US–Japan Relations in the Age of Trump', *Asian Security* 17(2): 195–215.

70. Since the publication of the 2017 National Security Strategy, US policymakers, analysts and commentators have refered to US–China and US–Russia relations as 'great powers competition', to describe the increasingly competitive nature of the interactions between the three states. The Biden administration has often substituted the term with 'strategic competition'. Japanese official documents have adopted the two definitions, used both in defence White Papers and Diplomatic Blue Books. In line with Abbondanza, the term 'super power competition' should be more appropriate to provide a more detailed illustration of the global power shifts. See again, Abbondanza, 'Middle Powers and Great Powers through History'.

71. The White House (2023), *Joint Statement of United States and Japan*. Washington, DC, 13 January

72. T. Satake and J. Hemmings (2018), 'Japan–Australia Security Cooperation in the Bilateral and Multilateral Contexts', *International Affairs* 94(4): 815–34.

73. C. Wallace (2018), 'Leaving (North-East) Asia? Japan's Southern Strategy', *International Affairs* 94(4): 883–904; J. F. Bradford (2021), 'Japanese Naval Activities in Southeast Asian Waters: Building on 50 Years of Maritime Security Capacity Building', *Asian Security* 17(1): 79–104.

74. During this period the Abe government sought also to improve the level of civil–military integration, encouraging a process of technological spin-off between civilian companies and the defence industry. On this issue, see Koshino, Y. (2021) Is Japan ready for civil–military 'integration'? *International Institute for Strategic Studies Analysis* 3 August https://www.iiss.org/blogs/analysis/2021/08/japan-civil-military-integration. For a classic work on this issue, see Samuels, '*Rich Nation, Strong Army*'.

75. Interviews with officials of Japanese Ministry of Defence (Strategic Planning Division, and Bureau of Defence Policy), Tokyo, November 2017; Interviews with officials of the National Security Secretariat, Tokyo, November 2017; Interviews with US Navy officers, 7th Fleet at Yokosuka Naval Base, January 2016.

76. Abe Shinzo was killed on 8 July 2022 by a former member of the JMSDF during a campaign speech in Nara.

77. Suga served as Abe's chief cabinet secretary between 2012 and 2020. Kishida was a member of the *kochikai* faction, which has traditionally promoted a more cautious approach to foreign and defence policies. However, Kishida, while serving as minister of foreign affairs (2012–2017) gradually aligned with Abe's policies.

78. Japanese Ministry of Defence (2020), *Defense of Japan*. Tokyo.

79. A. P. Liff (2015), 'Japan's Defense Policy: Abe the Evolutionary', *Washington Quarterly* 38(2): 79–99; G. Pugliese and A. Patalano (2020), 'Diplomatic and Security Practice under Abe Shinzō: The Case for Realpolitik Japan', *Australian Journal of International Affairs* 74(6): 615–32.

80. C. W. Hughes (2017), 'Japan's Strategic Trajectory and Collective Self-Defense: Essential Continuity or Radical Shift?' *Journal of Japanese Studies* 43(1): 93–126. The Basic Space Law of 2008 made it possible to use space for national security purposes, legalising the use of satellites in the BMD system.

81. A. Sakaki and S. Maslow (2020), 'Japan's New Arms Export Policies: Strategic Aspirations and Domestic Constraints', *Australian Journal of International Affairs* 74(6): 649–69.

82. Oros, *Japan's Security Renaissance*; Smith, *Japan Rearmed.*
83. The Izumo class includes two ships, the *Izumo* and the *Kaga* helicopter/aircraft carriers.
84. Sakaki and Maslow, 'Japan's New Arms Export Policies'.
85. Japanese Ministry of Defence (2013), *National Defense Program Guidelines for FY2013 and Beyond.* Tokyo.
86. Japanese Ministry of Defence (2014), *Defense of Japan 2014.* Tokyo.
87. Japanese Ministry of Foreign Affairs (2016), 'Japan's Legislation for Peace and Security'. Tokyo, available at: https://www.mofa.go.jp/files/000143304.pdf.
88. Fujishige, Uesugi and Honda, *Japan's Peacekeeping at a Crossroads.*
89. Ibid.
90. O'Shea and Maslow, '"Making the Alliance even Greater"'.
91. Japanese Ministry of Defence (2018), *National Defence Programme Guidelines 2019.* Tokyo.
92. Japanese Ministry of Defence (2020), *Defense of Japan 2020.* Tokyo.
93. N. Katagiri (2021), 'From Cyber Denial to Cyber Punishment: What Keeps Japanese Warriors from Active Defense Operations?' *Asian Security* 17(3): 331–48; P. Kallender and C. W. Hughes (2017), 'Japan's Emerging Trajectory as a "Cyber Power": From Securitization to Militarization of Cyberspace', *Journal of Strategic Studies* 40(1/2): 118–45.
94. J. L. Schoff and S. Romei (2019), *The New National Defense Program Guidelines: Aligning US and Japanese Defense Strategies for the Third Post-Cold War Era.* Washington DC: Sasakawa USA.
95. Ibid.
96. Interviews with officials of the Japanese Ministry of Defence (Strategic Planning Division, and Bureau of Defense Policy), Tokyo, November 2017; Interviews with officials of the National Security Secretariat, Tokyo, November 2017; National Institute Defence Studies, Tokyo, November 2017; Japanese Ministry of Defence, Tokyo, October 2018.
97. K. C. Wadsworth (2019), 'Should Japan Adopt Conventional Missile Strike Capabilities?' *Asia Policy* 26(2): 61–87.
98. J. D. Caverley and P. Dombrowski (2020), 'Policy Roundtable: The Future of Japanese Security and Defense', *Texas National Security Review*, available at: https://tnsr.org/roundtable/policy-roundtable-the-future-of-japanese-security-and-defense/#essay4, last accessed 6 August 2021.
99. J. Beale (2022), 'UK, Italy and Japan Link Up for a New Fighter Jet', BBC News, 8 December 2022, available at: https://www.bbc.com/news/uk-63908284.
100. Japanese Ministry of Defence (2022), *National Defence Strategy.* Tokyo.

Chapter 7

Conclusions

In the three decades since the end of the Cold War the defence policies of Italy, Germany and Japan have undergone remarkable processes of transformation that involved their military doctrines and force structure. Furthermore, the armed forces of the three countries have been deployed – to varying degrees – in a range of new missions, such as counterinsurgency, peacekeeping operations, disaster relief and anti-piracy operations, in addition to the existing roles of deterrence and territorial defence. The three countries were regarded as 'security consumers' during the Cold War, despite their significant military budgets and the considerable technological sophistication they accumulated during the 1970s and 1980s. Since the 1990s, the three states have evolved, to varying degrees, into active supporters and defenders of the international order. Each country has followed its own specific trajectory of evolution which, in turn, has been deeply affected by policy choices implemented during fundamental critical junctures. These decisions determined the development of new paths, opening the way to a phase for the reproduction and reinforcement of the trajectory. These conclusions look at the major findings of the empirical chapters, providing a first-cut comparison of the military transformation that occurred. While the purpose of this book is not to present a standard comparative analysis, there are certainly a few similarities and contrasts that can be highlighted.

7.1 How military doctrines and force structure evolved

Participation in Desert Storm in 1991 was a fundamental critical juncture for Italy. The direction taken at that time was reinforced in the following three decades, with Rome becoming a significant contributor to international PKOs, as well as COIN operations, in the 2000s and 2010s, in a wide area extending from the Balkans to Sahel and Afghanistan. For Germany the years between the intervention in Kosovo and participation in the ISAF operation marked the critical juncture that initiated a (slow) process of evolution in the country's defence policy. Although in 1991 Germany did not directly take part in Desert Storm, in 1999 the Bundeswehr played an active role in the NATO-led coalition in Kosovo, a role that was then further consolidated by participation in the NATO-led mission in Afghanistan. In this context, the German armed forces were involved for the first time in combat on the ground, assuming major responsibility in the multinational coalition. Berlin gradually began to move towards crisis management in the 2000s. However, military reluctance did not disappear, as the crisis in Libya in 2011 clearly demonstrated. The Russian annexation of Crimea was another crucial moment for German defence policy, partly because it led to the reconsideration of territorial defence as a key priority. In the Japanese case, two critical junctures can be identified which are completely different from the Italian and German cases. Both are defined by the overlapping of multiple external and domestic factors, rather than key catalytic events such as the First Gulf War or the intervention. In the period between 1996 and 1998 Japan experienced a deterioration in the external environment with the Third Taiwan Strait Crisis and the Taepodong Shock, a domestic political realignment with the return of the conservative LDP in power, and a major step in the consolidation of the alliance with Washington. Likewise, in 2012 the election of Abe Shinzo ended the short-lived interlude featuring the DPJ in power, after a sharp rise in the level of external threat determined by China's pressure on the Sekaku Islands and the acceleration of the North Korean nuclear and ballistic programme.

The Italian military doctrine was heavily shaped – and in turn influenced – by the approach to military interventions. Since the approval of the *New Defence Model* in 1991, emphasis began to be placed on 'deployability' and the capacity to conduct joint missions overseas, and power projection, thus breaking with the Cold War era approach rooted in territorial defence. This trend was reinforced in the 2000s with participation in high-intensity COIN operations in Iraq and Afghanistan. While Italy developed its own approach to COIN (from Somalia onwards), the national strategic reflection was still limited, and Rome essentially relied on NATO doctrines as its main references. On the whole, the highly demanding post-2001 missions (Iraq, Lebanon, Libya and, especially, Afghanistan) represented a crucial operational experience that, from the ground upwards, pushed for the transformation and adaptation of Italian defence in the direction of 'deployability' and crisis management. Since the mid-2010s, the migration crises stemming from civil wars and extensive instability in the 'Enlarged Mediterranean' added another element of change to Italian military doctrine. The Italian navy was given the task of patrolling the Mediterranean, conducting national missions such as 'Mare Nostrum' and taking part in EU missions such as Operation Sophia (followed by Operation Irini). Since the 2015 White Paper, as the 'war on terror' slowly came to an end, Italy began to focus heavily on the so-called Enlarged Mediterranean as the main vital area for its national interests. Overall, however, military deployment aboard did not stop, and the post-Cold War trajectory continued.

The transformation of German military doctrine was significantly slower compared with Italy. Due to the legacy of the Cold War doctrine, inspired by high-intensity territorial defence, and the 'delayed start' caused by the lack of direct involvement in Iraq in 1991, the German trajectory was quite different from the radical transformation promoted by Rome. Even during and after its participation in ISAF, the Bundeswehr did not develop an integrated doctrine for COIN and continued to regard fighting wars, peace support and humanitarian aid as different categories, rather than elements of a single 'continuum of conflict'. Even at the height of the 'war on terror', German military doctrine maintained a balance between *Verteidigungsarmee* (territorial defence) and an *Einsatzarmee* (expeditionary force for missions abroad). With regard to the latter, Germany sought to develop a 'comprehensive approach' that integrated military and non-military aspects. Russia's annexation of Crimea in 2014 halted the process of reorientation towards interventions abroad, with territorial defence once again playing a major role in German military doctrine.

During the last three decades Japan has deeply reconsidered its military doctrine based on the concept of 'defensive defence' (*senshubōei*). Japan began to contribute to UN-led PKOs and to perform other tasks, such as HA/DR and anti-piracy operations. As in the case of the Bundeswehr, however, the JSDF never considered out-of-area deployments as their main mission. The deterioration of the security environment surrounding Japan prompted it to develop a doctrine aimed at exercising deterrence in a wide spectrum of conflict situations, ranging from grey zone strategies to high-intensity warfare. Tokyo's desire to embrace the role of defender of the regional and global order also prompted it to consider providing 'proactive contributions to peace' in the region as a key element of the contemporary military doctrine of the JSDF.

If we look at how the military doctrines of the three countries have developed, we can see that Italy's trajectory has been rather unique compared with those of the other two countries. Rome, which since the 1980s had already been gradually moving towards a more dynamic military role in the Mediterranean, in 1991 embraced the will to turn its armed forces into an instrument geared, above all, to military missions abroad. The path towards deployability was thus established, and then reinforced in the following years through constant involvement in a wide range of operations. In contrast, Germany and Japan remained much more anchored to the needs of territorial defence and deterrence.

Force structure substantially evolved in each of the three countries. All three significantly reduced the total size of their forces and sought to rationalise and streamline them. With two laws passed in 2000 and 2004, Italy's armed forces suspended conscription (in line with the *New Defence Model* approved in 1991), with the aim of creating a smaller professional force better suited to deployment in PKOs or post-conflict situations. In Germany, the relevance of territorial defence also persisted in terms of force structure, with conscription being suspended one decade later than in Italy.

All three made efforts to reduce duplication and promote jointness and integration between services. The evolving requirements associated with emerging and consolidating military doctrines greatly impacted the allocation of resources to different services. In Japan, the ASDF and the MSDF increased their share of the total budget, compared with the GSDF. Vice versa, to comply with the requirements made necessary by their participation in the COIN operations during the 'war on terror', Italy and Germany allocated more resources to their ground forces.

Choices enacted in response to critical junctures were central in the process of adaptation of forces structure. As of the early 1990s, Italy began to develop a joint, deployable and highly professional force, seeking to implement the lessons learned during the Gulf War. To achieve this, it had to overcome a complex legacy constituted by a budget that was unbalanced in favour of personnel costs, a lack of proportion between the size of the forces and the resources available, and interservice rivalries. The Italian armed forces were still partially struggling with many of these problems during the 'war on terror'. The process of transformation towards a joint, deployable force was substantially boosted only after Kosovo, and adapted to the needs of COIN only during the war in Afghanistan.

In Germany also, the process of the evolution of force structure was hampered by constant resource constraints. Again, as in the case of Italy, Berlin developed two armies: a larger, less well-equipped component, and a smaller, better-equipped one for out-of-area missions. However, feedback from the operations abroad were much more limited in the case of Germany, which still dedicated considerable attention to territorial defence, including in terms of the composition of forces. The degree of modernisation (relating, for example, to the so-called 'revolution in military affairs') and reforms (such as for enhancing jointness) was extremely slow in German post-Cold War defence. Not until the new century did the Bundeswehr finally adapt, while conscription was suspended and the number of bases reduced. Yet when requirements from the ground were finally 'incorporated' into the reform projects after years of urgent demands, the Russian seizure of Crimea caused the regional and international scenario to change. After 2014, new attention was given to defence spending, but economic constraints on the defence budget remained in place. These constraints seem finally to have been eroded when Russia invaded Ukraine in 2022.

The JSDF has undergone a process of adaptation functional to the new requirements dictated by its new doctrine and by the challenges posed by China and North Korea. Especially after the two critical junctures of the late 1990s and 2010s, the deterioration in the external environment and the consolidation of the alliance led Japan to make a number of significant steps, such as introducing a BMD system, enhancing its C4ISR capabilities, developing amphibious capabilities, and acquiring the capacity to strike back at the enemy from a longer range. Moreover, considerable investment has been made in the fields of anti-submarine warfare, cyberwarfare and air interception.

New activism in terms of security policies, and new tasks assigned to the armed forces, did not translate into relevant expansion of the military budget, due to economic stagnation, the impact of financial crises and a general economic decline, as well as the persisting domestic political constraints.

During the post-Cold War period, Italy's military budget remained steadily between 1.5 per cent and 1.8 per cent of GDP.[1] Since 1995, that of Germany has never exceeded 1.5 per cent, averaging 1.3 per cent in the last two decades. Up to 2022, Japan remained faithful to its commitment not to spend more than 1 per cent of GDP in military expenditure, one of the remaining anti-militarist limits instituted in the post-war period. In the case of Italy and Japan, the lack of growth that characterised the post-Cold War period translated into a very slow increase in military budgets. Japan spent around US$44 billion in 1992 and US$49 billion in 2020, despite the sharp deterioration in the security environment and the rapid growth of China's military power. The National Security Strategy and the National Defence Strategies adopted in December 2022 called for a transition towards military expenditure of 2 per cent of GDP in the period 2023–2028. After the Russian invasion of Ukraine, also Germany and Italy shared the same commitment to 2 per cent GDP. However, it is hard to predict whether – and when – this significant budget increase will actually be enacted by the three governments.

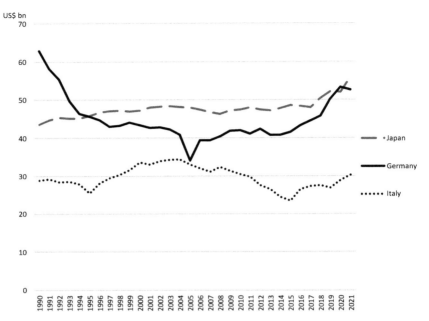

Graph 7.1 Military budget in Germany, Italy and Japan, 1991–2021, (US$ 2020)
Source: Authors' elaboration based on SIPRI annual reports.

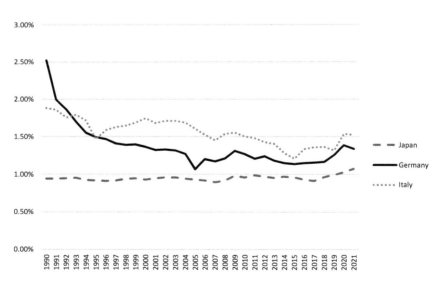

Graph 7.2 Military budget as a percentage of GDP in Germany, Italy and Japan, 1991–2021, 000 US$
Source: Authors' elaboration based on SIPRI annual reports.

Italy spent US$29 billion in 1991, reached a peak of almost US$34 billion during the first half of the 2000s, and subsequently implemented significant cuts in the aftermath of the Euro-crisis, bringing the amount to a minimum of US$25 billion in 2015. In 2020, the Italian military budget was lower than in 1991.[2] From 1991 to 2005, Germany steadily reduced its budget from US$56 to US$33 billion, then inverted the tendency during the Merkel years, reaching US%52 billion in 2020.

7.2 How domestic and international factors have shaped change

Empirical chapters show how a plurality of factors lie behind the trajectories described. From a domestic point of view, at first glance the three countries appear to have faced similar constraints, yet a more thorough analysis reveals that these similarities also conceal certain differences in how they effectively played out in affecting transformation.

The empirical analysis presented in Chapters 4, 5 and 6 highlights how the three countries addressed dissimilar critical junctures, which were then followed by different patterns of consolidation and institutionalisation, with diverse self-reinforcing feedbacks. Path dependence mechanisms well explain the similarities and differences in the evolution of the trajectories adopted by Germany, Japan and Italy in their respective post-Cold War defence policies. More specifically, along with the constant role played by 'legacies in action', the empirical chapters reveal how the dynamic interaction between international and domestic factors shaped the process of evolution (doctrines and force structure) of each path. The analysis examines this process in depth along the different junctures addressed by the three countries, looking at the interplay between international pressures (allies and perceived threats), and domestic and organisational drivers and constraints (from cultural factors to the different roles of the parliaments and the different military experiences and their feedbacks). What are the elements that shaped the trajectories? Let us now outline these factors.

In the three decades after the Cold War, Germany, Italy and Japan each developed narratives of active pacifism, embracing the idea that peace needed to be actively promoted. Italy, however, began this process earlier, and strategic cultures proved to be more 'malleable' than in Germany and Japan. While constantly referring to its military deployments as peace and stability missions, Italy eschewed any reference to terms associated with war and conflict, even when it took part in high-intensity COIN operations in Afghanistan and Iraq. Germany legitimised its new-found security role by drawing on its own traumatic past. To its Cold War *Friedenpolitik* it added references to the necessity of preventing mass atrocities and violations of human rights. The need to 'avoid a new Auschwitz' gave moral and political legitimacy to its participation in military interventions in Kosovo and Afghanistan. Japan framed its process of 'normalisation' (that is, overcoming part of the post-war institutional norms) as the will to defend the regional and global order, offering a proactive contribution to peace. In this context, the exercise of deterrence, the consolidation of the alliance with the United States and the establishing of 'minilateral' partnerships with other states in the region are regarded as steps towards consolidating a liberal international order and regional and global peace. This peace-oriented narrative also resulted in limitations to what the armed forces could do once deployed. The strictest limits regarded the JSDF, whose activities were narrowly defined in the Five Principles for Deployment, which requires a ceasefire and a UN mandate, and limits the use of weapons to self-defence. In Japan, legitimacy also came through engaging with domestic missions – the disaster relief operations following the earthquake and tsunami of 11 March 2011 were crucial in improving the perceived legitimacy of the JSDF. Additionally, the threat posed by China and North Korea also helped to convince the Japanese public of the need for a more robust defence policy.

In terms of institutional constraints, several restrictions are still in place in the three countries. The actual practices of parliamentary control, however, have proved to be rather different. In Germany, the Bundeswehr have largely remained the parliament's army, with the Bundestag closely monitoring missions right from inception to implementation. On quite a few occasions this has led German cabinets to adopt very cautious approaches, even when requested to intervene by allies (namely, the United States). Italy has a tradition of parliamentary government but has been relatively less constrained than Germany, with cabinets managing to circumvent parliamentary approval for missions in most cases, and leaving the former larger windows of opportunity. In Italy, the government has considerable autonomy in defence policy, and the very limited parliamentary oversight allows it to avoid a clear attribution of responsibility and potential audience costs. On the other hand, the Bundestag has had considerable control over the cabinet, both regarding the decision to deploy troops and also how forces have been employed on the ground (caveat, rules of engagement and so on). Thus, while in both countries public opinion has shared similar attitudes towards missions aboard (such as opposing combat operations), only in Germany the parliament adopted a tight monitoring of the government, actually limiting executive autonomy. In Japan, meanwhile, the activities geared to overseeing the Diet and the Diet members individually for defence policies have increased, partially compensating for the evolution of the bureaucratic mechanisms of oversight. The creation of an autonomous Ministry of Defence in 2007 relaxed the control of the JSDF by the Office of the Prime Minister and other ministries. With the creation of the National Security Council, the 2015 legislation concentrated the defence policy authorities in the hands of the prime minister and the core members of the NSC.[3] Article 9, despite attempts by conservative leaders such as Koizumi and Abe, has not been amended. Nevertheless, since 2015, its interpretation allows for 'collective self-defence' (in other words, the defence of US troops deployed in the area) if Japanese security is threatened.

Domestic politics had a large but rather counterintuitive effect on the process of military transformation. Significantly, no critical juncture was associated purely with domestic politics: when 'alternative' forces took power they did not bring about radical ruptures with established trajectories. In Italy, between the 1990s and the 2010s, both centre-right and centre-left coalitions confirmed the two main pillars of the country's foreign policy: 'Atlanticism' (pro-US orientation) and 'Europeanism' (alignment with the EU). The debate between the two coalitions, especially during the 'war on terror', largely focused on which one needed to come first. In the 1990s and 2000s the majority of former communists were eager to demonstrate their 'Atlanticist' credentials by embracing an active role for Italy in NATO and in US-led missions. Italy's military activism, therefore, was actively opposed only by pacifist NGOs and small parties on the extreme left of the political spectrum.[4] In 2018, Italy elected a government led by the Five Star Movement and the League, two populist, anti-establishment parties. During its fifteen months in power, the so-called 'Yellow–Green' government attempted to introduce a degree of discontinuity in Italian foreign policy by improving relations with Russia and China.[5] Nevertheless, it did not promote a relevant discontinuity with the trajectory of Italian defence policies, substantially confirming the overall orientation in terms of missions abroad and funding.[6] On the whole, a large bipartisan consensus has always marked the attitudes of the Italian parties towards post-Cold War defence policy.

During the three decades after the Cold War, Japan has been governed by the conservative LDP, with only two exceptions – the periods from 1993 to 1996[7] and from 2009 to 2012. On both occasions progressive forces sought to promote a higher degree of autonomy from the United States and put in place initiatives to complement the alliance with forms of cooperation with Asian partners, and on both occasions these attempts were undermined by the deterioration in the external environment, and bureaucratic resistance within the JSDF and defence and foreign affairs ministries. In 1997 and 2012, the return to power of the LDP, with

Hashimoto and, especially, with Abe, led to the reinforcement of the US–Japan alliance and a substantial acceleration in the evolution of Japanese defence policies.

The German domestic political scenario has been constantly shaped by a reluctant approach towards a more deployable Bundeswehr. A 'civilian narrative' has been adopted – and modified across time – to better address the perennial anti-militarism. On the whole, domestic 'concerns' have been prioritised during international crises, always limiting the military activism demanded by allies. In other words, constant 'negotiation' with the domestic constituency affected the decision-making process of German defence. Aside from opposition by radical left and radical right parties to greater military involvement in operations abroad, and to the modernisation of forces, the Social Democrats and the Greens did not enthusiastically support the missions in Kosovo and Afghanistan, while strongly backing the centre-left decision to avoid participating in the US-led mission in Iraq. The war in Libya, with Merkel's decision to not provide German military support despite a UNSC resolution, demonstrated how the bipartisan political reluctance to take part in combat operations continued to exist for decades in the post-Cold War era.

These processes cannot be described as merely a by-product of systemic transformation. Nor were they a reaction to an evolving threat environment. In this respect, Italy, Germany and Japan faced very different threat environments. Of the three, Italy enjoyed the most 'benign' environment. After the Cold War, it never faced a direct conventional military threat to its safety and integrity. Consequently, it was able to dedicate the bulk of its resources to develop an expeditionary military instrument, without having to give priority to territorial defence. The non-conventional challenges the country faced in the 2000s and 2010s, such as terrorism, widespread instability in the Mediterranean and illegal migrations, were not associated with any direct military threat to its territory. Although the Russian invasion of Ukraine in 2022 has led to a greater Italian military commitment to the eastern flank of NATO, the main priority is still the 'Enlarged Mediterranean', which continues to be regarded as the vital strategic region for Italy. The renewal of military missions in the region, public speeches, and documents by the Draghi government,[8] and new diplomatic missions demonstrate the continued importance of the 'southern front' for Italian national security (from energy scarcity to illegal migration).[9]

Germany's threat perception significantly improved after the end of the Cold War. The inclusion of Central and Eastern Europe in NATO and in the European Union pacified Germany's immediate neighbourhood and

helped to give Berlin the possibility of integrating its approach, largely oriented to territorial defence, with substantial crisis management and power-
projection tasks. Russia's use of force in Georgia (2008), its occupation of
Crimea (2014) and, ultimately, its invasion of Ukraine in 2022 partially
reversed this situation. Russia has progressively returned to the centre of
Germany's threat perception, together with the awareness that peace and
stability in Europe can no longer be taken for granted. More importantly,
the Russian invasion of Ukraine could represent a *Zeitenwende*, a turning
point in German history. Before the Bundestag (on 27 February 2022),
Chancellor Olaf Scholz announced the creation of a €100 billion special
defence fund, later approved by parliament, to re-build Germany's military.[10] Scholz stressed that the war in Ukraine represented a turning point
for Germany and for European security. While German public opinion
supported such view, and 'although the *Zeitenwende* will trigger significant
change, it is unclear which lessons exactly Germans will now be learning
and how far that adaptation will go'.[11]

Despite the resurgence of the Russian threat on the eastern borders
of Europe, Germany, and Italy, as NATO members, still enjoy an overwhelmingly favourable balance of power vis-à-vis Russia. Japan, on the
other hand, has had to deal with a constantly deteriorating threat environment and an increasingly unfavourable balance of power. At the end of
the Cold War, the Japanese military budget was three times larger than
China's. In 2021, the budget of China's PLA was five times higher than
that of the JSDF. Moreover, China has demonstrated its will to change,
albeit incrementally, the territorial status quo in the region, using grey
zone tactics in the South and East China Sea and posing a direct threat to
Japanese territory.

Alliance dynamics had an important impact on the processes of military transformation in the three countries. First of all, for Germany and
Japan in particular the reinforcing of NATO and the US–Japan alliance
ruled out any possible alternatives to a strong military and political relationship with the United States. Both for Germany and Japan alternative
scenarios were possible, albeit unlikely, in the early 1990s. The process
of re-unification of the Federal Republic and the Democratic Republic
could result in a neutralisation of the new German state and this could
lead either to the reaffirming and consolidating of the country's pacifist
approach to defence policies or, in the longer term, to a return to a more
muscular and independent stance by the German state. Similarly, before
the critical juncture of 1996–1998, both in Tokyo and in Washington
the utility of the US–Japan alliance was called into question. At that time,
Japanese 'neo-autonomists' argued in favour of an independent and active
security policy, while pacifists aspired to a neutralist and radically pacifist

identity. On the contrary, during the post-Cold War period, Italy never seriously considered an alternative to its NATO membership.

Since the Gulf War, alliance dynamics have entailed different forms of external pressures to contribute more and share a larger part of the burden of collective security, both regionally and globally. As we have seen, for Italy the Gulf War represented a fundamental critical juncture that shaped the future trajectory of the country's defence policy, while Germany and Japan resorted to 'chequebook diplomacy'. In the late 1990s, Italy and Germany contributed to NATO missions in the Balkans, and during the early 2000s the two countries were directly involved in the COIN operations in Afghanistan, within the framework of the NATO ISAF mission. Italy also actively participated in the attempt to stabilise and pacify Iraq, deploying troops in the country between 2003 and 2006 and between 2014 and 2022.[12] In 2006, NATO members pledged to commit 2 per cent of GDP to defence spending, and since 2014 there has been increased pressure to meet this threshold. Italy and Germany, however, never reached the target and the '2 per cent rule' become a source of dispute within the Alliance, especially during the Trump years.[13]

In the Japanese case, the 'external pressure' for burden-sharing did not focus primarily on deployment abroad – although, from Tokyo's perspective, the deployment of the JSDF to Iraq as well as its participation in the UN PKOs represented major departures from post-war pacifism. The reinforcing of the alliance led Tokyo to gradually assume more responsibility in the area surrounding Japan, particularly with regard to exercising deterrence against China and North Korea.

With the presidency of Donald Trump, the dynamics between the United States and its allies were unexpectedly reversed, arousing grave fears of abandonment in Japan and, to a lesser extent, in Germany. During the Trump administration, Chancellor Merkel and Prime Minister Abe strongly advocated the consolidation of the US-led liberal order and preserving the role of NATO and the US–Japan alliance in the face of the uncertainty generated by Trump's erratic alliance management.

Alliances played a key role also in terms of military doctrine, force structure and procurement. At doctrinal level, the reinforcing of the alliance favoured the transition from defensive defence to the exercise of deterrence, autonomously and jointly with US forces. This led to important new approaches, such as the concept of seamless coordination, promoted after 2015 to respond to China's so-called grey zone challenges. In turn, new requirements generated by the reinforcing of the alliance also created incentives to overcoming institutional limits in key sectors such as deployments abroad, intelligence sharing, use of space and the export of weapons.

In terms of interoperability, Japan started from a much lower base compared with NATO levels, since up to the 1990s the JSDF did not actively seek forms of integration with the US forces in Japan. Since the late 1990s, major procurement choices such as the BMD system, Aegis destroyers and F-35s demonstrated how increasing interoperability with US forces gradually became a necessary requirement for key Japanese platforms. Italy, meanwhile, thanks to its constant involvement in missions abroad, greatly increased the level of interoperability with allies. The war in Afghanistan clearly represents (partly also for Germany) the crucial moment that improved jointness in terms of procedures, assets and approaches, after years of very complex and demanding actions within the common NATO framework.

7.3 Ways to go

New events that seem to change the very environment in which the armed forces of Germany, Italy and Japan operate – from the Russian invasion of Ukraine to the 'permanent' Taiwan crisis – certainly call for further analyses of military transformation. According to this volume, only by taking into consideration the dynamic interaction between international factors, domestic drivers and operational experience we can properly assess the timing and direction of military transformation. The interplay between alliance dynamics, external pressures, cultural and institutional constraints, and operational experience (and their feedbacks) set the conditions that shaped the path.

Relying on historical institutionalism as a framework of analysis, the research has identified and illustrated the mechanisms behind the trajectories of the military transformation that occurred Italy, Germany and Japan in the post-Cold War era. We have provided empirical evidence on the different evolution of military doctrine and force structure in the three countries, examining the conditions of the critical junctures – when a given path is adopted – and the self-reinforcing dynamics responsible for distinct trajectories and for the patterns of institutionalisation. The empirical chapters have revealed how the legacies of the past largely shaped post-Cold War military transformation in Germany, Italy and Japan.

Thus, path-dependence mechanisms should be carefully taken into consideration if we want to understand the future evolution of German, Italian and Japanese defence policy. A key tenet of this book is that 'legacies in action' matter and the trajectories of change are more slow moving than declarations of policymakers in the wake of crises might lead to believe.

Germany's stance vis-à-vis the Ukraine War – such as Chancellor Scholz's immediate and strong reaction to the invasion and a call for Germany to assume a larger military role – might seem to indicate a possible *Zeitenwende*, a profound re-orientation of German defence policy. What we have showed here is that such evolution is part of a longer-term process in which German armed forces had already switched the pendulum back towards the more conventional territorial defence approach (versus crisis management) that is more coherent with their historical legacy. Also, the pace of change in the last three decades has been deeply influenced by previous decisions, for instance, related to military hardware, reducing the real margin of action for policymakers willing to induce change.

While Germany and Japan remained focused on 'territorial defence' for many years, the trajectory of Italian defence policy after 1989 was less slow and 'reluctant'. The book has analysed the process of transformation that occurred after the critical juncture of Desert Storm and the growing operational experience of Italian armed forces in interventions abroad. Maybe, the Russian invasion of Ukraine and the dramatic conclusion of long and complex missions related to the 'war on terror' could bring a re-thinking of the Italian 'expeditionary defence policy', with its patterns and priorities. On the one hand, the war in Ukraine could enhance further the recent process of growing defence spending, especially concerning the acquisition of new military equipment for conventional interstate warfare. Moreover, the narrative of political elites seems to be gradually shifting towards a widespread appeal for rising expenditure on defence. On the other hand, those potential changes could be still hindered by hesitant or openly hostile public attitudes regarding a larger defence budget. In addition, the Russian invasion of Ukraine could be exploited as an opportunity by those who are willing to maintain (or even increase) the number of Italian troops ahead of mounting threats, contrary to the reforms that attempted for decades – with very limited success – to reduce the size of the armed forces. Such a move could influence the sustainability of the military instrument, whose composition and unbalanced budget are indeed deeply affected by the features of the personnel (age, expenditures for pensions, etc.). On the whole, despite changes at regional and international level, to understand the future path we should still take into consideration the legacies of three decades of significant military transformation, starting from domestic dynamics and constraints.

Despite the geographical distance, the impact of the invasion of Ukraine has had a deep impact on Japan. First, the conflict has accelerated a process of strategic and ideological polarisation of the international order, an outcome that Tokyo had sought to avoid, seeking a cooperative relationship with Moscow up to 2022. In the aftermath of the invasion,

Japan joined the West in condemning the aggression, enforcing sanctions, severing economic and diplomatic contacts with Russia, and sending economic and logistical aid to Ukraine. Secondly, the Russian invasion testifies to how large-scale conflicts involving superpowers have returned to be a tangible possibility. Therefore, Japan should be prepared for it. In East Asia, Taiwan represents the most likely scenario in which war could emerge, due to the deterioration in US–China relations in the late 2010s and early 2020s. A Taiwan contingency could engulf the entire region, directly involving Japan. This implies doubling down on the trajectory established during the Abe period, continuing to strengthen deterrence and territorial defence. Finally, the Ukraine War has accelerated another key trajectory, regarding the expansion of the Japanese role of promoter and defender of the liberal international order. The violation of the territorial integrity of Ukraine is considered as a threat to a key pillar of the international order. Consequently, as articulated by Prime Minister Kishida, Japan's duty is to act in support of the principle of integrity and self-determination and to sustain Ukraine. Yet it is important to note that such help did not involve 'offensive weapons', but mainly economic and logistical supplies.

The evolution of international relations will affect the threat environment of the three countries investigated in this book. The war in Ukraine and the growing tension around Taiwan well highlight the actual risks of rising superpower rivalry as well as the challenges posed to the post-1945 US-led liberal international order (which is under attack also internally).

Our framework of analysis has emphasised the relevance of path-dependent mechanisms and the dynamic interplay between external and domestic factors to better understand the military transformation of Italy, Germany and Japan, all states with a very complex legacy in terms of military affairs. Further studies could assess the same process of transformation with a different comparative perceptive, in Europe and beyond. Qualitative but also quantitative methods could be employed for large-*n* studies on drivers of change for defence policy. Indeed, still relying on historical institutionalism or moving towards different frameworks, research could develop and then test specific hypotheses on the (international or domestic) conditions that foster or hinder military transformation. For instance, the growing literature on 'parliamentary war powers' could better interact with the vast scholarly debate on strategic culture and military affairs. In addition, the mounting FPA research on defence policy change could further exploit insights from public policy and organisational studies to assess causes and obstacles for change. Moreover, advancements can be derived from further integration of the findings and approaches of the literature on organisational learning within military transformation studies.

Notes

1. Sometimes also lower than 1.5 per cent, especially after the financial crisis. See Table 6.1.
2. All data are expressed in 2020 US$ and taken from the SIPRI database of military expenditures.
3. The four 'core members' of the NSC are the prime minister, the ministries of Foreign Affairs and Defence and the chief cabinet secretary.
4. Coticchia and Vignoli, 'Italian Political Parties and Military Operations'.
5. For a review on this point, see M. Pugliese, F. Ghiretti and A. Insisa (2022), 'Italy's Embrace of the Belt and Road Initiative', *International Affairs* 98(3): 1033–51.
6. Coticchia, 'A "Sovereignist Revolution"'?; M. Ceccorulli, F. Coticchia and S. Gianfreda (2022), 'The Government of Change? Migration and Defence Policy under Giuseppe Conte's I Cabinet', *Contemporary Italian Politics*, 1–19.
7. In 1993–1994 the Hosokawa government did not include the LDP; in 1994–1996 the grand coalition led by the Socialist Murayama Tomiichi included the LDP.
8. See, again, the new strategy (which was published several months after the Russian invasion of Ukraine) for the Mediterranean, available at: https://www.difesa.it/Il_Ministro/Documents/Strategia%20Mediterraneo%202022.pdf. The official document confirms how the 'Enlarged Mediterranean' still represents the vital strategic priority for Italian foreign and defence policy.
9. The Italian Chief of Defence of Armed Forces Adm Cavo Dragone emphasised the crucial task of monitoring the growing concerning presence of the Russian fleet in the Mediterranean, also as a consequence of the war in Ukraine. See G. Di Feo (2022), 'Intervista all'ammiraglio Cavo Dragone: "Così la marina ha respinto le navi russe nell'Adriatico"', *La Repubblica*, 20 August.
10. O. Scholz (2022), 'Policy Statement by Olaf Scholz, Chancellor of the Federal Republic of Germany and Member of the German Bundestag', 27 February, Berlin, available at: https://www.bundesregierung.de/breg-en/news/policy-statement-by-olaf-scholz-chancellor-of-the-federal-republic-of-germany-and-member-of-the-german-bundestag-27-february-2022-in-berlin-2008378.
11. T. Bunde (2022), 'Lessons (to be) Learned? Germany's Zeitenwende and European Security after the Russian Invasion of Ukraine', *Contemporary Security Policy* 43(3): 516–30. For a critical perspective, see K-H. Röhl, H. Bardt and B. Engels (2022), 'Zeitenwende für die Verteidigungswirtschaft? Sicherheitspolitik und Verteidigungsfähigkeit nach der russischen Invasion der Ukraine', *IW-Policy Paper*, No. 4, Berlin/Köln.
12. In May 2022, Italy assumed the command of the NATO mission in Iraq.
13. Italy did not reach 2 per cent, but it addressed the required levels in terms of 'contribution' (through missions abroad) and 'capabilities' (finally after 2019 reaching the mark of 20 per cent of the budget allocated to the funding of new procurement programmes).

List of Interviewees

Authors' anonymous interview with former staff member at the Ministry of Defence (2018–2019), Rome, 7 November 2019.

Authors' interview with a former member of the Weiszäcker Commission, Berlin, 16 April 2015.

Authors interview with a senior SWP researcher, Berlin, 9 April 2015.

Authors' interview with a ZMSBw researcher, Potsdam, 1 April 2015.

Authors' interview with Andrea Manciulli, Vice President of the Foreign Affairs Committee in the Chamber of Deputies, Florence, February 2016.

Authors' interview with EU–Navfor Med: Sophia Command, Rome, 10 July 2017.

Authors' interview with former staff member at the Ministry of Defence (2018–2019), Rome, 7 November 2019.

Authors' interview, anonymous high-level member of the Ministry of Defence, Rome, October 2019.

Authors' interview, Domenico Rossi, Undersecretary of Defence, 26 June 2017.

Authors' interview, Elisabetta Trenta, former Minister of Defence (2018–2019), Rome, 31 October 2019.

Authors' interview, former counter intelligence section chief and security officer at RC-C HQ, ISAF, 23 October 2019.

Authors' interview, former general staff officer, Ministry of Defence, Berlin, SWP, 26 November 2019.

Authors' interview, former German general, Berlin, SWP, 16 April 2015.

Authors' interview, former member of the Weizsäcker Commission, Berlin, SWP, 16 April 2015.

Authors' interview, German army officer, Potsdam, ZMSBw, 26 November 2019.

Authors' interview, journalist, expert on German defence, Berlin, 9 April 2015.

Authors' interview, researcher on German defence and public opinion, Potsdam, ZMSBw, 2 April 2015.

Authors' interview, researcher on German defence policy, Berlin, SWP, 9 April 2015.

Authors' interview, researcher on German defence policy, Potsdam, ZMSBw, 26 November 2019.

Authors' interview, researcher on German military operation in Afghanistan, Potsdam, ZMSBw, 28 November 2019.

Authors' interview, researcher, Italian Institute of International Affairs, Rome, 21 October 2019.

Authors' interview, Roberta Pinotti, former Minister of Defence (2014–2018), Genova, May 2018.

Authors' interviews with officials of the Japanese Ministry of Defence (Strategic Planning Division, and Bureau of Defence Policy), Tokyo, November 2017.

Authors' interviews with officials of the Japanese Ministry of Defence (Japan–US Defence Cooperation Division, Strategic Planning Division), November 2017.

Authors' interviews with officials of the Japanese Ministry of Defence (Strategic Planning Division), November 2017.

Authors' interviews with officials of the Japanese Ministry of Foreign Affairs (International Cooperation Bureau), October 2018.

Authors' interviews with officials of the National Security Secretariat, Tokyo, November 2017.

Authors' interviews with officials of the National Institute Defence Studies, Tokyo, November 2017

Authors' interviews with officials of the Japanese Ministry of Defence, Tokyo, October 2018.

Authors' interviews with officials of the National Security Secretariat, Tokyo, November 2017

Authors' interviews with US Navy officers, 7th Fleet, Yokosuka Naval Base, January 2016.

Authors' interviews with representatives of the Japanese Ministry of Foreign Affairs, October 2017.

Authors' interviews with representatives of the National Institute for Defence Studies (NIDS), November 2017.

Authors' telephone interview, Coordinator Italian Disarmament Network, 5 November 2019.

Authors' telephone interview, Domenico Rossi, former Undersecretary of Defence (2014–2018), June 2017.

Authors' telephone interview, European Council of Foreign Relations expert on Italian foreign policy, North Africa and Middle East, February 2017.

Authors' telephone interview, journalist, expert on Italian defence, 30 October 2019.

References

Abbondanza, G. (2020). 'The West's Policeman? Assessing Italy's Status in Global Peacekeeping', *International Spectator* 55(2): 127–41.

Abbondanza, G. (2020). 'Middle Powers and Great Powers through History: The Concept from Ancient Times to the Present Day', *History of Political Thought* 41(3): 397–418.

Abbondanza, G. (2021). 'The Odd Axis: Germany, Italy, and Japan as Awkward Great Powers', in G. Abbondanza and T. S. Wilkins (eds), *Awkward Powers: Escaping Traditional Great and Middle Power Theory*. London: Palgrave Macmillan, 3–39.

Adamsky, D. (2010). *The Culture of Military Innovation: The Impact of Cultural Factors on the Revolution in Military Affairs in Russia, the US and Israel*. Stanford, CA: Stanford University Press.

Allers, R. M. (2016). 'Are We Doing Enough? Change and Continuity in the German Approach to Crisis Management', *German Politics* 25(4): 519–40.

Altman, D. (2017). 'By Fait Accompli, Not Coercion: How States Wrest Territory from their Adversaries', *International Studies Quarterly* 61(4): 881–8.

Andreatta, F. (2001). 'Italy at the Crossroad: The Foreign Policy of a Medium Power after the Cold War', *Daedalus* 130: 45–66.

Archetti, C. (2017). 'Narrative Wars: Understanding Terrorism in the Era of Global Interconnectedness', in A. Miskimmon, B. O'Loughlin and L. Roselle (eds), *Forging the World: Strategic Narratives and International Relations*. Ann Arbor: University of Michigan Press, 218–45.

Armacost, M. H. (1969). *The Politics of Weapons Innovation: The Thor-Jupiter Controversy*. New York: Columbia University Press.

Armacost, M. H. (1996). *Friends or Rivals? The Insider's Account of US–Japan Relations*. New York: Columbia University Press.

Arthur, W. B. (1989). Competing Technologies, Increasing Returns, and Lock-in by Historical Events', *Economic Journal* 99(394): 116–31.

Arthur, W. B. (1994). *Increasing Returns and Path Dependence in the Economy*. Ann Arbor: University of Michigan Press.

Attinà, F. (2019). 'L'Italia e la crisi migratoria dell'Europa', in P. Isernia and F. Longo (eds), *La politica estera italiana nel nuovo millennio*. Bologna: Il Mulino, 181–202.

Auerswald, D. P. and S. M. Saideman (2014). *NATO in Afghanistan: Fighting Together, Fighting Alone*. Princeton, NJ: Princeton University Press.

Aust, H. and M. Vashakmadze (2008). 'Parliamentary Consent to the Use of German Armed Forces Abroad: The 2008 Decision of the Federal Constitutional Court in the AWACS/Turkey Case', *German Law Journal* 9(12): 2233–6.

Avant, D. D. (1994). *Political Institutions and Military Change: Lessons from Peripheral Wars*. Ithaca, NY: Cornell University Press.

Balfour, R. et al. (2016), 'Europe's Troublemakers: The Populist Challenge to Foreign Policy', European Policy Center, Brussels.

Baldini, G. and M. F. N. Giglioli (2019). 'Italy 2018: The Perfect Populist Storm?' *Parliamentary Affairs* 73(2): 365.

Barbin, J. (2015). *Imperialkriegführung im 21. Jahrhundert: Von Algier nach Bagdad. Die kolonialen Ursprünge der COIN-Doktrin*. Berlin: Miles-Verlag.

Barnes, D. L. (2017). *Architects of Occupation: American Experts and Planning for Postwar Japan*. Ithaca, NY: Cornell University Press.

Barno, D. and N. Bensahel (2020). *Adaptation Under Fire: How Military Change in Wartime*. New York: Oxford University Press.

Batacchi, P. (2020). 'Una nuova riforma per la Difesa.' *Rivista Italiana Difesa* 12/2021.

Battistelli, F. (2003). 'L'opinione pubblica italiana e la difesa', *Quaderni di sociologia* 32/2003: 8–36.

Battistelli, F. (2003). *Gli italiani e la guerra*. Roma: Carocci.

Battistelli, F., M. G. Galantino, L. F. Lucianetti and L. Striuli (2012). *Opinioni sulla guerra. L'opinione pubblica italiana e internazionale di fronte all'uso della forza*. Milan: Franco Angeli.

Battistelli, F. and P. Isernia (1990). *I movimenti pacifisti ed antinucleari in Italia 1980–1988*. Roma: Cemiss.

Baumann, R. and G. Hellmann (2001). 'Germany and the use of Military Force: "Total War", the "Culture of Restraint" and the Quest for Normality', *German Politics* 10(1): 61–82.

Becher, K. (2004). 'German Forces in International Military Operations', *Orbis* 48(3): 397–408.

Belloni, R., V. Della Sala and P. Viotti (eds) (2019). *Fear and Uncertainty in Europe: The Return to Realism?* Houndmills: Palgrave.

Bellucci, P. (1998). *Difesa, politica e società: la politica militare italiana tra obiezione di coscienza e professionalizzazione delle Forze armate*. Milano: FrancoAngeli.

Berenskoetter, F. and B. Giegerich (2010). 'From NATO to ESDP: A Social Constructivist Analysis of German Strategic Adjustment after the End of the Cold War, *Security Studies* 19(3): 407–52.

Berenskötter, F. and H. Stritzel (2021). '*Welche Macht darf es denn Sein?* Tracing "Power" in German Foreign Policy Discourse', *German Politics* 30(1): 31–50.

Beretta, S., A. Berkofsky and F. Rugge (eds) (2014). *Italy and Japan: How Similar Are They? A Comparative Analysis of Politics, Economics, and International Relations*. Berlin: Spinger.

Berger, T. U. (1998). *Cultures of Antimilitarism: National Security in Germany and Japan*. Baltimore, MA: Johns Hopkins University Press.

Berkofsky, A. (2011). 'Japan's December 2010 "National Defense Program Guidelines (Ndpg)": The "Big Bang" of Japanese Security and Defense Policies?' *Korean Review of International Studies* 14(1): 33–52.

Berman, E. and A. M. Matanock (2015). 'The Empiricists' Insurgency', *Annual Review of Political Science* 18: 443–64.

Betts, R. K. (2000). 'Is Strategy an Illusion?' *International Security* 25(2): 5–50.

Biba, S. (2021). 'Germany's Relations with the United States and China from a Strategic Triangle Perspective', *International Affairs* 97(6): 1905–24.

Biddle, S. and I. Oelrich (2016). 'Future Warfare in the Western Pacific: Chinese Antiaccess/Area Denial, US Airsea Battle, and Command of the Commons in East Asia', *International Security* 41(1): 7–48.

Biehl, H., B. Giegerich and A. Jonas (eds) (2013). *Strategic Cultures in Europe: Security and Defence Policies across the Continent*. Wiesbaden: Springer.

Biloslavo, F. (2012).'Solo ora lo ammettiamo: sulla Libia una pioggia di bombe', *Panorama* 12 December.

Bini, E., I. Londero and G. Iannuzzi (eds) (2017). *Nuclear Italy: An International History of Italian Nuclear Policies during the Cold War.* Trieste: EUT Edizioni.

Born, H. and H. Hänggi (2005). *The Use of Force under International Auspices.* Geneva: DCAF Policy Paper.

Boyd, J. P. and R. J. Samuels (2005). *Nine Lives? The Politics of Constitutional Reform in Japan.* Honolulu, HI: East West Center.

Bradford, J. F. (2021). 'Japanese Naval Activities in Southeast Asian Waters: Building on 50 Years of Maritime Security Capacity Building', *Asian Security* 17(1): 79–104.

Braw, E. (2021). 'Italy's Carabinieri Were the Perfect Force for the Kabul Evacuation', *Defense One,* 3 September.

Breuer, G. (2006). 'Between Ambitions and Financial Constraints: The Reform of the German Armed Forces', *German Politics* 15(2): 206–20.

Brighi, E. (2013). *Foreign Policy, Domestic Politics and International Relations: The Case of Italy.* New York: Routledge.

Brockmeier, S. (2013). 'Germany and the Intervention in Libya', *Survival* 55(6): 63–90.

Brummer, K. (2013). 'The Reluctant Peacekeeper: Governmental Politics and Germany's Participation in EUFOR RD Congo', *Foreign Policy Analysis* 9(1): 1–20.

Brummer, K. and K. Oppermann (2016). *Germany's Foreign Policy after the End of the Cold War: 'Becoming Normal?'* Oxford: Oxford Handbooks Online: Political Science, 1–30.

Brummer, K. and K. Oppermann (2021). 'Poliheuristic Theory and Germany's (Non) Participation in Multinational Military Interventions: The Non-compensatory Principle, Coalition Politics and Political Survival', *German Politics* 30(1): 106–21.

Buckley, R. (1995). *US–Japan Alliance Diplomacy 1945–1990.* Cambridge: Cambridge University Press.

Bulmer, S. and W. E. Paterson (2013). 'Germany as the EU's Reluctant Hegemon? Of Economic Strength and Political Constraints', *Journal of European Public Policy* 20(10): 1387–1405.

Bunde T. (2022). 'Lessons (to be) Learned? Germany's Zeitenwende and European Security after the Russian Invasion of Ukraine', *Contemporary Security Policy* 43(3): 516–30.

Bunde, T. and S. Eisentraut (2022). *Zeitenwende for the G7: Insights from the Munich Security Index Special G7 Edition*, Munich Security Brief No. 3, Munich Security Conference.

Bundesrat (Drucksacke 3330/19; 09.08.19) Gesetzentwurf der Bundesregierung – Entwurf eines Gesetzes über die Feststellung des Bundeshaushaltsplans für das Hausaltsjahr 2020 (Hausaltsgesetz 2020) – übersichten – Teil V: Personalübersichten.

Buras, P. and K. Longhurst (2004). 'The Berlin Republic, Iraq, and the Use of Force', *European Security* 13(3): 215–45.

Buszynski, L. (2013). *Negotiating with North Korea: The Six Party Talks and the Nuclear Issue.* London: Routledge.

Calligaris, L. (1990). 'La politica militare', in B. Dente (ed.), *Politiche pubbliche in Italia.* Bologna: Il Mulino, 65–82.

Calligaris, L. and C. M. Santoro (1986). *Obiettivo difesa: Strategia, direzione politica, comando operativo.* Bologna: Il Mulino.

Calossi, E., F. Calugi and F. Coticchia (2013). 'Peace and War in Political Discourse of Italian Marxist and post-Marxist Parties', *Contemporary Italian Politics* 5(3): 309–24.

Capoccia, G. (2016). 'Critical Junctures', in O. Fioretos, T. G. Falleti and A. Sheingate (eds), *The Oxford Handbook of Historical Institutionalism.* Oxford: Oxford University Press, 89–106.

Capoccia, G. and R. D. Kelemen (2007). 'The Study of Critical Junctures: Theory, Narrative and Counterfactuals in Historical Institutionalism', *World Politics* 59(3): 341–69.

Carati, A. and A. Locatelli (2017). 'Cui prodest? Italy's Questionable Involvement in Multilateral Military Operations amid Ethical Concerns and National Interest', *International Peacekeeping* 24(1): 86–107.

Carati, A., M. Merlati and D. Vignati (2021). 'Freer When Constrained? Italy and Transatlantic Relations during the Cold War', *Journal of Modern Italian Studies* 26(3): 314–32.

Carbone, M. (2007). 'The Domestic Foundations of Italy's Foreign and Development Policies', *West European Politics* 30(4): 903–23.

Carsten, P. (2020). 'Die Bundeswehr hat problem, ihren ETAT richting zu investieren', *Frankfurter Allgemeine Zeitung*, 8 December.

Carter, D. A. (2015). 'Forging the Shield: The US Army in Europe, 1951–1962', *US Army in the Cold War Series* 45(3): 232.

Cary, N. D. (2019). 'On the Political Decision-making Process see Helmut Schmidt, Euromissiles, and the Peace Movement', *Central European History* 52(1): 148–71.

Catalinac, A. (2016). *Electoral Reform and National Security in Japan: From Pork to Foreign Policy*. Cambridge: Cambridge University Press.

Catanzaro, A. and F. Coticchia (2018). *Al di là dell'Arcobaleno: I movimenti pacifisti italiani tra ideologie e contro-narrazioni strategiche*. Milano: Vita e Pensiero.

Catanzaro, A. and F. Coticchia (2021). 'The Fog of Words: Assessing the Problematic Relationship between Strategic Narratives, (Master) Frames, and Ideology', *Media, War & Conflict* 15(4): 427–49.

Catignani, S. (2012). '"Getting COIN" at the Tactical Level in Afghanistan: Reassessing Counterinsurgency Adaptation in the British Army', *Journal of Strategic Studies* 35(4): 513–39.

Caverley, J. D. and P. Dombrowski (2020). 'Policy Roundtable: The Future of Japanese Security and Defense', *Texas National Security Review*, available at: https://tnsr.org/roundtable/policy-roundtable-the-future-of-japanese-security-and-defense/#essay4.

Caviglia, D. and M. Cricco (2006). *La diplomazia italiana e gli equilibri mediterranei: la politica mediorientale dell'Italia dalla guerra dei Sei Giorni al conflitto dello Yom Kippur (1967–1973)*. Roma: Rubbettino Editore.

Ceccorulli, M. and F. Coticchia (2015). 'Multidimensional Threats and Military Engagement: The Case of the Italian Intervention in Libya', *Mediterranean Politics* 20(3): 303–21.

Ceccorulli, M. and F. Coticchia (2020). '"I'll Take Two": Migration, Terrorism, and the Italian Military Engagement in Niger and Libya', *Journal of Modern Italian Studies* 25(2): 174–96.

Ceccorulli, M., F. Coticchia and S. Gianfreda (2022). 'The Government of Change? Migration and Defence Policy under Giuseppe Conte's I Cabinet', *Contemporary Italian Politics*, 1–19.

Cerquetti, E. (1975). *Le forze armate italiane dal 1945 al 1975: Strutture e dottrine*. Milano: Feltrinelli.

Cha, V. D. (2016). *Powerplay: The Origins of the American Alliance System in Asia*. Princeton, NJ: Princeton University Press.

Cha, V. D. and D. C. Kang (2018). *Nuclear North Korea: A Debate on Engagement Strategies*. New York: Columbia University Press.

Chan, S. (1995). 'Grasping the Peace Dividend: Some Propositions on the Conversion of Swords into Plowshares', *Mershon International Studies Review* 39 (S1): 53–95.

Chijiwa, Y. (2016). 'Unfinished "Beyond-the-Threat Theory": Japan's "Basic Defence Force Concept" Revisited', *NIDS Journal of Defense and Security* (17): 83–101.

Christensen, T. J. (2015). *The China Challenge: Shaping the Choices of a Rising Power*. New York: W. W. Norton.

Cladi, L. and A. Locatelli (2019). 'Why did Italy Contribute to UNIFIL II? An Analytical Eclectic Analysis', *Italian Political Science Review* 49(1): 85–97.

Colby, E. A. and A. V. Mitchell (2020). 'The Age of Great-Power Competition', *Foreign Affairs* 99(1): 118–30.

Colley, T. (2017). 'Is Britain a Force for Good? Investigating British Citizens' Narrative Understanding of War', *Defence Studies* 17(1): 1–22.

Cordesman, A. H. (2001). *The Lessons and Non-Lessons of the Air and Missile Campaign Over Kosovo*. Westport, CT: Prager.

Cornish, P. (2009). 'The United States and Counterinsurgency: "Political First, Political Last, Political Always"', *International Affairs* 85(1): 61–79.

Cortright, D. (2008). *Peace: A History of Movements and Ideas*. Cambridge: Cambridge University Press.

Corum, J. (2004). 'Building a New Luftwaffe: The United States Air Force and Bundeswehr Planning for Rearmament, 1950–60', *Journal of Strategic Studies* 27(1): 89–113.

Coticchia, F. (2013). *Qualcosa è cambiato: L'evoluzione della politica di difesa italiana dall'Iraq alla Libia (1991–2011)*. Pisa: Pisa University Press.

Coticchia, F. (2014). *La guerra che non c'era: opinione pubblica e interventi militari italiani dall'Afghanistan alla Libia*. Milano, EGEA.

Coticchia, F. (2017). 'Running in Chains: The Transformation of Italian Defence Policy', in M. Evangelista (ed.), *Italy from Crisis to Crisis*. London: Routledge, 119–35.

Coticchia, F. (2019). 'Italy', in H. Meijer and M. Wyss (eds), *The Handbook of European Defense Policies and Armed Forces*. Oxford: Oxford University Press, 109–24.

Coticchia, F. (2019). 'Unheard Voices: International Relations Theory and Italian Defence Policy', in R. Belloni, V. Della Sala and P. Viotti (eds), *Fear and Uncertainty in Europe: The Return to Realism?* Houndmills: Palgrave, 131–50.

Coticchia, F. (2020). 'La Politica di Difesa', in G. Capano and A. Natalini (eds), *Le politiche pubbliche in Italia*. Bologna: Il Mulino, 77–94.

Coticchia, F. (2021). 'A "Sovereignist Revolution"? Italy's Foreign Policy under the "Yellow–Green" Government', *Comparative European Politics* 19(6): 739–59.

Coticchia, F. and M. Ceccorulli (2017). 'Stick to the Plan? Culture, Interests, Multidimensional Threats and Italian Defence Policy', *Italian Political Science Review* 47(2): 183–203.

Coticchia, F. and J. Davidson (2019). *Italian Foreign Policy during Matteo Renzi's Government: A Domestically-Focused Outsider and the World*. Lanham: Lexington.

Coticchia, F. and J. Davidson (2018). 'The Limits of Radical Parties in Coalition Foreign Policy', *Foreign Policy Analysis* 14(2): 149–68.

Coticchia, F. and F. N. Moro (2014). 'Transforming the Italian Armed Forces, 2001–2012: New Challenges and Budget Constraints', *International Spectator* 49(1): 133–48.

Coticchia, F. and F. N. Moro (2015). *The Transformation of Italian Armed Forces in Comparative Perspective: Adapt, Improvise, Overcome?* Abingdon: Routledge.

Coticchia, F. and F. N. Moro (2016). 'Learning from Others? Emulation and Change in the Italian Armed Forces since 2001', *Armed Forces & Society* 42(4): 696–718.

Coticchia, F. and F. N. Moro (2020). 'Aspiring and Reluctant Middle Powers?' in G. Giacomello and B. Verbeek (eds), *Middle Powers in Asia and Europe in the 21st Century*. Lanham, MD: Lexington Books, 57–76.

Coticchia, F. and F. N. Moro (2020). 'From Enthusiasm to Retreat: Italy and Military Missions Abroad after the Cold War', *IPS - Italian Political Science* 15(1): 114–31.

Coticchia, F. and F. N. Moro (2020). 'Peaceful Legislatures? Parliaments and Military Interventions after the Cold War: Insights from Germany and Italy', *International Relations* 34(4): 482–503.

Coticchia, F. and A. Ruggeri (2022). An International Peacekeeper: The Evolution of Italian Foreign and Defence Policy', *IAI Policy Paper*, 22/06, Osservatorio IAI-ISPI sulla Politica Estera italiana.

Coticchia, F. and V. Vignoli (2020). 'Populist Parties and Foreign Policy: The Case of Italy's Five Star Movement', *British Journal of Politics and International Relations* 22(3): 523–41.

Coticchia, F. and V. Vignoli (2020). 'Italian Political Parties and Military Operations: An Empirical Analysis on Voting Patterns', *Government and Opposition* 55(3): 456–73.

Cox, R. (1975). 'A New Self-Confidence in the Bundeswehr', *RUSI Journal* 120(4): 58–61.

Croci, O. and M. Valigi (2013). 'Continuity and Change in Italian Foreign Policy: The Case of the International Intervention in Libya', *Contemporary Italian Politics* 5(1): 38–54.

Cumming, A. J. (2010). *The Battle for Britain: Interservice Rivalry between the Royal Air Force and Royal Navy 1909–40.* Annapolis, MD: Naval Institute Press, 2015.

Cusumano E. and M. Villa (2021). 'From "Angels" to "Vice Smugglers": The Criminalization of Sea Rescue NGOs in Italy', *European Journal on Criminal Policy and Research* 27(1): 23–40.

Cuzzi, M. (2005). 'L'opinione pubblica e le clausole del trattato di Parigi', in P. Rainero and R. Albertini (eds), *Le forze armate e la nazione italiana.* Roma: Commissione Italiana di Storia Militare, 75–110.

D'Alema, M. (1999). *Kosovo, gli italiani e la guerra.* Milano: Mondadori.

D'Amore, C. (2001). *Governare la difesa: Parlamento e politica militare nell'Italia repubblicana.* Milano: Franco Angeli.

Dalgaard-Nielsen, A. (2005). 'The Test of Strategic Culture: Germany, Pacifism and Pre-emptive Strikes', *Security Dialogue* 36(3): 339–59.

Dalvi, S. (1998). 'The Post-Cold War Role of the Bundeswehr: A Product of Normative Influences', *European Security* 7(1): 97–116.

Daugherty, L. J. (2011). '"The Tip of the Spear": The Formation and Expansion of the Bundeswehr, 1949–1963', *Journal of Slavic Military Studies* 24(1): 147–77.

Davidson, J. (2011). *America's Allies and War: Kosovo, Afghanistan, and Iraq.* Houndmills: Palgrave.

Davidson, J. (2020). *America's Entangling Alliances: 1778 to the Present.* Washington, DC: Georgetown University Press.

De Leonardis, M. (2014). *Guerra Fredda e interessi nazionali.* Roma: Rubettino.

Defense Intelligence Agency (2019). *China Military Power: Modernizing a Defense Force to Fight and Win.* Washington, DC: Defense Intelligence Agency.

Della Porta, D. and D. Rucht (1992). 'Movimenti sociali e sistema politico: Un confronto tra Italia e Germania', *Rivista Italiana di Scienze Politiche* 22(3): 501–37.

Dentice, G. and F. Donelli (2021). 'Reasserting (Middle) Power by Looking Southwards: Italy's Policy Towards Africa', *Contemporary Italian Politics* 12(3): 331–51.

Denzin, N. K. and Y. S. Lincoln (2011), *The SAGE Handbook of Qualitative Research.* Los Angeles, CA: Sage.

Dessì, A. and F. Olmastroni (2017). 'Foreign Posture in Comparative Perspective: A Quantitative and Qualitative Appraisal of Italian Foreign and Defence Policy during the Renzi Government', *Contemporary Italian Politics* 9(2): 201–18

Destradi, S. and J. Plagemann (2019). 'Populism and International Relations: (Un)predictability, Personalisation, and the Reinforcement of Existing Trends in World Politics', *Review of International Studies* 45(5): 711–30.

Di Feo, G. (2022). 'Intervista all'ammiraglio Cavo Dragone: "Così la marina ha respinto le navi russe nell'Adriatico"', *La Repubblica* 20 August.

Di Nolfo, E. (2006). 'Guerra, Stato e Nazione nel secondo dopoguerra', in L. Goglia, R. Moro and L. Nuti (eds), *Guerra e Pace nell'Italia del Novecento.* Bologna: Il Mulino, 227–50.

Dian, M. (2014). *The Evolution of the US–Japan Alliance: The Eagle and the Chrysanthemum.* Oxford: Chandos.

Dian, M. (2015). 'The Pivot to Asia, Air–Sea Battle and Contested Commons in the Asia Pacific Region', *Pacific Review* 28(2): 237–57.

Dian, M. (2017). *Contested Memories in Chinese and Japanese Foreign Policy.* Oxford: Elsevier.

Dian, M. (2020). 'Japan, South Korea and the Rise of a Networked Security Architecture in East Asia', *International Politics* 57(2): 185–207.

Dian, M. (2020). 'Obama and Japan: An Endangered Legacy', in I. Parmar and O. Turner (eds), *The United States in the Indo-Pacific*. Manchester: Manchester University Press, 63–78.

Dian, M. and A. Kireeva (2022). 'Wedge Strategies in Russia–Japan Relations', *Pacific Review* 35(5): 853–83.

Dian, M. and H. Meijer (2020). 'Networking Hegemony: Alliance Dynamics in East Asia', *International Politics* 57(2): 131–49.

Diodato, E. and F. Niglia (2017). *Italy in International Relations: The Foreign Policy Conundrum*. Basingstoke: Palgrave Macmillan.

Doeser, F. (2018). 'Historical Experiences, Strategic Culture, and Strategic Behaviour: Poland in the anti-ISIS Coalition', *Defence Studies* 18(4): 454–73.

Doeser, F. and J. Eidenfalk (2019). 'Using Strategic Culture to Understand Participation in Expeditionary Operations: Australia, Poland, and the Coalition against the Islamic State', *Contemporary Security Policy* 40(1): 4–29.

Dower, J. W. (1988). *Empire and Aftermath: Yoshida Shigeru and the Japanese experience, 1878–1954*. Cambridge, MA: Harvard University Press.

Dower, J. W. (2000). *Embracing Defeat: Japan in the Wake of World War II*. New York: W. W. Norton.

Dower, J. W. and H. Tetsuo (2007). 'Japan's Red Purge: Lessons from a Saga of Suppression of Free Speech and Thought', *Asia-Pacific Journal: Japan Focus* 5(7): 1–7.

Doyle, M. W. (1986). 'Liberalism and World Politics', *American Political Science Review* 80(4): 1151–69.

Duffield, J. S. (1999). 'Political Culture and State Behavior: Why Germany Confounds Neorealism', *International Organization* (53)4: 765–803.

Dyson, T. (2007). *The Politics of German Defence and Security: Policy Leadership and Military Reform in the post-Cold War Era*. New York: Berghahn.

Dyson, T. (2008). 'Convergence and Divergence in Post-Cold War British, French and German Military Reforms: Between International Structure and Executive Autonomy', *Security Studies* 17(4): 725–74.

Dyson, T. (2010). *Neoclassical Realism and Defence Reform in post-Cold War Europe*. Basingstoke: Palgrave.

Dyson, T. (2011). 'Condemned Forever to Becoming and Never to Being? The Weise Commission and German Military Isomorphism', *German Politics* 20(4): 545–67.

Dyson, T. (2011). 'Managing Convergence: German Military Doctrine and Capabilities in the 21st Century', *Defence Studies* 11(2): 244–70.

Dyson, T. (2014). 'German Defence Policy under the Second Merkel Chancellorship', *German Politics* 23(4): 460–76.

Dyson, T. (2019). 'The Military as a Learning Organisation: Establishing the Fundamentals of Best-Practice in Lessons-Learned', *Defence Studies* 19(2): 107–29.

Eberle, J. and A. Miskimmon (2021). 'International Theory and German Foreign Policy: Introduction to a Special Issue', *German Politics* 30(1): 1–13.

Eberle, J. And A. Miskimmon (eds) (2022). *International Theory and German Foreign Policy*. London: Routledge.

Eldridge, R. D. and P. Midford (eds) (2017). *The Japanese Ground Self-defense Force: Search for Legitimacy*. New York: Palgrave Macmillan.

Ertola, E. (2020). *Democrazia e difesa: Il controllo parlamentare sulla politica militare (1948–2018)*. Milano: Unicopli.

Evangelista, M. (ed.) (2018). *Italy from Crisis to Crisis*. London: Routledge.

Evans, R. J. (1977). 'The Creation of the Bundeswehr: Ensuring Civilian Control', *RUSI Journal* 122(3): 33–7.

Everts, P. and P. Isernia (eds) (2015). *Public Opinion, Transatlantic Relations and the Use of Force*. Houndmills: Palgrave.

Farrell, T. (2005). *The Norms of War: Cultural Beliefs and Modern Conflict*. Boulder, CO: Lynne Rienner.

Farrell, T. and S. Gordon (2009). 'COIN Machine: The British Military in Afghanistan', *Orbis* 53(4): 665–83.

Farrell, T., S. Rynning and T. Terriff (2013). *Transforming Military Power since the Cold War: Britain, France, and the United States, 1991–2012*. Cambridge: Cambridge University Press.

Feaver, P. D. (2011). 'The Right to be Right: Civil–Military Relations and the Iraq Surge Decision', *International Security* 35(4): 87–125.

Federal Ministry of Defence (2006). *White Paper 2006 on German Security Policy and the Future of the Bundeswehr*. Berlin: Federal Ministry of Defence.

Fioretos, O., T. G. Falleti and A. Sheingate (eds) (2016). *The Oxford Handbook of Historical Institutionalism*. Oxford: Oxford University Press.

Fogarty, F. (2015). 'Backing the Bundeswehr: A Research Note Regarding the State of German Civil–Military Affairs', *Armed Forces & Society* 41(4): 742–55.

Foley, R. T., S. Griffin and H. McCartney (2011). '"Transformation in Contact": Learning the Lessons of Modern War', *International Affairs* 87(2): 253–70.

Foradori, P. (2018). 'Cops in Foreign Lands: Italy's Role in International Policing', *International Peacekeeping* 25(4): 497–527.

Franke, U. E. (2012). 'A Tale of Stumbling Blocks and Road Bumps: Germany's (non) Revolution in Military Affairs', *Comparative Strategy* 31(4): 353–75.

Freedman L. (2006). *The Transformation in Strategic Affairs*. London: Routledge.

Fujishige, H. N., Y. Uesugi and T. Honda T. (2022). *Japan's Peacekeeping at a Crossroads: Taking a Robust Stance or Remaining Hesitant?* Basingstoke: Palgrave Macmillan.

Gaddis, J. L. (2005). *Strategies of Containment: A Critical Appraisal of American National Security Policy during the Cold War*. New York: Oxford University Press.

Gala, M. (2015). 'The Euromissile Crisis and the Centrality of the "Zero Option"', in L. Nuti, F. Bozo, M. P. Rey and B. Rother (eds), *The Euromissile Crisis and the End of the Cold War*. New York: Woodrow Wilson Center Press.

Gala, M. (2017). 'Italy's Role in the Implementation of the Dual-Track Decision', in E. Bini, I. Londero and G. Iannuzzi (2017). *Nuclear Italy: An International History of Italian Nuclear Policies during the Cold War*. Trieste: EUT Edizioni, 151–62.

Garthoff, R. L. (1985). *Detente and Confrontation: American-Soviet Relations from Nixon to Reagan*. Washington, DC: Brookings Institution Press.

Geis, A., H. Müller and N. Schörnig (eds) (2013). *The Militant Face of Democracy: Liberal Forces for Good*. Cambridge: Cambridge University Press.

Gentili, A. (2011). 'La Russa: l'azione sta andando bene, ora avanti la politica e la diplomazia', *Il Messaggero*, 11 May.

German Federal Ministry of Defence (2010). 'Internal Deficit Review' (*Strukturkommission der Bundeswehr*), 12 April.

Gerring, J. (2010). 'Causal Mechanisms: Yes, But . . .', *Comparative Political Studies* 43(11): 1499–526.

Ghiselli, A. (2018). 'Revising China's Strategic Culture: Contemporary Cherry-Picking of Ancient Strategic Thought', *China Quarterly* 233: 166–85.

Giacomello, G. and B. Verbeek (eds) (2020). *Middle Powers in Asia and Europe in the 21st Century*. Lanham, MD: Lexington Books.

Giegerich, B. and M. Terhalle (2021). *The Responsibility to Defend: Rethinking Germany's Strategic Culture*. New York: Routledge.

Gilli, A. and M. Gilli (2019). 'Why China has Not Caught Up Yet: Military–Technological Superiority and the Limits of Imitation, Reverse Engineering, and Cyber Espionage', *International Security* 43(3): 141–9.

Gilli, A., A. R. Ungaro and A. Marrone (2015). 'The Italian White Paper for International Security and Defence', *RUSI Journal* 160(6): 34–41.

Giurlando, P. (2020). 'Populist Foreign Policy: The Case of Italy', *Canadian Foreign Policy Journal* 27(2): 251–67.

Goldman, E. O. and R. B. Andres (1999). 'Systemic Effects of Military Innovation and Diffusion', *Security Studies* 8(4): 79–125.

Gongora T. and H. von Riekhoff (2000). *Toward a Revolution in Military Affairs: Defence and Security at Dawn of the Twenty-First Century*. Westport, CT: Greenwood.

Graham, E. (2005). *Japan's Sea Lane Security: A Matter of Life and Death?* London: Routledge.

Gray, C. S. (1981). 'National. Style in Strategy: The American Example', *International Security* 6(2): 21–47.

Gray, C. S. (1999). 'Strategic Culture as Context: The First Generation of Theory Strikes Back', *Review of International Studies* 25(1): 49–69.

Greco, E. (1998). 'New Trends in Peacekeeping: The Operation Alba', *Security Dialogue* 29(2): 35–57.

Green, M. J. (2010). 'Japan's Confused Revolution', *Washington Quarterly* 33(1): 3–19.

Green, M. J. (2017). *By More than Providence: Grand Strategy and American Power in the Asia Pacific since 1783*. New York: Columbia University Press.

Green, M. J., K. Hicks, Z. Cooper, J. Schaus and J. Douglas (2017). *Countering Coercion in Maritime Asia: The Theory and Practice of Gray Zone Deterrence*. New York: Rowman & Littlefield.

Green, M. J. and K. Murata (1998). *The 1978 Guidelines for the US–Japan Defence Cooperation Process and the Historical Impact*. GWU Working Paper No. 17. Washington, DC: George Washington University.

Green, M. J. and N. Szechenyi (2012). 'US–Japan Relations: Back to Normal?' *Comparative Connections* 14(1): 1–10.

Griffin, S. (2017). 'Military Innovation Studies: Multidisciplinary or Lacking Discipline', *Journal of Strategic Studies* 40(1): 198–203.

Grissom, A. (2006). 'The Future of Military Innovation Studies', *Journal of Strategic Studies* 29(5): 905–34.

Grønning, B. E. M. (2018). 'Operational and Industrial Military Integration: Extending the Frontiers of the Japan–US Alliance', *International Affairs* 94(4): 755–72.

Gustafsson, K., L. Hagström and U. Hanssen (2018). 'Japan's Pacifism is dead', *Survival* 60(6): 137–58.

Guzzini, S. (ed.) (2012). *The Return of Geopolitics in Europe? Social Mechanisms and Foreign Policy Identity Crises*. Cambridge: Cambridge University Press.

Haesebrouck, T. and P. A. Mello (2020). 'Patterns of Political Ideology and Security Policy', *Foreign Policy Analysis* 16(4): 565–86.

Haftendorn, H. (1984). 'Germany and the Euromissile Debate', *International Journal* 40(1): 68–85.

Hagström, L. and U. Hanssen (2016). 'War is Peace: The Rearticulation of "Peace" in Japan's China Discourse', *Review of International Studies* 42(2): 266–86.

Hansel, M. and K. Oppermann (2016). 'Counterfactual Reasoning in Foreign Policy Analysis: The Case of German Nonparticipation in the Libya Intervention of 2011', *Foreign Policy Analysis* 12(2): 109–27.

Harnisch, S. (2009). '"The Politics of Domestication": A New Paradigm in German Foreign Policy', *German Politics* 18(4): 455–68.

Harold, S. W., Y. Nakagawa and J. Fukuda (2017). *The US–Japan Alliance and Deterring Gray Zone Coercion in the Maritime, Cyber, and Space Domains*. Santa Monica, CA: RAND Corp.

Hellmann, G. (2011). 'Normatively Disarmed, But Self-Confident', *Internationale Politik Global Edition* 3: 45–51.

Henke, M. E. (2019). *Constructing Allied Cooperation: Diplomacy, Payments, and Power in Multilateral Military Coalitions*. Ithaca, NY: Cornell University Press, 2019.

Herszenhorn, D. (2019), 'Trump Threatens to Punish Germany over Military Spending', *Politico*, 4 December, available at: https://politi.co/3Qv3J6Y.

Hikotani, T. (2018). 'The Japanese Diet and Defence Policy-making', *International Affairs* 94(4): 791–814.

Hoffmann, A. and K. Longhurst (1999). 'German Strategic Culture and the Changing Role of the Bundeswehr', *WeltTrends* 22: 145–62.

Hofmann, S. C. (2021). 'Beyond Culture and Power: The Role of Party Ideologies in German Foreign and Security Policy', *German Politics* 30(1): 51–71.

Hogan, M. J. (1998). *A Cross of Iron: Harry S. Truman and the Origins of the National Security State, 1945–1954*. New York: Cambridge University Press.

Horwood, I. (2010). *Interservice Rivalry and Airpower in the Vietnam War*. Fort Leavenworth, KS: Combat Studies Institute, US Army Command and General Staff College.

Hosoya, Y. (2019). 'FOIP 2.0: The Evolution of Japan's Free and Open Indo-Pacific Strategy', *Asia-Pacific Review* 26(1): 18–28.

Hughes, C. W. (2011). 'The Slow Death of Japanese Techno-Nationalism? Emerging Comparative Lessons for China's Defense Production', *Journal of Strategic Studies* 34(3): 451–79.

Hughes, C. W. (2012). 'The Democratic Party of Japan's New (but Failing) Grand Security Strategy: From "Reluctant Realism" to "Resentful Realism"?' *Journal of Japanese Studies* 38(1): 109–40.

Hughes, C. W. (2013). 'Japan, Ballistic Missile Defence and Remilitarisation', *Space Policy* 29(2): 128–34.

Hughes, C. W. (2015). *Japan's Foreign and Security Policy Under the 'Abe Doctrine': New Dynamism or New Dead End?* Basingstoke: Palgrave Macmillan.

Hughes, C. W. (2017). 'Japan's Strategic Trajectory and Collective Self-Defense: Essential Continuity or Radical Shift?' *Journal of Japanese Studies* 43(1): 93–126.

Hunter-Chester, D. (2016). *Creating Japan's Ground Self-Defense Force, 1945–2015: A Sword Well Made*. Lanham, MD: Lexington Books.

Huntington, S. P. (1961). 'Interservice Competition and the Political Roles of the Armed Services', *American Political Science Review* 55(1): 40–52.

Hyde, S. D. and E. N. Saunders (2020). 'Recapturing Regime Type in International Relations: Leaders, Institutions, and Agency Space', *International Organization* 74(2): 363–95.

Hyde-Price, A. (2004). 'European Security, Strategic Culture, and the Use of Force', *European Security* 13(4): 323–44.

Hyde-Price, A. G. V. (2015). 'The "Sleep-Walking Giant" Awakes: Resetting German Foreign and Security Policy', *European Security* 24(4): 600–16.

IAI-LASP (2017). *Gli Italiani e la politica estera*, available at: https://www.iai.it/sites/default/files/laps-iai_2017.pdf.

Ignazi, P., G. Giacomello and F. Coticchia (2012). *Italian Military Missions Abroad: Just Don't Call It War*. Houndmills: Palgrave Macmillan.

Ikenberry, G. J. (2018). 'The End of Liberal International Order?' *International Affairs* 94(1): 7–23.

Ilari, V. (1987). 'The New Model of Italian Defence, Doctrinal Options, Issues and Trends', *International Spectator* 22(2): 80–7.

Insisa, A. and G. Pugliese (2022). 'The Free and Open Indo-Pacific versus the Belt and Road: Spheres of Influence and Sino-Japanese Relations', *Pacific Review* 35(3): 557–85.

Iriye, A. (1990). 'Chinese–Japanese Relations, 1945–90', *China Quarterly* 124(4): 624–38.

Iriye, A. (1992). *China and Japan in the Global Setting*. Cambridge, MA: Harvard University Press.

Isastia, A. M. (2005). 'Forze armate e società. Il ritorno dei reduci tra indifferenza e rimozione', in P. Rainero and R. Albertini (eds), *Le forze armate e la nazione italiana*. Roma: Commissione Italiana di Storia Militare, 29–48.

Isernia, P. (1996). *Dove gli angeli non mettono piede: Opinione pubblica e politiche di sicurezza in Italia*. Milano: FrancoAngeli.

Isernia, P. and F. Longo (2017). 'The Italian Foreign Policy: Challenges and Continuities', *Italian Political Science Review* 47(2): 107–24.

Italian Ministry of Defence (1991). *Modello di difesa: Lineamenti di sviluppo delle FFAA negli anni 90*. Rome: Stato Maggiore della Difesa.

Italian Ministry of Defence (2002). *Il Libro Bianco della Difesa*. Rome: Stato Maggiore della Difesa.

Italian Ministry of Defence (2005). *Il concetto strategico del Capo di Stato Maggiore*. Rome: Stato Maggiore della Difesa.

Italian Ministry of Defence (2011). *Nuove Forze per un Nuovo Secolo*. Rome: Stato Maggiore della Difesa.

Italian Ministry of Defence (2013). *Direttiva Ministeriale in merito alla politica militare per l'anno 2013*. Rome: Stato Maggiore della Difesa.

Italian Ministry of Defence (2015). *Libro Bianco della Difesa e della Sicurezza*. Rome: Stato Maggiore della Difesa.

Italian Ministry of Defence (2020). *Documento Programmatico Pluriennale della Difesa per il Triennio 2020–2022*. Rome: Stato Maggiore della Difesa.

Italian Ministry of Defence (2022). *Strategia di Sicurezza e Difesa per il Mediterraneo*. Rome: Stato Maggiore della Difesa.

Italian Ministry of Defence (2022). *The Chief of Defence Strategic Concept*. Rome: Stato Maggiore della Difesa.

Izumikawa, Y. (2010). 'Explaining Japanese Antimilitarism: Normative and Realist Constraints on Japan's Security Policy', *International Security* 35(2): 123–60.

Japanese Ministry of Defence (2005). *National Defence Program Guidelines, FY 2005 and After*. Tokyo.

Japanese Ministry of Defence (2010). *National Defence Program Guidelines for FY2011*. Tokyo.

Japanese Ministry of Defence (2013). *National Defence Program Guidelines for FY 2013 and Beyond*. Tokyo.

Japanese Ministry of Defence (2013). *National Security Strategy*. Tokyo.

Japanese Ministry of Defence (2014). *Defence of Japan 2014*. Tokyo.

Japanese Ministry of Defence (2014). *National Defence Program Guidelines for FY 2014 and Beyond*. Tokyo.

Japanese Ministry of Defence (2018). *National Defence Programme Guidelines 2019*. Tokyo.

Japanese Ministry of Defence (2020). *Defence of Japan 2020*. Tokyo.

Japanese Ministry of Defence (2021). *Development of the Free and Open Indo Pacific Vision*. Tokyo, available at: https://www.mod.go.jp/en/d_act/exc/india_pacific/india_pacific-en.html.

Japanese Ministry of Defence (2022). *Defence of Japan 2022*. Tokyo.

Japanese Ministry of Defence (2022). *National Defence Program Guidelines (NDPG) and Medium Term Defence Program (MTDP)*, available at: https://www.mod.go.jp/en/d_policy/basis/guideline/index.html.

Japanese Ministry of Defence (2022). *National Defence Strategy*. Tokyo

Japanese Ministry of Foreign Affairs (1995). *National Defence Program Outline in and after FY 1996*. Tokyo.

Japanese Ministry of Foreign Affairs (2014). 'Cabinet Decision on Development of Seamless Security Legislation to Ensure Japan's Survival and Protect its People', available at: https://www.mofa.go.jp/fp/nsp/page23e_000273.html.

Japanese Ministry of Foreign Affairs (2016). *Japan's Legislation for Peace and Security. Tokyo*, available at: https://www.mofa.go.jp/files/000143304.pdf.

Japanese Ministry of Foreign Affairs (2022). *The National Security Strategy of Japan*, Tokyo.

Jeffrey, H. (1991). *War by Other Means: Soviet Power, West German Resistance, and the Battle of the Euromissiles*. New York: Free Press.

Jimbo, K. (2012). 'Japan's National Defence Planning for the New Security Environment: The 2010 National Defence Program Guidelines', *DTP Policy Briefs, 2012*, Policy Brief 3. La Jolla, CA: University of California Institute on Global Conflict and Cooperation.

Jimbo, K., R. Sahashi, S. Takahashi, Y. Sakata, M. Masuda and T. Yuzawa (2011). *Japan's Security Strategy toward China: Integration, Balancing and Deterrence in the Era of Power Shift*. Tokyo: Tokyo Foundation.

Joffe, J. (1990). 'Once More: The German Question', *Survival* 32(2): 129–40.

Johnson, J. (2017). 'Washington's Perceptions and Misperceptions of Beijing's Anti-access Area-denial (A2-AD) "Strategy": Implications for Military Escalation Control and Strategic Stability', *Pacific Review* 30(3): 271–88.

Johnston, A. I. (1995). 'Thinking about Strategic Culture', *International Security* 19(4): 32–64.

Johnston, A. I. (2013). 'How New and Assertive is China's New Assertiveness?' *International Security* 37(4): 7–28.

Jones, E. (2018). 'Italy, Its Populists and the EU', *Survival* 60(4): 113–22.

Juhasz, Z. (2001). 'German Public Opinion and the Use of Force in the Early Nineties', in P. Isernia and P. Everts (eds), *Public Opinion and the International Use of Force*. London: Routledge, 57–85.

Kaarbo, J. (2015). 'Foreign Policy Analysis Perspective on the Domestic Politics Turn in IR Theory', *International Studies Review* 17(2): 189–216.

Kaarbo, J. and R. K. Beasley (2008). 'Taking It to the Extreme: The Effect of Coalition Cabinets on Foreign Policy', *Foreign Policy Analysis* 4(1): 67–81.

Kallender, P. and C. W. Hughes (2017). 'Japan's Emerging Trajectory as a "Cyber Power": From Securitization to Militarization of Cyberspace', *Journal of Strategic Studies* 40(1/2): 118–45.

Katagiri, N. (2021). 'From Cyber Denial to Cyber Punishment: What Keeps Japanese Warriors from Active Defense Operations?' *Asian Security* 17(3): 331–48.

Katzenstein, P. J. (1996). *The Culture of National Security: Norms and Identity in World Politics*. New York: Columbia University Press.

Katzenstein, P. J. (ed.) (1997). *Tamed Power: Germany in Europe*. Ithaca, NY: Cornell University Press.

Kawana, S. and M. Takahashi (eds) (2020). *Exploring Base Politics: How Host Countries Shape the Network of US Overseas Bases*. London: Routledge.

Kawasaki, T. (2001). 'Japan and Two Theories of Military Doctrine Formation: Civilian Policymakers, Policy Preference, and the 1976 National Defence Program Outline', *International Relations of the Asia-Pacific* 1(1): 67–93.

Keohane, D. (2016). *Constrained Leadership*, Zurich: CSS ETH Zurich, available at: https://bit.ly/3QLtMGK.

Kier, E. (1995). 'Culture and Military Doctrine: France between the Wars', *International Security* 19(4): 65–93.

Kier, E. (2017). *Imagining War: French and British Military Doctrine between the Wars*. Princeton, NJ: Princeton University Press.

Kilcullen, D. (2010). *Counterinsurgency*. New York: Oxford University Press.

King, A. (2006). 'Towards a European Military Culture?' *Defence Studies* 6(3): 257–77.

Kissinger, H. A. (1979). *The White House Years*. Boston, MA: Little Brown.

Klein, B. (1988). 'Hegemony and Strategic Culture: American Power Projection and Alliance Defence Politics', *Review of International Studies* 14(2): 133–48.

Klos, D., H. Möllers and D. Stockfish (2013). 'The Military Services', in I. Wiesner (ed.), *German Defence Politics*. Baden-Baden: Nomos, 127–62.

Koshino, Y. (2021). 'Is Japan Ready for Civil–Military "Integration"'? *International Institute for Strategic Studies Analysis*, 3 August.

Krauss, E. S. and R. J. Pekkanen (2011). *The Rise and Fall of Japan's LDP: Political Party Organizations as Historical Institutions*. Ithaca, NY: Cornell University Press.

Krotz, U. (2015). *History and Foreign Policy in France and Germany*. Houndmills: Palgrave.

Kümmel, G. (2003). 'The Winds of Change: The Transition from Armed Forces for Peace to New Missions for the Bundeswehr and Its Impact on Civil–Military Relations', *Journal of Strategic Studies* 26(2): 9.

Kümmel, G. and N. Leonhard (2005). 'Casualties and Civil–Military Relations: The German Polity between Learning and Indifference', *Armed Forces & Society* 31(4): 513–35.

La Racine, R. B. (2005). 'Il rapporto tra la Marina e la Nazione', in P. Rainero and R. Albertini (eds), *Le forze armate e la nazione italiana*. Roma: Commissione Italiana di Storia Militare, 157–89.

Labanca, N. (2005). 'Nota sui bilanci militari della Repubblica', in P. Rainero and R. Albertini (eds), *Le forze armate e la nazione italiana*. Roma: Commissione Italiana di Storia Militare, 224–55.

Labanca, N. (ed.) (2009). *Le armi della Repubblica: dalla Liberazione ad oggi*. Turin: UTET.

Labanca, N. (2011). 'Defence Policy in the Italian Republic: Frames and Issues', UNISCI Discussion Papers', No. 25 (January), Madrid, 145–66.

LaFeber, W. (1998). *The Clash: US-Japanese Relations throughout History*. New York: W. W. Norton.

Laksmana, E. A. (2017). 'Threats and Civil–Military Relations: Explaining Singapore's "Trickle Down" Military Innovation', *Defence & Security Analysis* 33(4): 347–65.

Lanoszka, A. (2022). *Military Alliances in the Twenty-First Century*. New York: John Wiley.

Lantis, J. (2002). *Strategic Dilemmas and the Evolution of German Foreign Policy since Unification*. Santa Barbara, CA: Greenwood.

Lantis, J. S. (2002). 'Strategic Culture and National Security Policy', *International Studies Review* 4(3): 87–113.

Lantis, J. S. (2014). 'Strategic Cultures and Security Policies in the Asia-Pacific', *Contemporary Security Policy* 35(2): 166–86.

Large, D. C. (1996). *Germans to the Front: West German Rearmament in the Adenauer Era*. Chapel Hill: University of North Carolina Press.

Law Decree, 12 May 1995, n. 196, *Attuazione dell'art. 3 della legge 6 marzo 1992, n. 216, in materia di riordino dei ruoli, modifica alle norme di reclutamento, stato ed avanzamento del personale non direttivo delle Forze armate*.

Leffler, M. P. (1992). *A Preponderance of Power: National Security, the Truman Administration, and the Cold War*. Stanford, CA: Stanford University Press.

Lequesne, C. (2021). 'Populist Governments and Career Diplomats in the EU: The Challenge of Political Capture', *Comparative European Politics* 19(6): 779–95.

Liff, A. P. (2015). 'Japan's Defense Policy: Abe the Evolutionary', *Washington Quarterly* 38(2): 79–99.

Lim, Y. H. (2017). 'Expanding the Dragon's Reach: The Rise of China's Anti-access Naval Doctrine and Forces', *Journal of Strategic Studies* 40(1/2): 146–68.

Locatelli, A., F. N. Moro and F. Coticchia (2016). 'Renew or Reload? Continuity and Change in Italian Defence Policy', *EUI Working Papers Series*, EUI RSCAS 1.

Loi, B. (2004). *Peacekeeping: pace o guerra?* Firenze: Vallecchi.

Lombardi, B. (2011). 'The Berlusconi Government and Intervention in Libya', *International Spectator* 46(4): 31–44.

Long, A. (2016). *The Soul of Armies: Counterinsurgency Doctrine and Military Culture in the US and UK*. Ithaca, NY: Cornell University Press.

Longhurst, K. (2003). 'Why Aren't the Germans Debating the Draft? Path Dependency and the Persistence of Conscription', *German Politics* 12(2): 147–65.

Longhurst, K. (2004). *Germany and the Use of Force*. Manchester: Manchester University Press.

Longhurst, K. (2005). 'Endeavours to Restructure the Bundeswehr: The Reform of the German Armed Forces 1990–2003', *Defence & Security Analysis* 21(1): 21–35.

Longhurst, K. and A. Miskimmon (2007). 'Same Challenges, Diverging Responses: Germany, the UK and European Security', *German Politics* 16(1): 79–94.

Lungu, S. (2004). 'Military Modernisation and Political Choice: Germany and the US-Promoted Military Technological Revolution during the 1990s', *Defence & Security Analysis* 20(3): 261–72.

Lytle, M. A. and T. L. Cockman (1989). 'An Institutional Evolution: The Bundeswehr – A New German Army', *Defence Analysis* 5(3): 207–20.

Mahnken, T. G. (2011). 'China's anti-Access Strategy in Historical and Theoretical Perspective', *Journal of Strategic Studies* 34(3): 299–323.

Mahnken, T. G. (ed.) (2020). *Learning the Lessons of Modern War*. Stanford, CA: Stanford University Press.

Mahoney, J. (2000). 'Path Dependence in Historical Sociology', *Theory and Society* 29(4): 507–48.

Malici, A. (2006). 'Germans as Venutians: The Culture of German Foreign Policy Behavior', *Foreign Policy Analysis* 2(1): 37–62.

Mammarella, G. and P. Cacace (2008). *La politica estera dell'Italia: Dallo stato unitario ai giorni nostri*. Bari: Laterza.

Marrone, A. and M. Nones (eds) (2016). *Italy and the Security in the Mediterranean*. Roma: Nuova Cultura.

Martuscelli, C. (2022). 'Germany to Miss 2 percent NATO Defense Spending Target: Think Tank, 15 August, *Politico Europe*, available at: https://www.politico.eu/article /germany-to-miss-2-percent-nato-defense-spending-target-think-tank.

Maull, H. (2000). 'Germany and the Use of Force: Still a "Civilian Power"?' *Survival* 42(2): 56–80.

McCormack, G. and S. O. Norimatsu (2018). *Resistant Islands: Okinawa Confronts Japan and the United States*. New York: Rowman & Littlefield.

Mead, W. R. (2014). 'The Return of Geopolitics: The Revenge of the Revisionist Powers', *Foreign Affairs* 93(3): 69.

Mearsheimer, J. J. (2019). 'Bound to Fail: The Rise and Fall of the Liberal International Order', *International Security* 43(4): 7–50.

Mehrer, T. (2022). *Turn of Phrase: Germany's Zeitenwende*. ECFR, available at: https://ecfr .eu/article/turn-of-phrase-germanys-zeitenwende.

Mello, P. A. (2014). *Democratic Participation in Armed Conflict*. Houndmills: Palgrave.

Mello, P. A. and D. Peters (2018). 'Parliaments in Security Policy: Involvement, Politicisation, and Influence', *British Journal of Politics and International Relations* 20(1): 1–16.

Midford, P. (2018). 'Decentering from the US in Regional Security Multilateralism: Japan's 1991 Pivot', *Pacific Review* 31(4): 441–59.

Miskimmon, A. (2007). *Germany and the Common Foreign and Security Policy of the European Union*. New York: Palgrave.

Miskimmon, A. (2009). 'Falling into Line: The Legacy of Operation Allied Force on German Foreign Policy', *International Affairs* 85(3): 561–73.

Miskimmon, A. (2012). 'German Foreign Policy and the Libya Crisis', *German Politics* 21(4): 392–410.

Miskimmon, A., B. O'Loughlin and L. Roselle (2017). 'Conclusions', in A. Miskimmon, B. O'Loughlin and L. Roselle (eds), *Forging the World: Strategic Narratives and International Relations*. Ann Arbor: University of Michigan Press, 321.

Miyagi, Y. (2009). 'Foreign Policymaking under Koizumi: Norms and Japan's Role in the 2003 Iraq War', *Foreign Policy Analysis* 5(4): 349–66.

Monteleone, C. (2019). *Italy in Uncertain Times: Europeanizing Foreign Policy in the Declining Process of the American Hegemony*. London: Lexington Books.

Moro, F. N., L. Cicchi and F. Coticchia (2018). 'Through Military Lenses: Perception of Security Threats and Jointness in the Italian Air Force', *Defence Studies* 18(2): 207–228.

Mulloy, G. (2021). *Defenders of Japan: Post Imperial Armed Forces, 1946–2016*. London: Hurst.

Münch, P. (2015). *Die Bundeswehr in Afghanistan: Militärische Handlungslogik in internationalen Interventionen*. Freiburg im Breisgau: Rombach Verlag.

Murray, W. (1998). 'Armoured Warfare: The British, French and German Experiences', in W. R. Murray and A. R. Millett (eds), *Military Innovation in the Interwar Period*. Cambridge: Cambridge University Press, 6–49.

Murray, W. (1999). 'Does Military Culture Matter?' *Orbis* 43(1): 27–42.

Murray, W. (2001). *Military Adaptation in War*. Cambridge: Cambridge University Press.

Nascia, L. and M. Pianta (2009). 'La spesa militare in Italia, 1949–2008', in N. Labanca (ed.), *Le armi della Repubblica. Dalla Liberazione a oggi*. Turin: UTET, 177–208.

Noetzel, T. and B. Schreer (2008). 'All the Way? The Evolution of German Military Power', *International Affairs* 84(2), 211–21.

Noetzel, T. (2010). 'Germany', in T. Rid and T. Keneay (eds), *Understanding Counterinsurgency. Doctrine, Operations, and Challenges*. London: Routledge, 46–58.

Nones, M. and A. Marrone (2011). *La trasformazione delle Forze armate: il programma Forza NEC*. Roma: Carocci Army Report.

North, D. C. (1993). 'Toward a Theory of Institutional Change', *Political Economy: Institutions, Competition, and Representation* 31(4): 61–9.

Nuti, L. (1989). *L'esercito italiano nel secondo dopoguerra 1946–1950: La sua ricostruzione e l'assistenza militare alleata*. Rome: Stato maggiore dell'esercito, Ufficio storico.

Nuti, L. (1998). 'Commitment to NATO and Domestic Politics: The Italian Case and Some Comparative Remarks', *Contemporary European History* 7(3): 361–77.

Nuti, L. (2006). 'Linee generali della politica di difesa italiana (1945–1989)', in L. Goglia, R. Moro and L. Nuti (eds), *Guerra e Pace nell'Italia del Novecento*. Bologna: Il Mulino, 463–504.

Nuti, L. (2007). *La Sfida Nucleare: La Politica Estera Italiana e Le Armi Atomiche, 1945–1991*. Bologna: Il Mulino.

Nuti, L. (2016). 'Extended Deterrence and National Ambitions: Italy's Nuclear Policy, 1955–1962', *Journal of Strategic Studies* 39(4): 559–79.

Nye, J. S. (2001). 'The "Nye Report": Six Years Later', *International Relations of the Asia-Pacific* 1(1): 95–103.

Nuti, L., F. Bozo, M-P. Rey and B. Rother (eds) (2015). *The Euromissile Crisis and the End of the Cold War*. New York: Woodrow Wilson Center Press.

O'Shea, P. and S. Maslow (2021). '"Making the Alliance Even Greater": (Mis-)managing US–Japan Relations in the Age of Trump', *Asian Security* 17(2): 195–215.

Office of the Deputy Chief of Staff of the Army (2021). *Rapporto Esercito 2020*. Rome: Stato Maggiore dell'Esercito.

Office of the Prime Minister of Japan, *The Japanese Constitution*, available at: https://japa n.kantei.go.jp/constitution_and_government_of_japan/constitution_e.html.

Oktay, S. (2022). *Governing Abroad: Coalition Politics and Foreign Policy in Europe*. Ann Arbor: University of Michigan Press.

Oliva, G. (2016). '70 anni. 1946–2016. Le forze armate dell'Italia Repubblicana', *Informazioni della Difesa* 2/2016: 8–23.

Oppermann, K. (2012). 'National Role Conceptions, Domestic Constraints and the New "Normalcy" in German Foreign Policy: The Eurozone Crisis, Libya and Beyond', *German Politics* 21(4): 502–19.

Oppermann, K. and K. Brummer (2014). 'Patterns of Junior Partner Influence on the Foreign Policy of Coalition Governments', *British Journal of Politics and International Relations* 16(4): 555–71.

Oros, A. L. (2008). *Normalizing Japan: Politics, Identity, and the Evolution of Security Practice*. Stanford, CA: Stanford University Press.

Oros, A. L. (2017). *Japan's Security Renaissance: New Policies and Politics for the Twenty-first Century*. New York: Columbia University Press.

Page, S. E. (2006). 'Path Dependence', *Quarterly Journal of Political Science* 1(1): 87–115.

Palmer, G., T. London and P. Regan (2004). 'What's Stopping You? The Sources of Political Constraints on International Conflict Behaviour in Parliamentary Democracies', *International Interactions* 30(1): 1–24.

Panda, A. (2020). *Kim Jong Un and the Bomb: Survival and Deterrence in North Korea*. London: Hurst.

Panebianco, A. (1997). *Guerrieri Democratici*. Bologna: Il Mulino.

Panebianco, S. (ed.) (2016). *Sulle onde del Mediterraneo: Cambiamenti globali e risposte alle crisi migratorie*. Milano: Egea.

Pastorelli, P. (2011). 'De Gasperi, the Christian Democrats and the Atlantic Treaty', in E. Di Nolfo (ed.), *The Atlantic Pact Forty Years Later*. New York: De Gruyter, 209–19.

Patalano, A. (2008). 'Shielding the "Hot Gates": Submarine Warfare and Japanese Naval Strategy in the Cold War and Beyond (1976–2006)', *Journal of Strategic Studies* 31(6): 859–95.

Patalano, A. (2015). *Post-War Japan as a Sea Power: Imperial Legacy, Wartime Experience and the Making of a Navy*. London: Bloomsbury.

Patalano, A. (2019). '"The Silent Fight!: Submarine Rearmament and the Origins of Japan's Military Engagement with the Cold War, 1955–76', *Cold War History* 21(1): 1–21.

Pekkanen, S. and P. Kallender-Umezu (2010). *In Defense of Japan: From the Market to the Military in Space Policy*. Stanford, CA: Stanford University Press.

Petrilli, L. and V. Sinapi (2007). *Nassiriya, la vera storia*. Torino: Lindau.

Peyretti, E. (1998). *La politica è pace*. Assisi: Cittadella.

Pfaffenzeller, S. (2010). 'Conscription and Democracy: The Mythology of Civil–Military Relations', *Armed Forces & Society* 36(3): 481–504.

Pierson, P. (1996). 'The Path to European Integration: A Historical Institutionalist Analysis', *Comparative Political Studies* 29(2): 123–63.

Pierson, P. (2000). 'Increasing Returns, Path Dependence, and the Study of Politics', *American Political Science Review* 94(2): 251–67.

Pierson, P. (2000). 'Not Just What, But When: Timing and Sequence in Political Processes', *Studies in American Political Development* 14(1): 72–92.

Pierson, P. (2004). *Politics in Time: History, Institutions, and Social Analysis*. Princeton, NJ: Princeton University Press.

Pirani, P. (2010). 'The Way We Were: The Social Construction of the Italian Defence Policy', *Modern Italy* 15(2): 217–30.

Policy Guidelines for the Indo Pacific (*Leilinien zum Indo-Pazifik*), 1 September 2020.

Posen, B. (1986). *The Sources of Military Doctrine: France, Britain, and Germany between the World Wars*. Ithaca, NY: Cornell University Press.

Puglierin, J. (2021). 'After Merkel: Why Germany Must End Its Inertia on Defence and Security', *European Council on Foreign Relations*, 15 January.

Pugliese, G. and A. Patalano (2020). 'Diplomatic and Security Practice under Abe Shinzō: The Case for Realpolitik Japan', *Australian Journal of International Affairs* 74(6): 615–32.

Pugliese, M., F. Ghiretti and A. and Insisa (2022). 'Italy's Embrace of the Belt and Road Initiative', *International Affairs* 98(3): 1033–51.

Putnam, R. D. (1988). 'Diplomacy and Domestic Politics: The Logic of Two-Level Games', *International Organization* 42(3): 427–60.

Pyle, K. B. (1987). 'In Pursuit of a Grand Design: Nakasone between the Past and the Future', *Journal of Japanese Studies* 13(2): 243–70.

Pyle, K. B. (2007). *Japan Rising: The Resurgence of Japanese Power and Purpose*. New York: Public Affairs.

Rainero, P. and R. Albertini (eds) (2005). *Le forze armate e la nazione italiana*. Roma: Commissione Italiana di Storia Militare.

Rapp-Hooper, M. (2020). *Shields of the Republic: The Triumph and Peril of America's Alliances*. Cambridge, MA: Harvard University Press.

Rathbun, B. C. (2004). *Partisan Interventions: European Party Politics and Peace Enforcement in the Balkans*. Ithaca, NY: Cornell University Press.

Ratti, L. (2011). 'Italy as a Multilateral Actor: The Inescapable Destiny of a Middle Power', in M. Carbone (ed.). *Italy in the Post Cold War Order*. Lanham, MD: Lexington Books, 123–40.

Raunio, T. and W. Wagner (2017), 'Towards Parliamentarisation of Foreign and Security Policy?' *West European Politics* 40(1): 1–19.

Raunio, T. and W. Wagner (2020). 'The Party Politics of Foreign and Security Policy', *Foreign Policy Analysis* 16(4): 515–31.

Rid, T. (2007). 'The Bundeswehr's New Media Challenge', *Military Review*, July/August, 104–9.

Rink, M. (2015). *Die Bundeswehr 1950/55–1989*. Munich: De Gruyter Oldenbourg.

Risse-Kappen, T. (1994). 'Ideas do not Float Freely: Transnational Coalitions, Domestic Structures, and the End of the Cold War', *International Organization* 48(2): 185–214.

Rittberger, V. (2001). *German Foreign Policy since Unification: Theories and Case Studies*. Manchester: Manchester University Press.

Röhl, K-H., H. Bardt and B. Engels (2022). 'Zeitenwende für die Verteidigungswirtschaft? Sicherheitspolitik und Verteidigungsfähigkeit nach der russischen Invasion der Ukraine', *IW-Policy Paper* No. 4, Berlin/Köln.

Ronzitti, N. (2017). 'La legge italiana sulle missioni internazionali', *Rivista di diritto internazionale* 100(2): 474–95.

Rosa, P. (2012). *Tra pacifismo e Realpolitik*. Roma: Rubettino.

Rosa, P. (2014). 'The Accommodationist State: Strategic Culture and Italy's Military Behaviour', *International Relations* 28(1): 88–115.

Rosa, P. (2016). *Strategic Culture and Italy's Military Behaviour: Between Pacifism and Realpolitik*. Lanham, MD: Rowman & Littlefield.

Rosa, P. (2018). 'Patterns of Strategic Culture and the Italian Case', *International Politics* 55: 316–33.

Rosen, S. P. (1994). *Winning the Next War: Innovation and the Modern Military*. Ithaca, NY: Cornell University Press.

Rovner, J. (2014). 'Questions about COIN after Iraq and Afghanistan', in C. W. Gventer, D. M. Jones and M. L. R. Smith (eds), *The New Counter-insurgency Era in Critical Perspective*. London: Palgrave Macmillan, 299–318.

Ruffa, C. (2017). 'Military Cultures and Force Employment in Peace Operations', *Security Studies* 26(3): 394.

Rush, L. and L. B. Millington (2019). *The Carabinieri Command for the Protection of Cultural Property: Saving the World's Heritage*. Suffolk: Boydell Press.

Russell, J. (2020). *Innovation, Transformation, and War: Counterinsurgency Operations in Anbar and Ninewa Provinces, Iraq, 2005–2007*. Stanford, CA: Stanford University Press.

Ruzicic-Kessler, K. (2014). 'Italy and Yugoslavia: From Distrust to Friendship in Cold War Europe', *Journal of Modern Italian Studies* 19(5): 641–64.

Rynning, S. (2013). 'ISAF and NATO: Campaign Innovation and Organisational Adaptation', in T. Farrell, F. Osinga and J. A. Russell (eds), *Military Adaptation in Afghanistan*. Stanford, CA: Stanford University Press, 83–107.

Sakaki, A. and S. Maslow (2020). 'Japan's New Arms Export Policies: Strategic Aspirations and Domestic Constraints', *Australian Journal of International Affairs* 74(6): 649–69.

Sakaki, A., H. W. Maull, K. Lukner, E. S. Krauss and T. Berger (2019). *Reluctant Warriors: Germany, Japan and their U.S. Alliance Dilemma*. Washington, DC: Brookings Institution Press.

Salame, G. (1994). 'Torn between the Atlantic and the Mediterranean: Europe and the Middle East in the post-Cold War Era'. *Middle East Journal* 48(2): 226–49.

Samuels, R. J. (1994). *'Rich Nation, Strong Army': National Security and the Technological Transformation of Japan*. Ithaca, NY: Cornell University Press.

Samuels, R. J. (2003). *Machiavelli's Children: Leaders and Their Legacies in Italy and Japan*. Ithaca, NY: Cornell University Press.

Samuels, R. J. (2007). 'Securing Japan: The Current Discourse', *Journal of Japanese Studies* 33(1): 125–52.

Samuels, R. J. (2007). *Securing Japan: Tokyo's Grand Strategy and the future of East Asia*. Ithaca, NY: Cornell University Press.

Samuels, R. J. (2013). *3.11: Disaster and Change in Japan*. Ithaca, NY: Cornell University Press.

Sanding M. and R. Schlaffer (2015). *Die Bundeswehr 1955–2015: Sicherheitspolitik und Streitkräfte in der Demokratie*. Freiburg im Breisgau: Rombach.

Sangar, E. (2015). 'The Weight of the Past(s): The Impact of the Bundeswehr's Use of Historical Experience on Strategy-Making in Afghanistan', *Journal of Strategic Studies* 8(4): 411–44.

Santoro, C. M. (ed.) (1992). *L'Elmo di Scipio: Studi sul modello di difesa italiano*. Bologna: Il Mulino.

Sapolsky, H. M. (1971). *The Polaris System Development*. Cambridge, MA: Harvard University Press.

Sarotte, M. E. (2001). 'German Military Reform and EU Security', *Adelphi Paper 340*.

Satake, T. and J. Hemmings (2018). Japan–Australia Security Cooperation in the Bilateral and Multilateral Contexts', *International Affairs* 94(4): 815–34.

Schaller, M. (1985). *The American Occupation of Japan: The Origins of the Cold War in Asia*. Oxford: Oxford University Press.

Schaller, M. (1997). *Altered States: The United States and Japan since the Occupation*. Oxford: Oxford University Press.

Schieder, S. (2019). 'New Institutionalism and Foreign Policy', in K. Brummer, S. Harnisch, K. Oppermann and D. Panke (eds), *Foreign Policy as Public Policy*. Manchester: Manchester University Press, 122–39.

Schmitt, O. (2018). *Allies that Count: Junior Partners in Coalition Warfare*. Washington, DC: Georgetown University Press.

Schmitt, O. (2019). 'More Allies, Weaker Missions? How Junior Partners Contribute to Multinational Military Operations', *Contemporary Security Policy* 40(1): 70–84.

Schoff, J. L. (2017). *Uncommon Alliance for the Common Good: The United States and Japan after the Cold War*. Washington, DC: Carnegie Endowment for International Peace.

Schoff, J. L. and S. Romei (2019). *The New National Defense Program Guidelines: Aligning US and Japanese Defense Strategies for the Third Post-Cold War Era*. Washington DC: Sasakawa USA.

Scholz, O. (2022). 'Policy Statement by Olaf Scholz, Chancellor of the Federal Republic of Germany and Member of the German Bundestag', 27 February, Berlin, available at: https://www.bundesregierung.de/breg-en/news/policy-statement-by-olaf-scholz-chancellor-of-the-federal-republic-of-germany-and-member-of-the-german-bundestag-27-february-2022-in-berlin-2008378.

Schwenke, S. (2020). 'Changing Civil–Military Relations in Japan: 2009–2012', *Australian Journal of International Affairs* 74(6): 704–20.

Seaboyer, A. and I. Wiesner (2011). 'Budgeting for Defence', *Internationale Politik* 12(2): 30–6.

Seibert, B. (2012). 'A Quiet Revolution', *RUSI Journal* 157(1): 60–9.

Senato della Repubblica (2018). *In Difesa della Patria: Dai soldati di leva ai militari professionisti: come sta funzionando il nuovo modello delle Forze armate italiane?* Focus, Impact Assessment Office, available at: https://www.senato.it/service/PDF/PDFServer/BGT/01077449.pdf.

Seraphim, F. (2006). *In War Memory and Social Politics in Japan, 1945–2005*. Cambridge, MA: Harvard University Press.

Siddi , M. (2019). 'Italy's "Middle Power" Approach to Russia', *The International Spectator* 54(2): 123–8.

Silj, A. (1998). *L'alleato scomodo. I rapporti fra Roma e Washington nel Mediterraneo: Sigonella e Gheddafi*. Milan: Corbaccio.

Silove, N. (2016). 'The Pivot before the Pivot: US Strategy to Preserve the Power Balance in Asia', *International Security* 40(3): 45–88.

Simón, L., A. Lanoszka and H. Meijer (2021). 'Nodal Defence: The Changing Structure of US Alliance Systems in Europe and East Asia', *Journal of Strategic Studies* 44(3): 360–88.

SIPRI (2021). Military Expenditures Database, Stockholm, available at: https://www.sipri.org/databases/milex.

Slater, D. and E. Simmons (2010). 'Informative Regress: Critical Antecedents in Comparative Politics', *Comparative Political Studies* 43(7): 886–917.

Smith, E. T. (1983). 'The Fear of Subversion: The United States and the Inclusion of Italy in the North Atlantic Treaty', *Diplomatic History* 7(2): 139–56.

Smith, R. (2006). *The Utility of Force: The Art of World in the Modern World*. New York: Penguin.

Smith, S. (1986). 'Theories of Foreign Policy: An Historical Overview', *Review of International Studies* 12(1): 13–29.

Smith, S. A. (2019). *Japan Rearmed: The Politics of Military Power*. Cambridge, MA: Harvard University Press.

Snyder, D. B. (2002). 'Arming the Bundesmarine: The United States and the Build-up of the German Federal Navy, 1950–1960', *Journal of Military History* 66(2): 477–500.

Snyder, G. H. (1984). 'The Security Dilemma in Alliance Politics', *World Politics* 36(4): 461–95.

Snyder, G. H. (1997). *Alliance Politics*. Ithaca, NY: Cornell University Press.

Snyder, J. (1977). *The Soviet Strategic Culture*. Santa Monica, CA: Rand Corporation.

Snyder, J. (1984). 'Civil–Military Relations and the Cult of the Offensive, 1914 and 1984', *International Security* 9(1): 108–46.

Soave, P. (2017). 'Power vs. Diplomacy, Globalism vs. Regionalism: United States and Italy Facing International Terrorism. The Sidra Crisis, 1986', *Nuova Rivista Storica* 101(1): 161–79.

Soeters, J. L., D. J. Winslow and A. Weibull (2006). 'Military Culture', in G. Caforio (ed.), *Handbook of the Sociology of the Military*. Boston, MA: Springer, 237–54.

Soeya, Y. (1998). *Japan's Economic Diplomacy with China, 1945–1978*. Oxford: Oxford University Press.

Soifer, H. D. (2012). 'The Causal Logic of Critical Junctures', *Comparative Political Studies* 45(12): 1572–97.

Spiegel International (2010). 'German President Horst Köhler Resigns', 31 October, available at: http://www.spiegel.de/international/germany/controversy-over-afghanistan-remarks-german-president-horst-koehler-resigns-a-697785.html.

Stato Maggiore dell'Esercito (2008). *Army Report 2008*. Rome, 140.

Stato Maggiore dell'Esercito (2008). *Le Operazioni Contro-insurrezionali*. SME III RIF-COE.

Stato Maggiore della Difesa (2005). *La Trasformazione net-centrica*. Rome: Stato Maggiore della Difesa, 6.

Stinchcombe, A. L. (1987). *Constructing Social Theories*. Chicago, IL: University of Chicago Press.

Stockwin, J. A. (1968). *The Japanese Socialist Party and Neutralism: A Study of a Political Party and Its Foreign Policy*. Melbourne: Melbourne University Press.

Stockwin, J. A. (2000). 'The Social Democratic Party (Former Japan Socialist Party): A Turbulent History', in R. J. Hrebenar (ed.), *Japan's New Party System*. Boulder, CO: Westview, 209–51.

Swenson-Wright, J. (2005). *Unequal Allies? United States Security and Alliance Policy toward Japan, 1945–1960*. Stanford, CA: Stanford University Press.

Sydow, J., G. Schreyogg and J. Koch (2009). 'Organisational Path Dependence: Opening the Black Box', *Academy of Management Review* 34(4): 689–709.

Szczepanska, K. (2014). *The Politics of War Memory in Japan: Progressive Civil Society Groups and Contestation of Memory of the Asia-Pacific War*. London: Routledge.

Takahashi, S. (2019). 'Development of Grey-zone Deterrence: Concept Building and Lessons from Japan's Experience', *Pacific Review* 31(6): 787–810.

Tatsumi, Y. (2012). *Great Eastern Japan Earthquake: 'Lessons Learned' for Japanese Defense Policy*. Washington, DC: Stimson Center.

Thelen, K. (2004). *How Institutions Evolve: The Political Economy of Skills in Germany, Britain, the United States, and Japan*. New York: Cambridge University Press.

Thorsten, M. (2012). *Superhuman Japan: Knowledge, Nation and Culture in US–Japan Relations*. London: Routledge.

Tow, W. (1999). 'Strategic Cultures in Comparative Perspective', in K. Booth and R. Trood (eds), *Strategic Cultures in the Asia Pacific Region*. Basingstoke: Palgrave Macmillan, 320–44.

Trachtenberg, M. (1999). *A Constructed Peace: The Making of the European Settlement, 1945–1963*. Princeton, NJ: Princeton University Press.

Trachtenberg, M. and C. Gehrz (2003). 'America, Europe and German Rearmament, August–September 1950', in M. Trachtenberg (ed.), *Between Empire and Alliance: America and Europe during the Cold War*. New York: Rowman & Littlefield, 1–23.

Trauschweizer, I. W. (2008). 'Learning with an Ally: The U.S. Army and the Bundeswehr in the Cold War', *Journal of Military History* 72(2): 477–508.

Tucker, N. B. (1984). 'American Policy toward Sino-Japanese Trade in the Post-War Years: Politics and Prosperity', *Diplomatic History* 8(3): 183–208.

Ulatowski, R. (2022). 'Germany in the Indo-Pacific Region: Strengthening the Liberal Order and Regional Security', *International Affairs* 98(2): 383–402.

Uriu, R. M. (2009). *Clinton and Japan: The Impact of Revisionism on US Trade Policy*. Oxford: Oxford University Press.

van der Vorm, M. (2021). 'The Crucible of War: What Do We Know About Military Adaptation?' *Journal of Advanced Military Studies* 12(1): 197–209.

Van Orden, G. (1991). 'The Bundeswehr in Transition', *Survival* 33(4): 352–70.

Varsori, A. (1992). 'Italy and Western Defence 1948–55: The Elusive Ally', in B. Heuser and R. O'Neill (eds), *Securing Peace in Europe, 1945–62*. London: Palgrave Macmillan, 196–221.

Varsori, A. (2011). 'The First Stage of Negotiations: December 1947 to June 1948', in E. Di Nolfo (ed.), *The Atlantic Pact Forty Years Later*. New York: De Gruyter, 19–40.

Varsori, A. (2022). *Dalla rinasciata al declino. Storia internazionale dell'Italia repubblicana*. Bologna: Il Mulino.

Verbeek, J. A. and A. Zaslove (2015). 'The Impact of Populist Radical Right Parties on Foreign Policy: The Northern League as a Junior Coalition Partner in the Berlusconi Governments', *European Political Science Review* 7(4): 525–46.

Vignoli, V. (2022). *Conflitti consensuali: I partiti italiani e gli interventi militari*. Bologna: Il Mulino.

Vignoli, V. and F. Coticchia (2022). 'Italy's Military Operations Abroad (1945–2020): Data, Patterns, and Trends', *International Peacekeeping* 29(3): 436–62.

Wadsworth, K. C. (2019). 'Should Japan Adopt Conventional Missile Strike Capabilities?' *Asia Policy* 26(2): 61–87.

Wagner, W. (2018). 'Is There a Parliamentary Peace? Parliamentary Veto Power and Military Interventions from Kosovo to Daesh', *British Journal of Politics and International Relations* 20(1): 121–34.

Wagner, W., A. Herranz-Surrallés, J. Kaarbo and F. Ostermann (2017). 'The Party Politics of Legislative–Executive Relations in Security and Defence Policy', *West European Politics* 40(1): 20–40.

Wallace, C. (2018). 'Leaving (North-east) Asia? Japan's Southern Strategy', *International Affairs* 94(4): 883–904.

Weiss J. C. and J. L. Wallace (2021). 'Domestic Politics, China's Rise, and the Future of the Liberal International Order', *International Organization* 75(2): 635–64.

Weitsman, P. A. (2013). *Waging War: Alliances, Coalitions and Institutions of Interstate Violence*. Stanford, CA: Stanford University Press.

White House, The (2023). 'Joint Statement of United States and Japan', Washington, DC, 13 January.

Wiesner, I. (2011). *Importing the American Way of War? Network-centric Warfare in the UK and Germany*. Baden-Baden: Nomos Verlag.

Williams, D. and R. Kersten (eds) (2004). *The Left in the Shaping of Japanese Democracy: Essays in Honour of JAA Stockwin*. London: Routledge.

Wilsford, D. (1994). 'Path Dependency, or Why History Makes it Difficult but Not Impossible to Reform Health Care Systems in a Big Way', *Journal of Public Policy* 14(3): 251–83.

Wörner, M. (1974). 'Parliamentary Control of Defence: The German Example', *Survival* 16(1): 13–16.

Yuzawa, T. (2007). *Japan's Security Policy and the ASEAN Regional Forum: The Search for Multilateral Security in the Asia-Pacific*. London: Routledge.

Yuzawa, T. (2018). 'From a Decentering to Recentering Imperative: Japan's Approach to Asian Security Multilateralism', *Pacific Review* 31(4): 460–79.

Zisk, K. M. (1993). *Engaging the Enemy: Organization Theory and Soviet Military Innovation, 1955–1991*. Princeton, NJ: Princeton University Press.

Zürn, M. (2014). 'The Politicization of World Politics and its Effects: Eight Propositions', *European Political Science Review* 6(1): 47–71.

Index